The Name's Familiar II

The
Name's Familiar
II

By Laura Lee

PELICAN PUBLISHING COMPANY
Gretna 2001

Library of Congress Cataloging-in-Publication Data

Lee, Laura, 1969-
    The name's familiar II / by Laura Lee.
      p. cm.
    Includes index.
    ISBN 1-56554-822-1 (pbk. : alk. paper)
    1. English language—Eponyms—Dictionaries. 2. English
language—Etymology—Dictionaries. 3. Names, Personal—
Dictionaries. 4. Biography—Dictionaries. I. Title: Name's
familiar 2. II. Title: Name's familiar two. III. Title.

PE1596 .L43 2001
423'.1—dc21   00-065216

Printed in Canada
Published by Pelican Publishing Company, Inc.
1000 Burmaster Street, Gretna, Louisiana 70053

Contents

Acknowledgments

Thank you to the following people, who helped me find facts for this book:

La Vonne Gaw of the Graceland Archives

Elizabeth Harkin of the Northern Territory Holiday Centre in Australia

David Hoffman of the *Haight-Ashbury Free Press*

Christopher Lee of the Kansas State Historical Society, for information on Lawrence

Barry Levenson, curator of the Mt. Horeb Mustard Museum

Darryl Smith, who provided information on "Star Trek"

Introduction

Once you start paying attention to the people behind every-day words and phrases, you see them everywhere. At some point, though, you simply have to declare a book finished and send it on its merry way to the publisher, the printer, and the bookstore. Between the time that I finished *The Name's Familiar* and the time it was available, many months had passed. Almost immediately, however, I came across names that I had managed to overlook. I wanted to somehow paste them into the book, already en route to the printer. That was, of course, impossible.

So I started a file with a handful of extra names. Then the promotional interviews began. People called radio stations to ask me the stories behind brand names, song titles, and every-day words. Sometimes they stumped me. Very little time had passed, therefore, before I had a relatively sizeable new collec-tion of familiar names. How had I missed the people who gave their names to the Osterizer blender, Saudi Arabia, CliffsNotes, Little Debbie snack cakes, the Uzi submachine gun, chicken tetrazzini, the song "Barbara Ann," and Uncle Ben's rice?

This book will include a few entries I left out of *The Name's Familiar* because I decided, at the time, that they were not familiar enough. This is not because I've run out of familiar names but because I felt the stories behind some of the lesser-known words were interesting enough to warrant telling. For example, since most Americans have little worry of catching malaria, they are unaware of the various drugs used to treat it. One such drug, *artemisinin*, takes its name from Artemisia of Caria, a female botanist who lived more than three hundred years before Christ. She ruled Caria for more than three years after the death of her husband, the king, and built one of the Seven Wonders of the World. While "artemisinin" may not be a household word in, say, Idaho, I hope readers there and elsewhere will enjoy her story.

A few of the familiar faces from the previous book have returned as I uncovered new facts about them. Some of the biographies originally appeared in the two- or three-line "Shorts" section in the back of the book. Often a person who inspired one word or phrase eventually inspired many words and phrases. When I uncovered the origin of another term or related information that was interesting, entertaining, or just plain too good to leave out, I brought the person back for a second visit. Julius Caesar, for example, appeared in the first book as the origin of the *Julian calendar, July,* and the *Caesarian section,* but these are only a few of the words that derive from his name.

I hope you will enjoy this collection of familiar names as much as I enjoyed compiling it.

The Names

A

Abu-Bakr

Abu-Bakr, or Abu-Bekr, lived from A.D. 573 to 634. Because of his service to Mahomet, he was given the title "The Faithful." Upon Mahomet's death in 632 Abu-Bakr became his successor and took "Caliph" or successor as his new title. Abu-Bakr's own successor, Omar, took the title "Commander of the Faithful" or "Amir-al-Muninin." This popularized the use of the title "Commander of." Abu-Bakr became "Amir-al-Umara" or "ruler of rulers," the minister of finance was referred to as Amir-al-Ahgal, and the commander of Caravans to Mecca was the Amir-al-Hajj. The Christians who encountered such caravans assumed that Amir and al were one word—"amiral." They brought the word back to England, where later writers assumed that it was a misspelling of a Latin word beginning with the common "adm." Soon the British were appointing their own *admirals*. As Charles Earle Funk points out in his book *Thereby Hangs a Tale*, technically admiral should mean "commander of." Thus, if the original meaning were observed, "Admiral Smith" would actually be "Commander of Smith."

Adams, Fanny

Sweet Fanny Adams is a primarily British expression meaning something worthless or nothing at all. The story of how this came about is not for the faint of heart or weak of stomach. Adams was an eight-year-old girl who was found murdered and chopped into bits in 1867. What was left of her body was thrown into the river Wey at Alton in Hampshire. Her murderer, a man named Fred Baker, was publicly hanged for the crime. The case attracted much attention. It happened to occur around the same time the British Navy was introducing canned stew. The new process of canning meat was one of trial and error. Spoilage was common. By 1850, 111,108 pounds of tinned meat had been condemned in one English shipyard alone, prompting a Select Committee inquiry. Employing the type of black humor for which military men are often known, the unpalatable food was dubbed Fanny Adams, for obvious reasons. Over the years, "Fanny Adams" became "sweet Fanny Adams," or "Sweet F. A.," with the abbreviated form serving as a popular euphemism for an obscenity. To get a sense of this usage, here is a small excerpt from a recent article in London's *Daily Telegraph:*

> Paul Boateng was rebuked by the Speaker yesterday for saying "sweet FA" during Commons questions. The junior health minister was criticized by Betty Boothroyd for what she described as "most undesirable" language. . . . To gasps from the Chamber, Mr Boateng [had said]: "You did sweet FA about public health when you were in government. We are actually tackling those issues."

Boothroyd said she was not sure whether the language was unparliamentary "but it was certainly most undesirable." She said, "I hope that Members, and particularly ministers of the Crown, will use better language in this House." Music fans will recall that the rock band Sweet recorded an album called *Sweet Fanny Adams* in 1974.

Al-Khwarizm, Abu Abdullah Muhammad Ibn Musa

He was born at Khwarizm, a town south of the river Oxus in present-day Uzbekistan, some time around the year 813. When he was a child, his family immigrated to a place south of Baghdad. He grew up to be a gifted mathematician, astronomer, and geographer and wrote influential books on all those topics. Seventy geographers worked under the scholar, who revised Ptolemy's views on geography. The team produced the first map of the known world in the year 830. His other contributions include original work related to clocks, sundials, and astrolabes. It is his contributions in the field of mathematics, however, that make his name familiar. He is recognized as the founder of algebra, the name of which comes from his book, *Al-Jabr wa-al-Muqabilah.*

A Latin translation of this title introduced the new science to the West, and along with it Arabic numerals and the Hindu numeral zero. The book was used until the sixteenth century as the principal mathematical textbook of European universities. His pioneering work on the system of numerals is well known today as *algorithm*.

Albert of Saxe-Coburg-Gotha

"Poor dear Albert, how cruelly are they ill-using that dearest angel! Monsters! You Tories shall be punished. Revenge, revenge," wrote Queen Victoria in her diary eight days before her 1840 marriage to first cousin Prince Albert of Saxe-Coburg-Gotha. Albert, with whom she was very much in love, was not so beloved to the English people. He was German and seen as a foreigner despite being made a British citizen. He never was made an English peer. It was only after seventeen years of marriage that he was given an official title, prince consort. Together Albert and Victoria had nine children. The first, Victoria, was born in 1840 and would go on to be empress of Germany. The second was the Prince of Wales, later Edward VII. Their marriages and those of her grandchildren allied the British royal house with those of Russia, Greece, Denmark, Romania, and several of the German states. Albert's popularity began to grow in the late 1840s as he toured the nation's factories trying to find a means by which British workers could improve their lives and technology could be put to better use in industry. In 1849, Albert was given a heavy gold watch chain. He wore it from one pocket to a button of his vest. The fashion came to be known as the *Albert chain*. Albert's popularity reached its zenith in 1851 when he organized the first World's Fair, known as "The Great Exhibition." He had an exhibition hall designed and built for the event. The building, which was made up of more than three hundred thousand panes of glass supported by a cast-iron framework, was teasingly dubbed the "Crystal Palace." The name stuck. The exhibition earned a profit of £186,000, which was used to build, among other things, the *Victoria and Albert Museum*. After the exhibition, the palace was dismantled and moved across the Thames. Albert's admirers began to speak of erecting a statue to him in Hyde Park where the Crystal Palace had been. The suggestion embarrassed Albert, who had always downplayed his royal role. He wrote that he could say, "with perfect absence of humbug," that it would disturb his rides in the park "to see my own face staring down at me" and, if it was "an artistic monstrosity, like most of our monuments," he would be "permanently ridiculed and laughed at in effigy." In 1861, Albert contracted typhoid and died at the age of forty-two. Victoria's grief was so great that she did not appear in public for three years and did not open Parliament until 1866. Despite Albert's apparent modesty, his name now appears all over the map. *Lake Albert* in central Africa, discovered in 1864, bears his name as does the city of *Prince Albert* in central Saskatchewan, Canada. A number of commercial products were also given his name, most notably *Prince Albert tobacco,* the existence of which allowed children to call stores and ask if they had "Prince Albert in a can" and to reply "then you'd better let him out." Some Alberts that were not named for Queen Victoria's husband include *The Prince Albert coat,* which was named for his son, Albert Edward, later Edward VII, and *Alberta, Canada* (see next entry).

Alberta, Louise Caroline

Louise Caroline Alberta was born March 18, 1848 in Buckingham Palace, the fourth child of Queen Victoria and Albert, Prince Consort. On March 21, 1871, when she was twenty-three, she married the twenty-six-year-old John Campbell, ninth Duke of Argyll, and Marquis of Lorne, who was named governor general of Canada. He was thus given the task, in 1882, of naming one of four provisional districts of the North-West Territories, previously known as Assiniboia. Not only did he name the region for his wife, he also composed a fourteen-line poem for the occasion, which concluded with the following stanza: "In token of the love which thou hast shown/For this wide land of freedom, I have named/A province vast, and for its beauty famed/By thy dear name to be hereafter known./*Alberta* shall it be!" The princess also gave her first name to another Canadian geographical feature, *Lake Louise,* located in Banff National Park in southwest Alberta. Princess Louise died December 3, 1939 of natural causes at the age of ninety-one.

Alciatore, Antoine

French immigrant Antoine Alciatore was twenty-seven years old
when he traveled from New York to New Orleans with a dream
of opening a restaurant. After a brief stint in the kitchen of the
grand St. Charles Hotel, he opened a pension, a boardinghouse,
and a restaurant called, simply, *Antoine's*. He quickly built up a
following and was able to send to New York for his sweetheart,
Julie Freyss. She married Alciatore and bore him eighteen children. After Alciatore's death in 1874, his son Jules took over the
culinary duties. He created the restaurant's most famous dish,
oysters Rockefeller, so named because it was "as rich as" industrialist John D. Rockefeller. The restaurant itself gained literary fame when New Orleans author Frances Parkinson Keyes
used it in the title of her 1948 novel *Dinner at Antoine's*.

Allen, Ann

In 1824, a Virginian named John Allen and a New Yorker named
Elisha Rumsey became the first settlers on a wooded, 640-acre
parcel of land in Washtenaw County, Michigan. Coincidentally,
both men's wives went by the name "Ann." Rumsey's wife was
Mary Ann and Allen's was Ann Isabella. Local legend has it that
the two women spent many hours together chatting in a wild
grape arbor. Thus the new town was called Ann Arbor. This version of the tale is more charming that factual, however. It is
true that the town took its name from one or both of the original settlers' wives. Most sources say the name honors both
women, but University of Michigan professor emeritus Russell
Bidlack, who wrote a book about Ann Allen, claims she alone
was the inspiration for the name. John Allen, he said, wanted to
call the area Annapolis or Allensville, but his wife suggested
"Annarbour." In any case, the "Arbor" portion of the name
could not have been inspired by arbor chats between the two
Anns. Records show the name was chosen and recorded five
months before Ann Allen arrived in the region. Most likely
"arbor," which describes a shady spot, simply referred to one of
the features of the landscape. An even more creative tale on how
the town got its name involves a woman named Ann D'Arbeur
who supposedly led people through the wilderness surrounding
the Huron River long before Allen or Rumsey arrived. This

version of Michigan history is undoubtedly a myth. Ann Arbor is best known today as the location of the University of Michigan, which opened in 1841. Previously, the city lost a bid to become the state capital. Two points if you can name the city that won that honor. Answer: Lansing.

Alperin, Sharona

In 1978, Sharona Alperin was a senior at Fairfax High School in Los Angeles. She was just seventeen, and she had a steady boyfriend. One day a twenty-six-year-old musician named Doug Feiger came into the clothing store where she worked. He was immediately smitten with the young beauty, but Alperin rebuffed his advances. Feiger didn't give up so easily. He got together with Berton Averre, the lead guitarist of his band, The Knack, and wrote a song for her. It did the trick. Feiger managed to convince Alperin to leave her boyfriend and join him on tour. For the next three years she led the life of a rock star's girlfriend, touring, riding in limousines, and rubbing elbows with the rich and famous. The song, "My Sharona," helped make it all possible. The group's album *Get the Knack,* powered by the infectious, stuttering single, was marketed and hyped and sold enough copies to live up to its expectations. *Rolling Stone* magazine dubbed them "the new fab four." The album went gold in only thirteen days, platinum in less than seven weeks. "My Sharona" entered the singles charts on June 23, 1979 and reached number one nine weeks later on August 25, 1979, where it remained for six weeks. *Billboard* named it the number-one single of 1979. The "next Beatles," however, did not quite live up to that billing. Their next single, "Good Girls Don't," made it to number eleven on the charts. Their follow-up album yielded only one Top 40 hit, "Baby Talks Dirty," which peaked at number thirty-eight. They made one more album, a commercial failure, and the band called it quits. Alperin's romance with Feiger did not last either. After a brief engagement, they went their separate ways, but are reportedly still friends. Alperin continues to hobnob with celebrities. Today she is a Hollywood real-estate agent. She sells million-dollar homes to the Hollywood elite, including Claire Danes, Julianne Moore, and Leonardo DiCaprio.

Amherst, Jeffrey

Jeffrey Amherst was born January 29, 1717 in Kent, England. He joined the military and received a commission in the foot guards in 1731. He was chosen to be an aide-de-camp by Lord Ligonier and later the Duke of Cumberland. In 1758, he was given his own command with 14,000 soldiers in Canada. He captured Louisbourg on Cape Breton Island and received a promotion to chief command in America. Many of the regular British soldiers felt Amherst's new American recruits were good for nothing but a good laugh. One such officer, Dr. Richard Shuckburg, even wrote a little song to satirize them. He set it to the tune of an old martial air of the 1660s, "Nankee Doodle." He called his song "The Yankees Return to Camp." Amherst's combined American and British troops fared fairly well, however. Amherst drew up a plan that led to the capture of Quebec in late 1759 and Montreal in 1760. Canada thus remained in the British dominion. Amherst was named governor general of Canada and remained in that position until 1763. He turned his attention to fighting the Native American tribes. He used every tactic available to him, including biological warfare. "Could it not be contrived to send the smallpox among the disaffected tribes?" he asked a subordinate. In accordance, two chiefs were presented with "gifts" of blankets that had come from a hospital smallpox ward. Amherst wrote to Col. Henry Boquet and told him he did "well to try to Inoculate the Indians by means of Blankets, as well as to try Every other method that can serve to Extirpate this Execrable Race." At the beginning of the Revolutionary War, as George Washington took command of the Continental Army, a Harvard student named Edward Bands rewrote the lyrics of the song Shuckburg had written to make fun of Amherst's Americans. The result was the version of "Yankee Doodle" we still sing today. Amherst was created a baron in 1776 and a field marshal in 1796. He died in 1797 in his native England. *Amherst, Massachusetts, Amherst College,* and several other U.S. towns bear his name. *Amherst, Texas,* a northwest town with a population of 745, was named for the college. A group of Amherst, Massachusetts residents have recently petitioned to have the name changed because of Amherst's use of germ warfare. Those who would like to see the name changed suggest "Norwottuck" as a possible alternative. It is the name of the tribe that previously lived on the land that is now called Amherst. Another Massachusetts college, Williams College in Williamstown, known for its annual theater festival, faces a similar controversy. The town was named for Ephraim Williams, who allegedly cheated Native Americans out of land by making sure transactions were recorded incorrectly so they could later be nullified. Williamstown is located in the Berkshire Mountains, named for Berkshire County in England. It is one of the few English counties that does not take its name from a town. Instead it derives from Berroc, an ancient wood, which most likely took its name from the Celtic word "barro," meaning "hill." The mountain range is therefore rather redundantly named the "hill mountains." "Massachusetts" comes from the Massachusetts Indian tribe. It means "large hill place." So the Berkshires of western Massachusetts are the "hill mountains of the large hill place." Some other redundantly named places include the Rio Grande River (Rio Grande is Spanish for "Big River"), the Ganges River (it comes from the Hindi word "ganga" meaning "river"), and the Sahara Desert (Sahara comes from the Arabic for "brownish desert").

Amster, Lois

Lois Amster was a student at Granville High School in Cleveland, Ohio in the 1930s. She was a class beauty, the type the girls envied and boys wanted to date. One of her classmates was a boy named Jerry Siegel. He was skinny, wore glasses, and worked as a delivery boy to help support his family. He spent most of his time in a world of fantasy. He used his extra cash to buy comic books and his classroom time to gaze at Lois Amster. "He used to stare at me," Amster said. "Be we never had any social communication. He was unsophisticated. I thought I was more sophisticated." Siegel never did get up the courage to ask Amster out, which is probably a good thing. She would later confess to a *Time* magazine reporter that she would probably have laughed at him if he had. Instead, Siegel turned his daydreams into science-fiction tales, which he mimeographed and sold to other students. "As a high-school student," Siegel once said, "I thought that someday I might become a reporter, and I had crushes on several attractive girls who either didn't know I

existed or didn't care I existed. . . . It occurred to me: What if I
. . . had something special going for me, like jumping over
buildings or throwing cars around or something like that?" One
summer night in 1934, Siegel went over to his friend Joe
Shuster's house. He wove a tale of a man from a planet called
Krypton who landed on Earth to find he had superpowers. His
name was Superman. The character of Lois Lane, who fell for
the suave superhero but not his nerdy alter ego, was named in
honor of Lois Amster. Shuster illustrated Siegel's story. They
kept at it until they'd finished twelve newspaper comic strips.
They took it from syndicate to syndicate. It was rejected time
and time again. Even Detective Comics publisher Harry
Donenfeld, who would later buy the strip, called the first cover
"ridiculous." The cover, featuring Superman lifting a car over
his head, is now worth as much as $35,000 to collectors.
Superman went on to appear in more than 250 newspapers,
thirteen years of radio shows, three novels, seventeen animated
cartoons, a TV series with 104 episodes, a Broadway musical,
two movie serials of fifteen installments each, and five feature
films. So the little guy wins out in the end? Not exactly. When
DC Comics bought Superman in 1938, the contract called for
all rights in exchange for $10 a page. When it became an in-
stant hit, Siegel and Shuster sued to get their rights back. The
courts ruled against them and DC Comics fired them and hired
other people to work on Superman. They kept fighting until
the late 1970s. By then Warner Communications owned DC
Comics and they wanted to make a Superman movie. They
didn't want the adverse publicity they would surely get if they
continued to fight against Superman's creators. Superman, the
character, was estimated to be worth more than $1 billion.
Warner agreed to pay Siegel and Shuster $20,000 a year for life.
And what became of Lois Amster? She married an insurance
agent named Robert Rothschild and raised her children and
grandchildren in Cleveland.

Ångström, Anders Jonas

Anders Jonas Ångström was born August 13, 1814, in Lögdö,
Sweden. He earned a degree from the University of Uppsala,

where he became a physics lecturer in 1839. In 1843 he was made observer at Uppsala Observatory, and in 1858 he took the chair in physics at Uppsala, which he held until his death. He was one of the founders of spectroscopy, the science of measuring the emission and absorption of different wavelengths of visible and nonvisible light. In a paper delivered to the Stockholm Academy in 1853, he deduced that an incandescent gas emits light of the same wavelength as it will absorb. In 1862, he announced the presence of the element hydrogen in the sun's atmosphere. He was the first, in 1867, to examine the spectrum of the Aurora Borealis and to detect and measure the characteristic bright line in its yellow-green region, but he was mistaken in supposing that this same line is also to be seen in the zodiacal light. A year later, he published a famous map of the solar spectrum, which remained authoritative for many years despite its wavelength errors of about one part in 7,000. These arose because Ångström referred his measurements of wavelength to a meter bar that was slightly too short. He died June 21, 1874. The unit used in measuring the wavelength of light is called an *angstrom* in his honor.

Arbuckle, John

John Arbuckle, the son of a Scottish immigrant, began his career in 1860 with his brother Charles and uncle Duncan McDonald. They opened a grocery in Pittsburgh known as McDonald & Arbuckle. Four years later, John Arbuckle, then twenty-one, bought a coffee roaster. He sold his coffee in little packages that were widely mocked by competitors due to their resemblance to peanut bags. They didn't laugh long. Soon the grocery was employing fifty girls to pack and label the coffee, which he could not keep in the store. Advertisements for his first coffee brand, Ariosa, were not subtle. He circulated handbills featuring cartoons of his competitors' coffee with insects in it and a woman crying, "I see what killed my children." Somehow Arbuckle avoided being sued. In 1871, he left his brother Charles to open a factory in New York. McDonald retired and the company was renamed Arbuckle Brothers. John Arbuckle passed away in 1912 at the age of sixty-nine, leaving an estate worth $20 million. The business was transferred to his nephew, Will Jamison, and his two sisters, Mrs. Robert Jamison and Christina Arbuckle. To compete with the new coffee brands, Jamison knew he needed to offer a high-end coffee. He had just the thing, the personal favorite blend of John Arbuckle, who usually gave it as a Christmas gift to his closest friends. He hired the J. Walter Thompson ad agency to create the campaign for the product. They decided the new brand needed a name that did not remind consumers of Arbuckle Brothers' other products. They took inspiration for the name from the bags in which shipments of green coffee arrived. They were labeled *ABNY* for Arbuckle Brothers, New York. They decided to use those letters to make up the new name. The result could have been Bany or Naby coffee. Instead someone suggested adding a vowel to Yban and *Yuban* coffee was born. The brand was a hit in New York and Chicago and the family soon wanted to go national. The J. Walter Thompson admen presented the company with a thirty-three-page report that laid out "the opportunity for a nationally advertised coffee, and none is in so ideal a position to take advantage of it as Yuban." The agency proposed a five-year campaign that would cost about 1.5 cents per pound of coffee sold. Arbuckle Brothers turned the plan down saying "the effort and cost of going national was too great for them." By the end of the 1920s, other brands that did advertise nationally had taken center stage. Consumers ignored Yuban. The J. Walter Thompson agency dropped the Arbuckle account in favor of Maxwell House. In 1937, Arbuckle Brothers was sold to General Foods, which retired the Ariosa brand.

Arnold, Benedict

Born and raised in New England, Benedict Arnold grew up to be a patriotic soldier in the American army. He fought in the French and Indian War and the Battle of Lexington and Concord and led a band of 700 men through the Maine wilderness to attack Quebec. This last campaign was unsuccessful, and Arnold was wounded. Even so, he managed to regroup his soldiers into a naval fleet. Although they were outgunned and outnumbered, Arnold's men took the day. Eventually, however, Arnold's many injuries kept him from further combat. In 1778, George Washington appointed Arnold commander of Philadelphia. There Arnold met Margaret Shippen, a British loyalist. The pair fell in love and married. Shippen's loyalist views appealed to the soldier, who felt he should have been promoted because of his military heroics. Even though he didn't have the rank he thought he deserved, he did have the respect of his peers and could provide the British with information for which he expected to be well compensated. He asked for £10,000 in exchange for the plans for an American invasion of Canada. Arnold's plot was revealed when his British contact, John Andre, was captured. Andre was sentenced to death by hanging. Arnold and his wife escaped to England. Even among the British, however, his disloyalty earned him few friends. Benedict Arnold's name became synonymous with the word "traitor." He died penniless and nearly friendless. One place that sounds as though it was named for Benedict Arnold, but was not, is Ben Arnold, Texas. The east-central Texas town, with a population of 148, was once a stopping point on the San Antonio & Aransas Pass Railway. The notary was going over the documents for a land purchase along the railroad right of way and someone asked him to choose a name for the place. He named it after his three-year-old daughter, Bennie Arnold.

Artemisia of Caria

Artemisia lived in the fourth century B.C. Her name came from Artemis, the Greek goddess of the moon. Artemisia was betrothed, as was common practice for royalty in those days, to her brother Mausolus, king of Caria in southwestern Anatolia. He expanded his rule on the mainland of Asia Minor and in the islands at the expense of Athens, and developed Halicarnassus as a strategic and cultural center. For her part, Artemisia was known as a botanist and a patron of the arts. When Mausolus died, Artemisia was so distraught that she toasted him each day with a drink that contained some of his ashes. In 353 B.C., she erected a tomb for her husband/brother at Halicarnassus. It was over one hundred feet high, filled with riches, and surrounded by statues. The first *mausoleum* was counted among the Seven Wonders of the World. Although the mausoleum no longer stands, portions of it are preserved in the British Museum in London. But Artemisia was more than a grieving widow. She succeeded her husband to rule Caria. Her ability to rule was immediately tested. The Rhodians were offended at the idea of a woman ruling in Caria and they were sure it would be no trouble at all to dethrone her and capture the city. The queen was aware of their plans even before they arrived at the port of Halicarnassus. She told her people to shout and clap their hands as though they were going to surrender the city without a fight. The overly confident Rhodians left their ships and approached the city. Meanwhile, Artemisia brought her galleys out from her own secret little port. She had had a small canal cut so that she could seize the enemy's fleet while they were all entering the city. The Rhodians now had no means of escape and Artemisia had them put to death. She then used their ships to sail back to Rhodes. When the people of that city saw their ships returning adorned with wreaths of laurel (a sign of victory), they began celebrating and opened their gates, only to find the enemy was on board. Artemisia easily captured Rhodes. She died a year later. The herb *Artemisia annua,* a genus that includes the sagebrush and the wormwood, was named in honor of the ancient botanist and ruler. An anti-malarial drug, *artemisinin,* comes from the herb.

Astor, John Jacob

One of America's first self-made millionaires, John Jacob Astor was born July 17, 1763 in Waldorf, Germany. On the ship that brought him to America, Astor learned about the fur trade. In 1786 he opened a fur shop in New York City and founded the American Fur Company to manufacture the goods. A 1794 treaty between the U.S. and England opened up new markets in Canada and the Great Lakes region. The timing was fortuitous. Through a combination of shrewd dealings with Native American tribes and the use of skilled mountain men, Astor soon controlled much of the far-west beaver trade. By 1800, he had amassed $250,000. He was given permission to trade in ports monopolized by the British East India Company and was able to export to China. In 1811, he established the first permanent U.S. settlement on the Pacific coast. It was named *Fort Astoria*. The war of 1812, however, interfered with Astor's plans for the location. The fort was sold to the British in 1813. It was formally restored to the United States in 1818, but trade remained in British hands until the mid-1840s when pioneers followed the Oregon Trail to the spot. *Astoria, Oregon* sprang up around the fort. As of 1990, Astoria had a population of 10,069. Astor, meanwhile, invested in New York City real estate. It is here that his descendents would put their name on the map. By the 1840s, "rich as Astor" was a common expression for wealth. When he died in 1848, Astor had a fortune equal to $78 billion in today's money, making him the fourth richest American of all time, according to *Forbes American Heritage*. The top three were John D. Rockefeller with a net worth of $190 billion in modern currency, Andrew Carnegie with $100.5 billion, and Cornelius Vanderbilt with $95.9 billion. Bill Gates was fifth on the list with $61.8 billion. In his will, Astor bequeathed $400,000 for the foundation of a public library, the *Astor Library* in New York City. It consolidated with others as the New York Public Library in 1895. His son, William Backhouse Astor, born in 1792, inherited most of the estate. He expanded the library and invested heavily in real estate in Manhattan. When he was accused of being a slumlord, he renovated a number of the Astors' older tenements. He also doubled the family fortune, leaving a $50 million estate when he passed away in 1875. His son, John Jacob Astor, lived from 1822 to 1890. He was known for his philanthropy, giving generously to the Metropolitan Museum of Art, the Astor Library, and Trinity Church on Wall Street. A section of the Queens borough of New York, formerly known as Hallet's Cove, was renamed *Astoria* for this member of the prominent family. His son, William Waldorf Astor (the "Waldorf" being a reference to the Astors' native city in Germany), was born in 1848. His aunt Lina Caroline Webster Schermenhorn Astor was one of the most acclaimed hostesses of Fifth Avenue in her time. William Astor decided it would annoy Aunt Lina if he built a hotel across the street from where she entertained. He called it the *Waldorf*. It worked. She moved up the street, but her son John Jacob Astor IV built his own hotel on the spot that she vacated. He called his building the *Astoria*. This John Jacob was born in 1864, the great-grandson of the fur trader. Besides the Astoria, he built a number of New York's landmark hotels, including the Knickerbocker and the St. Regis. In 1912, he traveled to England, Egypt, and France with his second wife, Madeline, who was four months pregnant. The couple booked their return voyage on a new ship, the *Titanic*. According to a number of survivor accounts of the sinking of the ship, Astor asked Second Officer Lightoller if he could join his pregnant wife in the lifeboat. Lightoller replied, "No men are allowed in these boats until the women are loaded first." Thus, his career and life were cut short. The Waldorf and Astoria hotels eventually linked. A hall was built connecting them. The result became known as the *Waldorf-Astoria*. It was demolished in 1929 to make way for the Empire State Building, but was rebuilt on Park Avenue. The hotel is the source of a popular dish, the *Waldorf salad*. The Waldorf's Swiss chef, Oscar Tschirky, was credited with its creation.

Augustus, Frederick

George III's second son, Frederick Augustus, was born in 1763 and received the title Duke of York. As befitting a royal, Augustus spent his entire life as a high-ranking military official, even though he was known to be almost completely incompetent. He managed to remain popular among his subjects anyway. From 1793 to 1795 he commanded the unsuccessful English forces in Flanders, after which he was somehow made a field marshal. In 1798 he advanced to the role of commander in chief of the army. He led a disastrous expedition to the Netherlands a year later. He was forced to resign his command in 1809 after he was accused of selling army commissions with the help of his mistress, Mary Anne Clarke. He was cleared of the charges and reappointed in 1811. His infamous performance on the battle-field was immortalized in a familiar nursery rhyme:

Oh, the grand old Duke of York,

He had 10,000 men;
He marched up to the top of the hill,
And he marched them down again.
And when they were up, they were up,
And when they were down, they were down,
And when they were only halfway up,
They were neither up nor down.

York was also, briefly, the name of the city that is now known as Toronto. "Toronto" was a garbled French version of the original Mohawk name, "Tkaronto," meaning "where there are trees standing in the water." The expression described the area where the indigenous tribes drove stakes into the water to create fish weirs. In 1792, the lieutenant governor of Upper Canada, John Graves Simcoe, who disliked the Indian labels, gave a number of towns and landmarks good English names. He renamed Niagara-on-the-Lake, "Newark." He named a lake, *"Lake Simcoe,"* after his father, and he dubbed Toronto "York" in honor of the duke. After he went back to England, however, a petition was submitted to the legislature to reinstate the name "Toronto." The Duke of York may also be the source of the expression "put up your dukes." The theory is that his name became associated with fighting after he had a public duel with the future Duke of Richmond. Another theory is that he was known as a fan of boxing, which led boxers and boxing fans to call fists "dukes." It might also have derived from Cockney rhyming slang. Duke of York rhymed with forks, which were symbolic of fingers, which you fold over to make fists, thus, "dukes." Some word-watchers think it was another duke who gave us the expression. The first Duke of Wellington had a very large nose, the theory goes. Thus, "duke" became a slang expression for the nose and a "duke buster" was a fist. This, over time, was shortened to simply "dukes." While we're on the subject of dukes, you may think that John Wayne earned his nickname "The Duke" because of his fists. It actually came from a pet. "I had a dog named Duke," he once said. "Every fireman in town knew that hound, because he chased all the fire wagons. They knew the dog's name, but not mine, so the next thing I was Duke, too. I was named for a damn dog!" A fictional

film hero, Indiana Jones, got his name the same way. Director
George Lucas had a dog named Indiana. The movie *Indiana
Jones and the Last Crusade* makes a reference to that fact when
Indy's father, played by Sean Connery, says incredulously,
"Indiana? We named the dog Indiana."

Aurelius, Marcus

Marcus Aurelius, born Marcus Annius Verus, was born in the
year 121 in Rome. He was adopted by the emperor Antoninus
Pius in 138, and married his daughter Annia Galeria Faustina
a few years later. As the son of the emperor, Aurelius was educated by private tutors and studied poetry and rhetoric. At
about the age of twelve, he took an interest in Stoicism, a
school of philosophy founded by Zeno of Citium about three
hundred years before Christ. The Stoics got that name, incidentally, because the original group met in the Stoa Poecile at
Athens. The philosophy advocated the complete control of
one's passions and asserted that everything happens for the
best. Aurelius began an intense study of philosophy and law at
the age of twenty-five. He became emperor in 161 and elevated his brother to the status of co-emperor—the first time that
Rome had ever been ruled by two men. Aurelius, however, was
responsible for most of the management of the empire.
During his reign, increased attacks by barbarians along the
northern borders, especially on the Danube River, threatened
the stability of the empire and caused a constant financial
drain on the treasury. The returning soldiers brought an unexpected spoil of war along with them—the plague. Aurelius
responded to these troubles by building orphanages and hospitals as well as schools. He also reduced taxes, and tried to
humanize the criminal law system and the treatment of slaves.
At one point the emperor sold his own possessions to raise
money to ease the suffering of the empire's people. He did,
however, persecute the early Christians, whose religion was
against state law. Aurelius was very active in the defense of his
empire. He guarded Syria from invasion by the Parthians in
166, battled the German tribes on the Rhine-Danube frontier
in 167, and launched his last campaign to extend the empire's

boundaries to the north in 176. The plague caught up with him before he could push beyond the Vistla River. He died in Vindobona (now Vienna) on March 17, 180. He is best remembered for his *Meditations*, which have survived and are popular among those who study the Stoic philosophers. In the third century, Romans rebuilt a city in Gaul (now France) that had been destroyed when it revolted against Julius Caesar. The former Cenabium was dubbed "Aurelianum," in honor of Aurelius. The name evolved into *Orléans*. In 511 it became the capital of the Frankish kingdom. Under the Capetians, the first kings of France, the city became, after Paris, the principal residence of the French kings. Orléans, with the surrounding province, the Orléanais, constituted part of the small nucleus of the royal domain, and the name was given to two branches of the French royal line. One member of the house of Orléans, Philippe II, was regent of France from 1715 to 1723 during the minority of Louis XV. During this period, a group of French settlers arrived in what is now Louisiana. They named their settlement *Nouvelle Orléans* in Philippe's honor. The name was Anglicized to *New Orleans* in 1803. Trivia question for folk-music fans: What do Louisiana, the Illinois Central Railroad, and Arlo Guthrie have in common? Answer: The City of New Orleans. The song "The City of New Orleans," recorded by Arlo Guthrie, was written by Steve Goodman. It was inspired by a real-life trip on an Illinois Central Railroad train known as the City of New Orleans. Its lyrics about the "disappearin' railroad blues" were somewhat premature. The City of New Orleans still runs on a regular basis from Champaign, Illinois.

Avery, R. Stanton

Ray Stanton Avery was born in Oklahoma City in 1907, the son of a minister. He was blessed with great determination, if not great financial resources. He was so poor, in fact, that he lived in a rented chicken coop and worked as a clerk at the Midnight Mission in downtown Los Angeles to put himself through Pomona College. After dropping out for a year to live in China, Avery graduated in 1932. He experimented with a number of enterprises, including selling smoked Tahitian bananas, before stumbling onto the product that would make his fortune. He cut a hole at each end of a cigar box, filled it with glue, and pulled pieces of paper through. The paper came out with a glue backing so it could serve as a self-sticking label. He called the product "Kum Kleen Price Stickers." In 1935, during the height of the Great Depression, with a $100 investment from schoolteacher Dorothy Durfee, who would later become his wife, Avery bought a washing-machine motor, parts of a sewing machine, and a saber saw and fashioned a machine to punch out the self-stick labels. He rented a 100-square-foot loft in the Flower District and launched a company called Kum-Kleen Products. Avery would later say that there were benefits to starting a new business during the depression. Because so many people were out of work, Avery was able to employ talented, highly motivated people for $15 to $20 a week. They didn't know if the company would survive, but they were happy to have jobs. He would have to call on his ability to persevere again three years later when his plant was destroyed by fire. The $3,000 insurance money allowed him to rebuild and he took the opportunity to improve his label-making machinery. By the end of World War II, the company was generating more than $500,000 in annual sales. Avery said he owed his company's success to focusing on small day-to-day problems rather than setting a grand goal to be a Fortune 500 company. Of course the operation, by then called the *Avery Products Company,* was helped in no small part by the patent it held on adhesive labels. Until 1952, when the patent lapsed, Avery had no competition. Other manufacturers rushed into the market that year, but the competition only brought more attention to Avery's products. Sales actually doubled from $1 million to $2 million in a single year and rose to $5 million by 1956. Over the years, Avery amassed eighteen patents for such inventions as self-adhesive label dispensers and in-line label-making and printing machines. Even when the company had become sizeable, Avery kept an informal workplace and was known as "Stan" to his staff. He always took time to visit the factory floor and talk with employees. He would often share bits of his personal philosophy, which employees called "Avery's

Laws." These included: "When you stop making mistakes, you're in deep trouble"; "External pressures unite; internal pressures divide"; "If you have the power, you don't have to use it"; and "You're always down on what you're not up on." In 1990, Avery Products Corporation joined the smaller Dennison Manufacturing of Framingham, Massachusetts, which manufactured such products as Hi-Liter, Marks-A-Lot, Carters inks, glue sticks, mailers, and various paper products. Today, *Avery Dennison* has more than 16,100 employees in eighty-nine countries. Stan Avery remained active in his company until 1995 when he retired from the board of directors and took the title founder chairman emeritus. He passed away in 1997 at the age of ninety.

B

Baekeland, Leo Hendryk

Leo Baekeland was born November 14, 1863 in Belgium. His father, Charles, was an illiterate shoemaker, and wanted his son to follow him in his craft. Leo, however, was clearly destined for a career in science and academic study. When he wasn't making shoes, he was reading and studying. When he was only sixteen, he won a scholarship to the University of Ghent, from which he graduated in 1882. At age twenty-one he was awarded his doctorate in chemistry. In 1887 he became a professor of physics and chemistry at the University of Bruges, and in 1888 returned to Ghent as an assistant professor of chemistry. A year later he married the daughter of one of his college professors. The couple planned a trip to the United States for their honeymoon. They never went back to Belgium. Instead, Baekeland set up a laboratory in New York City. His first successful invention, in 1893, was a type of photographic printing paper that could be developed under artificial light. He called it Velox. In 1899 George Eastman's Kodak Corporation bought the invention and the manufacturing company from Baekeland for $750,000 (about $15 million in today's money). For his next project, Baekeland decided to work on creating a synthetic shellac. Shellac, at that time, was created with the help of resin-creating lac beetles. To make one pound required the output of 15,000 beetles for six months. By combining carbolic acid and formaldehyde he produced a material called phenolic resin. He discovered that it could be produced in a hard form that can also be molded by casting under heat and pressure. This early plastic he named *Bakelite*—a play on his name and the fact that the material was hardened by baking it in a mold. He also formed the *General Bakelite Company* to sell it. The substance became a symbol of modernism and was used everywhere in Art Deco style. Radios particularly helped make Bakelite a household word. The first Bakelite product, by the way, was the gearshift knob on the Rolls-Royce. In 1924, the inventor appeared on the cover of *Time* magazine, which predicted: "From the time that a man brushes his teeth in the morning with a Bakelite-handled brush until the moment when he removes his last cigarette from a Bakelite holder, extinguishes it in a Bakelite ashtray, and falls back upon a Bakelite bed, all that he touches, sees, uses will be made of this material of a thousand purposes." Eventually, however, newer plastics became more common. At age seventy-five, Baekeland sold General Bakelite to Union Carbide and retired to Florida.

Baker, James

As a physician, Dr. James Baker of Dorchester, Massachusetts, was introduced to cocoa beans as an ingredient for medicines in the mid-1700s. The beans were ground and sold to patients as an unsweetened cake. Although drinking chocolate was popular in Europe, only this far-from-delectable version of chocolate existed in the American colonies. In 1764, Dr. Baker befriended an Irish immigrant named John Hannon. Hannon was a chocolate maker by trade, and he complained to his wealthier friend that there were no chocolate mills in the New World. Baker decided to fund Hannon. The new partners were convinced that there would be a market for nonmedicinal forms of cocoa. In 1765, they opened a chocolate factory in Milton Lower Falls on the Neponset River in Massachusetts. They called their product "Hannon's Best Chocolate" and sold it with a money-back guarantee. In 1779, Hannon sailed for the West Indies to purchase more cocoa beans and was lost at sea. Baker went on without him. In 1780 the first chocolate to be called "Baker's" was unveiled, but it wasn't until 1824 that Baker's grandson Walter renamed the entire company *Baker's Chocolate*. The company is also responsible for another familiar name—*German chocolate cake,* one of many foods whose names belie their origins. The coconut-and-pecan confection was not German fare at all. The name originated from one of the key ingredients— Baker's German's Sweet Chocolate. Note that the "German" was possessive. That is because it came from the name of an employee, Samuel German, who, in 1852, developed the sweet chocolate.

Ballantine, George

George Ballantine was born in 1809 on the family farm outside Edinburgh, Scotland. Instead of following in the footsteps of his father and grandfather and becoming a farmer, Ballantine was apprenticed at age thirteen to a city grocer, Andrew Hunter. Hunter was a merchant of wines and spirits as well as flour, grains, and other foodstuffs. In his five years at the grocery, Ballantine learned about mechanizing, customer service, accounting, and whiskey. At the age of eighteen, Ballantine headed out into the world with a letter of reference from his former employer that said that the youth had served him "faithfully, assiduously and honestly." In 1827, Ballantine was able to set up his own shop in Edinburgh's Cowgate district. As the name suggests, Cowgate was mostly populated with meat markets and the cattlemen who supplied the animals for them. By 1831, he had earned enough to open a second shop in Candlemakers' Row, an area known for its skilled craftsmen. Five years later, he opened a third shop around the corner from the city's fashionable Princes Street. In 1842, Ballantine married Isabella Mann, the daughter of an Inverness grain merchant. The couple had two sons, George and Archibald. In 1853, Ballantine's friend, Andrew Usher, blended a whiskey from malts of different ages, and Ballantine quickly followed suit. He sold a number of whiskeys all with the name Ballantine on the label, including Old Glenlivet, Talisker, and Ballantine's Fine Old Highland Whiskey. By 1881, he was exporting them worldwide. That year his wife died, and he moved to Glasgow to open a new branch of the business. The Edinburgh business was handed down to Archibald and the Glasgow business to George Jr. George Ballantine died in 1891 at the age of eighty-two. His name lives on. Today, *Ballantine's Finest* is the number-one brand of Scotch in Europe and the third largest in the world.

Barbara

According to a report by Prof. H. A. Skinner, Barbara was a waitress in Munich. As the story goes, she contributed a urine specimen to organic chemist Adolf von Baeyer, who used it to synthesize a substance that he called *barbituric acid*, which is, in turn, the source of all *barbiturates*. It is also used in some plastics. Baeyer won the Nobel prize for chemistry for his work. Barbara may well be the stuff of myth, but scientists have been known to name things after patients who were research subjects or provided samples (*see* Lacks, Henrietta). In case you were curious about the origin of various drug names, most are shortened versions of the names of their chemical components. Benzedrine, for example, is a carbonate of benzyl-methyl-carbinamine. Its name derives from the "benz" in benzyl and the suffix "edrine" as in "ephedrine," an alkaloid drug. Novocain was first registered as a trademark in 1905. Its name comes from the Latin "novo" meaning "new" and "cocaine," suggesting the drug is a form of cocaine. It is, in fact, a form of procaine.

Barca, Hamilcar

In 247 B.C., Hamilcar Barca took command of the Carthaginian forces in Sicily during the First Punic War with Rome. Carthage had lost most of its Sicilian possessions. Barca made repeated raids on the Romans from mountain bases near Palermo. He mounted a number of naval expeditions against Sicily and northern Italy but the Carthaginians were eventually defeated. Barca negotiated the treaty that ended the war. He then returned to Africa, where his mercenary troops staged a revolt. It wasn't until 238 B.C. that he was able to defeat the rebels. His victory earned him a great deal of power as the leader of Carthage's ruling party and he was able to occupy Spain as a new base against Rome. There he founded the city of Acra Leuce, now Alicante, and probably founded the city the Romans called Barcino before his death in battle in 229 or 228 B.C. The Carthaginians were replaced by the Romans in the first century B.C. They made Tarraco (modern-day Tarragona) their regional capital. During the third century A.D. Barcino replaced Tarraco in importance and became the major Roman outpost in the area of Hispania Citerior. With the disintegration of the Roman Empire came the invasion of the Visigoths, who occupied Barcino in A.D. 415 and renamed the city Barcinona—a name that, over time, evolved into *Barcelona*.

Barcolo, Edward Joel

Edward Joel Barcolo began his career as a bookkeeper for a manufacturer of bed springs and metal bed frames based in Buffalo, New York. He was apparently good with money, because in 1896 he bought the assets of his former employer to form the *Barcolo Manufacturing Company*. The company claims to be the originator of the coffee break in 1902 and in 1912 it started the first in-house hot-lunch program for its employees. There were few regulations on manufacturing in those days and many furniture makers stuffed their mattresses with whatever material they had on hand, from sawdust to corncobs. In 1914 the state of New York began licensing the manufacture of mattresses. Barcolo's company received the first such license, and until the program was discontinued, Barcolo had a license bearing the number one. Around this time Barcolo bought a tool company. During World War I, most of the company's output was reserved for the war effort. Barcolo's plants made forged parts for military aircraft. One of Edward Barcolo's last acts before he retired from the company in 1939 was the purchase of a license to produce "scientifically articulated" furniture. Using adjustable hospital beds as a model, Dr. Anton Lorenz had created a model for a reclining chair. The design was first used to manufacture reclining wheelchairs for World War II soldiers. Following the war, the company released its first commercial reclining chair, which it dubbed the "Barcaloafer." The product's name was later changed to *Barcalounger*. No one at the company is sure why Barcolo's name was transformed into "Barca," but some speculate that anti-Italian sentiment following the war may have been a factor. In 1989 the Barcolo Manufacturing Company changed its name to match its most famous product. Based in North Carolina, it is now known as *Barcalounger, Inc.*

Bass, William

William Bass began his career as a beer distributor. In 1777, he decided to change focus and start brewing. He formed *Bass and Company Pale Ale* and adopted a red triangle for its logo. In 1876, Bass became the first company in Britain to file for trademark protection under the new Trademark Registration Act of 1875. It joined forces with Charrington United in 1967. By 1970, Bass had about a quarter of the British beer market. In case you were wondering what the difference is between "ale" and "beer," here's the lowdown on where the two terms come from. The word beer once just meant "drink." It comes from the Latin "biber," from which we also get "imbibe" and "beverage." "Ale" once referred to anything bitter. The word "alum" comes from the same source. It used to be, back in Anglo-Saxon times, that people generally referred to the intoxicating beverage as "ale." The term "beer" came into vogue in the sixteenth century and today is far more common than "ale." Bass Ale, incidentally, was one of only two beers to be stocked on the *Titanic*. According to experts, there are probably at least twelve thousand bottles of Bass at the bottom of the Atlantic.

Baudot, Jean-Maurice-Emile

Jean-Maurice-Emile Baudot was born in 1845 in Magneux, France. He grew up to work for the French Telegraph Administration. There he tried to create a more efficient means of transmitting telegraphic information. In 1874, he received a patent on a telegraph code in which each letter was represented by a five-unit combination of current-on or current-off signals of equal duration. This became known as the *Baudot Code* or International Telegraphic Code No. 1. It was a great improvement over Morse code, which it soon displaced as the most commonly used telegraphic alphabet. Around the turn of the century, another five-bit code, the Murray Code, was invented. It soon displaced Baudot as the most utilized code, and was dubbed International Telegraph Code No. 2. Since Baudot's name was already used in connection with five-bit telegraphic code, however, it soon came to be associated with International Telegraph Code No. 2 as well, and Murray's name was forgotten. A shortened version of the Frenchman's name, *baud*, was given to the unit that measures the speed of data transmissions—for example, a 2,400-baud modem.

Bauer, Eddie

Eddie Bauer was born on Orcas Island in 1900, the son of Russian immigrants. He began his career at the age of fourteen working in a Seattle sporting-goods store, Piper & Taft. At that time he was already well known for his skills as a hunter, fisher, and marksman. He continued those hobbies while drifting from job to job. He worked as everything from an auto mechanic to a saxophone player. In 1920, with twenty-five dollars to his name, he decided to turn his sports hobby into a career. He opened a Seattle business called Eddie Bauer's Tennis Shop. The shop sold the regular selection of tennis and badminton rackets, which he strung himself. To manufacture tournament-quality badminton shuttlecocks, Bauer used large quantities of feathers. One day he was looking at the feathers and an idea struck him—what if he were to use the feathers as insulation in jackets? Thus the first down jackets were created. Bauer was not surprised to find that there was great demand for such warm clothing among other outdoorsmen, but he soon discovered another group for whom the coats were valuable—pilots. At high altitudes in the aircraft of the day, pilots were chilled by bitter cold. Aviators like Charles Lindbergh became some of Eddie Bauer's most loyal customers. When World War II began, Bauer received a government contract to supply military pilots with high-altitude gear. Each of the items carried the Eddie Bauer label and many of the soldiers remembered the name. After the war they wrote to Bauer's shop in large numbers. This is how Eddie Bauer began selling clothes by mail order. Bauer retired in 1968. At that time Eddie Bauer's was still just one store. By 1998 it had become a chain of 477. The chain was purchased by Spiegel in 1988 and brings in more than half of the combined companies' sales. Although he lived to see his business grow to national prominence, Bauer himself refused to set foot in the company's new headquarters building. On occasion, however, he would sit in his Cadillac in the visitor's parking lot and talk to company officials. He spent his retirement raising champion Labrador retrievers with his wife, Stine. After fifty-six years of marriage, Stine died of cancer in 1986. Eddie Bauer died two weeks later on April 18, 1986. He was eighty-six. The official cause of death was cardiac arrest, but his son attributed his death to a broken heart.

Beaufort, Francis

Francis Beaufort was born in 1774 in Ireland, the son of a clergyman of Huguenot origin. His father had published in 1772 one of the earliest detailed maps of Ireland and brought his son up with a love of geography and topography. At the age of fourteen Francis was sent to study at the newly founded Dunsink Observatory with his father's friend Dr. Henry Ussher, professor of astronomy at Trinity College. He joined the East India Company in 1789, and a year later he enlisted in the Royal Navy. He served in the Napoleonic wars and was wounded in a battle off Malaga. The bullet remained in his lungs for the rest of his life, causing him intermittent chest pains. Even so, he remained in the military for the next twenty years, eventually becoming a rear admiral and hydrographer to the Royal Navy. In 1806 Beaufort drew up a scale to measure wind speed. It ranged from zero for dead calm up to twelve or hurricane force, or in Beaufort's words "that which no canvas could withstand." The *Beaufort scale* was officially adopted by the Admiralty in 1838. Part of the Arctic Ocean lying south and east of a line connecting Point Barrow, Alaska, and Lands End, Prince Patrick Island is known as the *Beaufort Sea,* also in the hydrographer's honor.

Beiler, Anne

Anne Beiler was raised in an Amish-Mennonite family in Lancaster County, Pennsylvania. "I would say the things I was taught as a child are still very dear to my heart," she says. "The principles we were taught growing up were just simple things— be nice to other people and use the golden rule and go the second mile. I've used those things in business, because I didn't know you couldn't or shouldn't." At the age of twelve, she made cakes and pies, which her family brought to farmers' markets in their horse-drawn buggy. When she was nineteen, she married Jonas Beiler. The couple moved to Texas and had two daughters before returning to Lancaster County in 1987 to open a free counseling center. To fund the project, Anne Beiler worked at a concession stand at a Maryland farmers' market. When the owner decided to sell, she borrowed $6,000 from her father-in-law and bought it and another market in Downingtown, Pennsylvania. There she sold a number of snack foods including pizza and ice cream, but by far the most popular items on the menu were the hand-rolled pretzels. She decided to drop everything else and concentrate on pretzels. In 1988 she named her business *Auntie Anne's*. With no advertising besides word of mouth, the company started to carve out a piece of the $1.1 billion pretzel industry. Soon, others were contacting the entrepreneur to ask about franchising. In early 1989 the first Auntie Anne's franchise opened. Today there are more than six hundred stores worldwide, located primarily in shopping malls. The Family Information Center opened in 1992. Trivia question for pretzel fans: Which U.S. state produces 75 percent of the world's pretzels? Answer: Pennsylvania.

Bendix, Vincent

Vincent Hugo Bendix was born August 12, 1881 in Moline, Illinois. He was the oldest of three children of Swedish immigrants Reverend Jann and Anna Bengtson. The couple changed their name to Bendix and moved to Chicago when Vincent was still a boy. At sixteen, Bendix left for New York City. There he found odd jobs, including working as an elevator operator. In his off hours he studied engineering. The first time he saw an "auto buggy," Bendix knew his calling. He returned to Chicago and got a job with one of the top auto makers in the city. He considered the job to be an apprenticeship. As soon as he was able, Bendix started his own company to manufacture and sell the "Bendix Motor Buggy." He managed to sell 7,000 of the vehicles before going bankrupt in 1909. Bendix was determined to make a success in the new automobile industry, but he decided a new approach was in order. With more and more companies entering the field, Bendix reasoned, it would be more profitable to sell products to other auto companies than to try to compete with his own car. He went to work to develop a method for starting a motor carriage without having to crank the engine. The Eclipse Manufacturing Company of Elmira, New York was impressed with Bendix's pushbutton starters. They paid the inventor a royalty and manufactured the items. They were installed in Chevrolets in 1914. Sales boomed as more and more auto makers opted to abandon the crank. Bendix's next inspiration was a personal tragedy. In 1922, his father was struck and killed by an automobile with defective brakes. Bendix studied braking systems and discovered a French system he believed to be superior to anything then available on the U.S. market. He bought the rights to manufacture the Perrot system and introduced four-wheel brakes. Bendix brakes were soon being used in 25 percent of American cars. In 1924, his company, *The Bendix Corporation,* went public. Since the firm sold components, not complete vehicles, Bendix was relatively unaffected by the depression. The company was thus able to buy a number of other firms in the 1930s. Primarily, Bendix bought aviation parts manufacturers. A new branch of the company, *Bendix Aviation Corporation,* was formed. Bendix celebrated his success with lavish spending. He bought an oceanfront mansion and a number of other residences. His office was equipped with its own maid, cook, butler, and barber. To finance this lifestyle, he sold off stock in his company to General Motors. By 1938 GM owned a majority of Bendix stock. Bendix himself was spending $250,000 a month. To stop this drain, GM removed Bendix from the day-to-day operations of the company that bore his name. The man who had once been worth $50 million found himself in debt to the tune of $13 million by 1939. He was forced to declare bankruptcy. He left The Bendix Corporation for good in 1942. Yet he was not willing to admit defeat. That same year he was able to start a new company, *Bendix Helicopter*. The venture reportedly earned him $1 million. Bendix died in 1945 at the age of sixty-three.

Benedict

Benedict and his twin sister (who became Saint Scholastica) were born in Norcia, Italy in the early fifth century to noble parents. He left his studies in Rome and moved into an underground cave, where he threw off his vestments and dressed in nothing but animal skins. It is said that he stayed alive by being fed by a magic raven. Tempted by sexual thoughts of a beautiful girl in Rome, Benedict threw himself naked onto a thorn bush. He never succumbed to such temptations again. Word of the religiously devoted man spread, and he was soon joined by disciples and students who formed a religious order known as the *Benedictines*. Their guiding principle was "to work is to pray." Benedict finally left his cave after a priest named Florentius tried to poison him by putting a toad in his drinking cup. When this failed, Florentius tried to tempt the monks by bringing a group of nude women to dance among them. Benedict did not take a relaxing vacation. He traveled instead to Monte Cassio, a malarial swamp, where he converted collapsing temples to Roman gods into oratories to John the Baptist and Martin of Tours. There he wrote what would come to be known as *The Rule of Saint Benedict*. In an age when monasteries were the only centers of literature, art, and scholarship, his rule quickly replaced all others in Western monasteries. The guide described how often the monks should pray and for how long, how much work they should do, how they should travel, and how they should receive guests. He believed people should retreat from the stress of the world and lead lives of solitude. Benedict had visions of the future. He predicted that Monte Cassio would be destroyed by the Lombards. His monastery was destroyed after his death, as he envisioned. It was rebuilt, but brought to the ground again during World War II by the Allies, who thought it was a German headquarters. After his death, Benedict became a saint. He is the patron of cave explorers, the dying, monks, farm workers, and all of Europe. It is an interesting twist of fate that a hermit monk who preached hard work and celibacy would give his name to a liqueur. Benedict's rule is known for its moderation and flexibility. So over time, the many branches of the order developed very differently from the others. Autonomous houses were formed over the succeeding centuries. One monastery of the Order of St. Benedict in France in the sixteenth century was home to herbalist Dom Vincelli. The fields surrounding the abbey at Fecamp were rich in herbs and the monk studied them to make medicines and balms. One of his tonics was called Elixir Benedictin. Another monk, Dom Bernardo, transcribed the recipe and stored it with other documents in the abbey. It remained there until the French Revolution. In 1789, the monastery at Fecamp was burned to the ground, but some valuables were salvaged, including the parchment with the formula for the elixir. Alexandre Le Grand inherited the old manuscripts in 1862. The formula listed twenty-eight ingredients, but it was incomplete. It did not explain how to treat the plants or what amounts to use. Le Grand began experimenting and searching through the other parchments, and in 1863 he announced he had recreated the drink. Le Grand called his liqueur *Benedictine*. He labeled each bottle D.O.M., which stood for Deo optimo maximo or "for the most good and great God." There are about seventy-five Benedictine monasteries in the United States today.

Bennett, James Gordon

James Gordon Bennett was born May 10, 1841. His father, a Scottish immigrant, with an initial investment of $500 launched a newspaper called the *New York Herald* in his cellar. By the time young Gordon Bennett came of age, the newspaper was successful and profitable. The younger Bennett took over as manager of the paper in 1867. He co-founded the Associated Press news service and financed Henry Stanley's expedition to Africa to find David Livingston. An avid yachter, he established the *James Gordon Bennett Cup,* a yachting trophy, and similar prizes for ballooning and aviation. The first air

race, held in 1909, was called *"The Gordon Bennett."* It was held
in Rheims, France, and was won by Glenn Curtiss. In England,
however, Bennett's name is familiar for an entirely different
reason. Called the "rogue and rambunctious heir," Bennett was
not blessed with great social graces. In 1876 he was engaged to
a beautiful American socialite, Caroline May. On New Year's
Day, 1877, he attended a party at her father's New York house
and became so drunk that he mistook the fireplace for a toilet.
May's brother challenged Bennett to a duel. Neither party was
physically injured, but Bennett had worn out his welcome in
New York. He moved to Paris, but he did not maintain a low
profile. He built a yacht at a cost, in today's money, of about two
million dollars. It had its own Turkish bath, a masseur on call
twenty-four hours a day, and a padded room holding a cow to
provide fresh milk for brandy milk punch. For fun, Bennett
liked to go into the city's most expensive restaurants and pull
the tablecloths off the tables, covering unsuspecting diners with
food. He would then pull out a large roll of money to pay for the
damages. As his reputation spread, restaurateurs would call out
the name "Gordon Bennett" as a warning whenever he walked
through the door. Even today in England, the name Gordon
Bennett is a euphemistic expletive signaling surprise. An
American name that stands in as a mild expletive is Sam Hill.
The expression supposedly comes from a Col. Samuel Hill of
Guilford, Connecticut. The 1946 text, *The Encyclopedia of
American Politics,* by Edwin V. Mitchell, says he was always
running for office and losing. Hence the expression *"run like
Sam Hill."* Apparently, Mitchell's book is the only record of
Hill's existence. The name can usually be found standing in
for "hell" in sentences like "Who in the Sam Hill was he?"

Bentley, Edmund Clerihew

Edmund Clerihew Bentley was born July 10, 1875 in London,
England. He attended St. Paul's School in London and there
met author G. K. Chesterton, who became his closest friend.
Next he attended the University of Oxford, where he studied
law. He soon abandoned the legal profession, however, in favor
of a career as a writer. He worked for the *Daily News* and then

for the *Daily Telegraph*. Fans of detective fiction know Bentley as the author of *Trent's Last Case*, written in a naturalistic style that replaced the romantic infallibility of Sherlock Holmes. The book has been said to mark the end of the Holmes era. Two decades later, Bentley revived this character in *Trent's Own Case* and a collection of short stories, *Trent Intervenes*. He is best known, however, for a form of verse he invented. The four-line, humorous verse usually contains the name of a well-known person and has lines of uneven length, an irregular meter, and usually an awkward, strained rhyme. As the *Encyclopedia Britannica* put it, "The humour of the form lies in its purpose-fully flat-footed inadequacy: both the verse and its treatment of the subject are off the mark, as in the work of a reluctant schoolboy." The form is called a *clerihew*. Here is an example:

Edmund's middle name was Clerihew,
A name possessed by very few.
But verses by Mr. Bentley
Succeeded eminently.

Bentley, Walter Owen

In 1905, sixteen-year-old Walter Owen Bentley, "W.O." to his friends, went to work at the Great Northern Railway Locomotive Works in Doncaster, England. In his spare time, Bentley and his brother took up motor racing. The pair won a gold medal in their very first event, the London to Edinburgh Trial. Bentley's passion for automobiles became more and more apparent so in 1912 his family decided to help him by finding a company that would import French racecars. One day, while he was at the factory, Bentley saw an aluminum paperweight on a desk and had a sudden flash of inspiration. Up to that point, engineers had always used cast iron to make engine pistons. Why not use lightweight aluminum instead? The brainstorm came only a year before the outbreak of World War I. During the war, Bentley worked for the Technical Board of the Royal Naval Air Service. His lightweight pistons were put to use in the *Sopwith Camel* and other military aircraft. Following the war, the pistons finally found their way into race-cars. Bentley Motors was created in 1919 to manufacture the

cars. In the 1920s Bentleys became famous for their many victories at important races, most notably Le Mans. The fame
helped make the Bentley a sought-after luxury automobile, a
fact that hurt the company in 1931 when the recession drasti-
cally reduced the number of people shopping for luxury
items. That year, Bentley fell into receivership. W. O. Bentley
expected Napier, another manufacturer of luxury vehicles, to
buy the company. At the last minute, however, another auto
maker came in with a slightly higher bid. That company was
Rolls-Royce. The former rival was not gracious in its victory.
According to Michael Scarlett of the *Daily Telegraph,* Bentley
wanted to go to work for Napier, but Rolls-Royce claimed he
was part of the assets they had purchased. They also claimed to
own Bentley's medals and trophies. As the story goes, a Rolls-
Royce executive told one of Bentley's winning drivers he could
keep only two of the racing trophies. The rest would be melted down. Bentley remained with the company, but he had little say in the design of Bentley motorcars. He became more
and more unhappy with the arrangement and, in 1935, when
his contract came up for renewal, he left the company that
bore his name. He passed away in 1971. His name, however,
continued to have value as a mark of driving luxury. In 1998,
two German auto makers, BMW and Volkswagen, went head to
head in an effort to buy Rolls-Royce/Bentley. In the resulting
deal, Volkswagen paid $790 million for the Rolls-Royce factory
in Crewe, England and its employees. For $65 million, BMW
purchased the Rolls-Royce name. Rolls-Royce and Bentley will
officially part company in 2003.

Bering, Vitus Jonassen

It all began because Peter the Great was embarrassed. During
his travels in Europe, some geographers had asked him how
much land there was in Russian Siberia. Peter didn't know. So
in 1725, shortly before his death, the czar commissioned Vitus
Bering, a Dane who served with the Russian Navy, to conduct
an expedition. His instructions read, in part: "You are to pro-
ceed . . . along the coast which extends to the north and which
seems, in all probability (since we don't know where it ends),

to be part of America. With this in view you are to try to find where it is joined to America, and to reach some city in European possession, and to inquire what it is called and to make note of it, and to secure exact information and to mark this on a map and then return home." Bering put together a crew of explorers, sailors, and shipbuilders. It took the men three years to make their way across the icy, roadless terrain, reach the shore, and build a ship, which they christened *St. Gabriel*. They sailed through a strait, which proved that Asia and America were not joined. They named it the *Bering Strait*. At its narrowest point, the Bering Strait is only thirty-six miles wide. The channel is usually completely frozen over from October to June. In the strait are two small islands about a mile apart. One of the islands is in American territory; the other is part of Siberia. The International Date Line now runs between them. Although the continents were not connected in Bering's time, it is believed that they used to be. Scientists believe that the Native Americans are the descendents of Asians who traversed the land bridge thousands of years ago. But back to Bering—after sailing through the strait that now bears his name, his crew continued towards Alaska but they were unable to see the land because of thick fog. Bering returned to St. Petersburg, made a report, and planned a follow-up mission. In 1741, the Great Northern Expedition began. Two ships, the *St. Peter* commanded by Bering and the *St. Paul* helmed by Alexei Chirikov, set sail towards America. The mission got off to an inauspicious start when Bering spent several days searching for a nonexistent landmass that his mapmakers had drawn on their maps for years even though they had no real reason to believe it was there. The *St. Peter* and *St. Paul* got separated from each other but they each continued towards Alaska. Members of both crews suffered from scurvy yet the ships reached American soil in July 1741. Chirikov's crew arrived first. He sent ashore a small boat carrying ten sailors who were to search for fresh water. They never returned. After a brief wait, the sick sailors headed back towards Russia, where they arrived on October 8. By the time they got back, twenty-one of the crew of eighty had perished. The *St. Peter* landed in Alaska on July 16. Bering saw the volcano of St. Elias but, much to the chagrin of his resident scientist, a German named Georg Wilhelm Stelle, he decided not to spend the winter there gathering data. Instead, the crew headed back towards Siberia. On the way, a number of crew members died of scurvy. Bering was himself suffering from the malady when they sighted what they thought was the shore of Kamachatka in Siberia. They landed on November 6 only to discover that they had actually run aground on a small island off the coast and that their ship was too badly battered to make the rest of the voyage. The crew was stranded there for the remainder of the winter. Many men died, including Vitus Bering. The island where he died is now known as *Bering Island*. The surviving members of the crew finally reached Kamachatka in summer 1742.

Bermúdez, Juan

In the early 1500s, possibly as early as 1503, a Spanish explorer named Juan Bermúdez discovered a group of islands in the West Atlantic clustered together in the shape of a fishhook. He called them "Islands of Devils" because of the strong winds in the area. Several years later, a navigator, Fernandez de Oviedo, sailed close to the islands and named them *"Bermudas"* in honor of Bermúdez. Spain was not especially interested in claiming the islands, however, because of the many hidden reefs. That, combined with strong winds, has made it one of the most difficult regions for sailors to navigate. In 1595, Sir Walter Raleigh passed Bermuda, describing it as being in "a hellish sea for thunder, lightning and storms." In 1609, a British ship was blown off course and shipwrecked on land the crew named Somers Isles. The event inspired William Shakespeare to write *The Tempest*. This is but a first chapter in the history of an area of the sea dubbed *The Bermuda Triangle* or The Devil's Triangle. The U.S. Board of Geographic Names does not recognize the Bermuda Triangle, which it describes as "an imaginary area located off the southeastern Atlantic coast of the United States." The apexes of the triangle are generally accepted to be Bermuda, Miami, Florida, and San Juan, Puerto Rico. Whether or not there is a magical area that causes planes and ships to disappear, there are definitely hazards in the Caribbean. Besides the wind and reefs, the triangle is one of only two areas in the world where a magnetic compass points towards true north. Normally it points toward magnetic north. If the compass variation is not compensated for, a navigator could become easily lost. Under the third charter of the Virginia Company, sixty British settlers colonized Bermuda in the 1700s. They imported Indian and African slaves until the practice was outlawed in 1807. Today, about three-fifths of the population of Bermuda is descended from slaves.

Bibb, John

John Bibb was the youngest son born to Richard and Lucy Booker Bibb. The Bibb family moved to Kentucky in 1798. Early on, Bibb demonstrated a keen intellect. He decided to become a lawyer and studied under Judge H. F. Broadnax. He put his legal career on hold when the War of 1812 broke out. He joined the Fourth Kentucky Volunteer Brigade. After a well-fought battle, he was promoted from private to major. Following the war, Bibb returned to Kentucky and in 1814 was admitted to the bar. He was elected to the Kentucky House of Representatives in 1827 and 1828. And, from 1830 to 1834, he served Kentucky as a state senator. He married Sarah P. Hopkins Horsley on August 24, 1831. Around 1856, the couple moved into a large house in Frankfort, Kentucky. Bibb took up gardening as a hobby. In his large backyard garden, he developed a new variety of lettuce. He called his lettuce "limestone." After his death in 1884, however, others dubbed it *Bibb lettuce* in his honor. In recent years, iceberg lettuce has overshadowed most of the other varieties in grocery stores, but there are, in fact, some eight hundred varieties. Bibb is the best known "butterhead lettuce." Such strains have a tight, small head and a more distinct flavor than iceberg.

Bidder, George Parker

George Parker Bidder was born in 1806, part of a family gifted with great powers of recall. One of his brothers knew the Bible by heart. Another, who worked as an actuary, had the misfortune of having all his books destroyed in a fire. He simply rewrote them all from memory over the course of six months. As a boy, Bidder's stonemason father exhibited him in England as the "calculating phenomenon." Members of the audience would try to stump the child prodigy with mathematical questions. At the age of twelve he was asked at one performance how many bulls' tails were needed to reach the moon. He replied, "One, if it's long enough." Not surprisingly, Bidder went on to study mathematics at Edinburgh University. In 1834, Bidder and a partner, Robert Stephenson, built the London to Birmingham Railway. Bidder also co-founded the Electric Telegraph Company, designed the Victoria Docks in London, engineered the Royal Danish Railway, and invented the railway swing bridge. Charles Dickens did not go to great lengths to disguise the identity of the inspiration for a character in his 1854 novel *Hard Times*. The character named "George Bitzer" was described by David E. E. Sloane in the *Dickens Studies Newsletter* as "one of Dickens's most grotesque representations of selfish calculation . . . Dickens may have been employing a cause celebre among the phrenologists of the 1830s as a source for his calculating traits and even his name. . . . The specific source appears to have been George Parker Bidder, practically undisguised in the minor name change."

Birch, John

John Birch was an air-force officer who was killed by Chinese Communists on August 25, 1945. In the view of the society that bears his name, he was "the first casualty of the Cold War." On December 9, 1958, a retired candy maker, Robert H. W. Welch, Jr., founded *The John Birch Society* to combat Communism and promote various ultraconservative causes. The group reached its peak of influence in the early 1960s. From an estimated 100,000 members in the early 1960s, membership dropped to 80,000 during the 1970s and then nose-dived during Ronald Reagan's presidency, hitting 15,000 in 1989. In recent years it has attracted some new members. In 1995, the group estimated its membership to be around 50,000. Fans of Bob Dylan will be familiar with his satire of the anti-Communist society: *"Talkin' John Birch Paranoid Blues."* Dylan canceled an appearance on "The Ed Sullivan Show" in the spring of 1963 when the network refused to permit him to perform the song.

Bolívar, Simón José Antonio de la Santísima Trinidad

Simón Bolívar was born in Caracas, Venezuela on July 24, 1783, into the aristocratic family of don Juan Vicente Bolívar y Ponte and doña María de la Concepción Palacios y Blanco. He received a classical education from personal tutors until he was orphaned at the age of nine. He remained in the care of an uncle until he was fifteen, when he was sent to Spain to study. In Spain, Bolívar met María Teresa Rodríguez del Toro y Alaysa, whom he married in 1802. Tragically, the union lasted only a year. Bolívar's bride died of yellow fever in 1803 shortly after the couple returned to Venezuela. The grief-stricken groom never remarried. Bolívar spent the next few years traveling between Venezuela, Spain, and the United States. In 1808, Napoleon installed his brother, Joseph, as king of Spain. This launched a great popular revolt known as the Peninsular War. That year, the Caracas junta declared its independence from Spain and Bolívar enthusiastically joined the rebel army under the command of Francisco de Miranda, but in 1812, his forces were defeated at Puerto Cabello, Venezuela and Bolívar soon had to flee to Cartagena in New Granada (now in Colombia). There, Bolívar wrote the *Manifiesto de Cartagena,* in which he argued that New Granada should help liberate Venezuela because they had a common cause. New Granada responded to the argument and in 1813, with New Granada's help, he invaded Venezuela. He entered Mérida on May 23 and was proclaimed "Liberator" by the people. In 1814, the Spanish recaptured Caracas and the revolutionaries were scattered by a royalist force. Bolívar escaped to Jamaica, where he wrote *La Carta de Jamaica (The Letter from Jamaica),* which advocated republican government throughout Spanish America, modeled after Great Britain. That same year, Bolívar traveled to Haiti and petitioned its president, Alexander Sabes Petión, to help the Spanish-American cause. With Haitian backing,

Bolívar launched an invasion of Venezuela. After a disastrous failure, he returned to Haiti. In 1817, he returned to his homeland to lead the revolutionary army. He recruited José Antonio Páez, who led an army of plainsmen and European veterans of the Napoleonic wars. The Battle of Boyaca of August 7, 1819 was a great victory for Bolívar. That year, Bolívar created the Angostura Congress, which founded Gran Colombia (a federation of present-day Venezuela, Colombia, Panama, and Ecuador). Bolívar became president. Several victories followed, leading up to the Battle of Ayacucho on December 9, 1824, which finally ended Spanish domination in the New World. On August 6, 1825, the land formerly known as Upper Peru became the *Republic of Bolivia,* making Bolívar one of the few people in history to have a country named in his honor while he was still alive. Bolívar wrote the constitution for his namesake land himself. Although he has become one of the most revered South American heroes, he was not universally loved in his day. On September 24, 1828, he barely escaped with his life after supporters of his vice-president, Francisco de Paula Santander, tried to assassinate him. The attack was foiled when Bolívar's mistress, Manuelita Saenz, signaled for him to leap to safety from a balcony at the National Palace. Disillusioned, bitter, penniless, surrounded by factional fighting, and suffering from tuberculosis, Simón Bolívar died on December 17, 1830,

Boole, George

George Boole was born in Lincoln, England on November 2, 1815. Precociously gifted in mathematics, he nonetheless had little formal training in it. His father, a tradesman, taught him basic math and how to make optical instruments. Boole began teaching at the tender age of sixteen. He opened his own school at twenty. For fun, he liked to read obscure mathmatical papers. In 1839, he began writing algebraic papers of his own. His first published work was *Researches on the Theory of Analytical Transformations,* which appeared in the *Cambridge Mathematical Journal.* The subject of the composition was differential equations and the algebraic problem of linear transformation, emphasizing the concept of invariance. After earning the esteem of his peers with several more publications, he was appointed professor of mathematics at Queen's College, County Cork in 1849 despite his lack of a college education. In 1859, he published a two-volume book called *A Treatise on Differential Equations*. It explained, in somewhat more complex terms, that any problem could be solved by proceeding in one direction or another. Therefore, the correct answer lay in the right combination of two digits, 0 and 1. The system became known as *boolean algebra*. Boole, by the way, was married to the bearer of another famous name, Mary Everest, the niece of George ("My Name Is on a Really Big Rock") Everest. Boole's name, however, might not have been heard outside of mathematics circles were it not for Claude E. Shannon, who in 1938 published an article based on the master's thesis he had written about Boole's binary system. Shannon showed that Boole's zeroes and ones could be used to represent the functions of switches in electronic circuits. As a result, boolean logic is the basis of all computers. Even many of us who do not routinely worry about the internal workings of our laptops use Boole's name when we use *boolean expressions* on Internet search engines.

Borghese

According to the *Boston Courier* of 1857 there was a man named Borghese who, in the 1830s, made a good living circulating counterfeit bills from nonexistent banks to people in the West. People referred to the money as Borghese currency. Some claim this term was eventually shortened to *bogus*. Robert Hendrickson, author of *Human Words*, believed there was some merit to the tale. He pointed out that the *Dictionary of Americanisms* traces the word bogus back to 1838, which would coincide with the career of Mr. Borghese as reported in the *Courier*. Other authors have identified an 1827 editorial of the *Plainsville Telegraph* of Plainsville, Ohio as the first printed occurrence of the word. If correct, this would mean the term existed long before Borghese. Other scholars have speculated that bogus comes from "tantrabogus," an Old Vermont term for bogeyman; "baggasse," a French word meaning counterfeit or illegitimate; "boghus," a gypsy word with a similar meaning; or "bagasse," a term for the refuse of sugarcane after the juice is extracted.

Bose, Amar

Amar Bose, the son of an Indian immigrant and an American schoolteacher, grew up in Philadelphia. The family found itself the target of discrimination in 1930s America. "There wasn't a restaurant in Philadelphia where I could be served," Bose would later say. "In those days you couldn't even rent a house." His father ran an import business and worked his way through Temple University by washing dishes and pumping gas. As soon as he was old enough, Amar helped the family economy. At thirteen, during World War II, as the political climate curtailed the import business, he earned money fixing radios. With most of the country's men overseas, there was great demand for repairmen. The business had soon grown to be one of the largest repair services in the city. In 1947, Bose entered the Massachusetts Institute of Technology. He earned both his bachelor's and master's of science degrees in 1952 and an Sc.D. in 1956. He stayed on as an assistant professor of electrical engineering after his graduation. His graduation present to himself was a stereo system. He tested a number of speakers, but didn't like the sound quality of any of them. So, with the help of his grad students, he launched a research project on psychoacoustics—the study of sounds as perceived by the human auditory system. The study showed that more than 80 percent of the music a person hears is first bounced off ceilings, walls, and floors. Sound channeled through speakers, however, was aimed right at the listener. So Bose designed a speaker that would reflect the sound rather than aiming it. He remained at MIT, but also hired one of his students, Sherwin Greenblatt, to help market his patented system. The first commercial product created by the Bose Corporation was a reflecting loudspeaker, released in 1968. His speakers came to be a favorite of audiophiles. *Fortune* magazine dubbed Bose speakers "so good you may think

Ol' Blue Eyes is in the back seat of your car." Not every publication was impressed with the Bose approach. In 1970, *Consumer Reports* critiqued the Bose 901 direct/reflecting loudspeaker, concluding, "Individual instruments heard through the 901 . . . tended to wander about the room." Bose sued the publication for "product disparagement." The court battle lasted thirteen years and went all the way to the Supreme Court. Bose lost. Over the next few decades the company came out with a number of innovative sound systems for homes, automobiles, and concert halls. It has also developed noise abatement systems and headsets for air travel. In 1994, after nine years of research, Bose introduced a system to allow designers to hear what a public place will sound like before it is built. Bose now sells more loudspeakers than any other audio equipment company, and its sound systems have been installed on the *QE2* and the space shuttle *Endeavor.* As of 1998, Amar Bose's estimated $550 million put him squarely on *Forbes* magazine's list of the 400 wealthiest Americans.

Boulle, Andre-Charles

Andre-Charles Boulle was born November 11, 1642 in Paris, France. As a young man Boulle studied drawing, painting, and sculpture and he put his training into practice as a furniture designer. He had gained such prominence by 1672 that Louis XIV named him royal cabinetmaker for the palace of Versailles. He became a favorite of European royals and nobility. Among his clients were King Philip V of Spain, the Duke of Bourbon, and the electors of Bavaria and Cologne. Boulle's elaborate designs used exotic woods from South America and India. Rosewood, ebony, satinwood, tulipwood, oak, and walnut were adorned with brass ornamentation. He employed and popularized marquetry, a process first used in sixteenth-century Italy. After he retired, his sons carried on the family tradition and further strengthened the association of the name Boulle with a kind of furniture. Eventually, any piece with some copper inlay on a black or red ground came to be described as *buhl work.* In 1993, a six-legged desk in ebony and chiseled bronze by Andre-Charles Boulle sold at an auction for $17 million.

Brach, Emil

In 1904, Emil J. Brach left his successful job with a Chicago candy company. With a capital of $1,000, he and his sons, Edwin and Frank, opened Palace of Sweets. At first they planned to sell candies in the store only. They soon discovered, however, that they would have to sell to other vendors as well if they were going to stay in business. With a name change to E. J. Brach & Sons, they started to sell caramels to shops along Chicago's Loop. Shortly thereafter they invented something that would make their product stand out among its competitors. It was not a new kind of sweet, but a new kind of packaging. The Brachs developed equipment that made it easy to wrap caramels and other candies individually. This method eventually made Brach's the biggest seller of bagged candies in the country.

Braniff, Thomas and Paul

The Braniff brothers, Thomas and Paul, were born in Kansas City, Missouri—Thomas Elmer in 1891 and Paul Revere in 1897. The family moved to Oklahoma City in 1900. Thomas demonstrated his ability for business early on when he joined his father's insurance business. Shortly thereafter he opened his own office with a partner. He built his company into one of the leading mortgage and insurance firms in the Southwest. In 1916 he bought out his partner to form the T. E. Braniff company. This evolved into the Braniff Investment Company. This enterprise was so successful that Thomas's company was able to build Oklahoma City's first skyscraper. Meanwhile, Paul's career had taken off in another direction. During the First World War, Paul enlisted in the army and served as an aviation mechanic. Stationed in France, he learned to fly. He would maintain an interest in aviation even after the war when he returned to the States and joined his brother's company. Back home he earned an official pilot's license from Orville Wright and bought his own airplane, a surplus "Jenny." He paid for his expensive hobby by charging curious passengers for short flights and by barnstorming. Paul convinced his older brother that aviation could be a viable business. In 1928 Tom agreed to give it a shot, and with four other investors, he bought an airplane and formed the Oklahoma Aero Club. This evolved into Paul R. Braniff, Inc. Paul was the first pilot of his namesake airline. In 1929 the airline merged with the Universal Aviation Company of St. Louis. After a year's hiatus to help a friend with a struggling airline in Mexico, Paul returned to the airline determined to help it expand. Four years later, he won an airmail contract that had been lost by United Airlines during reorganization. The airmail routes made Braniff's future secure, at least for the next few decades. Paul sold his interest in the airline to his brother in 1936 and retired from the company. In 1950, Braniff merged with Mid-Continent airlines. The only major airline to bear the name of its founder, Braniff celebrated its twenty-fifth anniversary in 1954. That same year both of the Braniff brothers passed away. Paul died of complications related to bone cancer, and Thomas was killed in a private airplane crash. The airline, however, was about to enter the most high profile period of its history. In 1965 Braniff hired interior designer Alexander Calder and couturier Emilio Pucci to give the airline a complete makeover. The company announced it was "the end of the plain plane." The campaign was the brainchild of Mary Wells, a savvy PR expert from New York, and Braniff's president, Harding Lawrence (whom she later married). Multicolored aircraft with matching air-hostess uniforms drew the attention of those who wanted to take part in fashionable flight. "Any airline that wants to outdo the Braniff razzmatazz is going to have to work hard," wrote *Business Week*. The airline did it again in 1977. This time the new look came courtesy of the famous designer Halston. Braniff's troubles began a year later with the deregulation of the airline industry. Fearing Congress would reverse its decision, Braniff acted fast. It launched a huge expansion, buying up airport gates and traffic routes at such a rate that it could not afford to pay the interest on its loans. By 1979, with fuel prices soaring, Braniff was faced with a loss of $9.8 million. By 1980 the company's interest payments alone totaled more than $92 million. It was forced to mortgage its entire fleet. A wealthy Chicago family bought the bankrupt airline in 1982 and tried to make it over into a discount carrier. That incarnation of Braniff also went bust. In 1991, Jeffrey Chodorow of Philadelphia and Arthur Cohen of Manhattan bought Braniff's name for $313,000 and the aircraft of the defunct Emerald Air of Houston. Former casino executive and amateur racecar driver Gregory B. Dix became the CEO of the last airline to call itself Braniff. This Braniff went bankrupt after only one month, but it kept operating and selling discount tickets until the summer of 1992, when it abruptly stopped flying, leaving ticket holders without flights or refunds. By 1995 the name *Braniff International Airlines* existed only as a case in bankruptcy court, where some nine hundred creditors sought reimbursement.

Braun, Max

Engineer Max Braun was born in East Prussia in 1890. He began his professional life making and selling electronic components from his apartment in Frankfurt, Germany in 1921. The radio industry was brand new and there were more than enough opportunities to sell his parts. By 1928, he'd become sufficiently established to move out of his home. Instead of just providing parts, he decided to go ahead and build entire radios himself. A year later he sold the first Braun radio. He was one of the first to incorporate receiver and speaker into one set. The company quickly became one of the largest German radio manufacturers. By 1932, his had also become one of the first companies to combine a radio and phonograph in a single set. In just a few years he would have a staff of 1,000 and win an award at the Paris World's Fair "for exceptional achievements in phonographs." All this time, however, another product was on his mind. It was a combination business idea and hobby. Braun was always tinkering with his electric shaver. He carried his prototype with him constantly. He worked it and reworked it. Finally, in 1949, he was ready to sell the world's first electric foil shaver. Mass production began a year later. Braun did not live long enough to see much of the success of his product. He died in 1951 and left the business to his sons Arthur and Erwin. In 1997, *The Braun Group* had sales of $1.744 billion and a profit of $304 million.

Bristol, William

In 1887 two men, William Bristol and John Ripley Myers, pooled their resources and bought a failing business, the Clinton Pharmaceutical Company, for $5,000. Bristol became president and Myers vice-president of the new venture, which was incorporated December 13, 1887. The project was not an immediate success; in fact, the company would not turn a profit until a year after Myers' death in 1899. That same year, the company became known as *Bristol-Myers*. The first big product for the company was Sal Hepatica, a laxative mineral salt. Shortly thereafter, they released Ipana toothpaste. The two products helped the company expand its regional presence to a national level. In 1924, Myers' heirs decided to share their part of the company and Bristol-Myers went public in 1929. In 1943, the company bought Cheplin Laboratories, which soon became a key supplier of penicillin for Allied soldiers. At that time, the largest penicillin production plant in the world, however, was owned by a company called Squibb. Originally known as E. R. Squibb and Sons, the firm had been formed in 1856 by Edward Robinson Squibb of Brooklyn, New York. In 1989, Squibb and Bristol-Myers merged, forming *Bristol-Myers Squibb*. The company owns such brands as Clairol and Excedrin, but some 70 percent of its $20 billion in sales comes from pharmaceuticals. And whatever happened to Ipana toothpaste? The product was a bestseller from 1936 to 1945. In 1957, Ipana Plus was released in a squeeze bottle instead of a tube. Its 1950s ad campaign, "Brusha brusha brusha, get the new Ipana," is familiar to a generation. New brands surfaced in the 1960s, however, that relegated Ipana to the back of the grocery-store shelf. In 1968, Bristol-Myers dropped the brand. It was sold to two Minnesota businessmen a year later. Initially the new Ipana did well. Eventually, however, sales lagged again. By 1991, the Ipana name had been acquired by Procter and Gamble, which launched a joint venture with a Turkish company. Ipana is now one of the top toothpastes in Turkey.

Brodie, Steve

Steve Brodie was a newsboy in Manhattan in the 1880s. As he

delivered his papers, he dreamed of seeing his own name on the front page. So determined was he to make this dream a reality—and to win a $200 bet—that on July 23, 1886, he jumped from the Brooklyn Bridge 130 feet into the East River. He was arrested the next day for "attempted suicide" but that was nothing more than a nuisance. His jump had made him an instant celebrity. Right away the Brooklyn Museum offered him $100 a week to be on exhibit as "the world's most courageous man." Next he put together a vaudeville act in which he shouted, "I'll save the girl!" and jumped from a cardboard bridge onto the stage while a stagehand threw confetti to simulate a splash. People kept asking him to recreate his famous jump for real, but he refused. Some people speculated that he'd lost his nerve, so he planned another stunt. On September 7, 1889, dressed in a rubber suit with steel bands, he swam in the rapids below Niagara Falls. He was swept away by the current and finally fished out a half-mile downstream, bruised and gasping for air. The stunt cemented Brodie's reputation as a daredevil, and he felt comfortable enough with his status to retire and open a saloon. There is a famous story about an encounter between Brodie and the father of boxer Gentleman Jim Corbett. Brodie had bet against Corbett in a heavyweight fight against John L. Sullivan. Corbett won the 1892 match, but Corbett's father, Patrick, was infuriated by Brodie. One day Corbett took his father into Brodie's saloon to introduce him. Patrick Corbett took one look at Steve Brodie and said with a sneer, "So you're the man who jumped over the Brooklyn Bridge." "Oh, no," Brodie corrected him. "I didn't jump over it; I jumped off it." "Oh," Corbett said. "I thought you jumped over it. Any damned fool could jump off it." In any case, the name "Brodie" survives in the expression *"to pull a brodie,"* meaning to blunder or take a wild chance.

Bronck, Jonas

In 1641, Jonas Bronck, a Swedish merchant sea captain, arrived in the area then known as New Netherlands with his bride and a small number of Dutch, Danish, and German indentured servants. He bought 500 acres of farmland in a region that had been called Keskeskeck by the Weckquasgeek, the indigenous Algonquin-speaking community that inhabited the area thousands of years prior to the arrival of the Dutch. Some accounts say the Weckquasgeek sold the property to the Dutch East India Company, which, in turn, sold it to Bronck. Some say that Bronck bought it directly from the Indians for 400 beads. In either case, Bronck and his servants built a small community of houses and barns. They cleared the fields, grew corn and tobacco, and grazed livestock. Bronck and his family were also known for their social skills. As the story goes, they often threw parties and the people who attended said they were going to the Broncks'. Eventually, this became shortened to *The Bronx*, which is why we still say "The Bronx" and not simply "Bronx" today (and why we don't say "The Brooklyn" and "The Manhattan"). Jonas Bronck died in 1643, and his small community dispersed. He gave his name to the *Bronx River*, and eventually to the northernmost of New York's boroughs. It is separated from Manhattan by the Harlem River and is bordered on the north by Westchester County, by the Hudson River to the west, the East River to the south, and Long Island Sound to the east. A celebrated Bronx landmark, Yankee Stadium, is probably the origin of the expression *"Bronx cheer."* The contemptuous sound may have been a common feature at the stadium in the 1920s.

Browning, John Moses

John M. Browning was born January 23, 1855, a descendent of one of America's ealiest settlers, Capt. John Browning, who arrived in the colonies in 1622 aboard the *Abigail.* Browning's father, Jonathon, had moved to Ogden, Utah three years prior to his birth to escape prejudice against Mormons. The Mormons at that time endorsed polygamy. John M. Browning's mother, Elizabeth Clark, was Jonathan Browning's second of three wives. In all, the man had twenty-two children, of which only two were from Elizabeth. The Browning clan ran a tannery and a small gun shop. Since this was a frontier family, it seemed natural for fourteen-year-old John to give his brother, Matthew, a rifle for his birthday. He constructed the weapon himself out of spare parts. Years later, he was repairing a complicated rifle and became frustrated. He said, "I could build a better gun than this." His father replied, "I know you could, John Moses. I'd like to see you try." So he did. He finished his single-shot rifle in 1879. It was an all-around eventful year for Browning. In April he married Rachel Teresa Child. On October 7 of that year he was granted U.S. Patent No. 220,271—the first of his eventual 128 gun patents. The single-shot earned him $8,000. "It made me so rich that I've never worried about money since," Browning would later say. "It gave me $8,000 worth of certainty that I could invent things for which people would pay large prices." A year later, following the death of his father, John and his brothers, Matthew, Jonathan Edmund, Thomas Samuel, William, and George, inherited the shop and expanded the business. Browning continued to develop new firearms into the 1920s. His last patent application, for a 9mm, short-recoil, locked-breech, exposed-hammer semiautomatic pistol, was filed June 28, 1923. John Moses Browning died of heart failure in 1926 at the age of seventy-one. The following year the J. M. and M. S. Browning Company was incorporated in Utah with the *Browning Arms Company* as a subsidiary.

Broyhill, James and Thomas

Thomas Broyhill, born in 1877, and James Edgar ("Ed") Broyhill, born in 1892, grew up on the family farm in North Carolina. Their father, Isaac, owned, in addition to the farm, a molasses mill and a grinding mill. Thomas grew up to work in the lumbering business. By the time he was in his early twenties he already had two sawmills of his own. Meanwhile, younger brother James was attending school. In 1913, at the age of twenty-one, he had decided he didn't want to stay on the farm all his life. He went to the Appalachian Training School to earn a high-school diploma, but was drafted to serve in World War I before he could complete his studies. Thomas's business continued to grow. He acquired a small firm known as the Lenoir Furniture Company. After the war, Ed Broyhill went to work for his brother's furniture-making company as a typist. During evenings and weekends, he sold life insurance to raise extra money. In 1926, Ed learned that the company that supplied chairs and rockers to

Lenoir Furniture had burned down. Sensing an opportunity, he mortgaged his house and used the $5,000 to found his own chair-making business in an old buggy shop. The gamble paid off. The Lenoir Chair Company took in almost $200,000 in its first year. Over the next several years, Ed continued to expand by purchasing a number of other furniture-making enterprises. He continued to work at brother Tom's company as well. In 1936, Tom had a heart attack and decided it was time to slow down. Ed, meanwhile, continued to expand operations. In 1941 he bought a bedroom-furniture manufacturer for $100,000. Tom thought his brother was "out of his mind." Ed, who now owned six plants, consolidated his operations under the name *Broyhill Furniture Factories,* later known as *Broyhill Furniture Industries.*

Brudenell, James Thomas

James Brudenell was born October 16, 1797, in Hambleden, England into a wealthy and titled family. He was the firstborn and only son of a family that also boasted seven daughters. "The Brudenells were proverbially good-looking," Richard Cavendish wrote in *History Today.* James was "undoubtedly badly spoiled," he continued. "Handsome, hot-tempered and lavishly be-whiskered, his three great passions in life were soldiering, hunting and women." Having been educated at Christ Church, Oxford, James entered the army against his parents' wishes in 1824. He quickly purchased a promotion, becoming lieutenant colonel of the Fifteenth Hussars by 1832. He was known for his temper, floggings, and court-martials. He often quarreled with his officers. He illegally placed one under arrest and was censured by the ensuing court-martial and forced to give up his command in 1834. Two years later, however, family influence secured him the command of the Eleventh Light Dragoons. The following year his father died and James inherited his title, becoming the seventh earl of Cardigan, as well as a small fortune—an income of £40,000 a year, which is roughly equivalent to £1.75 million in today's money. He spent a large portion of the money on new outfits for his soldiers. The splashy uniforms had tight red trousers, which earned the regiment the nickname

"Cherry Bums," and knitted woolen jackets that buttoned down the front. Earl Cardigan continued to do battle with his own officers. He even wounded one in a duel—Capt. Harvey Tuckett, whose wife Cardigan had seduced. He was later tried for wounding a junior officer in a duel, but escaped persecution on a technicality. He retained command of his regiment until his promotion to major general in 1854, but he was, as Saul David wrote in *The Life of Lord Cardigan,* "the most unpopular man in England." His public persona changed dramatically during the Crimean War. Cardigan was appointed commander of the Light Brigade. His brigade saw little action before October 25, 1854, when the celebrated charge of the Light Brigade took place. Thanks to a misunderstood order, 676 riders were sent to attack a Russian battery at the end of a valley bounded on three sides by enemy troops. Although Cardigan queried the ambiguous order from Lord Raglan that initiated the charge, when the order was repeated he led his men on the clearly suicidal mission. He is said to have muttered: "Here goes the last of the Brudenells." Later he wrote to his brother-in-law, "I considered it certain death, but I led straight and no man flinched." By the time the charge was finished only 195 men were still mounted. Overnight, Cardigan's act of bravery transformed his public image. He was appointed inspector general of cavalry, decorated by the queen, and celebrated in a poem by Alfred Lord Tennyson, "The Charge of the Light Brigade". Even the formerly ridiculed uniforms became stylish, the jacket being named cardigan in his honor.

Brue, Nordahl

In 1980, lawyer Nord Brue represented a construction company in Burlington, Vermont. He met a builder, Mike Dressel, and the two became friends. Dressel was a food fanatic with a taste for bagels. At the time, bagels were considered to be almost exclusively an ethnic food. They were not widely sold outside of Jewish communities in large metropolitan areas. Brue agreed with Dressel that there was a vast untapped market of potential bagel lovers out there. Bankers in six different states told the partners their plan would never work. They didn't listen. On February 4, 1983, Brue, Dressel, and James Briggs, a certified public accountant originally from Schenectady, opened the first *Bruegger's Bagel Bakery* across from the Rensselaer County Courthouse in Troy, New York, close to an area known as "Lawyer's Row." The name "Brue" is clearly seen in Bruegger's, but where did the "gger" come from? According to a company spokesperson, there are two theories. One is that Nord Brue's wife, Suzanne, simply thought the name would have more appeal if, in the spirit of Häagen-Dazs or Jordache, it had a foreign sound. Another is that "Bruegger" was an attempt to combine the names of the company founders, with Briggs contributing the two *g*s and Dressel, "well, they didn't have enough syllables for Dressel," said the spokesperson. Briggs did not stay with the company for long. By 1988, the *Albany Times Union* printed that he was "no longer a player." At the time, leaving the company probably seemed prudent. A restaurant is one of the hardest businesses to run successfully. Bruegger's had the additional challenge of trying to sell a product that, at the time, less than one-third of Americans had ever tasted. To combat this, the company spent more than half of its advertising budget giving away free bagels. "Our goal is to get people to try them," Brue told a *Times Union* reporter. "We want people to get into the habit of eating bagels." In its first year, the Troy store lost $10,000. It lost even more in the following two years. It would not turn a profit until 1987. Slowly, Americans did develop a taste for bagels. Today, in the words of a spokesman for a rival chain, Einstein Bros. Bagels, "bagels are the hottest thing since sliced bread. In fact, they are sliced bread." Annual per-capita consumption of bagels for breakfast grew 133 percent from 1984 through 1993 and Bruegger's benefited. By the end of the century, there were approximately 320 Bruegger's in twenty states.

Bunker, George

George Bunker, who sometimes spelled his name Buncker, was born in the late 1500s. The exact date is unknown because, according to family researcher Henry L. Bunker, his birth certificate is illegible. In 1624, George married Judith Major in

Bedfordshire, England. The couple had five children before emigrating to Charlestown, Massachusetts in 1632. Two more children would be born in America. The Bunkers were allotted a ten-acre parcel of land. One of his neighbors was John Harvard, the original benefactor of Harvard University. Bunker's property was later described in a deed thusly:

> Stands and is situate in Charlestown in the great throughfare street which goes from the neck of land into the market place. This house and garden stands right over against the way which goes up to the windmill hill, and that way which goes into Elbow Lane. The house is bounded on the front by the Street way or the West. And the house and garden are bounded on the East by the back street which goes to the pitt where the beasts drinke and where the creek begins to run on the back side of the Majors garden, into Charles River.

One of the pastures went over the summit of a large hill, which was given the name Bunker's Hill, later simply Bunker Hill. Judith Bunker died October, 10, 1646. She was buried in the family cemetery in the shadow of Bunker Hill. George Bunker was most likely buried there himself after his death in 1664, but no stone marks his grave. By the time a battle made his name familiar, only one of his descendents lived in the vicinity of Bunker Hill. Following the battles of Lexington and Concord in the American Revolution, the Continental forces learned of a British plan to capture the heights of Dorchester and Charlestown. William Prescott was sent to occupy Bunker Hill outside Charlestown. Prescott instead chose the neighboring Breed's Hill to the southeast. The fight went down in history, nonetheless, as the Battle of Bunker Hill. The battle was the first significant engagement of the war. The Americans actually lost the hill, but the Continental Army stood its ground for much longer than had been expected. There were heavy losses on the British side. The American defense heightened colonial morale and resistance.

Burke, William

The verb, *to burke,* used more in England than the United States, means to murder, especially by stifling. It is also applied metaphorically when speech is repressed or anything is quietly put down. The word comes from the surname of an Irish immigrant to Edinburgh, Scotland, William Burke. He and his partner, William Hare, were entrepreneurs of sorts. In the early 1800s, Edinburgh was one of the major centers of medical education in Europe. One of the main challenges facing medical instructors was how to teach anatomy when they were, by law, allowed to dissect only one body per year—and it had to be the body of an executed criminal. The problem was, there just weren't enough executed criminals to go around. A lucrative black market for corpses sprang up. Grave robbing was so common that people coined a nickname for them. They were called "resurrectionists" because they could raise the dead, and Burke and Hare were two of the best in the field. The noted anatomy professor Dr. Robert Knox was happy to pay for at least sixteen bodies. The general public, on the other hand, was not as happy with the arrangement. As Adam Lyal recounted in *The Trial of the Bodysnatchers,* "Watchtowers were constructed in some Edinburgh graveyards to protect those recently buried from exhumation. In addition to the towers, protective walls and iron bars can still be seen around some old Edinburgh graves." Eventually, Burke and Hare came to the conclusion that waiting for people to die, sneaking around the fences and guards, and digging up bodies was simply not the most efficient method of obtaining corpses. So they started to create their own by killing city residents. Apparently, they were careful to select victims who would not likely be missed. It is estimated that they murdered between thirteen and thirty individuals before they made the mistake of killing an elderly Irish immigrant named Mrs. Docherty, who was missed. The investigation of her murder led authorities to the former grave robbers. Fascination with gory cases involving serial killers is nothing new. The Edinburgh public was fascinated by the case. William Hare turned king's evidence and testified against his former partner in crime. Burke was found guilty and hanged a month later. The anatomists to whom the pair supplied bodies were never brought to trial. The rope that was used to hang Burke was snapped up by souvenir seekers who bought pieces by the inch from a hangman's assistant. Many rhymes and songs were written about the case. One example: "Up the close and doun the stair, But and ben with Burke and Hare, Burke's the butcher, Hare's the thief, Knox the boy that buys the beef."

Burpee, Washington Atlee

W. Atlee Burpee began his career with a mail-order chicken business. A poultry farmer who exhibited fancy chickens, turkeys, geese, ducks, and pigeons, Burpee had briefly attended medical school. He dropped out after he learned he could not stand to see people suffering. He returned to what he knew best and opened a poultry business in Philadelphia in 1876. Around this time he published a booklet, *The Pigeon Loft: How to Furnish and Manage It*. Interestingly, neither that title nor his "W. Atlee Burpee's Catalogue of High Class Land and Water Fowls" made him a household name. Things changed, however, when he decided to add some seeds to the catalog. Originally the seeds were there in case his customers needed them to feed the birds. He sold so many seeds that he decided to put out a separate catalog for them. He drew customers in by selling the seeds at amazingly low prices—a dollar's worth of vegetable seeds went for an introductory price of just twenty-five cents. He kept them coming back by providing information bulletins along with his catalogs. The company quickly moved from poultry to vegetables. Burpee was not only a deft marketer, he was also determined to provide the best and most innovative products to his customers. He introduced a variety of new vegetables including bush lima beans, Golden Bantam yellow sweet corn, the Big Boy tomato, and, in 1894, iceberg lettuce. Before iceberg, lettuce was seasonal. It appeared briefly in spring, again in fall. Burpee wanted to create a lettuce that could be on the shelf year round, so he began working with battavia lettuce to create a new strain. Because it was so big and round and didn't go to seed prematurely in hot weather Burpee decided it was "cool as an iceberg" and the name stuck. Iceberg lettuce is second only to potatoes in U.S.

vegetable sales. In 1992, each American ate more than twenty-six pounds of the stuff. The Burpee company became the world's largest seed business, but Burpee himself continued to live modestly until his death in 1915 at the age of fifty-eight. Now a subsidiary of the Ball seed business, Burpee ships 100 million packets of seeds and 7 million to 8 million catalogs a year.

Bush, A. J.

In 1891, A. J. Bush started a small cannery in Chestnut Hill, Tennessee. The operation, known as Bush Bros. & Co., sold canned tomatoes and other vegetables. Towards the turn of the century, it seemed clear that the vegetable business had low profit margins and little consumer loyalty. So the Bush family focused their attention on one product, baked beans. The gamble paid off, allowing the company to survive and feed the Bush family for four generations—a rare feat. Studies show that only 3 percent of family businesses survive and continue to be family owned for that long. The company survived in a highly competitive field despite what company spokesman Jay Bush calls "a full-scale frontal assault" from agribusiness giant ConAgra. In the early 1990s, *Bush's Baked Beans* were targeted by New England baked-bean makers who said the product did not deserve to be called "baked beans." According to Massachusetts health labeling rules, a "baked bean" is defined as "beans, with or without pork, in a sweetened sauce containing no tomato, and one which has been prepared by baking beans in sauce in open or loosely covered containers." Bush's Baked Beans, which are 40 percent cheaper than their rival BM Baked Beans, are soaked and blanched before being baked. Bush's won the day, and was able to sell its product under that name. A year later, the company brought in a new director of sales and marketing. Ron Dix, who had previously worked for a California wine merchant, arrived at a business with no advertising budget or marketing plan. He convinced the Bush family to take funds it had spent on trade promotions and use those on national advertising. A national campaign, featuring Jay Bush, the son of the company's chairman, was devised. The upper-level company members didn't like the idea, but Dix convinced them to give it a try. The ads with Bush eating the "secret family recipe" and saying "roll that beautiful bean footage" while his dog, Duke, looked on were a hit. Over the next two years, Bush's bean sales increased by 40 percent. Today, Jay Bush says wherever he goes people ask him, "Where's the dog?" Bush's now has 75 percent of the U.S. market for baked beans, with annual sales of more than two hundred million dollars. Trivia question for bean fans: Which state claims the baked bean as its "state bean"? Answer: Massachusetts. The bean was elevated to this status in 1993.

C

Caesar, Julius

Julius Caesar already made an appearance in *The Name's Familiar* as the origin of some everyday expressions. Although historians are skeptical, legend has it that he was cut from his mother's womb, the source of the term *caesarean section*. Caesar went on to make some revisions to the calendar in 46 B.C. Under the advice of an astronomer, who was either Egyptian or Greek, he reengineered the calendar so that the year would be in step with the seasons. In addition, he ordered the new year moved from March to the first day of Januarius, named after the Roman God Janus, whose two faces look both backward and forward in time. That year was called "The Year of Confusion," because eighty days were added to the year. When the start of the year was shifted, the names of the months lost their meaning. September or "seventh month" became the ninth month, October, the eighth month, became the tenth, and November, meaning ninth month, became the eleventh. The former fifth month, "Quintilus," was renamed Julius, or *July*, in Caesar's honor. The emperor also contributed to foreign languages. The Russian and German words for leader, czar and Kaiser, are derived from his name. Although the *Caesar salad* was not named for Julius (it was named for restaurateur Caesar Cardini, who invented the dish in 1924) Caesar did, indirectly, give his name to something edible, or more precisely, something potable. There was an ancient city in Spain called urbs Caesaris, Latin for "town of Caesar." Eventually the name evolved into a more Spanish pronunciation—Jerez, then Jerez de la Frontera. It became the center for the production of a specific type of wine named after the town. The English, in turn, Anglicized the name into Sherris. Assuming incorrectly that this was a plural noun, the drink came to be known as *sherry.*

Calvin, John

John Calvin or Cauvin was born in 1509 in France. He studied in Paris in preparation for an ecclesiastical career. His views began to change, however, and he found he disagreed with powers in Rome. At his father's insistence, in 1528, he changed his field of study to law. When his father died in 1531 he embarked on his own path. He studied the classics and Hebrew and became interested in the growing rebellion against conservative theology. He developed and preached a philosophy that thrift, industry, sobriety, and responsibility were essential to the achievement of the reign of God on earth. His followers, known as *Calvinists,* believed dancing and music to be sinful. They sported conservative dress and believed in the value of hard work. The influence of *Calvinism* spread throughout the entire Western world. John Calvin also lent his name to a popular comic—Calvin and Hobbes. Bill Waterson chose the reformer's name and that of philosopher Thomas Hobbes for his famous strip. It ran from 1985 to 1995, appearing in more than twenty-four hundred papers.

Carvelas, Thomas

Thomas Carvelas's family immigrated to the United States from Greece when he was four years old. The family later Americanized their last name to Carvel and settled in Manhattan. Carvel held a number of very odd jobs, including working as a drummer in a Dixieland band and as a test driver for Studebaker, before contracting tuberculosis at age twenty-six. The prognosis was not good. Doctors told the young man he had only three months to live. He proved them wrong. When he had recovered, he decided to move to the country. He borrowed $15 from his future wife and bought ice cream to sell from his home. One day, as he returned from his supplier in The Bronx, he blew out a tire in Hartsdale, New York. To keep the product from melting, he quickly sold it from the back of his truck. It did so well that he decided to stay there. Eventually, he'd earned enough to buy a nearby storefront to serve as a more permanent ice-cream stand. By 1950 the original shop had grown into a franchise of twenty-one Carvel ice-cream stores. By 1989, Carvel Ice Cream was able to fetch $80 million. It was purchased by the international banking firm Investcorp. Tom Carvel died less than a year later at age eighty-four. Carvel Corporation had sales of $212 million in 1998. The company no longer relies exclusively on its ice cream/bakery franchisees—it now sells cakes in some forty-five hundred supermarkets as well.

Catherine of Alexandria

As legend has it, Catherine was a beautiful Egyptian queen who converted to Christianity after a visit by the Blessed Virgin. She mystically married Christ and refused to temporally marry her suitor, the Roman emperor Maxentius. In response, Maxentius summoned a team of philosophers to try to talk her out of such foolishness. Instead, she convinced them to give up their pagan religion and become Christians. The emporer was not amused. He had all the scholars immediately put to death. Yet he still wanted to marry Catherine. He thought perhaps torture would win her over and he had her strapped to a spiked wheel, the torturous device now known as a *Catherine wheel*. It broke down and killed bystanders. After some other form of torture, she was beheaded. Milk flowed from her severed head instead of blood. Her body, it was said, was transported by angels to Mount Sinai. Scholars now doubt whether Catherine existed. There was no ancient cult of the saint and no early texts or works of art referring to her before the ninth century. After that time, however, she became a very popular martyr-saint. In England, sixty-two churches were dedicated to her. There are 170 medieval bells that bear her name. She inspired numerous poems, plays, books, and murals. She has also, in name, become a part of many Gothic-style churches. There a decorated circular window, often glazed with stained glass, is known as either a "rose window" or a *Catherine wheel window*. A firework that spins like a wheel as it explodes is also known as a *Catherine wheel*. An amusement-park ride and a rock band bear the name as well.

Chappell, Tom

Tom Chappell, the son of a textile-company manager, was born in Pittsfield, Massachusetts in 1943. At age eleven, he earned $25 posing for a *Saturday Evening Post* cover by local artist Norman Rockwell. He dressed in the role of an altar boy. He went on to study English at Trinity College. While a student there, he met a high-school student named Kate. After a first date at a Ravi Shankar concert, they fell in love and were married in 1966. They wanted to get back to nature, so they moved to Kennebunk, Maine. In 1970, they borrowed $5,000 from a friend to create a laundry detergent without phosphates. Using the profits, they enlisted the help of scientists to blend a toothpaste free of artificial sweeteners, dyes, and additives. The line of products grew to include mouthwash and deodorant. It took twenty years for the toothpaste to win the American Dental Association's seal of approval. Tom Chappell says this was because the company is against animal testing and the dental organization was slow to accept the results of tests on human volunteers. Besides being all natural, the toothpastes have unusual flavors like fennel and cinnamint, which was invented by the Chappells' son Matt when he was fourteen. Today, Tom's of Maine employs 120 people and earns revenues of $30 million. Although the toothpaste is not at risk of putting Crest or Colgate out of business, it has captured 1 percent of the market and is the brand of choice of such celebrities as Sting and Brendan Fraser.

Chase, Caleb

Caleb Chase grew up on Cape Cod and worked in his father's grocery until he was twenty-four. He then moved to Boston, where, in 1864, he went into business as a coffee roaster. James Sanborn moved to Boston three years later having worked various odd jobs in his native Maine. In Massachusetts, Sanborn set himself up as a coffee seller. He met Caleb Chase and the two decided to combine forces in 1867. Their new enterprise was called *Chase & Sanborn*. The pair poured almost all their profits back into the company. They soon had branches in Chicago and Montreal. By 1882 they were selling 100,000 pounds of coffee a month. They hired local selling agents throughout the nation and Canada to tout the benefits of Chase & Sanborn's sealed cans, a first in the industry. Advertising was always a priority. Chase and Sanborn, themselves, continued with the company until 1899. When they retired they handed over leadership to Charles Sias, known as the "Barnum of Coffee." The company thrived in the early part of the twentieth century. It continued to expand, opening new factories. By 1929, the company was taking in $12 million a year. The Royal Baking Powder Company bought it up. It was then swallowed by the Fleischman Company. Over the next few decades, two newer brands, Folgers and Maxwell House, started to dominate the market. Chase & Sanborn's portion of the market dropped to .6 percent. The brand changed hands a number of times. Hills Brothers Coffee Company bought it in 1984. It was later bought by Procter and Gamble and General Foods. In 1986, a market study showed that although Chase & Sanborn had not been advertised for fifteen years, about 88 percent of consumers in the Northeast and Southeast recognized the name. In 1999, Chase & Sanborn was purchased by the Sara Lee Corporation, which also owns Hills Brothers and Chock Full O' Nuts. The three brands together have annual sales of about $280 million.

Chase, Salmon Portland

Salmon Portland Chase was born in Cornish, New Hampshire in 1808. During his early years, Chase was taught by his uncle, Bishop Philander Chase of the Protestant Episcopal Church. He then went to Dartmouth College, graduated in 1826, and was admitted to the bar three years later. He opened his first legal practice in Cincinnati, Ohio. He quickly earned himself the nickname "attorney general for fugitive slaves" because he so frequently defended runaway slaves. His antislavery beliefs led him into politics. In 1849 he was elected to the U.S. Senate, where he opposed proslavery measures like the Compromise of 1850 and the Kansas-Nebraska Act. While his career flourished, his personal life was rife with difficulty. He had three wives who each died in rapid succession, and four of his six daughters died as babies. Despite these personal hardships, he was elected governor of Ohio in 1855 and it seemed the presidency could not be far away. His abolitionist views were not popular with all people, however. His 1856 and 1860 bids for Republican nomination were unsuccessful. He was instead elected once again to the Senate in 1861, but he served only two days before resigning to become Abraham Lincoln's secretary of the treasury. In that Civil War-torn era, Chase was put in charge of a treasury that was nearly bankrupt. In 1862 he issued federal paper money, or "greenbacks." A year later, he established the national banking system. Although he went on to hold a variety of political offices, and to staunchly support the rights of former slaves in the South, Chase would ultimately be remembered for his contributions to the Treasury Department. Chase died in New York City on May 7, 1873. Five years later, former schoolteacher John Thompson opened a bank named after the statesman. *Chase National Bank* would become the country's third largest bank and establish a network of overseas offices. In 1955 it merged with the Bank of Manhattan, which had been formed by Aaron Burr. Forty years later, the *Chase Manhattan Corporation* merged with Chemical Banking Corporation. The $11.5 million merger moved the combined corporation ahead of Citibank to become the nation's largest bank. When the entities merged, the name Chase remained.

Chesebrough, Robert

Robert Chesebrough, born in 1837, was an engineer and kerosene dealer. In 1859, the use of kerosene as fuel was eclipsed by the success of Edwin L. Drake, who drilled the first oil well at Titusville, Pennsylvania. Just ten years after California's Gold Rush, a new breed of prospector filled western Pennsylvania seeking "black gold." Some, like John D. Rockefeller, accumulated vast fortunes. Most, including Drake, died broke. Sensing his livelihood was in danger, Chesebrough rode out to Titusville to check out the competition. While there, he heard a rumor that the residue that accumulated on the pump rods held miraculous healing powers. He collected a sample and reduced the material to a white jelly. He tested it by cutting and burning himself, then smearing the ointment over the wounds. The cuts and blisters did seem to heal quickly. He named the goo Vaseline, a combination of the German word for water and the Greek word for olive oil. He first gave it away free to anyone who would take it. Soon, they were coming back for more. By 1880, Vaseline was a fixture in homes across the country. That year Chesebrough incorporated his company and a year later sold out to his major supplier, the Standard Oil Company. The Standard Oil trust was dissolved in 1911 and Chesebrough was on its own again. Chesebrough was a true believer in his product. He ate a spoonful of Vaseline each day until his death at the age of ninety-six. Many years after its founder's death, in 1955, Chesebrough merged with the company formed by Theron T. Pond, creating *Chesebrough-Pond's, Inc.* It, in turn, merged with Unilever in 1987.

Choiseul, César, comte Du Plessis-Praslin

César Choiseul, who lived from 1598 to 1675, was a French general also known as the *maréchal* Du Plessis and the count of Plessis-Praslin. He served as ambassador to Turin and commanded the army in Lombardy during the Thirty Years War. That conflict also marked the beginning of the military career of Henri de La Tour d'Auvergne, also known as Vicomte de Turenne. As explained in *The Name's Familiar,* Turenne was a brigadier in that war and was lauded as a hero after his capture of Turin in 1640. Legend has it that the soldier was the source of the term *tureen.* During one of the war's battles, the viscount, having no dishes, used his helmet for a soup bowl. The soldiers began calling any large serving dish a "tureen." Many etymologists dispute this claim, however, speculating that it comes from the French word for an earthenware container—*terrine.* In any case, Choiseul and Turenne would soon find themselves on opposite sides of an armed conflict. In 1648, France was split by a civil war known as the Fronde. Named for the "sling" of a children's game played in the streets of Paris, The Fronde began as a rebellion against new policies begun by Cardinal de Richelieu, chief minister of Louis XIII. The changes weakened the powers of the nobility, and many of the aristocrats rebelled. Turenne sided with the rebellion. He allied himself with the

Spaniards, who were at war with France, and waged war in Champagne. Choiseul, meanwhile, had been given command of the royal forces and was fighting against the Spanish. He came up against Turenne's forces at Rethel in the Battle of Champ Blanc, October 15, 1650. His superior forces completely defeated Turenne, who only narrowly escaped capture. Choiseul was made a duke in 1665. While this episode of French history is not part of everyday conversation in America, the count of Plessis-Praslin is often invoked in reference to a favorite confection—pecans stirred into a boiling sugar syrup, or *pralines*.

Choteau, Pierre

Pierre Choteau, Jr., was born in St. Louis on January 19, 1789. His father had established a trading post, where his son worked briefly. By the 1820s, however, the younger Pierre Choteau had gone off on his own to trade with the Indians of the Upper Mississippi and Missouri valleys. In 1831 Choteau joined a company that was the Western agent for John Jacob Astor's American Fur Company. Soon Choteau had earned enough to buy out Astor's share, almost monopolizing trade with the Indians. He built a settlement where the Missouri River meets the Bad River. The spot was known as Fort Pierre. A town dubbed simply Pierre sprang up on the opposite bank of the Missouri. The name became official in 1832. The people of South Dakota pronounce the name of their capital city as "peer." The name *Dakota*, incidentally, comes from a Sioux tribe that once inhabited the region. North and South Dakota were simultaneously admitted to the Union on November 2, 1889. Pres. Benjamin Harrison made sure no one could see which paper he signed first. North Dakota is usually listed first, as number thirty-nine to South Dakota's forty, because *N* comes before *S* in the alphabet. Trivia question for Dakota fans: What is the state bird of South Dakota? Answer: The Chinese ring-necked pheasant.

Cincinnatus, Lucius Quinctius

In 1458 B.C., the Roman Army was surrounded by an Italic tribe known as the Aequi. The Roman Senate, in desperation, set out to find someone to lead the empire through the crisis. They chose Lucius Quinctius Cincinnatus. When Senate members arrived at his farm, Cincinnatus was hard at work, digging a ditch. He was named dictator. He addressed the people, suspended all civic affairs and business, and ordered all men of military age to report to the Campus Martius. Cincinnatus and his men surprised the enemy at night and were victorious. After celebrating his triumph in Rome, he resigned his dictatorship and returned to his farm. The story of his selfless devotion to the republic, and especially of giving up power when the crisis was ended, made him the stuff of legend—so much so that in May 1783, a number of officers who had served in the American Revolutionary War formed an organization called the Society of the Cincinnati. Membership was open to Revolutionary officers and their eldest male descendents. George Washington was elected its first president. Washington was often compared to the Roman general. He emulated the legendary figure by resigning as commander in chief at the end of the war and by refusing to run for a third term as the country's president. Most of the chapters of the society folded by 1835, but the group left a lasting impression on the state of Ohio. In 1787, Congress adopted the Northwest Ordinance, which opened the land between the Alleghenies and the Mississippi River to settlement. On December 28, 1788, eleven families arrived to settle a 747-acre plot along the Licking River. John Filson, an early surveyor, called the town Losantville." It did not retain the name long. In 1790, Gen. Arthur St. Clair, the first governor of the Northwest Territory, responsible for a number of place names, including *St. Clair County, Alabama; St. Clair County, Illinois; St. Clair County, Michigan;* and *St. Clair County, Missouri,* renamed the area *Cincinnati* for the society. "Cincinnatus," incidentally, derives from the Latin "cincinnus," meaning "lock of hair," and "natus," meaning "born." The Ohio city's name, therefore, means "born hairy."

Coel

Old King Cole may have been a real person, a king of the Britons before England as we know it today existed. Coel probably defended his land against the Picts and Scots and earned the affection of the Romans, who were still in charge of a good deal of the world at that time. The 1729 *History of Great Britain* mentions three English kings named Cole or Coel. One was, the book said, "a popular man in his day . . . and ascended to the throne of Britain on the death of Asclepoid" in the third century. He is said to have built Colchester, although this is probably not the case. The twelfth-century chronicler Geoffrey Monmouth said Coel had a daughter who was skilled in music, but most experts are leery of believing Monmouth's facts. Another candidate for the Cole of the rhyme is a clothier named Cole-brook. He was a rich man who had more than four hundred people in his service. He was commonly known as "Old Cole," according to the nineteenth-century authority on popular music, William Chappell. His story was told in the 1598 bestseller *The pleasant Historie of Thomas of Reading: or, The Sixe worthie Yeomen of the West.* The earliest version of the rhyme appeared in 1709, although Old Cole showed up in Elizabethan dramas, Dekker's *Satiromastix* in 1602 and *The Malcontent* by John Martson in 1604. A number of variations of the song appeared in the 1700s, when it was probably the eighteenth-century version of a hit single. Here's a version of the rhyme as it appeared in 1776: "Old King Cowl was a jolly old soul, and a jolly old soul was he. Old King Cowl, he had a brown bowl, and they brought him in fiddlers three."

Cointreau, Edouard-Jean and Adolphe

Two brothers, Edouard-Jean and Adolphe Cointreau, opened a distillery in Angers, France in 1849. They produced a spirit called *Cointreau,* although it would not be recognizable to modern-day fans of the drink. This prototype was made with only regional fruits. Edouard-Jean's son Edouard would later join the operation. The young man wanted to bring new life to the product by blending exotic fruits. "I have searched passionately for the quintessential flavor of Cointreau," he would say. "I wanted to combine crystal-clear purity with the subtlety of tastes obtained from the perfect harmony of sweet and bitter orange peels." His formula called for two distillations, during which orange peel is soaked in alcohol for several weeks. To ensure the high standard of the final product, each time the liquid is distilled, the head and the tail are discarded and only the heart is retained. Finally, water, sugar, and other ingredients are added. Today 13 million bottles of Cointreau are sold each year in more than two hundred countries.

Coleman, William Coffin

William Coffin Coleman remembered the night that he first saw an alcohol lamp. It was a cold winter night in 1899, and he would recall seeing the lamp's brilliant glow as "the most important moment" of his life. Most shops, in those days, were lit with oil wicks. This lamp was designed so that as the alcohol vaporized it escaped through a tiny opening in the generator and entered a burner where it mixed with the air and ignited. The "force feeding" of alcohol kept impurities out of the supply line because any particles that got into the generator were trapped inside a porous wick. Thus, the lamp burned with greater heat and intensity than any lamp Coleman had seen. At the time Coleman was selling typewriters in Brockton, Alabama to earn enough money to go to law school. His parents had to read him the textbooks he could afford because he had lost 25 percent of the vision in one eye and 50 percent in the other. He made it his mission to find out more about the lamp that allowed him to see at night. It was another month before Coleman tracked down the salesman in Caruthersville, Missouri. Through the salesman he got in touch with the lamp's manufacturers, who offered him a job. On January 1, 1900, Coleman went to work selling lamps in Kingfisher, a city in the Oklahoma Territory. He was stunned by the poor reception he got in town. He had visited sixty businesses and sold only two lanterns. Finally, a tavern owner explained the problem. A traveling salesmen had passed through the territory selling gas lamps. The gas lamps became clogged with carbon and stopped working, but by that time, the salesman had moved on. Coleman quickly changed his strategy. Clearly, the people of Kingfisher were not going to trust another lamp salesman. Instead of selling the lamps at $15 each, he decided to rent them for $1 a week. This way, if a lamp didn't work, the customer didn't have to pay for it. He was sure, though, that the lamps would work and that he would keep collecting $1 a week. He quickly rented out all of his lanterns and used the money to buy hundreds more. He formed a business called the Hydro-Carbon Light Company, which earned enough within the year to buy the patent rights to the original lamp for $3,000. Coleman's adaptability paid off a second time when electric light became a household fixture. He changed directions and targeted his lanterns to campers, hunters, and outdoorsmen. The Coleman Company, as it came to be called, added sleeping bags, outdoor stoves, and other supplies to its line. In 1997, the company that began by renting lanterns for $1 a week reported revenues of $1.1 billion.

Comstock, Anthony

Anthony Comstock was born March 7, 1844 in New Canaan, Connecticut. Connecticut was then known as "The Blue Law State." The first "blue laws," a series of statutes limiting what people could do on Sunday, were passed in the seventeenth century in the settlement of New Haven. They were so called because they were printed on blue paper. The expression "bluenose," which first appeared in print in 1809 in the writings of Washington Irving, may derive from "blue law." Comstock, a Union Army veteran, began working with the Young Men's Christian Association in New York City in 1872. A year later, when he was twenty-nine, he founded an organization known as the New York Society for the Suppression of Vice. He remained secretary of the organization until his death in 1915. He lobbied for a statute that came to be known as the *Comstock Law*. It banned "obscene" materials from the mails without defining what was "obscene." Comstock took it upon himself to define it. Stamping out any and all obscenity was his mission. For the most part, he focused on nudes in art and photography. He would personally cart art dealers to jail if they refused to remove paintings with nudes in them from their galleries. Comstock was responsible for the destruction of 160 tons of literature and pictures. He was said to have boasted of the number of people he had driven to suicide. He had Walt Whitman fired from the Department of the Interior for writing *Leaves of Grass*. He once arrested a woman for a message she wrote to her husband on a postcard. When he had George Bernard Shaw's play *Mrs. Warren's Profession* banned after one showing, the playwright coined the word *"Comstockery,"* which *Merriam-Webster's Dictionary* defines as "strict censorship of materials considered obscene or censorious opposition to alleged immorality (as in literature)." Comstock also inspired the Watch and Ward Society of Boston, which, in turn, inspired the expression "banned in Boston." Many publishers, in the 1920s, discovered that having a book banned in Boston almost guaranteed bestseller status in other cities. Publishers would print *"banned in Boston"* right on the covers of their books. As the Watch and Ward Society started to wield less power, "banned in Boston" remained as a joking description of slightly naughty books. Eventually Comstock's zealousness was his downfall. In 1915, he had some store employees arrested for dressing their mannequins right in the department store window where everyone could see. The judge looked at Comstock and said, "Mr. Comstock, I think you're nuts." The crusader never got over the embarrassment. The expression "to Bowdlerize," meaning to censor a literary work, came to us by way of Thomas Bowdler, known for his expurgated versions of Shakespeare's plays. The phrase "book burner" did not come into common use until 1933, in the wake of a burning in Nazi Germany in which 20,000 books were destroyed. In case you were curious about the origin of other expressions related to prudishness and censorship, "Goody Two Shoes" came from a British nursery rhyme probably written by Oliver Goldsmith. In the story, Little Goody Two Shoes owned only one shoe. When she got another she showed it to everyone with a delighted, "Two shoes!" How that evolved to its present meaning, an overly sweet, too-good-to-be-true type of person, is unclear. And while we're talking about Goody Two Shoes, you might wonder who the original "Smart Aleck" was. The answer is, no one knows. *The Oxford English Dictionary* traces the phrase to the U.S. in the mid-1860s, but makes no identification of the mysterious person. Some have suggested that the term derives from a character, Dr. Smart-Allick, created by British humorist J. B. Morton. Since the expression was in use before Morton was born, however, the character had to have taken his name from the familiar expression, not the other way around.

Converse, Marquis

Marquis Mills Converse was born October 25, 1861 into a family that traces its lineage all the way back to Edward III of England. His immigrant ancestor was a Puritan devoted to a simple pious life in the New World. Converse grew up on a farm in New Hampshire. In 1880, he left for the big city and got a job at a Boston department store. In six years he had risen to the post of general superintendent. He decided to return home, where he would be a big fish in a smaller pond. He bought a general store, but missed city life. He sold it only four years later. Back in Boston, in 1890, he and a partner opened a wholesale rubber-boot company, which they called Converse and Pike. The business was also short-lived. Converse took a job with another rubber-shoe maker. When it was swallowed up by U.S. Rubber, he decided to open his own business again. In 1908, he used $100,000 of his own money and $250,000 others had invested and opened a rubber-shoe company in Malden, Massachusetts. By 1910, the Converse Rubber Shoe Company was churning out 4,000 pairs of overshoes and boots a day. Boots were, of course, primarily seasonal attire. To keep the cash flowing year round, Converse added canvas tennis shoes to his product line in 1915. That year he also started making hard-rubber tires. In the 1920s, as solid tires were replaced by the air-filled variety, the tire manufacturing division began to lose money. Converse attempted to quickly change over to balloon tires, but he did not have the proper equipment, and the majority of the shipments were being returned. Converse did not give up on the tires—that is, until the Converse Rubber Shoe Company had lost so much money that it was forced into receivership in 1928. It was purchased by a businessman and avid sportsman named Mitchell Kaufman. Marquis Mills Converse died two years later at the age of sixty-nine. Kaufman was killed himself in a hunting accident in Maine in 1930. Converse, the company, went through a number of owners before being spun off into an independent, publicly traded company in 1994. These days its products are sold worldwide through more than nine thousand shoe and sporting-goods stores. NBA basketball stars Dennis Rodman, Julius ("Dr. J") Erving, and Larry Bird have all worn and endorsed Converse's gym shoes.

Crow, James

James C. Crow was born in Scotland in 1789. There he earned a medical degree and was a practicing physician before massive debt caused him to flee to the United States. He arrived in Kentucky around 1825. There, he worked briefly in the distillery of Col. Willis Field. Next he moved to the town of Millville and was hired as master distiller at the Oscar Pepper Distillery. In the 1820s, distillers were beginning to discover that aging whiskey in charred oak barrels gave the liquor a sweeter mellower flavor and a deeper color. Crow quickly adopted the practice. He also discovered, around 1835, that if he used some of the leftover mash from a previous batch of whiskey, he could have greater control over the fermentation process. As the first person to use the so-called "sour mash" process, Crow is generally credited as the "father of bourbon." Crow insisted on selling only aged whiskey, unusual in his day. The earliest description of a Kentucky whiskey being red, rather than a more yellow hue, was in a letter by a Kentucky politician describing James Crow's concoction. The "red likker" was a favorite of such notables as Henry Clay, Andrew Jackson, John Calhoun, Ulysses S. Grant, William Henry Harrison, and Daniel Webster. It sold for twenty-five cents a gallon during a time when most distillers got only fifteen cents a gallon. Crow never owned his own distillery. After twenty years with Oscar Pepper, Crow went to work at the Johnson Distillery. He died suddenly on the job in 1856. He was sixty-seven and left no heirs. After Oscar Pepper died, his son sold the remainder of Dr. Crow's whiskey to E. H. Taylor, who built the *Old Crow Distillery* to make *Old Crow Bourbon*.

Cueva, Fernandez de la

In 1706, Fernandez de la Cueva was the viceroy of New Spain. As such, he was responsible for preliminary approval of applications for the establishment of Spanish villas in the New World. Spanish regulations said a minimum of thirty families had to reside in an area before it could be listed as a villa. Spanish settlers had been arriving in the area now known as New Mexico in great numbers in the late 1600s and early 1700s and Cueva fielded many requests. One petition, however, caught his attention. It came from Don Francisco Cuervo y Valdez, who lived in an area previously known as Bosque Grance de San Francisco Xavier. The establishment actually boasted only eighteen families. Cuervo decided that listing the exact minimum—thirty—would be too suspicious, so his petition claimed there were thirty-five families. He also included something else designed to get his application past Cueva—he proposed the settlement be named Alburquerque in honor of the Duke of Alburquerque—Fernandez de la Cueva. The request was granted. Eventually the first r fell out of use and the eighteen-family settlement has grown into the roughly 384,700-resident *Albuquerque, New Mexico.* There are a number of theories as to why the r disappeared from the duke's title. Legend has it that a sign painter for the railroad omitted it either accidentally or because he didn't have enough room for the whole name. Adrian Room, the author of a number of books on word origins, suggests that the lost r may be the result of confusion with Alfonso Albuquerque, the Portuguese viceroy of Portuguese India, who was better known. Another theory is that it simply fell out of use because it was nearly inaudible when spoken.

D

Daimler, Gottlieb Wilhelm

Gottlieb Wilhelm Daimler was born March 17, 1834 in Würtemberg, Germany. His career path began when he became a gunsmith's apprentice at the age of fourteen. He went on to technical school and formal training as a mechanical engineer at the Stuttgart Polytechnic in 1859. Thanks to the generosity of a benefactor from Stuttgart, Daimler was able to travel to England, then to France, where he may have seen Lenoir's newly developed gas engine. He worked for a number of engineering firms after that. In 1863, he joined the firm of Bruderhaus Maschinen-Fabrik in Reutlingen as a manager. There he met a sixteen-year-old named William Maybach. Daimler was impressed with his work. In 1872, Daimler left Bruderhaus Maschinen-Fabrik to become technical director in the firm of Nikolaus A. Otto, who had invented the four-stroke internal-combustion engine. One of his first acts was to hire his friend Maybach as chief designer. After a decade with Otto, Daimler and Maybach decided to open their own shop in Daimler's summer house. They patented one of the first successful high-speed internal-combustion engines and developed a carburetor that made possible the use of gasoline as fuel. Their innovative engines were first put to use on bicycles in 1885. The first four-wheeled vehicle to make use of a Daimler engine was a converted horse-drawn carriage, which was fitted with a one-cylinder engine in 1886. The next vehicle so equipped was a boat in 1887. It was 1889 before they specifically designed an automobile. A year later they founded Daimler Motoren Gesellschaft. In 1893, Daimler met an Englishman who was impressed by his four-stroke engine. This man established the Daimler Motor Syndicate in London the same year. Daimler and Maybach both retired in 1894 to concentrate on technical and commercial development work, only to rejoin the firm the following year. Maybach was then named technical director of the Daimler Motor Company. Daimler passed away March 6, 1900, eleven days before his sixty-sixth birthday. He was said to be weakened physically by quarrels within Daimler Motoren Gesellschaft. The company published the following obituary:

> This morning the chairman of our supervisory board, Kommerzienrat Gottlieb Daimler, died peacefully after severe illness. We mourn the inventor and founder of the automotive industry. It is first and foremost to his energy and untiring commitment that we owe the development of new means of transport to the degree of perfection it has reached today. It will be his heritage for all time to come. We will always honor the memory of our loyal friend with gratitude.

Maybach would live for another twenty-nine productive years. In 1901, working for the Daimler company, he designed an automobile that was named for the daughter of a dealer. Her name, Mercedes, became famous worldwide. In 1924 *Daimler-Benz* was formed. The German branch of Daimler never did manufacture cars with the founder's name on them. The same was not true in Britain. There, the name Daimler could be found on luxury vehicles. The first royal car was a Daimler purchased by the Prince of Wales. England's Daimler changed hands twice, ending up as the property of Jaguar in the 1950s. In this country, the name Daimler did not become familiar until Daimler bought Chrysler in 1998 for more than thirty-eight billion dollars, creating the new *Daimler-Chrysler*. The company manufactures Chryslers, Jeeps, and Mercedes-Benz but it does not have the right to produce a car called Daimler. That right belongs to the Ford Motor Company, which bought Jaguar in 1989. Daimler-Chrysler does plan to produce a car with the name of its other founder. The *Mercedes Maybach* is on the drawing board for 2002.

Dallas, George Mifflin

George Mifflin Dallas was born in Philadelphia, July 10, 1792.

He graduated from Princeton in 1810 with a law degree and quickly joined the political arena. In 1813 he was secretary to Albert Gallatin on a mission to Russia aimed at settling the War of 1812. He served as mayor of Philadelphia and U.S. district attorney for eastern Pennsylvania and in 1831 became a senator. In 1844, he was elected vice-president under eleventh president James K. Polk. He presided over the Senate during the Mexican War. Dallas died in Philadelphia on December 31, 1864. Although there is disagreement among historians as to the origin of the name of the city of Dallas, Dallas County, Texas, mapped out in 1846, was definitely named for the vice-president. The origin of the city's name is a little more mysterious. According to Bill Bradfield and Clare Bradfield, authors of *Muleshoe and More,* a book about the origin of Texas place names, Dallas's first settler, John Neely Bryan, established a trading post at the three forks of the Trinity River. A small settlement sprang up, with a general store and a tavern. When the Republic of Texas determined there was sufficient population to warrant the establishment of a post office, Bryan was appointed postmaster. He named the office for "my friend Dallas," but never said which friend Dallas he had in mind.

Dalton, John

John Dalton, the son of a Quaker weaver, was born September 6, 1766 in Cumberland, England. He became a teacher and took charge of a Quaker school at the ripe old age of twelve. He went on to teach mathematics and natural philosophy at New College in Manchester. He was influenced by a fellow Quaker who was a wealthy maker of meteorological instruments. In 1787, Dalton started keeping a diary of meteorological observations. He published *Meteorological Observations and Essays* in 1793. He continued to publish treatises on meteorology throughout his career. One of his studies produced a law of partial pressures that says the total pressure of a mixture of gases equals the sum of the pressures of the individual gases in the mixture. Scientists know this today as *Dalton's Law.* The scientist's name is most commonly known in connection with his studies of color blindness. Both Dalton and his brother shared the affliction. He published an account of his observations in 1794 in a work titled *Extraordinary Facts Relating to the Vision of Colours*. It was the first description of the problem. As a result, *daltonism* became synonymous with color blindness, especially the inability to distinguish between red and green. Dalton remained at New College until 1800 when he became secretary of the Manchester Literary and Philosophical Society and taught privately on the side. He continued to collect meteorological observations until his death in 1844. In his will, he left his eyes to science for further study of color blindness.

D'Arbanville, Patti

Patti D'Arbanville was born in Greenwich Village. Her parents, George, a bartender, and Jean Egan, an artist, never married. They split up when Patti was fifteen. She dropped out of school and spent her days playing chess in a cafe. She found herself cast in two Andy Warhol movies, *Flesh* and *L'Amour*. She made her way to London and at eighteen was working as a model. There she met musician Cat Stevens. They had their first date the day Neil Armstrong walked on the moon. The relationship was apparently stormy. Stevens wrote two songs for D'Arbanville. The first, "Wild World," includes the lyrics, "If you want to leave/Take good care." That song reached number eleven in the U.S. *Billboard* charts in 1970, but was not a hit in England. In the second song he wrote for her, he actually imagined her dead: "Though in your grave you lie/I'll always be with you." That song, titled *"Lady D'Arbanville,"* did not chart in the U.S. but stayed on the U.K. charts for thirteen weeks, reaching number eight at its peak. Perhaps not surprisingly, the relationship did not endure. D'Arbanville continued to have a colorful life both personally and professionally. In 1975 she married French actor Roger Mirmont. The marriage ended after only two years. In 1980, she married actor-singer Steve Curry. A year later, she became romantically involved with another actor, Don Johnson. They became parents to a daughter. She later married New York City firefighter Terry Quinn and had three more children. Professionally she has appeared in the television series "New York Undercover,"

"Wiseguy," "Another World," and "The Guiding Light." She has appeared in numerous films, including *Wired.*

Davies, Peter Llewellyn

Peter Davies was the third son born to Arthur Llewellyn Davies, a young barrister, and the former Sylvia Jocelyn du Maurier, the daughter of George du Maurier, author of the 1891 novel *Peter Ibbetson,* which was the inspiration for the child's name. Peter was still a baby when his mother found herself seated next to writer J. M. Barrie at a New Year's Eve party given by Sir George and Lady Lewis. The Lewises counted some of the most prestigious people of London among their friends. Barrie caught Sylvia Davies in the act of hiding some desserts under her coat. He was impressed when she did not apologize. Instead she said, "It's for my youngest, Peter." In the course of their conversation, Barrie learned that he had met the Davies' oldest son, George, during his frequent walks in Kensington Gardens. George had mentioned a funny man who wiggled his ears and told stories about pirates and buried treasure. As it happened, George had influenced one of the characters in Barrie's new play, *The Little Minister.* Barrie was invited to the Davies' home. He became a frequent guest and a good friend to the children. He often took walks with the older boys, George and Jack, but most frequently with George. As they walked Barrie wove a story about the baby. He explained that before there were baby carriages infants could fly. Children were all once birds, and the reason there were bars on the windows and in front of the fire was that children sometimes forgot they no longer had wings and would try to fly up the chimney or out the window. When no one was watching Peter, he said, he would fly to Kensington Gardens. When George asked him why Peter would stay in his stroller if he could fly, the author shifted the story. He came up with a new character drawn from his own childhood experiences. When Barrie was six, his older brother, David, who had always been his mother's favorite, was killed in a skating accident at the age of thirteen. From that day forward Barrie was fascinated by the idea that David would never grow up. He used that as the basis for a new character. A newly published play, *Pan and the Young Shepherd,* which began with the line, "Boy, boy, wilt thou be a boy forever?" gave him further inspiration. He dubbed the boy who wouldn't grow up *Peter Pan.* As the story took shape, Barrie used Mr. and Mrs. Davies as the prototypes for Mr. and Mrs. Darling. Another child, Margaret Henley, the daughter of the poet and editor W. E. Henley, also found her way into Barrie's works. She used to call Barrie "my friendly." Because she couldn't pronounce her *r*s correctly, "friendly" came out sounding like "fwendy." Tragically, the girl died when she was only six. But Barrie immortalized her in the character Wendy, a name that he coined. The play made it instantly popular. Margaret was also the inspiration for the character "Reddy" in his novel *Sentimental Tommie.* The play *Peter Pan* was first performed December 27, 1904. It was performed every year at Christmas in London until its run was interrupted by war from 1939 to 1940. It then continued until 1969. Barrie asked that the royalties from its production be given to the Great Ormond Street Hospital for Sick Children in London. The arrangement was legally in place until 1988, when it finally expired. The British Parliament changed the copyright law to allow the contract to continue. The hospital continues to receive money from productions of *Peter Pan.* Steven Spielberg's movie *Hook* paid an estimated half-million dollars to the charity. Peter Davies grew up to be a successful publisher, but he could never shake the association with "the boy who never grew up." He was depressed and withdrawn. He finally took his own life at the age of sixty-three by jumping under an approaching subway train. The *Daily Express* of London, in its obituary for Peter Davies, said that he would always be best remembered as the Boy Who Never Grew Up. Peter Pan "was a gift to him from playwright Sir James Barrie, and Peter Davies hated it all his life," the obituary continued. "But he was never allowed to forget it until, as a shy, retiring publisher, he fell to his death on Tuesday night."

Davis, Dwight

Dwight Filley Davis was born in 1879 to a wealthy St. Louis

family. At the age of fifteen, he took up tennis during a summer trip to Massachusetts. The sport became his passion. Within a year he was entering national championships. In 1896 he enrolled at Harvard University, which his two brothers attended. A hard-hitting lefthander, Davis won his first national tennis title in August 1899. At the time tennis was considered to be a rich man's sport. Davis wanted to change that. He traveled to California and staged competitions between players from the East and West coasts in hopes of drumming up interest. Davis then spoke to Dr. James Dwight, president of the National Lawn Tennis Association. He offered to pay for a silver cup if the association would invite different countries to compete for it. Dwight sent a letter to British tennis officials, who immediately accepted the challenge. The first matches were played five months later at the Longwood Cricket Club. Although the formal name of the competition is the International Lawn Tennis Challenge Trophy, most people know it by the name of the trophy itself—*The Davis Cup.* Today 129 countries compete for the cup, making it the largest annual team competition in sports. John McEnroe, in a foreword to the book *The Davis Cup,* by Richard Evans, wrote: "The Davis Cup offered me more immediate pleasure than almost anything else I accomplished in my career. My parents had brought me up to believe that it was an honor to be asked to play for and represent your country." Less familiar are the details of Davis's life off the tennis court. He worked for two presidents and served as secretary of war under Calvin Coolidge and as governor general of the Philippines under Herbert Hoover. As commissioner of the St. Louis Parks department he was responsible for building public parks and tennis courts and organizing athletics. Before his death in 1945 at the age of sixty-six, he was honored for heroism in World War I. He is buried in Arlington National Cemetery.

Davis, James Garfield

James Garfield Davis was described by his grandson as a "big, opinionated, stubborn" man. The grandson in question is Jim Davis. Davis was a sickly child, unable to work on the family farm in Indiana when he was growing up. To keep him occupied, his mother gave him pencils and paper and encouraged him to draw. Draw he did. He kept right on drawing in high school, through college, and into his first job as an assistant to Tom Ryan, the creator of a comic strip called "Tumbleweeds." A few years later, Davis went to New York to sell a comic of his own. "Gnorm Gnat" didn't catch on. The top syndicates told him no one would identify with the stip's main character, an insect. Davis did some market research by looking at the funny pages. It was true; there were no hit comic strips about bugs. There were, however, plenty about dogs. Instead of going up against the likes of Snoopy and Marmaduke, he decided to make his strip's main character a cat. He fashioned the feline after his grandfather and named it *Garfield.* It debuted on June 19, 1978 in forty-one newspapers and became one of the biggest cartoon hits of the 1980s. While we're on the subject of cartoon character names, Yogi Bear clearly took his name from baseball great Yogi Berra, right? Well, it depends on whom you ask. Shortly after Hanna-Barberra introduced the smarter-than-the-average-bear, the baseball player sued for defamation of character. Hanna-Barberra insists there was no connection between the two. "We never thought of Yogi Berra when we named Yogi Bear," a straight-faced executive was quoted as saying. "It was just a coincidence." But as Walter M. Brasch put it in his book *Cartoon Monikers,* "Whether coincidence or not, it is difficult to find anyone else in the industry who believes it." In any case, Yogi Berra dropped his suit and never took the cartoon bear to court. Bugs Bunny's nemesis, Elmer Fudd, took his name from a song lyric. The early 1920s hit contained the line "It's a treat to beat you on the Mississippi mud, Uncle Fudd." Elmer Fudd first appeared on screen in the 1938 *A Feud There Was.*

Dawson, James

Although the film *Titanic* documents a real-life event, the sinking of the great passenger liner on her maiden voyage in 1912, the main characters in director James Cameron's story are entirely fictional. By telling the story of a romance between a young first-class woman—statistically the most likely person to survive the sinking of the ship—and a third-class male passenger—most likely to perish—the director could give the viewer a limited number of characters to follow while at the same time showing all facets of life on *Titanic*. His female protagonist, whom he named Rose DeWitt Bukater, would be in one of the luxury suites on the liner. The rooms occupied by Rose, her mother, and Rose's fiancé, Caledon Hockley, were B52, B54, and B56. These were staterooms on the real *Titanic*. They were originally booked by millionaire J. P. Morgan. Morgan had a controlling interest in International Mercantile Marine, a conglomerate that owned the White Star Line, which in turn owned the *Titanic*. Morgan canceled his reservation at the last minute, however, and did not sail on the doomed liner. By putting his fictional characters in these rooms Cameron could effectively place them in the center of things without changing history too much. Caledon Hockley's name, by the way, comes from two small towns (Caledon and Hockley) near Orangeville, Ontario, Canada, where Cameron's aunt and uncle live. For his leading man, the third-class passenger, he chose the name Jack Dawson. He would later learn that a J. Dawson had, in fact, gone down with the *Titanic*. Although his given name was James, he always signed his name simply *J. Dawson*. In 1912, the young Dubliner came to Southampton, England looking for work. He was fair haired with a thick mustache that made him look older than his twenty-three years. He chose Southampton because it had been a flourishing seaport since the opening of a rail line from London in the 1840s. While ports in Liverpool were known for cargo shipping, Southampton was known as the hub of Britain's passenger and postal ships. The population had nearly quadrupled since the rail line had been opened, as seamen, stokers, and stewards moved there. The news of a new line of huge ships, each larger than the last, which White Star originally planned to call *Olympic, Titanic,* and *Gigantic,* meant even more work would be available. But in early 1912 a coal strike had stopped much shipping traffic. The new wonder ship, *Titanic,* would be one of the few vessels afloat. The *Titanic*'s call for workers was definitely a boon to the area. The "floating palace" would need more than nine hundred workers: waiters and waitresses, chefs, bakers, and engine-room workers. J. Dawson fell into this final category of employee. He was a trimmer, someone who stows the coal on board. As part of the so-called "black gang," Dawson would earn £5.10 for the voyage. Very few members of the ship's black gang survived. Most were needed to secure the vessel and shut her down after the collision. Those who were not were still deep in the bowels of the ship, far from the decks. When his body was recovered in the chilly waters of the North Atlantic, Dawson was still wearing his coal-stained shirt and denim pants. He was listed as body number 227 and described as looking "about thirty." His body was unclaimed, probably because his family could not afford to have it shipped back to England. In all, only 59 of the recovered bodies that were sent to Halifax, Nova Scotia, were claimed. Dawson was interred, with the rest of the unclaimed, in Fairview cemetery, with a simple grey granite stone paid for and erected by the White Star Line. Although he was not actually the prototype of James Cameron's Jack Dawson character, the similarity in their names has brought a great deal of attention to the real J. Dawson's grave. Mourners now frequently leave flowers and tributes to this J. Dawson, one of the otherwise forgotten victims of the 1912 disaster.

Dayton, Jonathan

Jonathan Dayton was born in what is now Elizabeth, New Jersey in 1760. His father, Elias, was a prominent merchant and colonial official who had served as a militia officer in the French and Indian War. Two of Dayton's classmates were Alexander Hamilton and Aaron Burr. He went on to attend the College of New Jersey, which would later be known as Princeton, but his studies were interrupted by political upheaval. In 1774, Dayton joined his father in a committee to enforce a boycott on British goods. When New Jersey rejected the rule of royal governor William Franklin a year later, they helped to raise a militia to fight against the British. Elias Dayton was put in charge of the Third New Jersey Regiment. He gave his fifteen-year-old son a position in his unit as an ensign. By 1777, Dayton was a seventeen-year-old lieutenant. He and his father endured the cold and hunger of Valley Forge. In October 1780, Jonathan Dayton was captured by British loyalists and was held prisoner in New York for several months. When he was released, he returned to duty. Elias Dayton was soon promoted to brigadier general and Jonathan Dayton was promoted to captain. Both remained in service until the army was discharged in 1783. Following the war, Dayton did what any young man with an exemplary war record and a father with influential connections would do. He entered politics. He became Elizabethtown's representative in the New Jersey legislature. When his father was invited to be a delegate to the Constitutional Convention in Philadelphia in 1787, he declined in favor of his son. Jonathan Dayton became one of the youngest members of the Convention. He went on to serve a term in the U.S. Senate. Ironically, his political career was cut short by the very thing that made his name a household word. He invested heavily in land speculation in Ohio. He owned more than a million acres in the region. This involvement led him to lend money to his old schoolmate, Aaron Burr. In 1807, the public discovered Burr had been involved in illegal activities. Dayton was also suspected. Even though a grand jury would later determine he had done nothing wrong, the damage was done. Dayton's political career was over. His name, however, had become attached to a town in Ohio. Today, *Dayton, Ohio* has a population of 182,044.

Dearborn, Henry

Henry Dearborn was born in 1751 at his grandfather's garrison house in North Hampton, New Hampshire. He grew up in Epping, New Hampshire, then studied medicine under Dr. Hall Jackson of Portsmouth, who also taught him military tactics. When tensions arose between the American colonies and Britain, Dearborn became a medic in the Continental Army. On April 20, 1775, Dearborn's wife gave birth to a daughter. The same day, he heard the news of the events at Lexington and Concord. A few hours later he marched to Cambridge with his regiment. During his military service, he kept a journal, which provided a valuable account of some of the most important battles of the war. Dearborn fought at the Battle of Bunker Hill and was then assigned to take part in a push to make Canada a fourteenth colony under the leadership of Benedict Arnold. The plan called for General Montgomery to move north from Ticonderoga while Arnold led an expedition through Maine to meet with Montgomery in Quebec. The trek was a disaster. It rained steadily for days, turning the terrain to mud and changing the shape of the rivers by which the army planned to navigate. They waded through icy swamps and found themselves lost, starving, and suffering from exposure. The low point came when several fellow soldiers forced Dearborn to surrender his dog so they could make a meal of it. When they finally arrived at a settlement, Dearborn was struck down with pneumonia. The army continued to Quebec without him. He recovered enough to join them in late December, just in time for a frigid battle in the ice and snow in which Montgomery was killed and Arnold wounded. The army found itself disoriented and lost once again. Dearborn was one of many prisoners taken that day. He was paroled two years later. He immediately rejoined the fighting. He joined a regiment that was erecting a line of defense to control the Hudson River. Dearborn was given command of the light infantry. The first battle, September 19, 1777, was a draw. In the second engagement, October 7, the Americans drove back the British line. Benedict Arnold was soon called in and with his regiment's assistance the Americans were able to cause the rest of the British line to collapse. The victory was a turning point for the Americans in the war. Next Dearborn joined George Washington at Valley Forge. He went on to join an expedition against the Indians in New York. In 1781 he was at Yorktown to witness the surrender of Cornwallis. After the war, Dearborn went into politics. He served as marshal for the District of Maine, Massachusetts congressman, major general in the War of 1812, ambassador to Portugal, and secretary of war. In this last role he issued an order "for erecting barracks and a strong stockade at Chikago with a view to the establishment of a Post." The name of the Illinois city dates back to pre-Revolutionary War times. It was recorded as early as 1688 in a French text as *Chigagou*. The name was never popular, however, because it came from an Algonquin word meaning "stinking." It probably earned that name from the indigenous skunks, the wild onion plants, or stagnant water in the area. The city was briefly named Fort Dearborn, but it did not stick. In 1830, "Chicago" was officially adopted. When the War of 1812 began, Dearborn, now a major general, attempted to invade Canada again. He was no more successful in these attempts than he had been during the Revolution, and he was removed from command by Pres. James Madison in 1813. Henry Dearborn passed away in 1829. His name does remain on the map, however, in southeastern Michigan. A stagecoach stop on the Sauk Trail between Detroit and Chicago grew into a community in the early 1800s. Originally known as Ten Eyck, then Bucklin, then Pekin, it was dubbed Dearbornville when it was charted in 1833. It was incorporated as *Dearborn* in 1893. Dearborn, Michigan is primarily known as the birthplace of industrialist Henry Ford and as the headquarters of the modern-day Ford Motor Company.

Dell, Michael

Michael Dell has never been accused of being lazy. The son of an orthodontist and a stockbroker, Dell grew up in Texas. In 1973, when he was only eight years old, he tried to graduate from high school by taking an equivalency test, but his parents wouldn't hear of it. Dell had to be satisfied with starting his career while still in school. He earned his first $2,000 at the age of twelve by talking neighbors into consigning parts of their stamp collections to him. Using the hunt-and-peck method, he typed out a catalog and advertised "Dell's Stamps" in a trade journal. He began speculating in gold, silver, and stocks at age thirteen. He bought his first computer, an Apple II, two years later and immediately tore it apart to see how it worked. In high school, he sold subscriptions to the *Houston Post* by tracking down new households through marriage licenses. He sent the couples a personalized letter offering a free two-week subscription, and most signed up after the trial period. He earned

$18,000 that way by the time he was seventeen. With his prof-
its, he bought himself a BMW, which he paid for with cash. In
1983, he entered the University of Texas as a biology student.
He thought he would become a doctor. He soon learned,
however, that local computer dealers were getting more IBM
PCs than they could sell. So Dell offered to buy surplus stock
at cost. Working from his dorm room, Dell added features to
each model and sold them through tiny ads in the local newspaper. "I used to drive the UPS man crazy because he had to
haul all my incoming equipment up twenty-seven flights of
stairs," Dell once told a reporter for the *Dallas Morning News*.
"He used to give me a lot of dirty looks." His parents were not
sure about his new venture, so when they came to visit, he
would hide the computers in his roommate's bathtub. He
promised his parents that if the "computer thing" didn't work
out by the end of his freshman year, he would put extra effort
into finishing his biology degree. By the following spring, he
was selling $50,000 worth of personal computers a month and
he dropped out of school. His parents were not too disap-
pointed. The year he would have graduated, 1987, Dell
earned $159 million. His company, *Dell Computer Corporation,*
joined the Fortune 500 list when Dell was only twenty-seven,
making him the youngest CEO ever to head a Fortune 500
company. He became a billionaire by the age of thirty-one. By
the time he was thirty-four, he was rated the sixth wealthiest
man in America by *Fortune* magazine. His estimated fortune of
$15 billion is more than Bill Gates was worth at the same age.
Today, Dell is overwhelmed with requests to speak to executives from well-established companies about doing business in
the computer age. In 1999 he was averaging about fifteen
hundred such requests a year. Michael Winkleman, executive
editor of *Chief Executive* magazine, says he is popular because
Bill Gates is too "nerdy." "Dell is much more accessible, better
looking," he told *USA Today*. "For older guys, he's a surrogate
son. For younger guys, he's who they want to be." Dell, the
company, is now one of the world's top PC makers and the
world's top direct-sale computer vendor with on-line sales of
$14 million a day.

Den, Kenjoro

Kenjoro Den, Rokuro Aoyama, and Meitaro Takeuchi were three of the major financiers of a young Japanese man named Masujiro Hashimoto who, in 1912, founded the Kwaishinsha Motor Car Company. In honor of their contributions, the company gave its cars a name based on the first initial of each man's last name. The result was the DAT. In 1926, Kwaishinsha merged with a company called Jidosha Seizo. The new company was named DAT Jidosha Seizo Company Limited. It continued to produce DAT automobiles. Four years later, after a reorganization, the directors of the company decided they should choose a new name for their automotive line. They called it "son of DAT" or "Datson." It was soon discovered, however, that when Japanese consumers pronounced "son," it sounded very similar to the Japanese word for "loss." So, in 1932, the name was modified to *Datsun*. The name of the parent company changed as well. DAT Jidosha Seizo had been purchased by a foundry company in 1931 and it was separated again from this parent company. It moved to a new site at Yokohama and was funded by a holding company named Nihon Sagyo. Financial traders knew the company by its stock exchange listing letters, Ni-San. In May of 1934, the name of the auto company was officially changed to Nissan Motor Company Limited. The automobiles it produced continued to be labeled Datsun.

Denver, James W.

James W. Denver was born October 23, 1817 in Virginia. When he was fourteen, his family moved to a farm outside Wilmington, Ohio. He studied surveying and in 1841 headed to Missouri in hopes of finding work as a surveyor. He returned to Ohio in 1842 to study law at the University of Cincinnati. After his graduation, he practiced law for a time in Xenia, Ohio. There, he edited a local Democratic newspaper called the *Thomas Jefferson*. After only a few months, however, the restless Denver had wanderlust again. He returned to Missouri and opened a law office with a partner. In 1847, Denver raised a company of soldiers to fight in the war with Mexico. When the war ended, he led a party of prospectors to California. He was elected a California senator in 1852. During his term a local newspaper editor named Edward Gilbert severely criticized one of Denver's projects. Denver challenged the reporter to a duel and on August 2, 1852, Gilbert was killed in the competition. No legal action was ever taken against Denver for Gilbert's death. He continued to be as popular as he had been before. He was elected secretary of state of California in 1853 and in 1855 was elected to the U.S. Congress. President Buchanan appointed Denver Commissioner on Indian Affairs in 1857. In that capacity, Denver negotiated treaties with the Indians of the "Bleeding Kansas Territory." He was named governor of that region in 1858. At about this time, a Georgia miner named William Green Russell struck gold in "Pikes Peak Country." Word of his discovery spread to California, which was full of prospectors who had had little luck in the gold rush of 1849. As many as 100,000 people flooded the region hoping to get rich quick. The gold of what would become Colorado, however, was buried in the mountains. Mining equipment and skills were required to extract it. As quickly as they came, most of the prospectors turned around and headed for home. Not wanting to face the long trek back, however, many of them ended up staying in two new settlements on the banks of Cherry Creek near Russell's original lode. On the west side of the creek was the community of Auraria, the Latin word for gold. (This is why the elemental symbol for gold is Au.) On the other side was the settlement of the St. Charles Town Company. In 1858, however, Gen. William H. Larimer renamed the community in honor of James Denver, whom he admired for bringing order to the frontier. On April 3, 1860, the residents of Auraria voted to merge with their neighbors across the creek. *Denver, Colorado* was the result. New deposits of gold were found in the area in 1859, bringing more settlers into the city and assuring its survival. James Denver continued to be involved in national politics. When the Civil War broke out, he was commissioned a brigadier general of volunteers by President Lincoln and placed in command of troops in Kansas. He served under Gen. Ulysses S. Grant until his retirement in

1863. In 1876 and 1884 Denver launched unsuccessful bids for the Democratic nomination for president of the United States. The party felt the fact that he had killed a man might be used against him. Denver died in Washington, D.C. August 9, 1892.

Di Leilo, Alfredo

Alfredo Di Leilo was an Italian restaurateur and chef. In 1914, when his wife was recuperating from the birth of their child, he decided to make her a special dish. He lovingly topped noodles with a rich combination of butter, cream, and Parmesan cheese. It was not only a hit at home. Patrons of the restaurant enjoyed it too. When it became a favorite dish of actors Douglas Fairbanks and Mary Pickford, *fettuccine Alfredo* received the publicity it needed to make Alfredo a household name. The dish made headlines again in 1994, albeit in a less flattering way. After testing the levels of fat in various popular foods, Jayne Hurley of the Center for Science in the Public Interest, a consumer-advocacy group based in Washington, D.C., announced: "Fettuccine Alfredo is the worst dish we've seen in twenty-three years of evaluating foods. It's a heart attack on a plate."

Diebold, Charles

The Great Chicago Fire of 1871 destroyed over 12,450 buildings and killed an estimated 250 people. Among the few things to survive the inferno were 878 safes made by a company founded by German immigrants Charles Diebold and Fred Bahman in 1859. Although Bahman's name was still over the door, he had left the company a number of years before the fire. When Chicagoans rebuilt their shops and offices, they bought Diebold safes in large numbers. Around the same time, a new partner, Jacob Kienzle, joined the operation. With new demand, the firm moved to a larger facility in Canton, Ohio and changed its name to Diebold & Kienzle. Two years later a man named John W. Norris joined up and the company changed its name again, this time to Diebold, Norris and Company. That same year, the company got its first order to supply a complete bank vault. The $100,000 vault measured thirty by twenty-five by nine feet and required eighteen train cars to move it to San Francisco. The extravagant project took manpower away from the production of smaller safes and cost so much to transport that it bankrupted the company. Charles Diebold rose from the ashes again. On July 29, 1876 he launched his new venture, the Diebold Safe and Lock Company, with W. W. Clark as president and Charles Diebold as plant superintendent. This version of the Diebold company was populated almost entirely with German immigrants. German was the only language spoken in the plants and offices. During World War I, the firm that had been dubbed "Little Germany" focused all its attention on military production. The production of armor plating for military vehicles and shell components brought an increase in revenue to the company. In the 1930s, the firm worked with the Lake Erie Chemical Company to develop a system to discharge tear gas in bank lobbies to help stop the notorious John Dillinger and his gang. In 1943, the company changed its name to Diebold, Incorporated. Eliot Ness, former crime fighter of "The Untouchables" fame, became chairman of the company's board of directors in 1944 and held the post until 1951. Today, along with safes, Diebold, Inc. is the second largest manufacturer of automated teller machines (ATMs) in the U.S. It also sells portable bank offices (MicroBranch) and similar products that automate bank transactions and enable them to be conducted from remote locations at any time of the day. Trivia question for quiz-show fans: A Diebold safe protected the questions for what 1955 television quiz show? Answer: "The $64,000 Question."

Dior, Christian

Christian Dior was born January 21, 1905, in a small resort town on the coast of Normandy, France. He was the second of five children of a well-to-do fertilizer manufacturer, Alexandre Dior, and his wife, Madeline. Christian adored his fashion-conscious mother. While his brothers were engaging in typically male pursuits, Christian was helping his mother decorate and work in the garden. As a teenager, Christian Dior wanted to be an architect and to attend the Académie des Beaux-Arts. His parents, however, did not approve of the choice of career and sent their son the Faculty of Political Science. In his free time, however, Dior hung out at Le Boeuf sur le Toit, a bar known for its avant-garde clientele. Pablo Picasso, Eric Satie, Salvador Dali, and Jean Cocteau frequented the establishment. After his required military service, Dior opened an art gallery with a friend. His timing was not ideal. The stock-market crash in America had worldwide repercussions. Not only did the gallery close, but the family fertilizer business went bust as well. Madeline Dior fell ill and died at the age of fifty-one. The combined misfortunes were too much for Dior. He became weak and contracted tuberculosis. Some friends sent him away to Ibiza to recover. When he returned he got a job behind the scenes in the Parisian fashion business. After a brief service in the military reserves during World War II, he returned to the business as an assistant to the famous designer Pierre Balmain. In 1946, a wealthy friend, Marcel Boussac, offered Dior financial backing to strike out on his own. His debut collection, dubbed "The New Look," was called revolutionary. Christian Dior's name would thereafter be synonymous with designer fashion. Interestingly, the designer's personal fashion sense was decidedly low key. *Life Magazine* once said he would be "instantly picked by anyone familiar with whodunits as the character least likely to be suspected M. Dior."

Dixie, Johan

Was the first Dixieland in Manhattan? It's possible, say some word watchers. According to an 1885 edition of the *Charlestown Courier:*

> When slavery existed in New York, one [Johan] Dixie owned a large tract of land on Manhattan Island, and a large number of slaves. The increase of the slaves and of the abolition sentiment caused an emigration of the slaves to more through and secure slave sections, and the Negroes who were thus sent off (many being born there) naturally looked back to their old houses, where they had lived in clover, with feelings of regret, as they could not imagine any place like Dixie's. Hence it became synonymous with an ideal location combining ease, comfort and material happiness of every description.

As difficult as it is to imagine any slave farm inspiring such warm nostalgia, many experts believe it is the most likely origin of the term Dixie. Robert Hendrickson, author of *Human Words,* calls it "somewhat less doubtful than other theories." At least one other theory places the origin of Dixie in New York. In 1872, *New York Weekly* claimed that Dixie was associated with a children's game of tag that was first played in New York City, although it didn't give any evidence to back the story up. A more complicated explanation is that it comes from the French word for ten—*dix.* The idea is that the word *dix* appeared on ten-dollar bills issued by a New Orleans bank before the Civil War. The money flowed throughout the South, earning it the name "the land of dixes," which evolved into Dixieland. The simplest explanation is that it derives from the Mason-Dixon line, which divides the Northern from the Southern states. Whatever the origin, the first recorded use of the expression was the song "Johnny Roach," written by an Ohio minstrel named Daniel D. Emmett. The song was first performed in February 1859. Emmett never said he originated the word, so it was probably in use before that time. What Emmett undoubtedly did do was to popularize the term with a song he first performed later the same year. It was called "Away Down South in Dixie," or simply "Dixie." It was said that Emmett wrote the song on his violin "while looking out on the cold dreary streets of New York City and wishing he were in Dixie." Perhaps the most famous story about the song involves Abraham Lincoln. On April 10, 1865, when the White House received news that Robert E. Lee had surrendered, people flocked to hear what the president would say. Lincoln appeared and promised to say a few words. But first, he said, turning towards the members of a band that had come to the celebration, he would like to hear them play "Dixie." The crowd was incredulous. Why "Dixie," of all songs? Lincoln replied, "'Dixie' is one of the best tunes I have ever heard, and now we have captured it." There was a great cheer from the crowd, and the band played "Dixie."

Dorn, Prairie

Around 1969, Prairie Dorn was an actress. One day, Fran Brill, one of Jim Henson's Muppeteers, was sitting in an agent's office trying to get representation. As she waited, she flipped through the stack of head shots on the desk and noticed one belonging to "Prairie Dorn." "I couldn't believe that someone had this name, 'Prairie,'" Brill told David Borgenicht, author of *Sesame Street: Unpaved.* She went back to Henson and told him about the name. They decided to use it for one of their "Sesame Street" characters, a puppet of a young girl. "Obviously, we didn't want to use this poor actress's name, 'Dorn,' so she became Prairie Dawn," Brill said. Oscar the Grouch was also inspired by a real person, albeit not a person named Oscar. The idea for the character came when Jim Henson and "Sesame Street"'s director, Jon Stone, were having lunch at a restaurant called Oscar's Tavern in Manhattan. The waiter there was so rude and grouchy that, in Borgenicht's words, "going to Oscar's became a sort of masochistic form of lunchtime entertainment for them. They immortalized him as the world's most famous grouch." Oscar's voice was inspired by another real person, a New York cab driver who took Caroll Spinney, who played both Oscar and Big Bird, to the studio during the show's first season. Spinney imitated the man's gruff voice, and used it for the grouch from that day on. When the Muppet made his first appearance on the new show in 1969, he was orange. When he returned for the second season he was his now-familiar green color. Another Muppet, Zoe, introduced in 1983 as a female counterpart to Elmo, indirectly took her name from "Sesame Street"'s new executive producer, Michael Loman. Loman's nickname is Frannie. Someone suggested it for the new Muppet's name. Loman didn't like the idea of having a Muppet with his name, but he didn't stray too far afield. He thought of J. D. Salinger's book *Franny and Zooey.* He suggested using the Zooey (or Zoe) instead of the Franny (Frannie). "Sesame Street" best-buddies Ernie and Bert are widely believed to have been named for characters in the 1946 film *It's a Wonderful Life,* but the show's creators say it is just a coincidence. The producers of the Christmas special "Elmo Saves Christmas" used footage from the film, however. In the scene, Ernie and Bert walk past a pile of television sets showing the film. James Stewart's character, George Bailey, yells, "Bert! Ernie! What's with you two?" The Muppets do a double take on hearing their names. The oldest "Sesame Street" character is Kermit the Frog. Kermit first appeared in Jim Henson's 1955 television show "Sam and Friends." The first Kermit Muppet was made from the material of Henson's mother's spring coat, with two halves of a Ping-Pong ball for eyes. Trivia question for "Sesame Street" fans: What is Ernie and Bert's address? Answer: They live in the basement apartment at 123 Sesame Street.

Dracula, Vlad

Born in Transylvania in 1432, Vlad IV was prince of Walachia, a region south of the Transylvanian Alps. He was the son of Vlad Dracul, or "Vlad the Devil." Dracula means the devil's son. He first seized the Walachian throne briefly in 1448. He captured it again in 1456 and ruled until 1460, earning himself another nickname, Vlad Tepes, or "Vlad the Impaler," for his method of disposing of enemies. He skewered them and put them on display for the invading Turks to see. He was also known to boil in oil, mutilate, or decapitate enemies. He is remembered with some fondness by some in his own country, however. Besides stacking the severed heads of Turkish enemies, he developed commerce, and strengthened the army. In 1462, the Impaler was deposed by the Ottoman Sultan Muhammad II. Vlad sought aid from the Hungarian king Mathias Corvinus but instead he was jailed in Hungary for 12 years. In late 1476, Vlad, with Transylvanian aid, regained the Walachian throne. He did not have much time to celebrate his victory. The same year Vlad was killed by the Ottoman-supported prince, Laiota Basarab. More than 400 years later, a novelist named Bram Stoker would adopt the prince's name for his vampire character. In the 100 years since its publication, the novel *Dracula* has never been out of print and its central character has become a part of our culture.

Dreyer, William

At the age of eighteen, in 1906, William Dreyer earned his passage to the United States from Germany by working as a galley boy on the steamer SS *Kaiser Wilhelm*. On the last night of his journey, he made a special dessert of fresh fruit, gelatin, and sugar that was a hit with the passengers. Taking this reaction as a sign, Dreyer found a job making ice cream and candy in New York. He met a fellow German immigrant named Albina. They fell in love, got married, and decided to start their new life together out West. They made their way across the country selling confections and ice cream in various places to earn enough to move on. Finally they arrived in California, where they ran out of West. In Oakland, Dreyer met a candy maker named Joe Edy. The two men joined forces in 1928. Because Edy's name was better known in Oakland and because their new factory was located on Grand Avenue, they called their product Edy's Grand Ice Cream. In the 1930s, Dreyer experimented with new ice-cream flavors. One night he used his wife's good sewing scissors to chop up walnuts and marshmallows, which he added to chocolate ice cream. She forgave him for the misuse of her scissors because Rocky Road was an instant sensation. The partners developed a line of sherbets out of necessity during World War II when butterfat and cane sugar became scarce. In 1946, Edy and Dreyer went their separate ways. Dreyer, along with his son Bill, renamed the company Dreyer's Grand Ice Cream. William Dreyer retired in 1953. A decade later, Bill Dreyer sold the company. It changed hands a second time in 1976. The new owners invested in building a direct store-distribution system and they were able to expand quickly—too quickly, perhaps. Their rise caught the attention of Kraft Foods, which owned rival ice-cream maker Breyer's. Kraft felt Dreyer's sounded similar enough to Breyer's to create confusion. Dreyer's agreed to sell their products east of the Rocky Mountains under their original name, *Edy's Grand Ice Cream*. West of the Rockies it is still known as *Dreyer's Grand Ice Cream*. As of 1997, Dreyer's had annual sales of almost eight hundred million dollars.

Dubonnet, Joseph

In 1846, a Parisian chemist named Joseph Dubonnet concocted a fortified wine containing quinine. The resulting mixture had the properties of a tonic and stimulant. Quinine is bitter, so Dubonnet laced the wine with sweet, spicy ingredients to make it palatable. It is said to include bitter orange rind, chamomile, cinnamon, and green coffee beans. Dubonnet soon became popular as an aperitif and is now known all over the world. It is produced in the Roussillon region of France. It takes up to two years to produce. It is widely used in the preparation of cocktails, especially those with a vodka or gin base. Despite Dubonnet's French heritage, American supplies have been produced in the United States since the Second World War. American-produced Dubonnet is made from California wine that has been fortified with grape brandy to 19 percent alcohol.

Dun, Robert

Robert Graham Dun grew up in a family of limited means. He was raised along with four brothers and sisters on what little money had been left after their father's death when Dun was only nine. At the age of sixteen he started working as a clerk in a general store. He remained at the store for about five years. In 1851 his brother-in-law Benjamin Douglass offered him a position with the Mercantile Agency. Dun leapt at the opportunity. Founded in 1841 by Lewis Tappan in Northampton, Massachusetts, the agency was one of the first credit-reporting companies in the country. Douglass had taken the reins in 1849. With the railroad and telegraph making the world seem smaller, more and more Americans were heading West. So Douglass opened branch offices in that area. Meanwhile, across town, John M. Bradstreet was launching another credit-reporting company. Bradstreet managed to steal clients from the Mercantile Agency by creating a loose-leaf-bound system of coded reports. Mercantile's clients had to physically come to the office to get credit reports. So one of the first things Dun did when he got his shot at running Mercantile in 1859 was to release a comprehensive reference book. The book, creatively dubbed the *Reference Book,* featured credit information on 20,268 firms. It sold for $200, and that was back in the days when $200 was a lot to spend on a book. Despite its cost, the *Reference Book was popular.* Dun was thus able to recapture some of the clients his agency had lost to Bradstreet's. Dun also changed the way credit reports were written. Previously, they were based on assessments of men's characters. Dun wanted his agencies' reports to be less subjective, so he had his reporters use statistical ratings and capital worth as measures. John Bradstreet died in 1863 and his son took charge of the agency. In 1865, Dun established his agency's first print shop. Two years later, his company became the first business to use typewriters. In 1874, he placed an order for 100 typewriters with the brand-new Remington typewriter company. It was that company's first commercial order. Robert Dun died of cirrhosis in 1900 at the age of seventy-four. His obituary said, "R. G. Dun is known all over the world, and he has established an institution that will probably live as long as commerce lives." The Great Depression left both Dun and Bradstreet's agencies in bad shape, however. In 1930 a small credit-reporting company founded by Arthur D. Whiteside merged with R. G. Dun & Company. Whiteside became the CEO. Two years later, he orchestrated the merger of former competitors Dun and Bradstreet. Today, *Dun & Bradstreet* maintains a global database covering more than 55 million companies.

E/F

Eden, George

George Eden was born into an aristocratic family on August 25, 1784 on Eden Farm near Beckenham, Kent, England. He succeeded to his father's baronies in 1814, becoming the second Baron Auckland, and Baron Eden of Norwood. He served as Board of Trade president and lord of the Admiralty before being selected by his friend Lord Melbourne (for whom Melbourne, Australia was named) to be governor general of India. Lord Auckland arrived in India with his sisters Emily and Fanny. With Russia making advances into Afghanistan, England was concerned that the nation could be a threat to British India. Lord Auckland, who had participated in the first Afghan War, was chosen to stop that from happening. His mission was to restore the exiled Afghan king, Shah Shoja, who was living in the Punjab. But first he made a commercial treaty with the sitting Afghan ruler, Dost Mohammad. Auckland gained influence, in the words of the *Encyclopedia Britannica,* "with threats and a disregard of treaties." Shoja occupied the Afghan capital, Kabul, in 1839. This was the height of Auckland's status. He was made an earl for his successes. At the same time, England was having trouble with a settlement in another part of the world—New Zealand. New Zealand was first sighted in 1642 by a Dutch explorer named Abel Tasman (for whom Tasmania was named). Tasman called his discovery Staaten Landt meaning Land of the States, in other words, Land of the Netherlands. It is important to note, however, that this newly discovered land was no secret to the people who already lived there, the Maori. They called their land

Aotearoa—the Land of the Long White Cloud. Tasman was forced to abandon his exploration of the land when a number of members of his crew were killed by Maori who interpreted their trumpet calls as a battle cry. The following year, the Dutch dubbed the land Nieuw Zeeland or "new sea-land," a reference to the Dutch province of Zeeland, which consists largely of islands. It appeared as a jagged line on European maps, but few explorers, upon hearing of Tasman's reception, were inclined to go there. The next Europeans to arrive were the British, under the leadership of explorer James Cook in 1769. In the early 1800s, the Europeans and the Maori were able to make a kind of precarious peace. The British set up a prison, and whaling settlements sprang up on the eastern shore of the North Island. A Maori chief, Hongi Hika, invited British missionaries to establish a small settlement there as well. Little by little, however, the foreigners began to arrive in larger numbers. Battles erupted between various Maori tribes and the settlers. In February 1840 the British decided to send a naval force, commanded by Capt. William Hobson, to suppress the growing fighting. Hobson addressed a large gathering of Maori chiefs at Waitangi on February 6. The Waitangi Treaty guaranteed the Maori possession of their forests and fisheries in exchange for recognition of British rule. The Maori believed, for no other reason than that the treaty said so, that they would be left undisturbed on their tribal lands. It is still a point of contention to this day. With British rule established, Hobson, who had been supported financially by Lord Auckland, named the new capital city—not yet built—*Auckland.* (The capital was transferred to Wellington in 1865.) Lord Auckland's prominence quickly waned after this. Although he was considered to be an excellent administrator of India—he extended irrigation, inaugurated famine relief, and expanded training and education—his efforts in Afghanistan ended in the death or capture of 5,000 British troops. The problem was that Shah Shoja was not popular enough to rule on his own. To keep him in power, the British installed its own armies. The Afghans were not happy to have a foreign occupying army in their midst and they staged a number of revolts. After two years of fighting, the British garrison was overwhelmed in 1841. Auckland, blamed for the losses, was recalled from his post in 1842. He died seven years later at the age of sixty-five. His sister Emily was more successful in India. She wrote two novels, *The Semi-detached House* and *The Semi-attached Couple*. She also took the opportunity to draw the people of India. Her watercolors were lithographed by Lowes Dickson and published by J. Dickinson in 1844 under the title *Princes and People of India*.

Elmira

According to town legend, a rambunctious little girl lived in an unnamed New York town. Her mother was always calling after her: "Elmira! Elmira!" It was such a frequent sound that the neighbors decided to name the town *Elmira, New York*. As an aside, the town of Eleva, Wisconsin did not get its name from a person, as might be suspected. It took its name from a half-painted sign. The winter closed in earlier than expected one year as workmen were painting a sign for the town's large grain elevator. They only got as far as *ELEVA* when they had to stop until spring. The sign was the most prominent marker in town, however, and by the time the winter had ended, most people thought Eleva was the name of the town. Now it is. Another interesting geographical name is Enough, Missouri. The town was named by postal authorities after 200 names had been rejected. Another Missouri town name has a similar origin. The local postmaster selected dozens of names for his town, which were rejected. He was told he should pick a peculiar name. That's how it came to be called Peculiar, Missouri. Kansas, meanwhile, has two cities named for members of the St. Louis Browns baseball team. In the 1880s, workers from the Missouri Pacific Railroad were building a new line through the state. In honor of their winning team, they named fourteen of the stations after players. A dozen of the cities have been renamed but Bushong, named for pitcher Doc Bushong, and Latham, named for shortstop Arlie Latham, are still on the map. Titusville, Florida was named for Henry Titus, who, in 1873, won the right to name the town in a game of dominoes against Charles Rice. Truth or Consequences, New Mexico, may be the only city in America named for a game show. In 1950 the radio quiz show offered prizes to any city that would change its name. Hot Springs, New Mexico took them up on the offer.

Entenmann, William

William Entenmann was a German immigrant. He arrived in America in 1898 and opened a bakery in Flatbush, New York. He delivered the cakes and bread door to door with a horse and buggy. In the early 1900s, Entenmann moved his business to the country when his son, William, Jr., contracted rheumatic fever. At the new bakery in Bay Shore, Long Island, William, Jr., met a nineteen-year-old salesgirl, Martha Schneider. The couple were married and had three sons, Robert, Charles, and William. The children went to work for the family shop as soon as they were able. When their father offered to send them to college to learn a new trade, they all decided to stick with the bakery. William Entenmann II died of a heart attack in 1951 and Martha and her sons took over the operation of the business. They decided to phase out delivery routes and to sell to supermarkets. To make the products more attractive, they put them in a box with a clear top. Most baked goods in supermarkets of the day were sold in white boxes that revealed nothing of the contents. These turned out to be good decisions. Entenmann's went public in 1976 with Martha's picture on the stock certificates. Two years later the Entenmanns decided the business had become too big for the family and they sold it to Warner-Lambert for $233 million. In 1982 it was sold to General Foods for $315 million. General Foods was, in turn, bought up by Philip Morris, making Entenmann's a part of Kraft Foods. In 1997 Entenmann's became the property of Bestfoods. A year later, when Entenmann's celebrated its 100th anniversary, *Newsday* tallied up the quantities of some of the baked goods the company had sold over the course of a century in business. It included 620 million chocolate-chip cookies, a little more than 2 cookies for every person in the United States; 190 million pounds of apples in their apple pies, which would weigh twice as much as the

Titanic; 700 million all-butter loaf cakes, enough to reach from New York to Beijing and back seven times; and 780 million donuts, enough to circle the planet twice.

Escherich, Theodor

Little is known about Theodor Escherich except that he was a German physician. In 1885, while working in Munich, he identified a strain of bacteria that is commonly found in animals' intestines. Unlike other bacteria being studied at the time, this strain, which he called *Bacterium coli,* seemed to live in the body without causing disease. The bacterium was later named *Escherichia coli,* or *E. coli* for short. One of the greatest benefits of the discovery of *E. coli* has been in guaranteeing the quality of water supplies. Bacteria that cause such dangerous diseases as cholera and dysentery can exist in public water supplies in such sparse amounts that it is hard to detect but can still cause illness. Water systems instead test for the presence of *E. coli.* The bacterium, if discovered, may not be dangerous in itself but indicates that sewage may have gotten into the water and other contaminants may therefore be present.

Evans, Bob

Bob Evans was born May 30, 1918 on a farm in a small town outside Bowling Green, Ohio. His father opened a chain of markets. Eventually the family moved to Gallipolis, Ohio, where young Bob worked in one of the family stores. He grew up and went to veterinary school at Ohio State University. His education was interrupted, however, by World War II. When Evans came back from the war, he opened a truck stop. War shortages limited the amount of sausage he could buy, so he started making his own from the livestock on his family farm. Customers liked his homemade sausage better than anything he'd sold before, so he started to sell it in ten-pound tubs. Truckers carried it with them to other parts of the country and word spread. Evans wisely decided to focus entirely on sausage making. He borrowed $1,000 from his dad and in 1950 built a sausage plant. He was not sure the gamble would pay off. He hedged his bets by putting large doors at either end of the building so that he could resell the property for use as a machine shed if it failed. Since his father ran a chain of grocery stores in West Virginia and Ohio, Evans had natural distribution for his sausages. It wasn't long, however, before many other grocers were stocking the product. In 1962, Evans got into the restaurant business. His restaurant was called the Sausage Shop and it was located right on the farm where he and his family now lived. Along with sausage, the restaurant sold meals using his wife Jewell's personal recipes. When he built a second restaurant off his property he constructed it to look like a barn and called it Bob Evans Farms. Evans retired in 1986. Still run by family members, Bob Evans Farms now operates about 430 restaurants in twenty states.

Faber, Eberhard

Eberhard Faber grew up in Nuremberg, Germany in the early 1800s. Nuremberg could be called "the birthplace of the pencil." The first mass-produced pencils were made there in 1662, although people had been writing with lead rods since Roman times. Graphite came into use after the discovery of a large deposit in Borrowdale, England in 1564. It is softer and leaves a darker line than lead and was soon the material of choice for writing. By then, people were so used to referring to their writing rods as "lead" that the expression remained. We call the writing material in pencils "lead" to this day even though it is actually a mixture of graphite and clay. In 1756, Eberhard Faber's great-grandfather, Casper, perfected a process of binding powdered graphite and encasing it in wood. So when Faber moved to New York City and opened an import business he naturally included pencils in his inventory. At that time, most pencils were imported from Europe. Although such notables as Benjamin Franklin and George Washington were pencil fans, most Americans preferred goose-quill pens. The first American wood-cased pencils were made by William Monroe, a Concord, Massachusetts cabinetmaker in 1812. Faber gambled that it was just a matter of time before pencils were popular in America. He started manufacturing his own in 1861. His first factory was located in New York on the site of the present United Nations building. That plant was destroyed by fire in 1872, and Faber rebuilt in Brooklyn. Pencil popularity picked up during the Civil War. Soldiers in the field could not always find inkwells for their quills. They started to carry pencils with them as they marched so they could write letters home. When Faber died in 1879, pencils were a household fixture and Eberhard Faber was a household name, so much so that his son John legally changed his name to Eberhard. The second Eberhard Faber took charge of the company after his father's death. In 1893, he started painting the pencils. Have you ever wondered why pencils are usually yellow? It was no accident. In the 1800s, Chinese graphite was reputed to be the best in the world. Americans associated the color yellow with China, so yellow pencils conveyed the message that they contained top-quality Chinese graphite. Yellow pencils outsold all the others and became the standard. These days, about 75 percent of the pencils sold in the U.S. are yellow. According to Doug Gelbert, author of *So Who the Heck Was Oscar Mayer?*, the Eberhard Faber company once staged an experiment. They manufactured 1,000 identical pencils. Half were painted green, the other half yellow. The preference for yellow pencils was so strong that most of the green pencils were returned with complaints that they broke easily and were not as durable as the yellow ones. Today's standard pencil can draw a line thirty-five miles long and can write an average of 45,000 words. What gives the pencil its distinctive smell? The answer is incense cedar, one of the most commonly used pencil woods. More than two billion pencils are used in the U.S. each year. Do Americans make more mistakes than their European counterparts? It's possible. According to the Incense Cedar Institute, most U.S. pencils have erasers while most European models don't. While we're on the subject of Americans and pencils—during the Space Race in the 1960s, the National Aeronautics and Space Administration spent about $241 million and months of research to develop a ballpoint pen to write in the zero-gravity confines of its space capsules. Soviet astronauts came up with another solution. They used a pencil.

Faberge, Peter Carl

Peter Carl Faberge was born in St. Petersburg in 1846, the son of jeweler Gustav Faberge. There was no question that young Peter would take over the family business one day. He trained with a master goldsmith in Frankfurt, and when he was twenty-four he took charge of the store. In 1872 he married Augusta Jakobs, the daughter of an overseer at the Imperial Furniture Workshop. The couple had four sons. The family lived modestly in an apartment above the small store. Yet Faberge had his eye on the imperial palace. He wanted to capture the attention of Russia's imperial family, who were, needless to say, a potential gold mine for a jeweler. He first got their business by offering free repairs, but soon he caught the empress's eye with his craftsmanship. He was named court goldsmith in 1885, a title that cemented his reputation throughout Europe as a fine jeweler. That same year Czar Alexander III asked Faberge to create a jewel-encrusted Easter egg that he could give as a gift to his wife, Empress Maria Federovna. More delicate eggs were soon requested, and they became a favorite of the imperial family, who offered them as gifts to each other and to visiting heads of state. In all, Faberge's company made fifty of the finely crafted items for the imperial family and another seven for the wealthy Kelkh family. According to Leah Popper, an expert on decorative arts quoted in the *Jerusalem Post,* Faberge did not create any of the eggs himself, but he inspected every item before it left the workshop. But the Faberges did not live happily ever after. In 1917 the Russian Revolution made "court goldsmith" a dangerous occupation. Czar Nicholas II and his family were executed by Bolsheviks in 1918. The Faberges were forced to flee for their lives. Faberge escaped by acting as a British courier and settled in Switzerland, where he died two years later. His sons tried to continue in the family tradition, but times had changed and they had little success. Later an American perfume company, Unilever, bought the Faberge name and continued the tradition of producing *Faberge eggs.* Today, original Faberge works are expensive and prized works of art. More of Faberge's works can be now found in the United States than in Russia.

As Russians tried to escape the nation's communist borders, Faberge works were continually confiscated. Josef Stalin sold most of the treasures to capitalist art dealers in America. Malcolm Forbes has the largest collection of original Faberge eggs in the world.

Fassert, Barbara Ann

When Barbara Ann Fassert was just thirteen, her brother Fred wrote a song for their other brother Charles' band, the Regents. One day in 1960 she was sitting in their Bronx kitchen with her mother and her brothers came in to play it for her. "Barbara Ann/Take my hand," they sang. "When they said my name, I was so excited," she told *People* magazine. "I thought, 'I'm a movie star!'" The Regents took the song "Barbara Ann" to number thirteen on the *Billboard* charts in 1961. Five years later the Beach Boys made it an even bigger hit. Their version peaked at number two in 1966. The original Regents disbanded in 1975. Charles Fassert went on to own his own recording company. Fred became a New York City building inspector and Barbara Ann married a Bronx supermarket owner, Pat Rizzo, and had three children.

Filene, William

William Filene was born in 1830 in the Polish city of Posen, then part of Prussia. His father earned enough selling ribbons to send his two sons to Berlin to study law. A pair of tragedies, the death of William's brother and a bloody uprising in Posen, caused the distraught William to renounce Judaism and emigrate to England and finally the United States. At age eighteen, he found himself in Boston, where he worked as a tailor, eventually earning enough to open his own shop in 1851. In 1856 he moved to Salem and met and married a Bavarian immigrant named Clara Ballin. They had four sons and a daughter. During the Civil War, Filene moved to New York to open a dry-goods store, which failed. So the family returned to Massachusetts, this time to Lynn, where Filene opened two small stores, one for men's wear, one for women. When Filene fell ill in 1879, two of his sons, Edward Albert and Abraham

Lincoln, who went by his middle name, took over the majority of the business. In 1881, the family sold the small shops in Lynn to buy a more modern shop, "with its genuine white marble floor and most artistic windows," in Boston. As their father's health deteriorated, the brothers took over more of the responsibility until William Filene finally passed away in 1901. In 1908 Edward Albert moved all of the sale items to the basement of the store and marked them down further and further the longer they remained in the store, thus creating the first "bargain basement." Filene's Basement became a landmark of its own and, more recently, a separate company of its own. In 1988 May Department Stores Company bought Filene's department store, but not the bargain basements, which became Filene's Basement Corporation.

Fingerhut, Manny

Manny Fingerhut was born November 20, 1914, one of five children of Russian immigrants. The Fingerhuts had planned to join relatives in Indianapolis when they came to America in 1902. They knew little English, and they accidentally bought tickets to Minneapolis instead. There, they settled. Fingerhut's father died when he was still a boy. So he helped support the family by selling newspapers. In 1933 he took a job as a bookkeeper for a car dealership. He worked his way up to manager before World War II interrupted his career. He served in France, then returned to his former business. It was not satisfying, however. After a short time, he decided to quit and join his brother, William, who made car-seat covers. In 1948, the brothers expanded the small operation and called their venture *Fingerhut*. They found selling the covers through face-to-face visits was difficult. So within a year they printed up a catalog and started selling them by mail. This was much more effective. Manny expanded his mailing list and began to ship catalogs to other states. Within four years, annual sales from the catalog were close to one million dollars and the brothers abandoned personal sales calls completely. In 1957, Fingerhut was approached by an agency that represented a group of manufacturers who wanted to pool their resources and sell their own products directly to consumers. Manny agreed to add their products to his catalogs. William Fingerhut retired and sold his share of the business to Manny in 1967. He took the company public in 1970. Manny Fingerhut retired in 1978. When he died, in 1995, Fingerhut sales were roughly two billion dollars a year.

Fleer, Frank

When German immigrant Frank H. Fleer founded a candy company in Philadelphia in 1885, chewing gum was just coming into vogue in America. People had been chewing on wads of sticky stuff since ancient Greece. New England Indians chewed on a substance taken from the pulp of the spruce tree. The first white settlers adopted the practice, but it would be another hundred years before anyone tried to manufacture the gum commercially. In 1848, a man named John Curtis went into business to sell "State of Maine Pure Spruce Gum." The great candy-buying public was not unduly impressed with the stuff. It was, well, too sprucey. Two years later, Curtis tried again with a paraffin-based chew. It tasted better, or more specifically, it didn't taste like anything. It didn't have the texture of spruce, though, and was not a hit. On December 28, 1869, William Finley Semple of Mount Vernon, Ohio, was issued a patent for a chewing gum made from rubber and "other articles," but he never manufactured it. The next breakthrough in the world of chewing gum came in 1870. Thomas Adams, a commercial photographer in New York, began experimenting with the sap of the Chiclezapote tree. Mexicans had been chewing the stuff for years and legend has it that Adams got his first sample of it from Santa Anna, who brought it to the United States when he was exiled. Adams spent two years trying to make a practical product from the rubbery material. He tried to make toys, tires, and rain boots but failed in every endeavor. Finally he took a piece, stuck it in his mouth, and found he liked it. He added flavoring and opened the world's first chewing-gum factory. Around the time Fleer went into business, Adams' factory employed 250 workers. Chewing gum was definitely a hit. Not surprisingly, it met with some resistance. The *New York Sun*, in 1890, condemned the new practice: "The habit has reached such a stage now that makes it impossible for a New Yorker to go to the theater or the church, or enter the street cars of the railway train, or walk on a fashionable promenade without meeting men and women whose jaws are working with the activity of the gum chewing victim. And the spectacle is maintained in the face of frequent reminders that gum-chewing especially in public, is an essentially vulgar indulgence that not only shows bad breeding, but spoils a pretty countenance and detracts form the dignity of those who practice the habit." Fleer decided to produce its own chewing gum in 1906. The product was called Blibber Blubber. The company would not come out with a breakthrough chewing gum until an accountant started playing around with the gum mixtures at the Philadelphia plant. "I was supposed to be doing something else," Walter Diemer said, "and ended up with something with bubbles." Diemer's mixture was less sticky than regular chewing gum, and more stretchy. The result was that it could be used for blowing bubbles. The twenty-three-year-old inventor carried five pounds of the substance to a grocery store, where he taught the staff to blow bubbles. The gum sold out in a single afternoon. Fleer decided to wrap up the first bubble gum and sell it under the name Dubble Bubble. It was pink, and most bubble gum since that time has been the same color. Why? The only food coloring Diemer had on hand was red. Today most gum is made from latex rubber taken from the sapodilla tree of Central and South America. The dried latex is kneaded into a hot mix of sugar and corn syrup, flavored, then pressed and cut into strips. While Dubble Bubble remains popular to this day, Fleer's name is most associated with the thin, dry sticks of gum that come packaged with baseball cards. Fleer first offered "famous pictures" with some of its candy in 1923. One of the famous people included was Babe Ruth, but the set is so rare, no one knows the entire list of 120 celebrities. Fleer's next trading-card set was a Cops and Robbers set sold with bubble gum. Fleer's first complete entry into the baseball card industry was the eighty-card 1959 Ted Williams set. Other sets were issued off and on until 1981. Fleer has been continually producing sports cards since that time. A group of investors bought the company from the Fleer family in 1989. Trivia question for chewing-gum fans: How many sticks of gum does the average American chew in a year? Answer: 300. There is good news for gum chewers. Researchers at the prestigious Mayo Clinic have discovered that chewing gum can raise your metabolic rate by as much as 20 percent and can help you lose weight. Of course, to lose weight you must chew sugarless gum. And you have to do a lot of chewing. To lose eleven pounds you'll have to chew gum every waking hour for a full year.

Foster, Richard

Not surprisingly, with a dish as tasty and dramatic as *bananas Foster,* a number of people have stepped forward to take the credit. Bananas Foster, which consists of sliced bananas in a sauce of butter, rum, and banana cordial, flamed for effect, and poured over ice cream, is a favorite New Orleans creation. In the 1950s, New Orleans was the major port of entry for bananas, which were being shipped from Central and South America. With a new fruit that was plentiful and inexpensive, it made sense for a restaurant to come up with creative ways to serve it. It is generally agreed that the dish was first served at Brennan's, a restaurant owned by Owen Edward Brennan, who challenged his chef, Paul Blange, to come up with a banana dish. (The *Toronto Star* credited another restaurant, Antoine's, with inventing the concoction, but the restaurant itself makes no such claim. *See* Antoine Alciatore entry for more on Antoine's.) According to Brennan's, the restaurant simultaneously received a request from *Holiday Magazine* to provide a recipe for a feature article on the establishment. They provided the recipe for a new dish, which they say was named for Richard Foster, a friend of Brennan's and a loyal customer. Foster, who had served with Brennan on the New Orleans Crime Commission, was the owner of the Foster Awning Company. The article brought greater publicity to both the establishment and the dish. Bananas Foster has become a trademark part of the New Orleans-style breakfast served at Brennan's. It is the most requested item on the menu. Each year 35,000 pounds of bananas are flamed there. Joan Foster

Dames, a feature writer for the *St. Louis Post-Dispatch,* however, claims that her father, Albert Steere Foster, was not only the namesake, but the inventor of bananas Foster. In her version of the story, Albert Steere Foster was an amateur chef in New Orleans. He became friends with a number of the area's professional chefs and, in the early 1930s, he whipped up his rum-soaked banana split in the kitchen of one of the area restaurants. The chef there thought it was great and called it bananas Foster for its inventor. Despite the writer's insistence that the family legend is true, Martha Barnette, author of *Ladyfingers and Nun's Tummies,* which chronicles the origins of the names of popular foods, gives her nod to Richard Foster.

Foster, W. M. and R. R.

Foster's Lager bills itself as "Australian for 'beer.'" Each can is printed with the Southern Cross. The Australian brew once had Crocodile Dundee himself, Paul Hogan, as a spokesman. They even sponsor boomerang contests. You might be surprised to learn, then, that the company was started by a pair of American brothers of Irish descent. The Fosters, remembered only as W. M. and R. R., moved to Australia and started the Foster's Brewing Company in 1888. They were better at brewing beer than managing money. After a few years they were broke. They sold their company to a local syndicate that has since become the Foster's Brewing Group. They moved back to America and were, in the words of the company, "never heard from again." They were not the only Americans to create "Australian" products. The Outback Steakhouse, complete with boomerangs on the walls, "Aussie-Tizers" on the menu, and commercials dubbed in thick Australian accents, was founded in 1987 in Florida by veteran restaurateurs Robert Basham, Timothy Gannon, and Chris Sullivan. The partners got the idea for the theme that year when *Crocodile Dundee II* was the big movie in theaters and Australia was preparing for its bicentennial. None of the men had ever even been down under. They rejected the names "Dundee's" and "Sydney's" before arriving at Outback, which had "a rugged, outdoorsy quality" and "good marketing potential . . . it provided a real point of differentiation." In

1999, there were 616 Outback Steakhouses in the world, earning $124 million. Plans are under way to open the first Outback Steakhouse in Sydney, Australia. One change is being made to the menu of the Australian version of the restaurant—kookaburra wings, a popular item on the American menu, are being renamed. The kookaburra is Australia's national bird. Leaving the item on the menu would be equivalent to an Australian chain bringing an American-themed restaurant to the U.S. with "bald-eagle wings" on the menu.

Freund, Madeleine

Madeleine Freund, known as Mimi to her friends, was the daughter of a banker. At seventeen she went into a convent, but she found the life was not for her. After leaving the convent, she got a job as an artist's model at Ervine Metzl's studio. There, in 1933, she met Ludwig Bemelmans. Bemelmans had come to the United States from Germany in 1914 at the age of sixteen. A talented, eccentric, and struggling artist, Bemelmans described himself as "a six-year-old, really." He was immediately smitten with the young model. She was, he would later write, "extremely photogenic, but she dislikes clothes, fashion hairdressers and fashionable people, and she blooms like the night-flowering jasmine, a bittersweet perfume." Bemelmans borrowed five dollars from Metzl and took her to the movies that day. They were married a year later and about a year after that they welcomed a daughter, Barbara. Slowly, but surely, Bemelmans' economic situation improved. His work was starting to be purchased by *The Saturday Evening Post* and *Town and Country*. He covered celebrities, restaurants, and travel and thus spent a lot of time at the theater and restaurants. Meanwhile, he was inspired by his daughter to write children's stories. He wrote about the girl in *Town and Country* and compiled albums of the letters they exchanged when he was away. One evening in the late 1930s, the Bemelmans were at Pete's Tavern in New York and Bemelmans was inspired to write a little story. It began: "In an old house in Paris that was covered with vines/Lived twelve little girls in two straight lines." "The smallest one" he named after his wife, but changed the spelling to *Madeline* to make it simpler. When Bemelmans first offered the story to his editor at Viking, May Massee, she turned it down saying it was "too sophisticated for children." He took it to Simon & Schuster, who published it. After all these years, *Madeline* still consistently ranks in the top selling books for children. As to the origins of another favorite children's tale: The children's story *Paddington Bear* was written by Michael Bond when he and his wife were living near the Paddington railway station. Paddington means "Padda's farm." The district of west-central London has had the name for so long that no one remembers who Padda was.

Fuchs, Wilhelm

William Fuchs was born January 1, 1879 in the Hungarian town of Tulchava. His family moved to the United States shortly after his birth. In New York, they Americanized their names and Fuchs became William Fox. Fox started working when he was only six years old selling shoelaces, candy, and stove blacking on the streets to help support his family. He dropped out of school five years later, at the age of eleven, and went to work in the city's garment district. He married in 1899, when he was twenty, and added two daughters to the family. In 1903, Fox saw something that would change his life—his first motion picture. He was so excited that he decided to open his own nickelodeon. He took his life savings of $1,700 and opened a 146-seat theater in Brooklyn. He also formed the Greater New York Film Rental Company to rent films to other theaters. The theater was a success. In just five years, Fox made $50,000. He used the money to open a string of theaters in the city. Soon Fox was ready to make his own films. He launched Fox Productions. Its first film, *Life's Shop Window*, was released in 1914. The next year he expanded the venture into the Fox Film Corporation and established a Hollywood studio. He came up against a formidable obstacle in the person of Thomas Edison, who had, along with several major film companies, set up the Motion Picture Patents Company in 1909 to preserve their control over the production of film and equipment. Fox led antitrust efforts and was finally able, in 1917, to prompt the government to open the industry to independent film producers. During World War I, Fox launched Fox Newsreel. In 1923, he bought the West Coast Theater Chain and created Fox Theaters Corporation. Talking pictures were a new phenomenon. Fox worked with inventor Theodore Case and developed a number of innovations in sound technology. The studio developed a process known as Movietone. The results were applied to the reels of Fox Movietone News in 1926. The talking newsreels worked well and soon Fox was producing sound features as well. William Fox retired in 1928. In 1929 he was injured in an automobile accident. While he was recovering, the stock market crashed, and he lost control of the company. In 1935, Fox Productions merged with Twentieth Century Pictures, forming Twentieth Century Fox. In the 1980s, Fox Corporation launched the Fox Television Network.

Fujita, Tetsuya

Tetsuya Theodore Fujita was born October 23, 1920 in Kitakyushu City, Japan. He earned a bachelor's degree in mechanical engineering in 1943 from Meiji College of Technology and a doctoral degree from Tokyo University in 1953. Later that year, he joined the University of Chicago as a research associate in the meteorology department. He remained at the institution and became an American citizen. He held a number of positions during his tenure, notably in the Wind Research Laboratory. He traveled the United States studying wind systems and examining the aftermath of tornadoes, earning himself the nickname "Mr. Tornado." Colleagues said he never used computers and preferred to do his calculations himself. In 1976 he investigated the Eastern Airlines Flight 66 accident at New York's JFK Airport and determined it was the result of a deadly form of wind shear he called "microbursts." Initially other meteorologists were skeptical about his conclusions, but he was proved correct. The important discovery led to the installation of Doppler radar equipment in major airports and helped prevent microburst accidents that previously had killed more than five hundred airline passengers. He was most known, however, for his classification of the intensity of tornadoes known as the *Fujita tornado scale.* The scale ranges from F0 to F5, although the researcher did allow for the remote possibility of an F6 storm. At the low end of the scale, an F0 has winds of 40-72 mph and can do moderate damage to signs, chimneys, and tree limbs (little consolation, of course, if the tree limb happens to fall through your roof). An F5, on the other extreme, blows in with winds of 261-318 mph. It can lift houses off their foundations and throw automobiles in the air. On average, only one F5 tornado hits the United States each year. Despite popular belief, mobile homes do not attract tornadoes by magnetism or any other means. The reason mobile homes are so frequently damaged in tornadoes is that they are built to be mobile, so even winds of moderate intensity on the Fujita scale can topple them. Safety experts say you're safer outside in a ditch than in a mobile home in a tornado. For his pioneering work, Fujita received the Order of the Sacred Treasure, Gold and Silver Star from the Japanese government in 1991. He passed away in 1998 at the age of seventy-eight.

G

Gainsborough, Thomas

Thomas Gainsborough was born in 1727 in Suffolk, England. His father, a maker of woolen goods, sent him to London at the age of thirteen to study landscape painting. He worked as an assistant to the French painter and engraver Hubert Gravelot, who was then an important figure in London art circles. He married a woman named Margaret Burr in 1746 and the couple moved back to Suffolk, where they would have two daughters. Although landscape painting was Gainsborough's forte and his first love, like most artists of his day, he relied on income earned from painting portraits of important people. He moved to Bath in 1759, where he was popular in theatrical and musical circles. There he discovered the work of Anthony Van Dyck, who would greatly influence his later work. He painted one of his most famous works, *The Blue Boy*, in Bath around 1770. Four years later, he moved to London, where he gained the attention of the royal family and was commissioned to paint the king and queen. He died in 1788 in London. The *Encyclopedia Britannica* summed up his life's work by saying: "Of all the 18th Century English painters, Thomas Gainsborough was the most inventive and original, always prepared to experiment with new ideas and techniques." He was, the entry says, "the most versatile English painter of the 18th Century." For the purposes of this book, however, we are interested in his contribution to language, not art. As a portrait painter, Gainsborough captured the images of many of England's most fashionable people. His name has been applied to one of the fashions that appear frequently in his work—a wide-brimmed, oversized hat, turned up at the side with a plume. We call such a garment a *Gainsborough hat.*

Gal, Uziel

On May 14, 1948, immediately following the proclamation of the State of Israel, war broke out. Arab forces from Egypt, Transjordan, Iraq, Syria, and Lebanon occupied the areas in southern and eastern Palestine that were not apportioned to the Jews, plus a small Jewish quarter of the Old City of Jerusalem. The Israelis won control of the main road to Jerusalem through the Judaean Hills, and by early 1949, they had occupied all of the Negev up to the former Egypt-Palestine frontier, with the exception of the Gaza Strip. The fighting continued until July 1949, when a temporary border was fixed. That conflict is now known as the first Arab-Israeli war. Uziel Gal, an Israeli army officer, did not think that it would be the last. (He was quite right.) He went to work to design a new submachine gun like some Czech models he had seen. His weapon contained the magazine in the pistol grip. It was easy to manufacture from stamped metal, compact, easy to load, and reasonably stable and accurate even when fired automatically. The *Uzi submachine gun* was introduced in 1952.

Gannett, Frank

Frank Ernest Gannett was born September 15, 1876 in New York's Finger Lakes area. He got his first job as a paperboy for the *Democrat and Chronicle* of Rochester, New York when he was only nine. His parents ran hotels and moved frequently, and Gannett continued to hold paper routes as they went from city to city. As he was making deliveries in Italian neighborhoods, he learned that immigrants had trouble addressing envelopes to family members back home in English. Still a young teenager, Gannett sold rubber stamps bearing names and addresses of European families. When he was fifteen, his parents announced they were moving again. Gannett decided to stay put and finish high school. With his family background, he was able to get a job at a local hotel as a waiter and bookkeeper. He was awarded a scholarship to attend Cornell University in 1894. At

Cornell he worked on the student newspaper and held an unpaid internship at the *Syracuse Herald*. Meanwhile, he sold news items to papers in other cities. He was able to graduate with a savings of $1,000 and a paying job at the *Herald*. After a year, he was hired as city editor of the *Ithaca Daily News*. A Pittsburgh, Pennsylvania newspaper was sufficiently impressed with his work to hire him away. He became the paper's editor in chief, but he didn't remain long. By 1906 he was back in New York. There he learned that one of the owners of the *Elmira Gazette* had put his share up for sale. Gannett scrounged up the asking price and became a part owner of his own paper. A year later he bought the *Elmira Star*. The combined paper was called the *Star-Gazette*. Five years later he bought the *Ithaca Journal*, which later merged with the *Ithaca News* to create the *Ithaca Journal-News*. He then created the *Rochester Times-Union* by buying and merging the city's *Union and Advertiser* and the *Evening Times*. In 1924, Gannett bought out his two partners and created the Gannett Company. In 1940 he ran, unsuccessfully, for the Republican presidential nomination. He financed his campaign by selling stock to employees. The first public offering of Gannett stock would not be until 1967. *The Gannett News Service* was founded in 1943 as the Gannett National Service. Gannett kept buying up newspapers until his retirement in 1957. He died shortly thereafter at the age of eighty-one. The Gannett Company is now the largest newspaper publisher in the U.S. with nearly seventy-five newspapers with a combined circulation of almost seven million.

Garrison, Edward

Edward R. Garrison was born in New Haven, Connecticut February 9, 1868. As a boy he dreamed of being a jockey, and at the age of fourteen he took the first steps towards this dream by becoming a blacksmith's apprentice. He soon was taken under the wing of trainer Fr. Bill Daly, who gave his student the nickname "Jack Snapper." The Jack didn't stick, but the young rider was forever after known as Snapper Garrison. He became one of the most famous riders of his day. He won nearly seven hundred races and $2 million in purses in his fifteen years riding. In 1894, he was paid $23,500 to ride for August Belmont—the highest retainer ever paid for a jockey up to that time. He introduced a number of practices to the sport, including the "Yankee seat"—the familiar pose where the jockey stands high in the stirrups and crouches over the horse's mane. Garrison's name became part of the lexicon in 1882. In that year's Suburban he trailed behind the other riders until the last furlong. Then, in a burst of energy, he brought his mount, Montana, ahead of all the others to win the race. He repeated the technique in later races. Eventually any race that was won at the last minute from behind became known as a *Garrison finish*. After retiring from racing, Garrison stayed on the track as a trainer and official until his death at the age of sixty-two of heart failure in October 1930. Edward ("Snapper") Garrison was among the first inductees in 1955 to the Hall of Fame at the National Museum of Racing in Saratoga Springs, New York.

Gelbfisz, Samuel

Samuel Gelbfisz was born in the Jewish section of Warsaw, Poland, the eldest of six children of a struggling used-furniture dealer. He described his life in his native country as "poor, poor, poor." In 1895, he made his way to England, where relatives Anglicized his name to Samuel Goldfish. There he begged or stole enough money for a ticket in steerage across the Atlantic. He traveled alone to the United States and arrived in 1898. He was probably nineteen when he arrived, depending on which source you believe for his year of birth. Goldfish moved to Gloversville, New York, which was, at the time, the capital of the U.S. leather-glove industry. By the time he was thirty, he owned a prosperous glove business. Now a big Goldfish in a small pond, he decided to take on the big city. He moved to Manhattan and married the sister of theatrical producer Jesse L. Lasky. Goldfish convinced Lasky and Cecil B. DeMille to go into movie producing. The new company later became the nucleus of Paramount Pictures. But when Goldfish's marriage dissolved, so did his partnership with his ex-wife's brother. In 1916, Goldfish formed a new film company with Archibald and Edgar Selwyn. They named it Goldwyn Pictures Corporation, from the first syllable of Goldfish's name and the last of Selwyn. Goldfish changed his own name again to match that of his company and became Samuel Goldwyn. The judge who granted the request for the name change was Judge Learned Hand, who commented: "A self-made man may prefer a self-made name." Goldwyn hired an advertising agency to come up with a trademark. One agency man, Howard Dietz, was a Columbia University graduate. Inspiration struck Dietz as he was attending a Columbia football game. As the team mascot, Leo the lion, came on the field to cheerleaders' cries of "Roar! Roar! Roar!" a light bulb appeared over his head. What better trademark for the king of production companies than the king of the beasts? It was up to Volney Phifer, Hollywood's premier animal trainer, to supply a lion to roar on cue. Goldwyn took out full-page ads in *The Saturday Evening Post.* The ad featured Leo the lion surrounded by a loop of film and the Latin motto *Ars Gratia Artis,* meaning "Art Is Beholden to the Artists." The ads promised "Pictures built upon the strong foundation of intelligence and refinement." In the early 1920s, Marcus Loew, owner of a theater chain, Loew's Inc., bought the famous Metro Studio. Loew was born in 1870 to Austrian parents in New York City. A school dropout at the age of nine, Loew made his initial fortune with a chain of penny arcades. This evolved into a nickelodeon chain. By 1912 Loew's Theatrical Enterprises consisted of 400 cinemas all across the country. By 1924, with Metro Studios a part of his collection, he turned his eye towards Goldwyn Pictures. Loew began negotiations to acquire the company through an exchange of stock. The main holdout in the endeavor was Goldwyn. He was fiercely independent and as famous for his temper as for his ambition. He didn't want any part of the deal. So he was forced out of the company that bears his name. Goldwyn Pictures bought out his shares for cash, the deal went through without him, and Metro-Goldwyn Pictures Corporation was formed. Goldwyn formed his own company, Samuel Goldwyn Productions, a year later and became an independent producer. Producer Louis B. Mayer was brought on board to direct operations at Metro-Goldwyn. Mayer was born Lazar Meir in Ukraine, not far from Kiev. A Jewish family of

Austro-Hungarian origin, the Meirs were victims of repeated anti-Jewish pogroms, until they left for England in 1886. They traveled on to Canada and the finally the U.S. With his Anglicized name, Louis Mayer took American citizenship and resolved thereafter to celebrate his birthday on the Fourth of July. He opened a single nickelodeon in 1907. Within ten years it grew into a successful production company. As the vice-president and general manager of a new company, he was given a choice of having his pictures bear the credit line "Produced by Louis B. Mayer for the Metro-Goldwyn Corporation" or "Produced by Metro-Goldwyn-Mayer." He chose the latter and MGM was born. As for Leo the lion, he came along to MGM. He made his sound debut in MGM's first sound picture, *White Shadows in the South Seas,* which premiered July 31, 1928. The movie had only one piece of human dialog—the word "hello." According to *People* magazine, the lion "survived train wrecks, a Mississippi flood, a California earthquake and a plane crash in Arizona during various promotional tours." Volney Phifer retired from Hollywood in the 1930s. He bought a farm in Gillette, New Jersey and took his famous lion with him. When Leo died in 1938 at the age of twenty-three, he was buried in the front yard and a small, blank block of granite marked the grave. A group of Leo fans is now campaigning to restore the lion's tombstone, which had been removed by later owners.

George

Although he is the patron saint of England, Saint George was actually martyred in Palestine shortly before the accession of the emperor Constantine. Legend has it that George slew a fearful fire-breathing dragon that lived in a lake near Silena in Libya. Many armies had failed to kill the beast, and to appease it, the villagers selected a young woman to sacrifice. The daughter of a king was chosen to be the dragon's lunch, but George came to the rescue, killing the creature with his lance. The people were so impressed by the feat that they were instantly converted to Christianity. Although the king offered George a large sum of money for his troubles, the hero gave it to the poor and went on his way. He was a celebrated figure in the Middle East during the Crusades and it is likely that the Crusaders brought the reverence for George back to England. In 1222 the National Council at Oxford established George's feast day as April 23. More than a century later, King Edward III made George the patron of England and founded an order of knights, which he called the Knights of St. George. The red cross of Saint George graces the Union Jack. Ironically, Saint George became the focus of a popular curse—"by Saint George!" ("By Saint Louis!" was another common term.) When Henry VIII banned the Catholic Church from England so he could get a divorce, the saints went out with it and "by Saint George" became *by George!*

George I

By the end of the 1600s, William III was ill and childless; his sister-in-law, the prospective queen, Anne, had just lost her only remaining child out of seventeen. Abroad the supporters of the exiled king, James II, were numerous and active. Without an act that spelled out exactly who should take the throne, there would likely be much bloodshed while the question was resolved. For years in England the Catholics and the Protestants had been at odds, and sometimes at war, over what should be the official religion of the land. By the late 1600s, Protestantism, in the form of the Church of England, had become the officially recognized church and there was a Protestant king on the throne. The majority of the English people didn't want a return to Catholicism and the battles that were likely to erupt. They would rather have a foreigner on the throne than a Catholic. So, in 1701 Parliament passed the Act of Settlement, which decreed that, if neither William or Anne had children, the crown was to pass to Sophia, electress of Hanover and granddaughter of James I, and to "the heirs of her body being Protestants," thus passing over the Catholics who would normally be in the line of succession. Sophia died before Anne, so on August 1, 1714, the electress's son Georg Ludwig, also known as George Louis, became king. George, a German, could not speak English and communicated with his cabinet in French. He seemingly had little interest in Britain before assuming the throne. In 1682 he had married his cousin Sophia Dorothea, an entirely political move. They were said to hate one another. They managed to have two children together, although George spent most of his time with a variety of mistresses. When his wife took a lover of her own, however, George was unforgiving. He had the man killed and Sophia imprisoned. She was locked in Ahlden Castle when George came to England and remained there until her death in 1726. Not everyone, of course, believed the line of succession should have passed over the Catholics. Those who wanted to see James Edward, also known as "the Pretender," take over as monarch rebelled in 1715 and 1719 but were easily suppressed. Even so, George was not popular in England. The British knew about his two greedy German mistresses and speculated at how many others there must be. Those stories and rumors of how he treated his wife inspired a rhyme: *Georgie Porgie*/pudding and pie/kissed the girls and made them cry./When the boys came out to play/Georgie Porgie ran away.

Gettys, James

Between 1736 and 1760, an area known as the Marsh Creek Settlement in Pennsylvania was settled by Scots-Irish families. Samuel Gettys owned a large farmstead in the region. After the Revolutionary War, Samuel's middle son, James, bought a 116-acre tract of land from his father's farm and built a town square with 210 lots surrounding it. The town was thus named *Gettysburg*. Located between some of the larger cities of Pennsylvania and Maryland, Gettysburg became strategically important during the Civil War and was the site of a bloody battle. Militarily, the earlier battle of Antietam was more important, but Gettysburg is more remembered thanks to a speech given by Pres. Abraham Lincoln on November 11, 1863. No one would have guessed when he delivered his address that it would become one of the most familiar pieces of oratory in U.S. history. Certainly Lincoln did not anticipate it. The speech itself says, "The world will little note, nor long remember, what we say here." Newspapers of the day panned the speech. The *Chicago Times* printed the following review of the

Gettysburg Address: "The cheek of every American must tingle with shame as he reads the silly, flat and dish-watery utterances of the man who has been pointed out to intelligent foreigners as the President of the United States."

Gimlette, Thomas

Sir Thomas D. Gimlette was a British naval surgeon who served from 1879 to 1917. Tired of trying to decide "what do you do with a drunken sailor," Gimlette diluted the sailor's favorite, straight gin, with lime juice. The resulting cocktail came to be known as a gimlet. At least that's one story. Another story of the drink's origin says that British sailors concocted the gin-and-lime-juice blend to help fight scurvy. This version of the tale points not to a Mr. Gimlette, but to a corkscrewlike tool called a gimlet, which was supposedly used to open the juice containers. The gimlet was a favorite drink of Raymond Chandler's fictional detective Philip Marlowe. In the 1953 novel *The Long Goodbye,* the sultry Terry Lennox introduces the cocktail to Marlowe by saying the drink "beats a Martini hollow."

Glidden, Francis

Francis Harrington Glidden was born May 24, 1832 in New Castle, Maine. A high-school dropout at the age of fourteen, he went to work for his brother's general store. Three years later, he joined his uncle's shipping business. After the loss of his left eye in an accident, Glidden decided the life of the sea was too dangerous. In 1852, at the age of twenty, he went back to Maine and dry goods. He married Winifred Kavanagh Waters and the couple eventually had eight children. His store, however, did not fare well. It went under in 1859 and the family moved to Alabama, where Glidden entered the steamship business. The Gliddens got caught up in the Civil War when Glidden was drafted into the Confederate army. During the war, a ship on which Glidden was stationed was seized by General Polk at Lewis Ferry. Polk was killed by cannon fire shortly thereafter, and Glidden was able to return to his family in Mobile, which was, by then, occupied by the Union army. By the end of the year, the Gliddens were able to get out

of the South and return to New England. In Maine, Glidden
went back to work at his brother's dry-goods store. After only a
few months, he was approached by a New York City varnish-
making firm, William Tilden & Nephew. The company needed
a salesman in Ohio. Glidden packed up the family once again
and they set out for Cleveland. Another new varnish business,
founded by Mr. Sherwin and Mr. Williams, was capturing most
of Ohio's market. So in 1875, Glidden, then forty-three, joined
forces with two other varnish makers, Levi C. Brackett and
Thomas N. Bolles, to create Glidden, Brackett & Company.
From a one-story building manned by one employee, the company produced 1,000 gallons of varnish each week and delivered it to customers throughout Cleveland with a horse and
wagon. Two years later, both Brackett and Bolles retired.
Glidden was briefly joined by a man named William Joy and
the business became known as the Glidden and Joy Varnish
Company. Joy sold his interest in the company to Glidden in
1892. Two years later, the organization was renamed simply the
Glidden Varnish Company. The company grew and prospered.
In 1895, Glidden decided to go after the consumer market.
Previously the company had only made industrial varnishes
such as coatings for furniture, pianos, and carriages. He introduced a line of colored varnish and, in 1903, Jap-A-Lac, which
became a favorite paint for home use. Two years later, fire
destroyed Glidden's entire plant. He built another factory and
was back to work with little delay. Sales reached $2 million a
year, thanks in part to advertising in such women's publications
as *Ladies' Home Journal.* In 1917, a syndicate bought Glidden
out. He died on September 24, 1922 at the age of ninety.
Glidden's company went on to be one of the world's leading
paint manufacturers.

Godot

Theater goers have long speculated on the origin of Godot in
the title of Samuel Beckett's play *Waiting for Godot.* According
to Andre Bernard, author of *Now All We Need Is a Title,* there
may have been a real person behind the name. The story,
which Beckett has neither confirmed nor denied, is that one

day the writer ran into a large group of people watching the annual Tour de France bicycle race even though there seemed to be no more bicycles going past. When Beckett asked what they were doing they said they were waiting for Godot, the oldest and last competitor in the race. Another story is that Beckett got the inspiration on the corner of Godot de Mauroy, a Parisian street known for its prostitutes. One of the women approached the writer and when he turned her down she asked whom he was waiting for, Godot? Another theory is that Godot takes its name from a character in a minor drama of Honoré de Balzac's in which the bourgeois characters await the arrival of a certain M. Godeau, with whom they have placed their savings. They expect him to bring them great fortune, but he never arrives and the characters wait in vain. One thing is clear, Godot does not stand for God. "If Godot were God, I would have called him that," Beckett said. In fact, he has said, "I do not know who Godot is. I do not even know if he exists." In any case, the play was written in French. The French word *Dieu* has little resemblance to the English God or Godot.

Golgi, Camillio

In 1872, thirty-year-old Camillio Golgi was working as a physician at the home for incurables in Abbiategrasso, Italy. The young scientist did not have a vast laboratory at his disposal and he was trying to do something that had never been done before. He wanted to understand how the brain functioned. Each time he tried to look at brain cells under the microscope he saw nothing that gave him any clue as to how the brain worked—that is, until a fortuitous accident occurred. One day he knocked a small lump of the brain tissue he was studying into a dish of silver nitrate. He didn't bother to remove it at first. He was too involved in his experiments. In fact, the tissue stayed in the nitrate for several weeks. When Golgi finally got around to removing the sample he noticed that the brain tissue was now shot through with shining streaks. The stained cells revealed all of their structure. This allowed him to study nerve cells in greater detail than ever before. His accident allowed him to make numerous discoveries, which were named after him. First was a kind of nerve cell now known as the *Golgi cell*. In 1876, after a move to the University of Pavia, he found and described the point at which sensory nerve fibers end in rich branchings encapsulated within a tendon. This is called the *Golgi tendon spindle*. In 1883, he discovered the presence in nerve cells of an irregular network of small fibers, cavities, and granules, now known as the *Golgi apparatus*. Golgi received a share of the Nobel prize in physiology or medicine in 1906 for his pioneering work on the nervous system. Another unexpected result was that the Golgi apparatus ended up being the unlikely subject of a song by the rock band Phish.

Gore, Wilbert

After receiving a bachelor's degree in chemical engineering and a master's in physical chemistry from the University of Utah, Wilbert L. Gore, "Bill" for short, got a job at Remington Arms. The chemical giant DuPont had a large ownership stake in the arms company and, in the early 1940s, Gore transferred to DuPont's Experimental Station as a research supervisor. He became part of a team to develop applications for polytetrafluoroethylene, "PTFE" for short, also known as Teflon. The first batch of the stuff was brewed on April 6, 1938 by DuPont scientist Dr. Roy Plunkett. Plunkett was experimenting with Freon in the hopes of developing a better coolant gas. He left one batch of this gas overnight in a container. When he arrived the next day, the gas had been transformed into a waxy and very slippery solid, which he discovered was impervious to a number of corrosive chemicals. Full-scale commercial production of Teflon did not begin for another decade. Gore believed PTFE could be used to insulate wire and electronics cables. He brought his work home with him to a basement lab. One of his children, Bob, was living at home while studying chemical engineering at the University of Delaware. He suggested that his father try bonding Teflon to a Teflon sealant tape made by 3M. Bill Gore was skeptical about the idea, but he tried it anyway. Early one morning, after working all night on the problem, the elder Gore burst into his son's room shouting, "It works! It works!" For four months Bill Gore tried to convince

DuPont that he had developed a worthwhile product. The company was not interested in selling finished Teflon goods, so on their twenty-third wedding anniversary, January 1, 1958, Bill and Genevieve Gore used their savings to found their own company, W. L. Gore & Associates. Eleven years later, Bob Gore had a doctorate in chemical engineering from the University of Minnesota. He had joined the company officially in 1964 as a research assistant. He was "trying to make something different" with Teflon. So he pulled on a burning-hot Teflon rod while it baked. (He used oven mitts. Kids, don't try this at home.) He found that PTFE could be stretched when heated. Pretty soon everyone in the plant was reaching into the oven to see for himself. The result was a superstrong porous material. The company at first imagined it would be used for tennis-racket strings or fish-tank pumps. It wasn't long, however, before the material was transformed into a fabric laminate. Introduced in 1976, *Gore-Tex* fabric is, in the words of the company, "the original waterproof/breathable fabric that revolutionized the outdoor sportswear market." After many years of making fabrics for outdoor enthusiasts, W. L. Gore began licensing manufacturers to use the Gore-Tex material and label in 1989. The name Gore-Tex became so well known that the company has recently taken out ads to remind journalists that it is a registered trademark. The private company had sales of $1.3 billion in 1998. It employs 6,000 workers at plants in the United States and abroad. Although the expanded PTFE material is used in everything from medical equipment to dental floss, the fabric division now garners more sales than any of the company's other divisions.

Goyathlay

Goyathlay is an Apache name meaning "He Who Yawns." The young man of that name was born in 1829. He grew up to be a brave warrior and leader. Mexican settlers had so much respect for the Apache leader that they dubbed him Geronimo, after Saint Jerome, the desert dweller. In 1850, Geronimo's family was killed by the Spanish, and he declared his own personal war against the white man. He was chased by American and

Mexican forces, but his knowledge of the deserts and mountains kept him always one step ahead of his pursuers. He was able to elude capture this way until 1886, when Generals George Crook and Nelson Miles finally captured him and took him to Florida. Now an old man, Geronimo was done fighting. He settled in Oklahoma, and sold Geronimo souvenirs. He died there in 1909 of natural causes. His name became familiar to a new generation thanks to a 1939 movie starring Preston Foster as Captain Starett and Chief Thundercloud as Geronimo. In 1940, four soldiers from the army's Parachute Test Platoon saw the film the night before they were to test a new mass-exit parachute technique. After the film, Privates Leo C. Brown, Aubrey Eberhardt, Lester C. McLaney, and John A. Ward discussed the next day's jump. One of the men teased Eberhardt, saying he would be so scared he wouldn't be able to remember his name. Eberhardt said that not only would he be able to remember his own name, he would remember the name of the subject of the movie they had just seen. The next day as he jumped from the airplane Eberhardt shouted, "Geronimo!" Soon after, all of the men of the platoon were shouting the warrior's name as they jumped. The tradition was passed on to other units and over time to civilians as well.

Gray, John

John Gray, a carpenter's son, dropped out of school at the age of thirteen but taught himself French, German, Spanish, and Latin. He worked as a metal craftsman and then at the post office, tracing lost letters. A respected, established employee of the Foreign Office by day, John Gray led a secret life by night. He spent his evenings in the dark bars where the "the spirit of London in the 1890s found its fullest and freest expression." His circle included what we would today call practitioners of an "alternative lifestyle." Sometime around 1889, he met Oscar Wilde, the noted playwright who would later be tried and imprisoned for homosexuality. The two became friends and, by most accounts, lovers. Gray included a poem to Wilde in his first book of poems, *Silverpoints,* which was published in 1893. Gray felt deeply guilty about the relationship and, after his conversion to Catholicism in 1890, he did all he could to distance himself from the playwright. When Wilde was brought to trial in 1895, Gray appointed his own lawyer to be in court in case his name came up. John Gray is believed to be the model for Oscar Wilde's character Dorian Gray, who had a secret double life in the form of a portrait in the attic. Gray sued the *Star* newspaper, which identified him as the original Dorian Gray. He won the case in spite of the fact that he had signed letters to Wilde as "Dorian." Few people were convinced, however, by the outcome of the trial. After persuading a fellow artist from his darker days to convert to Catholicism on his deathbed, John Gray was moved to become a priest. He studied at Scots College at Rome and was ordained in 1901. He was first assigned to an Edinburgh slum where he tended the sick and the destitute. Six years later he became the parish priest of St. Peter's in Edinburgh. He tried to remove all traces of his former life. He even bought up every book of his old poems he could find so that they would no longer be in circulation. When he died in 1934, his funeral was attended by 100 priests, a choir of Benedictine monks, and the entire cathedral chapter of St. Andrews and Edinburgh. The mass was performed by the archbishop.

Grey, Charles

Charles, the second earl Grey, was born on March 13, 1764 in Northumberland, England. He got his education at Eton and Cambridge and at age twenty-two was elected member of Parliament. Although he was born with blue blood, in the wake of the French Revolution Grey took a radical stance and was instrumental in forming the Society of the Friends of the People to encourage demands for parliamentary reform. In 1794 Grey married an Irish girl, Mary Elizabeth Ponsonby. Over the next twenty-five years, the couple had fifteen children. In 1806, Grey got another title: First Lord of the Admiralty. Later that same year he became foreign secretary and leader of the Whig Party. Partly because of his Irish-Catholic wife, Grey was a staunch campaigner for Catholic emancipation. In 1830, he became prime minister. In that role he secured passage of the Reform Bill of 1832 by threatening to force William IV to create enough Whig peers to carry it in the House of Lords. The bill enfranchised middle-class voters. The following year, Grey abolished slavery in the British Empire. Around this time, a merchant named George Charlton prepared a special blend of tea for the earl. *Earl Grey tea* was first sold to the public in 1836, and if the television program "Star Trek: The Next Generation" is to be believed, it will still be popular in the twenty-fourth century. It is the favorite drink of Captain Piccard of the starship *Enterprise*. For some companies today, however, the name "Earl Grey" is not enough to sell tea. In 1995, a company called Republic of Tea introduced an "Earl Greyer" tea. A few months later, Celestial Seasonings Inc. tried to top them by introducing "Earl Greyest" tea. The famous Canadian football prize, *The Grey Cup*, was named for Charles Grey's grandson, the fourth earl Grey, Albert Henry George Grey.

Grey, Maurice

More than five thousand years ago in what we now call Pakistan, cooks began using brown and yellow mustard seeds to spice up their food. The use of seeds in cooking spread throughout India and eastward to China. It may have been Julius Caesar's troops who brought the first mustard seeds from Asia to the French wine country. There, in the city of Dijon, chefs began to mix milled mustard seed with fine wine vinegar creating the blend we now know as Dijon mustard. Years later, in Dijon, a man named Maurice Grey invented a device that made the mass production of fine-textured mustard possible. The machine could crush, grind, and sieve the seed in virtually one operation. Using Grey's device, a mustard maker could churn out fifty kilograms a day, as opposed to about sixteen kilograms under the old system. Grey was awarded two medals for his invention in 1855, and in 1860 was granted a Royal Appointment. Six years later, he formed a partnership with another Dijon mustard maker, Auguste Poupon. Poupon provided the financial backing to put Grey's machine into use. Grey Poupon Dijon Mustard earned a place on international tables. In America, Grey Poupon came to

be known as the Rolls-Royce of mustards thanks to a clever television advertisement featuring a pair of aristocrats in limousines.
One asks the other, "Pardon me, but do you have any Grey
Poupon?" "I always felt regal when I held a jar of the condiment
in my hand," Erma Bombeck once wrote. She went on to
describe her temptation to stop in traffic, roll down her car window, and ask the neighboring driver for the condiment.
"Somehow it wasn't the same sitting in an '85 Wagoneer and
talking to the occupant of a cement truck," she wrote. Interestingly, as French as Grey Poupon seems to Americans, a
spoof of the famous advertisement was one of the few things that
didn't translate in the French version of the movie *Wayne's
World*. French audiences were not familiar with Grey Poupon or
its commercial. The scene where Wayne and Garth approach a
man in a Rolls-Royce and ask for the mustard was replaced with
a line from a popular commercial for an Italian economy car:
"You, you would look good in a Fiat Uno."

Grolier, Jean

Although he was not a printer or writer, Jean Grolier, Vicomte
d'Auigsy, had a passion for books. He served as the treasurer
for Francis I and was later ambassador to Italy. There he met
the printer Aldus Manutius and began collecting books, eventually accumulating 3,000 richly bound volumes. The library
remained in his family until 1675. By the end of the seventeenth century, book collecting had become common in
Europe and many auctions were held. The Groliers held such
an auction with the contents of their library. The books, which
bear the words *J. Grolerii et amicorum,* are collector's items
today. In 1884 a club was founded in New York City "for the
study and promotion of the arts pertaining to the production
of books." It was named *The Grolier Club*. Robert Hoe, a noted
collector, was the organization's first president. Today, rich,
ornate book bindings are called *Grolier bindings* in memory of
the early collector. The American publisher *Grolier, Inc.* is also
named for him. *Grolier's Encyclopedia Americana* was the first
encyclopedia published in the United States. In 1996 the company had 2,000 employees and sales of $465 million.

Grumman, Leroy

Leroy Grumman, whose red hair earned him the nickname "Red Mike," was born January 4, 1895, in Huntington, New York. He graduated second in his class at Huntington High School and went on to earn a degree in mechanical engineering from Cornell University in 1916. Then he joined the Naval Reserve and took a course in airplane inspection for pilot trainees at the Massachusetts Institute of Technology, followed by advanced flight training in Pensacola, Florida. Aviation was still in its infancy, and being trained as a pilot required some daring. Grumman was "very, very reticent," according to his flight instructor, Raymond P. Applegate. Yet he completed his training to become "Naval Aviator No. 1216" and a flight instructor in his own right. He then returned to MIT to study aeronautical engineering. Following World War I, in 1919, Loening Aeronautical Engineering Company in New York City won a government contract to build fifty monoplanes. Grumman was sent by the navy to oversee construction. The Loenings were sufficiently impressed with the aviator that they decided to hire him. It was at Loening that Grumman met a man named Jake Swirbul. Swirbul had came to the company in 1924 in much the same way as Grumman had—as a civilian inspector for the Air Corps. Five years later the Loenings sold their company to Keystone Aircraft, which announced it would move all operations to Pennsylvania. Grumman and Swirbul didn't want to move, so they decided to start their own company instead. Grumman mortgaged his house and Swirbul asked his mom for a $6,000 loan. With the money they bought an abandoned auto showroom-garage. Because Grumman had invested more money, the company was named the Grumman Aeronautical Engineering Company. It was launched January 2, 1930, only weeks after the stock-market crash that signaled the beginning of the Great Depression. The early years of the company were difficult. A few navy contracts were the only thing keeping it afloat. According to company legend, the owners were actually forced to pick up scrap metal from the side of the road to use in the shop. Grumman managed to stay in business through the depression to thrive during the

Second World War. The Grumman Hellcat was the only fighter aircraft developed by the United States during the war. Production soared, and the manufacturer thrived for the next few decades making planes for both the military and private pilots. Grumman retired from the company in 1966, at the age of seventy-one. He passed away in 1987. Seven years later the Grumman company was acquired by Northrop.

Guidroz, Jenny

Jenny Guidroz was born in Berwick, Louisiana in 1932, the youngest of six children. Her father worked three part-time jobs and her mother raised chickens to make ends meet during those difficult depression years. Young Jenny started training to become a dental hygienist, but she dropped out of school to marry a race-boat driver. The couple had two children. In an effort to lose the forty-five pounds she'd gained during her pregnancies, she got a job at a New Orleans gym. She lost the weight and became the manager of the entire operation. Her marriage was unsuccessful. After her divorce, she mortgaged her house to open her own gym. She eventually sold the business and, in 1970, went to work for Sid's Body Contour Center. The New Orleans gym was run by Sid Craig, a navy veteran and former dance teacher. Slowly, a romance developed between Sid and Jenny and the couple were married in 1979. The Craigs sold Body Contour in 1982, but they soon found they missed running their own gym. Since their agreement with Nutri/System, who had bought their operation, prohibited them from competing for at least two years, the Craigs moved to Australia and opened the first Jenny Craig Weight Loss Program. By the end of the first year, there were 50 such centers in Australia. As soon as they were legally able, they returned to the United States and opened 14 branches in Los Angeles. Jenny Craig now owns or franchises about 650 centers in North America, Australia, New Zealand, and Puerto Rico.

Guisewhite, Cathy

In 1976, twenty-six-year-old Cathy Guisewhite was a successful career woman. She was a vice-president at an advertising agency, but she felt her personal life was in disarray. One night as she sat by the phone, waiting for her boyfriend to call, feeling fat and unattractive, she started to laugh at herself and decided to draw some humorous pictures of "how pathetic" she'd become. She kept illustrating her anxieties and sending them to her parents. They found the drawings far from pathetic. They saved them and encouraged her to try to sell them as a comic strip. As it happened, Universal Press Syndicate had its eyes open for a strip dealing with women's issues. They bought the strip and named it after its author. *Cathy* now runs in nearly fifteen hundred newspapers worldwide. Guisewhite now says that if she had known the strip would be so popular she would never have let them name it after her. "When I show Cathy sobbing next to the phone Saturday night, eating a pint of Häagen-Dazs," she says, "I just don' t necessarily want people to know it was me."

Gunhildr

Who was Gunhildr? Possibly a Scandinavian woman whose identity has been lost in time. Many scholars suggest that she was the wife or sweetheart of a soldier who named a weapon after her. Her name appeared in English in 1309 in a description of munitions at Windsor Castle, which listed, in the English of the Middle Ages, a large ballista called Domina Guinilda or "Lady Gunhilda." "There are other instances of bestowing female personal names on engines of war," says *The Oxford English Dictionary*, "but there was no distinguished woman called Guinilda in the 14th Century and it is highly probable that this name may have come down from Scandinavian times." What etymologists do know is that Guinilda went from being associated with cannonballs to gunpowder and finally smaller weapons. The name was eventually shortened to gunne and then to *gun*. While we're on the subject of guns and munitions, have you ever wondered what a "smithereen" is? It is something that people and things are "blown to," but it is almost never used in any other context. Smithereens, almost exclusively a plural noun, are tiny pieces. The word comes from the Irish "smidirin" meaning "a fragment or a particle." "Smidgen" comes from the same word.

Gurney, Goldsworthy

Goldsworthy Gurney was a medical doctor and a prolific inventor. He was born in 1793 in Cornwall. His gifts for science, music, and engineering were evident at an early age. He was an exceptional student. He took over the medical practice of his tutor before his twentieth birthday and married a year later. Running a medical practice was not enough to occupy Gurney's mind. As a hobby he began experimenting with sea sand. He thought the lime in the sand might have many uses. Meanwhile he tinkered with musical instruments, combining pianos and organs. Most notable was a piano with glass instead of wires, which he displayed at the Regents Park Exhibition. In 1820, he and his family moved to London. He found work as a surgeon and as a lecturer at the Surrey Institution in Chemistry and Natural Philosophy. In London he developed an "oxyhydrogen blow pipe." The blow pipe would allow Gurney to use gasses for power. In 1825 he took out a patent for a steam carriage, but he was unable to interest any investors in the concept. He built the carriages himself and they were soon a common sight in London. Next he returned to his experiments with lime. He thought it might be used for lighting. The limelight was especially useful in the theater, hence the expression "in the limelight." He also developed a light for ship-to-shore signaling, a fire extinguisher for use in mines, and a system for ventilating mineshafts with steam jets. He invented the Gurney stove to heat the Houses of Commons. For this work he was knighted in 1863. Unfortunately he was paralyzed shortly thereafter and died in 1875 at the age of eighty-two. Was he the source of the word *gurney*, meaning a medical bed on wheels? The answer is a definite "maybe." *The American Heritage Dictionary* lists gurney as being "possibly" derived from the name Gurney. William S. Haubrich, author of the book *Medical Meanings: A Glossary of Word Origins*, offers only an educated guess. "With all these accomplishments," he writes, "who is to say that he did not also come up with the idea of a wheeled stretcher?"

Gwinnett, Button

Due to his untimely death, the name Button Gwinnett became

synonymous with scarcity as in the expression "rarer than a Button Gwinnett." The expression, which has, itself, become rare, refers to the value of his autograph, which fetches as much as $150,000. Gwinnett was one of the men who signed the Declaration of Independence, but he didn't have time to sign much else. He was killed in a duel less than a year later. The scarcity of his signature is the best known fact about Gwinnett. Even historians in his home state, Georgia, have few facts about his life, and what they do know is not particularly flattering. He was born in 1735 and came to Savannah, Georgia with his wife, Anne Bourne, in 1765. The couple had three daughters: Amelia, Ann, and Elizabeth Ann. Gwinnett worked in the "import-export business." It was apparently not very successful, as Gwinnett was heavily in debt. He became involved in Revolutionary politics and became a leader of Georgia's Continental battalion in 1776. In less than a year, fierce opposition forced him to resign from the post and accept an election to the Continental Congress. Gwinnett's greatest rival was Gen. Lachlan McIntosh, who was named leader of the Georgia forces, a post Gwinnett very much wanted. McIntosh was not fond of Gwinnett either. On the floor of the Georgia Assembly on May 15, 1777 he called him a "scoundrel and a lying rascal." In response, Gwinnett challenged McIntosh to a duel. The two met before sunrise the next day in a Savannah pasture and faced each other, standing ten to twelve feet apart. At the signal, they fired and both were hit in the leg. Gwinnett died of an infection to his injured leg four days later. There is some controversy as to whether Gwinnett was actually buried in Savannah's Colonial Cemetery. Several years ago an amateur archaeologist dug up the bones to see if they really belonged to the man with the famous signature. Results of his dig were inconclusive. Regardless of the facts of his life, as one of three Georgians to sign the Declaration of Independence, Button Gwinnett is honored in Georgia, where a county bears his name. A nine-foot statue of the patriot now graces the roof of the Mall of Georgia. As Milo Ippolito, a reporter for the *Atlanta Journal-Constitution*, put it, Gwinnett may be known to Georgians of the future as "that guy on the roof of the mall."

H

Haight, Henry

Henry Haight was a member of a prominent San Francisco family in the 1850s. Brother Samuel was a member of the military, Fletcher was a lawyer and judge, and Henry was the manager of an early banking firm, Page, Bacon and Company. He gave generously for the establishment of a Protestant orphanage and was instrumental in its foundation. In the late 1860s, the residents of San Francisco asked their Board of Supervisors to develop park grounds in the city. The result would be Golden Gate Park. It was another Henry Haight, Fletcher's son who had risen to prominence as California governor after the Civil War, who appointed the first San Francisco Park Commission. A special Committee on Outside Lands was formed to build parks and settle property disputes. The committee mapped out a formerly remote area on the western end of the city, an area early Spanish settlers had dubbed "tierra de las pulgas" or "land of the fleas." Several of the streets in the new district were named for members of the committee, including Ashbury Street, named for Monroe Ashbury. The intersection of Ashbury and Haight streets became the epicenter of a district that would come to be known as *Haight-Ashbury,* or *"The Haight."* Historians disagree on which Henry gave his name to the street and the district. Many assume that it was the governor who was so honored, but the Museum of the City of San Francisco says it was the banker who gave his name to the famous street. Haight-Ashbury was one of the few districts to survive the great San Francisco earthquake of 1906. After the disaster, many wealthy residents moved to the area. Today, however, Haight-Ashbury is best known as the setting of the "Summer of Love." It was, in the words of Barney Hoskyns, author of *Beneath the Diamond Sky: Haight-Ashbury 1965-1970*, "the mecca, the ultimate hub of hippiedom, home to thousands of patchouli-scented, mocassin-wearing love children, and to the bands whose trippy, blissed-out jams mesmerised them each night in the city's psychedelic ballrooms." Even today, hundreds of tourists come to Haight-Ashbury to look for the "hippies." They can still be found there among the estimated population of seven hundred fifty thousand.

Halajian, Peter Paul

Peter Paul Halajian, an Armenian immigrant, began his career working for a rubber company in Naugatuck Valley, Connecticut. Paid by the piece, Halajian rushed to meet his quota so he could join his two daughters who operated a fruit stand. With whatever time he had left over, Halajian would walk up and down train platforms selling homemade candy from a basket. Halajian saved the money he made and invested it in two small candy shops in Torrington and Naugatuck, Connecticut. After a few years, his brother-in-law, Calvin K. Kazanjian, suggested not selling candy retail, but manufacturing it to sell wholesale. A number of their friends from the Armenian community, George Shamlian, Jacob Hagopian, Harry Kazanjian, and Jacob Chouljian, put up $1,000 each. Thus, "Peter Paul Candy Manufacturing Company of Connecticut" was born. Their first confection was called the "Konabar," which contained fruit, nuts, coconut, and chocolate. A year later, in 1922, the company introduced the Mounds bar. Mounds' original slogan was, "What a bar of candy for 5 cents!" After the war, the price of the bar went up to ten cents, so the slogan had to be changed. Next was "Indescribably Delicious" and "Honest to Goodness Chocolate." The company moved to a larger factory in 1922 to keep up with growing demand for its products. Peter Paul Halajian died in 1927, but the company that bears his name continued. During World War II Peter Paul was faced with severe shortages of sugar and coconut, which had been shipped from the

Philippines before war broke out. The company decided to cease production of its lesser-selling bars and concentrate on Mounds. Following the war, Peter Paul introduced Almond Joy. In 1978, Peter Paul merged with Cadbury. Ten years later Peter Paul/Cadbury was purchased by Hershey.

Hale, Alan

On July 22, 1995, thirty-seven-year-old Alan Hale was watching the night sky. Hale had been fascinated with outer space since he was a boy. As he grew up in the 1960s, his imagination was sparked by Neil Armstrong's moonwalk and by the fictional journeys of Capt. James T. Kirk. After he earned a Ph.D. in astronomy, however, he discovered that jobs in the field are rare. The only related employment he was able to find was at a science museum. He commuted three hours a day for a $23,000 salary with no health benefits and a mandatory two-week unpaid vacation. Frustrated, he gave up on astronomy as a career. He had not worked in his field in three years that July evening. He gazed into a telescope that sat on the driveway of his Cloudcroft, New Mexico home. By midnight he'd tracked a pair of known comets, then focused on a star cluster in the constellation Sagittarius. He could just make out a fuzzy object and he decided to keep watching it. It was 12:55 A.M. Meanwhile, in Arizona, construction worker Thomas Bopp was having an amateur star-watching party. Bopp, too, had been fascinated with the stars since he was a boy. He would later tell ABC News that "I told my father that someday when I grow up and become an astronomer I'll find something important." That night Bopp also had set his sights on the star cluster known as M70. At about the same time that he was spotting a formerly uncataloged object, Alan Hale was sending an e-mail message to the International Astronomical Union in Cambridge. Hale woke his wife, Eva, and their son, Zachary, and asked them to come see his comet. Eva came down to look, but Zachary mumbled something and went back to sleep. Twenty minutes after Hale sent news of his discovery to the union, Bopp telegrammed word of his own observation. As it was the practice of the Astronomical Union to credit codiscoverers, the comet became officially known as *Hale-Bopp*. It was the brightest comet to pass near the earth in more than twenty years. Initially both astronomers were thrilled with their discovery and resultant fame. They appeared on TV talk shows and made personal appearances across the country. "Every amateur astronomer fantasizes about this," Hale told reporter Dan Williams. Bopp told ABC, "It's a spiritual experience. It touches the very heart of your being." The names Hale and Bopp would soon take on an eerie significance when members of a religious cult known as Heaven's Gate staged a mass suicide in the belief that Hale-Bopp was a "marker . . . for the arrival of the spacecraft from the Level Above Human to take us home." Hale's enthusiasm began to wane by 1998 when he found he was still unemployed. He made headlines again that year when he posted an open letter on the Internet saying that he could not encourage young people to pursue a career in science because of a lack of jobs.

Hammond, Laurens

Laurens Hammond was born in Evanston, Illinois in 1895, the youngest of four children and the only son of Chicago banker William Andrew Hammond and Idea Louise Strong, an Episcopal priest's daughter. On December 21, 1896, the First National Bank of Illinois, of which William Hammond was vice-president, failed due to "excessive holdings of worthless securities of the Calumet Electric Railway Company." Hammond, who served as director of the railway system, was accused of causing the crash by approving loans to the failing company to his own advantage. The matter was never resolved because investigations into Hammond stopped on January 2, 1897 when he committed suicide by drowning himself in Lake Michigan. Laurens Hammond was less than two years old at the time. In 1898, his mother took the children to Europe. She became a noted artist and the children were educated at a number of schools in Germany and France. Hammond and his siblings grew up to be multilingual. In 1909, however, it became apparent that war was going to break out in Europe, so the Hammonds returned to the United States. Laurens

Hammond received a degree in mechanical engineering from Cornell University in 1916. He would go on to hold 110 electrical and mechanical patents for a diverse collection of devices. One of the most unusual was an electric bridge table that used a rubber finger to shuffle playing cards. In the early 1930s, Hammond set out to improve the punch clocks used in factories. When he was tinkering with the electromechanical clock, he discovered he could get tones and harmonies, so he changed direction and started to design an electronic organ even though he couldn't play an instrument nor "even carry a tune." He brought in a number of employees with musical backgrounds to act as "ears" and help him refine his invention. The prototype organ was completed in 1933 and was patented on April 24, 1934. The first production model, "serial number one," was constructed in early 1935 and shipped to Hammond's agency in Kansas City, where a salesman named Bob Pierce drove it from town to town in the Midwest for the next three years and demonstrated it with the assistance of a maintenance man and an organist. They rode in a van "hitting every little burg with a population over 100," Pierce recounted in his book, *Pierce Piano Atlas.* "We demonstrated the Model A on university campuses and radio stations, for women's clubs, in music stores and churches and even mortuaries. The only places we avoided were the gin mills." Although the company's marketing materials would later claim George Gershwin was the first to buy a *Hammond organ,* the company's first customer was actually the industrialist Henry Ford, who placed a pre-production order for six of the instruments. Hammond organs became associated with ballparks and old-time gospel music. Hammond stepped down as the president of the company that bears his name in 1955 but he remained involved in operations until 1960. He retired to West Cornwall, Connecticut in 1960 and died July 3, 1973 at the age of seventy-eight.

Handwerker, Nathan

Nathan Handwerker was a Polish immigrant. He arrived in New York in 1912. He made ends meet by working two jobs. On weekdays he was a delivery boy for Max's Busy Bee restaurant.

The job earned him $4.50 a week. On the weekends, he worked at Charles Feltman's German Gardens restaurant in Coney Island behind the counter. One day, while he was minding his business, slicing rolls behind the counter, two singing waiters, Jimmy Durante and Eddie Cantor, not wanting to pay ten cents for a hot dog, tried to talk Handwerker into opening his own hot-dog shop. He decided to take their advice. With his life savings of $300, he invested in a hot-dog stand and worked eighteen to twenty hours a day with his nineteen-year-old bride, Ida. He sold his hot dogs for a nickel, half the price of the hot dogs at the German Gardens. They were an immediate hit. When competitors started to whisper that he couldn't possibly sell a quality hot dog for that price, Handwerker hired college students to sit at the counter wearing white doctor's uniforms complete with stethoscopes. When people saw that doctors were eating there, the rumors about a lack of quality subsided. Interestingly, the entrepreneur didn't name his stand until 1921. When he heard Sophie Tucker perform the hit song "Nathan, Nathan, Why You Waitin'?" he decided his name would do nicely and *Nathan's Hot Dogs* was born. In 1968, with a chain consisting of only three restaurants, Nathan's went public. Handwerker retired in 1972 and passed away in 1974 at the age of eighty-three. The chain was sold by the Handwerker family in 1987. By 1997 it had 300 locations in twenty-two states, generating sales of nearly $116 million. That year Nathan's announced plans to open its first overseas shops in Israel.

Harrington, John

In 1596, Sir John Harrington of England invented a "water closet" for his godmother, Queen Elizabeth I. That year he published a treatise, "The Metamorphosis of Ajax," which described his design of the flush, overflow pipe, and cistern. The invention was not widely adopted in Harrington's time because there were no sewers yet to carry the waste away. It is widely believed that the use of the name "john" for a toilet comes from John Harrington. The privy was first called by that name in the 1650s. According to Stuart Berg Flexner, author of

Listening to America: An Illustrated History of Words and Phrases from Our Lively and Splendid Past, however, "there is no scholarly evidence that his name was given to the device and privies had already long been given men's names." Prior to the 1600s it had already been called a "jake," he said. The most famous name associated with the flush toilet is probably that of Thomas Crapper, who improved upon John Harrington's designs in the 1880s. Crapper is an old Yorkshire name meaning "cropper." The Crappers, a family of sailors, lived in the little town of Thorne, England. In 1837, they had a son Thomas. At the age of eleven, Thomas Crapper walked 165 miles to London and took work as a plumber's apprentice. By 1861 he had his own business, Thomas Crapper & Co., Marlborough Works. He held nine patents—four for improvements to drains, three for water closets, one for manhole covers, and the last for pipe joints. The most famous product attributed to Crapper was "The Silent Valveless Water Waste Preventer." The product that allowed a toilet to flush effectively when the cistern was only half-full was actually patented to one of Crapper's employees, Albert Gilbin. Crapper most likely bought the patent rights from Gilbin and marketed the device. Queen Victoria was sufficiently impressed by Crapper's reputation to invite him to install the drains and plumbing in her royal home. Contrary to popular myth, however, he was never knighted and therefore cannot accurately be called Sir Thomas Crapper. Crapper man-hole covers can be found all over the U.K.; there is even one in Westminster Abbey. Crapper retired in 1904 and sold his shop to two partners, who operated the company under the Crapper name until 1966. He passed away January 27, 1910. Whether or not Crapper is the source of the expletive that seems to derive from his name is still a subject of scholarly debate. *The Oxford English Dictionary,* the most authoritative etymological reference, lists thirty-nine euphemisms for lavatory. Thomas Crapper is associated with one such euphemism. *The OED* records the earliest use of a slang term resembling Crapper's name and referring to rubbish or waste as occurring in 1846 when Crapper was a mere nine years old and not yet a famous plumber. According to Dr. Andy Gibbons, historian of the

International Thomas Crapper Society, possible sources of the word are a Low German word referring to vile and inedible fish or a Middle English word for residue or rubbish, originally used in connection with grain. Just how common this usage was is a subject of much debate. Thomas Crapper's prominence probably did have a role in giving the existing expression greater currency. World War I doughboys passing through England saw the words "T. Crapper-Chelsea" printed on toilet tanks and used his last name to refer to the lavatory (from the Latin *lavatorium,* a place for washing). They brought the expression home with them. The use of Crapper's name in association with a water closet was most likely combined with the already current term "crap" to give us a word with all its current shades of meaning. "The case either way is not proven with any great finality," writes Nigel Rees, author of *The Cassell Dictionary of Word and Phrase Origins.* "It would be of great assistance if a precise use of the word crapper could be found earlier than the 1932 citation (from *American Speech*) which is the best the OED2 can do." If you have an interest in this subject, you might want to visit the American Sanitary Plumbing Museum. The museum, located in Worcester, Massachusetts, is a treasure trove of flush-toilet, sink, and bathroom history. It features antique plumbing tools, early tubs, even an exhibit of antique toilet paper. Admission is free.

Harris, David

David Harris grew up in Fresno, California, the son of a lawyer. As a boy he dreamed of being an army soldier. In high school he was an honor student who was on the football team and in the debate club. The popular six-foot-two blond left for Stanford University, where his life changed dramatically. He came to Stanford in 1963, the year President Kennedy was shot. The debates over civil rights and the war in Vietnam were becoming heated. Harris served briefly as a voting-rights volunteer in Mississippi and in the fall of 1965 first demonstrated against the war. In 1966, he was elected president of the student body. Three months later, Harris sent his draft cards back to the government with a letter saying he would not take part in the war. Opposition to the war became his primary concern. He left college to make it his full-time career. He got a job at a Menlo Park bookstore. The owner also served as business manager for a folksinger named Joan Baez. Since Baez was a prominent antiwar activist the owner suggested Harris hit her up for money for his cause. Their common passion turned into a romance, and they were married in 1968. A year later Harris was sent to jail for resisting the draft. The couple's son, Gabriel, was born five months later. Baez wrote a song for her martyr-husband, *"A Song for David,"* the lyrics of which begin: "In my heart I will wait/by the stony gate/and the little one in my arms will sleep./Every rising of the moon/makes the years grow late/and the love in our hearts will keep." Yet the marriage did not last. Three months after Harris was released from jail, they went their separate ways. "Our relationship was defined by a larger situation—the Vietnam War," he told *People* magazine. He went on to marry writer Lacey Fosburgh and to have another child, Sophie. He is the author of a 1996 book about Vietnam—*Our War: What We Did in Vietnam and What It Did to Us.* He told *People* that he does not own a copy of "A Song for David," which he also never heard in prison. "I don't know the lyrics," he said. "I never identified with it."

Harris, John

John Harris of Yorkshire, England, was an early settler in this country. He arrived in Pennsylvania prior to 1698. In 1727 he bought 100 acres of land for five pounds and established a ferry across the Susquehanna River. The region came to be known as John Harris's Ferry. In 1733 he obtained a grant of 300 acres of land near his home, and bought an additional 300 adjoining acres. He is recorded in some official histories of *Harrisburg*, the city that bears his name and that of his son, as William Penn's ambassador to the Native Americans. He was also said to carry on a considerable trade with the local tribes. Historic records show, however, that relations between Harris and certain tribes were strained, to say the least. Evelyn Bartow's *Bartow Genealogy* reports that in 1718 Harris was captured by Indians and tied to a tree to be burned, but was rescued. In

1763, Harris wrote to governor John Penn and asked him to remove the Indians of the village of Conestoga. "The Indians here I hope your Honor will be pleased to have removed to some other place, as I do not like their company." They were described in a text of the day as "a miserable set of savages." Governor Penn, however, refused to move them. A group of citizens known as the Paxton Boys, "as no assistance or protection could be had from the government, took measures to destroy every one. . . . In the destruction of the Conestogas several well known, blood-thirsty savages lurking there were killed." John Harris remained in the area. He built a mansion, which he willed to his son, John Harris, Jr., who expanded it and, in one of its rooms, mapped out plans for the town that would be called Harrisburg. In his plan, the younger Harris provided 3 acres for use by the Commonwealth for a state capitol. Harrisburg officially became the capital in 1812. It now has a population of roughly fifty-six thousand people.

Harris, Mary

Mary Harris was born in Cork, Ireland, on May 1, 1830. She was brought to North America sometime after 1835 and attended school in Toronto, Ontario. She later worked as a schoolteacher in Monroe, Michigan, and Memphis, Tennessee. Around 1860, she met George Jones, a member of the Iron Molders' Union, in Memphis and fell in love. They were married and had four children. Tragically, in 1867, Mary Jones lost her entire family to a yellow fever epidemic. She moved to Chicago and started a dressmaking business, only to be wiped out by the Great Chicago Fire in 1871. Shortly thereafter, she started attending meetings of the newly formed Knights of Labor and discovered a calling. For the next fifty years, she traveled around the country speaking out and organizing workers. She traveled wherever a large strike was happening, from railroad yards in Pittsburgh to mines in West Virginia. In 1902, she led a march of Pennsylvania coal miners' wives who fended off potential strikebreakers with brooms and mops. A year later, she attempted to bring attention to the problem of child labor by leading a parade of young textile

workers from Kensington, Pennsylvania, to Pres. Theodore
Roosevelt's Long Island home. In 1905 she helped found the
Industrial Workers of the World. She had a number of run-ins
with the law, including a 1913 conviction in a West Virginia military court for conspiracy to commit murder. She was sentenced to twenty years in jail, but the governor set it aside. In
1923, at the age of 93, she was still working with striking coal
miners. On her 100th birthday she was honored by a reception
at her home in Silver Spring, Maryland. One of her former
enemies, John D. Rockefeller, sent her a telegram of congrat-
ulations. "I could never die," she once said, "because when I
get to heaven, I'm gonna tell that carpenter fella about the
mine operators in West Virginia, and He'll send me back down
to organize the workers." She did die, however, six months
after her 100th birthday, on November 30, 1930. Forty years
later, her name was put on the masthead of a new magazine.
Mother Jones was produced by a nonprofit institution funded by
a board who wished to create a forum for crusading left-wing
journalism. The magazine won three National Magazine
Awards in its first four years.

Hassenfeld, Henry and Helal

Siblings Henry and Helal Hassenfeld went into business
together as Hassenfeld Brothers in 1923. The modest shop
sold textile remnants and later school supplies such as pencil
boxes and tote bags. By 1939 the family business was taking in
$500,000 a year. Henry's son, Merrill, became president of the
company in 1943. Under his direction they began to sell
crayons, paint sets, and a few toys like nurse kits. The few toys
sold well, so Hassenfeld continued to add more to the inventory. Then, in 1952, Hassenfeld got wind of a toy created by
New York designer George Lerner. The idea was so simple that
Lerner originally planned to sell it to a cereal company to give
away in boxes. A small packet contained interchangeable eyes,
noses, and lips that could be pressed into a household potato.
The Hassenfelds thought Mr. Potato Head had a great deal of
potential. They offered Lerner a $500 advance and a 5 royalty
royalty on future sales. The original toy had twenty-eight plastic

face and body parts and a page of instructions. The idea was not entirely original. "Make a face" kits for kids had been around as long as toys, but the design of Mr. Potato Head, and clever marketing by the Hassenfelds, made it a hit. The company quickly followed up with Mrs. Potato Head and potato babies. The company, its name now shortened to *Hasbro,* aggressively marketed the spud family. They claim that Mr. Potato Head was the first toy advertised on television. Their biggest rival, Mattel, maintains that one of their products—a Mickey Mouse guitar—was the first toy to appear in its own TV ad. The Potato Head family and friends did not acquire their plastic bodies until 1964. Out of the estimated six thousand toys released each year, the trade association Toy Manufacturers of America keeps a list of about fifty it considers to be classic. Mr. Potato Head routinely appears on the list. The famous spud gave up smoking in 1987. Until that year, Mr. Potato Head always came with a pipe. Concerned parents, who felt the toy encouraged smoking, finally convinced Hasbro to leave the pipe out of the packages. Hasbro's next big success was a toy that seemed destined to fail—an answer to Mattel's Barbie doll marketed to boys. In 1963 Barbie was clearly a hit. Don Levine, then the executive director of Hasbro, came up with the idea of a soldier doll. Originally, the plan was to make a different doll for each branch of the armed services. Each would have its own name. The marketing department, however, felt is was important to have only one name for the line. As he was trying to come up with the perfect label, Levine was flipping through television channels and came across the 1945 film *The Story of G. I. Joe.* He had found the name. There were naturally worries about marketing a doll—always considered a feminine toy—to boys. To solve the problem they coined a new term: "action figure." "The offending 'd' word would be banned from the language of everyone on the development team," wrote John Michling in *GI Joe.* "Once the new term was coined, anyone using the word 'doll' in reference to the movable soldier was subject to Levine's wrath." For Joe to be a true action figure, he needed to have a fully articulated body. The body was modeled after wooden artists' mannequins. The head was designed by artist Phil Kraczkowski, who had previously designed the Kennedy-Johnson inaugural medal. He was paid $600 for the job. Joe was a hit. Its sales hit a high point in 1964. Then, in the late 1960s, during the Vietnam War, G. I. Joe came under fire from critics who saw him as a toy that glorified war and violence. Sales fell to less than a third of their previous level. Joe made a comeback in 1982. From 1982 to 1995 he brought in roughly $600 million. Hasbro, once a small family business, became a public company in 1968. Today it owns such brands as Parker Brothers, Play-Doh, Nerf, Milton Bradley, and Playskool.

Hauer, Barbara

Barbara Hauer, the daughter of German immigrants, was born December 3, 1766 in Lancaster, Pennsylvania. When she was about ten, the family moved to Frederick, Maryland. There she married John C. Frietschie. His name, and consequently her name, was sometimes spelled Fritchie. The events of most of Barbara Frietschie's life were not recorded for posterity, and the events for which she is most remembered probably did not happen. In September 1862, during the Civil War, the Northern Virginia Army spent the night in Frederick during Gen. Robert E. Lee's invasion of Maryland. When they marched out of town on September 10, they passed Frietschie's house. Frietschie, who was known to be a patriot, must have done or said something to the Confederate troops. She may have waved a Union flag from her second-story window, and there was probably a small incident of some kind. Frietschie died soon afterwards on December 18, 1862. The people of Frederick started talking about her, and the story of her defiant act was told and retold and most likely embellished a great deal. One person to hear the tale was novelist Emma D. E. N. Southworth. She passed it along to the poet John Greenleaf Whittier. Whittier created a stirring poem from the event. "Barbara Fritchie" appeared in *The Atlantic Monthly* in October 1863. As Whittier told it, Gen. Stonewall Jackson himself marched past Frietschie's home. Seeing her Union banner waving, the troops shot it full of holes. Frietschie picked up the flag. "Shoot, if you must, this old gray head. But spare your country's flag," she said. Jackson ordered his men to cease fire. "Who touches a hair of yon gray head dies like a dog! March on!" The poem and its heroine have become part of our national heritage. The only problem is, it never happened, at least not to Frietschie. Historic records show that Jackson never passed her house, but some Civil War scholars think another woman may have defied his troops. A woman named Mary Quantrill and her daughter stood in front of their home and waved Union flags as Jackson's men marched by. In the aftermath of that eventful day, as neighbors recalled what had happened, they shared stories of people who had defied the Confederates. Quantrill's story was most likely told along with the story of the incident involving Barbara Frietschie. By the time Union troops heard the gossip, the details had become muddled. They told the story of Frietschie's courage and Quantrill's name was forgotten.

Heaviside, Oliver

Oliver Heaviside was born in London, on May 18, 1850. His uncle, Charles Wheatstone, a pioneer of the telegraph, would talk to Oliver about science and electricity as he grew up. In the late 1800s, electricity was seen as the technology of the future, and young people were excited about it in much the same way they are today about computers. Heaviside did not let the fact that he had only an elementary education interfere with his fascination with modern inventions. When he was twenty he got a job with the Great Northern Telegraph Company. After only four years, however, problems with his hearing forced him to leave the job. Undaunted, he traveled to Denmark to further study the telegraph. Unable to find work upon his return, he lived with his parents and his brother. He continued to work with theoretical mathematics and the science of electricity. His theories were so advanced that they were rejected by some mathematicians and scientists. The electrical journals also rejected his writings because they felt they were too abstract. So he published his findings himself in a three-volume collection called *Electromagnetic Theory*. Among his theories was a method of reducing signal distortion in a telegraph cable by adding small inductance coils throughout its length. The theory that gave his name currency, however, was the suggestion that part of the atmosphere might act as a good reflector of electrical waves, thus making long-distance transmission of signals possible. In 1892, another scientist, Edward Appleton, proved that such a layer did, in fact, exist. This part of the atmosphere, about one hundred kilometers or sixty-two miles above the ground, is now called the "ionosphere," but it was previously known as the *Heaviside layer*. The reason you can hear AM radio stations from miles away at night is that the signals bounce off the ionosphere. Because the ionosphere changes when it isn't being hit by the sun, the radio waves bounce better after dark. FM radio and television waves go right through that layer of the atmosphere. Although "ionosphere" is more current today, the term Heaviside layer is still familiar to fans of the musical *Cats,* which features the old Grizabella rising toward the heavens on a giant tire while the kitty chorus sings, "Up, up, up to the Heaviside layer."

Hell, Maximilian

One of the privileges explorers have long enjoyed is naming their discoveries. In recent times the naming of landmarks has moved beyond the surface of the earth. The various features on the moon's surface have also been given names. One such name is a lunar plain called Hell. The name was not chosen as a description of the uninhabited terrain. It was given in honor of a Hungarian Jesuit astronomer, Maximilian Hell. Hell was born May 15, 1720. Engineering was prized in his family. His father was the chief engineer of the local mines and his brother invented a machine to pump water out of the mineshafts. Hell entered the Society of Jesus at Trentschin, Hungary at age eighteen. After his novitiate he was sent to Vienna, where he began with the expected range of theological and philosophical education. In a few years, however, he was incorporating science, especially mathematics and astronomy, into his studies. He became an assistant to Fr. Joseph Franz, the director of the observatory at Vienna. In 1751 was ordained a priest. A year later, he became a professor of mathematics at Klausenberg. His popular lectures are said to have increased the interest in astronomy in Europe. One of Hell's theories involved the use of magnetic fields to cure pain. Although this theory was later debunked, it greatly inspired a young man named Franz Mesmer, who gave us the word *mesmerize*. Hell continued to teach for three years. Father Hell was so successful in setting up small observatories that in 1755 Maria Theresa of Austria and Hungary named him her court astronomer and commissioned him to organize a great central observatory in Vienna. In addition, he published a number of books with long titles in Latin. These were primarily on astronomy but he also wrote about algebra and mathematics. The most important of his works was an annual publication, *Ephemerides astronomicæ ad meridianem Vindobonensem,* which he began in 1757 and continued for many years. By 1767 his reputation as a scientist had grown to the point that King Christian VII of Denmark and Norway invited him to direct a scientific expedition to the island station Vardø near Lapland within the Arctic Circle. The team would gather data from the 1769 transit of Venus, which crosses the face of the sun about twice a century. By observing the contact points of the sun with Venus from different vantage points on earth, they hoped to be able to compute the solar parallax, which could then be used to compute the sun's distance from the earth. His team's data would be combined with observations taken in California, Tahiti, Batavia, Manila, and Peking. On June 3, 1769, Hell and his team made their observations. That done, they remained in the arctic for eight months to collect data on meteorology, oceanography, zoology, geography, natural history, and linguistics. Since his team was already in the arctic, Hell did not want to pass up the opportunity for study and he hoped to publish an encyclopedia on the region. Astronomers back home were getting impatient. The French Academy accused him of having nothing to report and of waiting so that he could make up figures to correspond with the observations made elsewhere. Hell's observations were finally published in 1772. Sometime later, an astronomer named Carl Littrow became one of Hell's successors at the observatory. He looked into Hell's data and claimed that the figures had been falsified. He based his accusation on the fact that some of the information was recorded in a different-colored ink, which suggested that some of the data had been copied over. Hell was discredited and his reputation was destroyed. He fell ill with pneumonia in March 1792 and died in Vienna on April 14, 1792. It would be another century before his name would be cleared. American astronomer Simon Newcomb was studying Venus in 1883. He reexamined Littrow's evidence and found, among other things, that Littrow was color-blind and could therefore not tell if the pens had been of a different color. In 1922 the International Astronomical Union was formed to officially name the features of the moon. The National Air and Space Museum catalog now identifies about sixteen hundred points on the moon's surface. Maximilian Hell became one of thirty-five Jesuits honored with a piece of lunar topography. The moon is not the only heavenly body to bear human names. Scientists seem to have a great deal of fun naming asteroids. *The Asteroid Name Encyclopedia,* by Jacob Schwartz, contains an alphabetical listing of thousands of asteroid names. Along with the many objects named for scientists and their friends and family there are asteroids named for musician Eric Clapton and four asteroids named for each of the Beatles. According to Schwartz, Asteroids "Adolph" and "Germany" were discovered at the beginning of the twentieth century and traveled together in longitude and declination during Hitler's twenty years in power, and when Bill Clinton, Ross Perot, and George Bush were in a close race for the presidency in 1992, asteroids with their first names were in a close forty-degree arc and Bill led the pack.

Hepplewhite, George

George Hepplewhite died in 1786, never knowing that his name would be familiar to furniture collectors for years to come. From his workshop in England, he designed furniture that he admitted was not particularly original but showed the "prevailing fashion" in English furniture of the time. He based his own designs on those of Scottish-born Robert Adam, the noted architect and designer, and his brother James. His style was characterized by the use of inlaid ornamentation and shield, oval, and interlaced heart-shaped chair backs. He was not considered especially noteworthy in his time. He was mentioned in a trade directory in 1786 with the name misspelled as "Kepplewhite & Son." No pieces of his own work have been confirmed to exist because at that time few pieces were signed or labeled. It was his widow, Alice, and his son who were responsible for his posthumous recognition. They published his now-famous book, *Cabinet-maker's and Upholsterer's Guide*, two years after his death. The book has been the inspiration for many furniture makers, who copied the designs and said they were in the *Hepplewhite style*. Hepplewhite's guide also inspired the design of the first refrigerator. An early-nineteenth-century Maryland farmer named Thomas Moore took a design for a water cooler from the book and adapted it. He patented his icebox on January 27, 1803. Later that year he published *An Essay on the Most Eligible Construction of Ice-Houses, Also a Description of the Newly Invented Machine Called the Refrigerator.* The essay predicted the new device would be used to carry meats and dairy products to market, keep foods fresh in the store, and preserve foods in the home until mealtime. He was right, but it would be another twenty-seven years before iceboxes would be sold for home use.

Herod

Herod the Great was born around 73 B.C. He was a practicing Jew of Arab descent. He was appointed king of Judea by Rome in 37 B.C. The Jews always regarded him as an outsider, thus, Herod was not popular. He made many efforts in the beginning to win their favor. He built theaters, aqueducts, ports, and the second Temple in Jerusalem. As he got older, Herod became unstable and violent. He would change his will on a whim when his children pleased or displeased him. He had his wife and three of his sons executed. According to the Gospel of Matthew, Herod ordered the massacre of newborn children. William Shakespeare coined the phrase to *"out-Herod Herod"* in the play *Hamlet.* The expression became popular by the nineteenth century. About fifteen hundred other words and phrases were coined by the bard—so many, in fact, that two authors, Jeffrey McQuain and Stanley Malless, were able to compile a book on the subject. It is called *Coined by Shakespeare*. Some of his inventions include anchovy, rant, leapfrog (the game), to drug (as a verb), arouse, numb, epileptic, bedroom, impede, remorseless, and zany.

Hillegass, Cliff

Cliff Hillegass was born in the rural town of Rising, Nebraska. As a boy, he suffered an illness that left him bedridden for two months. He spent the time reading and developed a love of classic literature. As a graduate student at the University of Nebraska, Hillegass married a woman named Catherine and began his career in earnest as a bookstore representative for Long's College Bookstore. One of the people the met through he job was Jack Cole, who owned the Book People, a Canadian textbook manufacturer that also produced a line of study guides called "Cole's Notes." Cole suggested Hillegass release something similar in the States. The Hillegasses took this advice. They got a loan and, in August 1958, started producing and marketing *CliffsNotes* from their basement. CliffsNotes quickly became the best-selling study guides in America and the bane of English teachers everywhere. These days the company sells more than five million notes a year. In 1998 it was sold to IDG Books, makers of the famous "For Dummies" series.

Hills, Austin Herbert

For most of their youth, Austin Herbert and Reuben Wilmarth Hills of Maine were without a father. When they were just boys their father, a ship maker, took off to California in search of gold. He sent for his wife and children in 1873. By then, Austin was twenty-two and Reuben was seventeen. Three years later, the brothers opened a stall at San Francisco's Bay City Market. After five years they had put aside enough to open a coffee store, which they named the Arabian Coffee and Spice Mills. To draw crowds, they would roast the beans in front of the store. The smell of fresh coffee and the activity brought people in. As coffee prices rose, they decided to put most of their energy into wholesale accounts. They sold the coffee under the name *Hills Brothers*. By 1886, they had dropped the retail end of the business completely. Around this time, a roving artist stopped in the Hills' store. He offered to draw a figure to represent their Arabian Roast Coffee. He drew a turbaned man in a long, flowing robe drinking a cup of coffee. The icon still graces the Hills Brothers coffee can to this day. In July 1900, Reuben Hills decided to try applying to coffee a process he used on butter shipments. It was the first time coffee came in vacuum-packed containers. The business continued to grow until 1906, when the San Francisco earthquake destroyed their plant and offices. It took them two years to get back on their feet. Hills Brothers was officially incorporated in 1914. The name was changed to Hills Bros. Coffee, Inc. in 1929. It grew to be the third largest coffee roaster in the country, but in the late 1950s it started to lose market share. Marketing surveys said that people believed the brand was declining in quality and that the Arab icon was old-fashioned. In 1965, an internal Brand Image Study stated, "Throughout the Western Zone, Hills Bros. was seen as a poor quality coffee or a brand that was declining in popularity." It was sold to a Brazilian cooperative in 1976. It has changed hands more than once since then. Today the brand is owned by the Sara Lee Corporation, which also owns Chock Full O' Nuts and Chase & Sanborn.

Himmelstein, Lena

Lena Himmelstein was born in Lithuania in 1879. It was then part of czarist Russia. Only ten days after she was born, her mother died and she was sent to live with her grandparents. Growing up she witnessed "cruel Russian persecutions." As soon as she had the chance, at age sixteen, she accepted an invitation by a distant relative to travel to America. What her benefactors neglected to tell her was that they had given her passage because they expected her to marry their son. Lena was not taken with the young man and had no intention of marrying him so she ran away. The young immigrant, who spoke no English, joined her sister Anna, who was working for $1 a week in a New York sweatshop making "beautiful lingerie for fast women." By the time she was twenty she had learned English and machine sewing and had worked her way up to a job that brought in $15 a week. Around this time she met a jeweler from Brooklyn named David Bryant. They married and Lena joined him working in his shop. She gave birth to a son, Raphael, on February 3, 1900. Six months later David Bryant died, a victim of tuberculosis. At the age of twenty, Lena Bryant was a widow and the mother of an infant. The profits from the shop had gone to the doctors and Lena was forced to pawn her wedding gift from her husband—a pair of diamond earrings—to make a down payment on a sewing machine. She moved into a small apartment with her sister and, with Raphael on her knee, she sewed dresses and lingerie to sell to local ladies. She delivered the completed garments herself and eventually earned enough to open an official shop on Fifth Avenue. Lena, Anna, and Raphael lived behind the shop, which sold primarily bridal gowns. One day a regular customer came into the shop. She had a delicate problem. She was expecting a baby and she didn't know what she would wear. Maternity clothes as we know them today did not exist in turn-of-the-century New York. Pregnant women were not expected to be seen in public. Lena designed a comfortable maternity dress for her customer, which she sold for $18. Shortly thereafter, Anna was married and her husband agreed to lend his new sister-in-law $300 to open a bank account and buy a new shop. When she went to the bank she was so nervous that she misspelled her name on the deposit slip. She was too embarrassed to correct the mistake, so she decided instead to call her new shop *Lane Bryant*. The first Lane Bryant store employed employed women. In 1909, Lena was married again, to an engineer named Albert Malsin. The couple had a daughter and two sons over the course of the next four years. Malsin took over the business operations of Lane Bryant, while Lena continued to design the clothes. By 1910, Lane Bryant was earning $50,000 a year, primarily from maternity clothes. Malsin decided the company should focus all its attention on the maternity line. The only problem was that they couldn't find a newspaper that would advertise that kind of clothing. It wasn't until 1911 that the

New York Herald agreed to carry an ad that began: "Maternity wardrobes that do not attract attention . . ." The day the ad ran, the store's entire stock of maternity wear was depleted. Slowly, over time, women stopped asking to have the garments mailed in plain brown wrappings and hiding their faces as they walked in the shop. In 1916, the business was incorporated as Lane Bryant, Inc. A year later sales passed $1,000,000. Malsin decided that it was time to bring back other types of clothing. Women had been writing to Lane Bryant for some time asking them to make clothing in large sizes. "Won't some ingenious man please take pity on us poor stout women?" wrote one. "It seems as if some way should be found for us to walk into a store and buy comfortable and also stylish clothes as easily as our slimmer sisters do." Malsin looked at the measurements of 4,500 of the company's customers and combined them with measurements of more than 200,000 women holding insurance policies. He saw that 40 percent of the women were larger than the ideal figure of the day and no one was designing clothing for them. Although she was a petite woman herself, Lena designed a line of clothing for larger women. When Albert Malsin died in 1923, the plus-size clothing line had surpassed the maternity business in sales. The first Lane Bryant catalog was mailed in 1924 and featured a silk dress for $7.95. Lena Bryant Malsin turned over the directorship of the company to her sons but kept an office in the New York store until her death at age seventy-two of a heart attack on September 26, 1951. By 1967, large-sized clothing accounted for more than 95 percent of the company's annual sales. Eventually, Lane Bryant got out of the maternity business altogether. In the 1980s, Lane Bryant was acquired by The Limited, which aggressively launched retail stores under the Lane Bryant name and then spun off the catalog business in 1993. The catalog company Brylane, now a separate entity from the shops, bought a number of other catalogs including KingSize (big men's clothing), Lerner, and Chadwick's. According to *Forbes,* Brylane is the world's largest, most profitable major catalog company. Sales from its ten catalogs topped $1.3 billion in 1997. Its customer list is the longest in the business and includes 22 million names. Plus-sized fashions have become a $24 billion industry.

Hogan, Robert

In 1965, Albert S. Ruddy and Bernard Fein decided to create a television situation comedy with the unlikely setting of a World War II prisoner of war camp. The plot would revolve around an American soldier and his fellow prisoners who were always able to outsmart and sabotage their German captors. For the central role, Fein thought of his friend Robert Hogan, who was then a struggling actor. He thought he'd give his friend a leg up on the competition by actually naming the main character Bob Hogan. "One night I was talking to Bernie on the phone," Hogan recalled, "and he said they changed the name of the show [to "Hogan's Heroes"]. Good name. He said, half-jokingly, that it might do me some good." But the network wanted a "name" actor, not just an actor whose name was the title of the show. One of the actors to be considered for the role was Walter Matthau. Producer Ed Feldman rejected the idea, saying, "He can't do comedy." Actor Van Johnson turned the series down. Richard Dawson was briefly considered for the role of Hogan, but he had a British accent, so the series creators opted to make him a British prisoner named Peter Newkirk and to make Hogan an all-American hero. The role went to Bob Crane, who had left "The Donna Reed Show" after arguments over money. Another interesting casting choice was John Banner. The actor who played the Nazi Schultz was actually Jewish. Robert Clary, who played the French prisoner LeBeau, had been interned in Nazi concentration camps as a boy. Robert Hogan, the actor, did appear on the series twice as a guest star, but that was the extent of his involvement. "I cannot tell you how many people, on hearing my name, say, 'Oh, one of Hogan's Heroes, huh?'" he once said. "You can't tell everyone and they really don't care so I smile and weakly nod." Hogan went on to bigger and better things. He played Scott Banning on "Days of Our Lives" from 1970 to 1971, commanded the *Sea Tiger* as Lieutenant Commander Haller during the second season of "Operation Petticoat," and has appeared on more than one hundred television series including "Law and Order," "M*A*S*H," "Hill Street Blues," and "Murder, She Wrote." "Hogan's Heroes" ran from September 17, 1965 to July 4, 1971 and for years in syndication. In the late 1990s, it became a surprise cult hit in Germany, where it is called "A Cage Full of Heroes." The Nazi characters in the German version speak with regional dialects and, with liberal translation, are made to look even more ridiculous than they did in the American version. The "Heil Hitler" salute, illegal in Germany, was replaced with phrases like "Heil Schnitzler" and "Adios." It is one of the few American sitcoms to succeed in the German market. "Seinfeld," for example, one of America's most successful shows, was canceled there after less than a year.

Hood, Robin

Was there a real Robin Hood? Maybe, maybe not. No one knows for sure who the inspiration for the folk hero who robs from the rich and gives to the poor was. Yet scholars have suggested a number of candidates. One of the earliest surviving references to the hero is a ballad called "A Gest of Robyn Hode." It describes a "comely" king named Edward who meets Robin Hood while he is traveling around the country. The king pardons him and Robin Hood goes to work in his court. After a little more than a year, however, Robin Hood becomes bored with his respectable life and returns to robbery. One of the earliest possible Robin Hoods was Eustace the Monk. He was born in the late 1100s and lived in a monastery near Nottingham. He left his order when his father was murdered and lived as a hermit in Sherwood Forest. His hermitage changed his direction in life dramatically. He became a soldier of fortune and a pirate. He continued his successful pirate career until 1217 when he was defeated in the battle of Sandwich and beheaded by King Henry III. Although he was well known for his thievery, there is no record that Eustace ever gave to the poor. Another Robin Hood candidate is found in a record from 1225, which lists a "Robert Hod, fugitive" who had chattels worth thirty-two sous and six deniers. The same outlaw turns up in entries for later years, once under the nickname Hobbehod. Some scholars believe this was the same man known as Robert of Wetherby, described as an "outlaw and evildoer of our land." Records show he was hunted down and hung by a chain. In 1852, clergyman Joseph Hunter published a book in which he recounted the existence of a real man named Robyn Hood who served as a porter in the court of King Edward II for seven months in 1324. The book suggested that this was the same man recorded as "Robert Hood" of Wakefield, Yorkshire in 1316. Wakefield is close to the home of the legendary Robin Hood. In addition, Robert had a wife named Matilda, which two Elizabethan plays listed as the real name of Maid Marian. Hunter's theory is that Robert Hood took part in a rebellion against King Edward II led by Thomas of Lancaster in 1322. This was how Robert or Robyn became an outlaw. The second part of the story is pure speculation, however. There are no records that indicate that Robert Hood or Robyn Hood were the same man nor that either man was a criminal. One of these real historical figures may have been the prototype of the legendary character. On the other hand, in the words of the *Encyclopedia Britannica,* "None of the various claims identifying Robin Hood with a particular historical figure has gained much support, and the outlaw's existence may never have been anything but legendary."

Hooligan, Patrick

Patrick Hooligan was the best known member of an Irish family living in London. The family, it was said, was rowdy and they often caused trouble in their neighborhood. Patrick was especially notorious for his bad behavior. He was a sometime bouncer and thief who ended his life in prison after killing a policeman. His exploits became the subject of Clarence Rook's 1899 book, *The Hooligan Nights.* "The man must have had a forceful personality," he wrote of Patrick Hooligan. "A fascination which elevated him into a type. It was doubtless the combination of skill and strength, a certain exuberance of lawlessness, an utter absence of scruple in his dealings, which marked him out as a leader among men." Maybe it was the sound of his name, or the simple need for a descriptive word that his name was able to fill, but Hooligan quickly entered the English language. According to *The Oxford English Dictionary*, the word "hooligan" started to appear in London police-court reports in the summer of 1898. Within a week the papers were using such words as "Hooliganism," "hooliganesque," "Hooliganic," and the verb "to hooligan." It was the subject of a song, "The Hooligans," and a comic strip about a simple-minded hobo called "Happy Hooligan." It quickly found its way into literature. Because of its connotations, the name Hooligan, according to a researcher in the 1970s, is extinct. Most people with that name changed it to Holohan, Holland, or Nolan. Other once-proud names have suffered similar fates. As reported in *The Name's Familiar*, the family of French physician Joseph Guillotin (who championed but did not invent the device that was named for him) petitioned the government to change the name of the machine. When their petition was not granted they changed their name instead. Many relatives of the Civil War general Joseph Hooker (whose troops' personal habits helped popularize the word "hooker" for "professional" women) have also changed their names. Recently, according to Paul Dickson's *What's in a Name?* a family that signed its letter "Respectable Hookers" wrote to Ann Landers asking people to stop using their name in reference to prostitutes. The columnist replied, "I hate to be pessimistic, but I see no hope for your crusade." He also records the tale of a man named Archie Outlaw who petitioned a New York court for a name change when he was charged with selling heroin. Outlaw felt he couldn't get a fair trial with his last name. The court granted his petition. He changed his name to Simmons—and then pled guilty. A similar case involved a man who identified himself as Darryl Wayne Thief. He was appearing in court, charged with arson. One of the court officers was skeptical about his name. Thief finally admitted he had given a false name. As it turns out, his real name was Crook, but he had changed it to Thief because he thought Crook gave people the wrong impression. Author Vladimir Nabokov told *Life Magazine* in 1964, "It is odd, and probably my fault, that no people seem to name their daughter

Lolita anymore. I have heard of young female poodles being given that name since 1956, but of no human beings." This author personally recalls a conversation between two people who were trying to determine another man's age. "He must have been born before World War II," they decided, "because since the war there have been no Adolphs." The name Hitler also took a hit. Before Hitler became chancellor of Germany in 1933, there were twenty-two families named Hitler or Hittler listed in the New York telephone directories. By the end of the war there were none. Ironically, most of the former American Hitlers were Jewish. In 1998, the Wolf Files on ABCnews.com told the story of one stubborn Adolf Hittler who was alive and well and living in Austria. The then-sixty-one-year-old retired school-bus driver said he was often teased about his name, but he did not change it because he thought it would be an insult to his parents. The first name Judas, once a common and respected name (there were three Judases besides Iscariot in the Bible), has also virtually disappeared. In case you were wondering if there was a Mr. Hoodlum, the answer is maybe. According to *The Oxford English Dictionary*, "The name originated in San Francisco around 1870-1872 and began to excite attention elsewhere in the U.S. about 1877 by which time its origin was lost and many fictitious stories, concocted to account for it, were current in the newspapers." One of the more entertaining of these stories comes from John Bartlett, who reported, without any evidence, that in 1871 a newspaper reporter was assigned to cover the crimes of a gang leader named Muldoon. Out of fear for his safety, the reporter changed the spelling of the name by writing it backwards. A printer who read the *N* in Noodlum as an *H* accidentally created the word "hoodlum."

Hoosier, Samuel

It is possible that a man named Samuel Hoosier was the first Indiana Hoosier. *The Dictionary of Historical Allusions & Eponyms,* by Dorothy Auchter, says, Hoosier contracted Indiana laborers to work on the Louisville and Portland Canal. The workers came to be known as "Hoosier's men." This is only one of a number of theories as to the origin of the term, however. Another theory is that the word derives from "who's there," something backwoods folks would shout when city folks came knocking on the door. Yet another theory is that it comes from an old English dialect word, "hoozer," which referred to anything big. In America, big frontiersmen, the type of people who populated Indiana in the 1800s, came to be known as Hoosiers. Auchter, however, favors the explanation that it derived from "hoojee," meaning a dirty or vagrant person. Eventually the country people adopted the term for themselves and it evolved into Hoosier.

Horch, August

August Horch was born October 12, 1868, in Winningen, Germany. As a young man he was an apprentice to a blacksmith. Later, he attended engineering school in Mittwalda. In 1896 he signed on as an engineer with Carl Benz, who was then one of the most influential automakers in the world. After only three years with Benz, Horch decided to try running his own company. He left his position as manager of motor construction at Benz and founded August Horch and Cie in Cologne. Within a year he had built his first car. By 1908, his business was turning out more than one hundred automobiles a year. But Horch had begun his enterprise with more enthusiasm than accounting knowledge, and financial difficulties in 1909 forced him to sell the company that bore his name. He started over. This time, however, he did not have the right to produce cars under the name Horch. He decided to dub his new venture with the Latin translation of his name. In English, Horch means "listen" or "hear." In Latin that translates to *Audi*. In 1998, *USA Today* reported that Volkswagen was considering reintroducing the Horch name to the car-buying public. The name would grace a new line of luxury automobiles. The name is well known in Europe, if not America. The main drawback to the name, *USA Today* reported, was that Adolf Hitler favored Horch sedans and was often pictured riding in them. "That's not a great selling point," said Garel Rhys, professor at Cardiff University in Wales.

Horner, Jack

Jack Horner was a steward to the abbot of Glastonbury during the reign of Henry VIII. As the story goes, Horner delivered the deeds to the king at the dissolution of the monasteries. One version holds that Jack Horner was sent as a courier with the deeds concealed in a pie. He lifted the corner of the crust and pulled out a "plum"—the deed to the manor of Mells, which is still owned by Horner's descendents. Barry Fowler, chairman of the parish council of Kilmersdon, England, home of *Jack and Jill*, put it this way in an interview with National Public Radio: "Jack Horner was by no means the likely guy to inherit the money or to inherit the estate. But we understand that there was an argument between the more important members—the members of the family that were likely to inherit—and he just sat in the corner. And having been a bad boy, I think, perhaps the black heart of the family, he ended up getting the inheritance." Most likely, Horner achieved this through deception of some sort. In any case, he was immortalized by *Mother Goose* in the rhyme *"Little Jack Horner*/sat in a corner/eating his Christmas pie./He put in his thumb,/pulled out a plum,/and said, 'What a good boy am I!'"* Katherine Elwes Thomas, author of the 1930 book *The Real Personages of Mother Goose,* speculates that Jack Horner was also the Jack of the rhyme *"The House That Jack Built."* Her source for this information was the Horner family. *The Oxford Dictionary of Nursery Rhymes,* on the other hand, does not connect the two Jacks. "The House That Jack Built," it says, is more than two hundred years old and is one of the most parodied of any nursery rhyme. At least two entire publications were devoted to its meaning, but, editors Iona and Peter Opie report, "facts to go on are meagre." As for the Jack who jumped over the candlestick, no one is sure who he was, if in fact there was a "Jack" at all. What we do know is that the rhyme refers to an old fortune-telling game. In England it was once a Saint Catherine's Day tradition for people to jump a candlestick for luck. A lighted candle was placed on the floor. When a person jumped over it, if he didn't blow it out, he was supposed to have good luck for the rest of the year.

Hubert

One Good Friday, sometime around the year 700, Hubert, a hanger-on at the court of King Pepin, decided to skip church and indulge his passion for hunting instead. In the woods he stopped in his tracks when he came across a stag with a crucifix between its antlers. Hubert's wife died soon afterwards in childbirth and Hubert was wracked with guilt. He placed himself and his new son in the service of Saint Lambert. Lambert was assassinated and Hubert succeeded him. He died at Tervueren on May 30, 727 following injuries incurred while hunting. Hubert became the patron saint of hunters and dogs. Centuries later, a satirical character appeared, modeled on the saint. *Mother Hubbard* appeared for the first time in 1590 in *Mother Hubbard's Tale.* The story was familiar to a woman named Sarah Martin, who, in 1805, published a poem with the character's name. "Old Mother Hubbard/went to the cupboard/to fetch her poor dog a bone/but when she came there/the cupboard was bare/and so the poor dog had none," it began. Scholars believe Martin based her immortal rhyme on a poem that had been published two years earlier, *"Old Dame Trot."* Judge for yourself: "Old Dame Trot/some cold fish had got,/which for pussy/she kept in store./When she looked there was none./The cold fish had gone./For puss had been there before."

I/J

Iams, Paul

Paul Iams first made headlines in his native Dayton, Ohio when he was a student at Steele High School in 1933. That year he became the first player from Dayton to win the state tennis championship. After graduating, he went to Ohio State, where he lettered three years on the tennis team. He was studying business but said he "specialized in tennis." After earning a marketing degree in 1937, he went to work as "an ordinary laborer" at Procter and Gamble. He joined the navy after the Pearl Harbor attack but he was sent back to the States when he caught yellow fever. He spent the rest of the war stationed in San Francisco. His first shot at entrepreneurship was the E.Z. Orange Soft Drink Company based in Minneapolis. It was short-lived. When it failed to catch on, he returned to Ohio, where he worked at a mink ranch and for his father's feed store in Tipp City. During this period Iams taught himself all he could about animal nutrition. Most pet food at the time was not very nutritious. The top supermarket brands competed mostly on cost. Iams saw an opportunity. He would develop a premium pet food. Instead of trying to get supermarkets to buy it, he would go to veterinarians, breeders, and pet stores. "In hindsight, I find it amazing that Ralston Purina and others didn't spot this market, but none of them did," marketing expert Sam Hill told *Fortune* magazine in 1997. "A couple of guys in Dayton outsmarted a whole bunch of very sophisticated marketers." Iams chose the word "Eukanuba" as the name for his dog food. The expression was used in the postwar years, popularized by musician Hoagy Carmichael. Pronounced

181

"U-kanuba," it was a favorite expression of one of Paul Iams' friends. He usually used it when he saw an attractive woman walking by, a variation on "hubba hubba." Even though the brand was not carried in most grocery stores and it cost about 25 percent more than supermarket brands, it struck a chord with consumers. Gourmet pet food is now the fastest-growing segment of the $10.1 billion U.S. pet-food industry. In 1970, Clayton ("Clay") Mathile joined the company as an executive. He quickly rose to the post of general manager. Company legend has it that Iams chose Mathile as his successor when Mathile beat him in a poker game. Another addition to the Iams staff was Kersee, a golden retriever, who was made "vice-president of canine communications." The dog was made the official greeter at the headquarters. In 1982, with annual sales of $10 million, Iams sold the company to Mathile and retired to Sun City West, Arizona. Under Mathile's leadership, Iams grew. By 1999, Iams had more than two thousand employees. It marketed its products in seventy-seven countries resulting in sales of about $800 million. Iams was purchased by Paul Iams' first employer, Procter and Gamble, in August 1999 for $20.5 billion.

Ibn-Ziyad, Tariq

After the sudden death of King Wittiza in Spain, a rebellious baron named Roderic seized the throne and proclaimed himself king. The Iberian Peninsula was in great turmoil. In the north, the rebel Basques threatened to break away from Spain and create their own nation. In the hopes of keeping peace, church leaders reluctantly gave their blessing to Roderic's coronation. King Wittiza's sons appealed to the Muslims of North Africa for assistance against Roderic. The Arab commander Musa, however, saw it as an opportunity for conquest. The first Muslim incursion into Iberia was in 710, when a small reconnaissance force landed at the southernmost point of the peninsula. The following year a former slave, Tariq ibn-Ziyad, commanding an army of 7,000 Berbers from Morocco, landed near a huge rock at the entrance of the Mediterranean. As soon as his men were safely on shore, he burned the fleet that had transported them and gave his troops a rousing speech in

which he told them that there was now no option of retreat—
they had nowhere to go but forward.

> Oh my warriors, whither would you flee? Behind you is the sea,
> before you, the enemy. You have left now only the hope of your
> courage and your constancy. Your enemy is before you, pro-
> tected by an innumerable army; he has men in abundance, but
> you, as your only aid, have your own swords, and, as your only
> chance for life, such chance as you can snatch from the hands
> of your enemy. If the absolute want to which you are reduced is
> prolonged ever so little, if you delay to seize immediate success,
> your good fortune will vanish, and your enemies, whom your
> very presence has filled with fear, will take courage. Put far from
> you the disgrace from which you flee in dreams, and attack this
> monarch who has left his strongly fortified city to meet you.
> Here is a splendid opportunity to defeat him, if you will consent
> to expose yourselves freely to death.

In fact, the Moors met with little resistance. Roderic had made
many enemies in Spain, including persecuted Jews. Tariq's
fighters established control over the coastline. Roderic, distracted by fighting with the Basques, took some time to re-
spond to the invasion. He finally returned to the south with a
small band of men. They were easily overwhelmed and defeated in an ambush. Roderic was killed on July 19, 711. The rock
where Tariq's men landed was dubbed "Jabal Tariq," or Tariq's
Mount, which Christians later mangled into *Gibraltar.*

Ivo of Kermartin

There are two popular rhymes that mention "Saint Ives." The
less familiar of the two in this country is a French verse: "Saint
Yves was a lawyer, and a Breton as well/But not a liar, strange
to tell." The rhyme refers to Ivo of Kermartin, who was, as it
suggests, a lawyer in Brittany. He offered his services free to the
poor and oppressed. For his selfless giving he was sainted and
is remembered as the patron saint of Brittany, judges, lawyers,
and orphans. The other verse that mentions Saint Ives begins,
"As I was going to Saint Ives, I met a man with seven wives."
This rhyme refers to the town in Cornwall. It was named for a
different saint, a woman known as Saint Ia, Ja, or Hya. Little is
recorded about her life. She was a noble Irish virgin. Legend

has it that she went down to the seashore to depart for Cornwall from her native Ireland with other saints. They were afraid that she was too young for such a hazardous journey, so they left without her. She was frightened and upset to be left alone. Just then, she noticed a little leaf floating on the water. She touched it with the rod she was carrying to see if it would sink. It did not. Instead, it grew big enough for her to sit on it. She used the leaf to float across the Channel, arriving before the others. The legend goes on to say she founded the church of Saint Ives, which is dedicated to her.

Jacks, David

David Jacks was born in Scotland and arrived in New York to start a new life in the early 1800s. He followed the '49ers out to California, where he sold dry goods to gold miners. He finally settled in Monterey, where he became one of the richest men and largest landowners in the area. There he learned about a creamy white cheese that had been introduced to the region by Spanish missionaries. The local farmers called it "queso del pais" or "country cheese." Jacks added it to the line of goods in his shop and, in 1882, he started to ship it from his dairy to San Francisco. Before shipping he branded it with the city of origin and his last name. People began to ask for the cheese in that way and eventually the s on Jacks was dropped. It was thereafter known as *Monterey Jack*. The California Milk Advisory Board calls it "the most significant popular cheese created in the U.S." At least one-third of California's cheese makers produce Monterey Jack or variations like pepper jack. David Jacks, himself, was not as popular. He acquired much of his land by lending money to people who were not likely to be able to repay him. He would then quickly foreclose on their property. When he died, his obituary in one San Francisco newspaper called him "one of the most hated men in the Monterey county." On the other hand, Jacks gave generously to Stanford University and the University of the Pacific. He was most proud of his fifty years as a Sunday school teacher and boasted he was "the oldest Sunday-school teacher in continuous service in the state."

Jaeger, Gustav

Gustav Jaeger was a professor of zoology at Stuttgart University when he published an influential book called *Health Culture* in the mid-1800s. The book theorized that people would be healthier if they dressed in clothing made entirely of animal hair, especially wool. The idea was that such garments would keep the body at its natural temperature while linen and cotton garments would bring on disease. It was claimed that even including a linen label in an otherwise woolen suit could give the wearer a sore throat. In the summer, many Jaegerites, clad entirely in wool, would drop from exhaustion. The treatment for such a spell was to cover the victim with a woolen blanket to prevent chills. One man who was influenced by Jaeger's theories was Lewis Tomalin, a London accountant, who came across a copy of *Health Culture* in 1880 and translated it into English. Interest in the wool theory grew in England, where there was a need for appropriate attire. Tomalin opened the first *Jaeger shop* to meet the need. He began by selling woolen underwear in 1884. In the 1900s he expanded the line to include dresses, skirts, and sweaters. In 1950 the company finally broke away from its original purpose and added natural fibers, synthetics, and blends to its clothing line.

James II

James, the second surviving son of Charles I and Henrietta Maria, was born October 14, 1633. He was named Duke of York. After Charles I was executed, the family went into exile in the Netherlands. James joined the French army in April 1652 and served in four campaigns under the French general Vicomte de Turenne. When his brother, Charles II, concluded an alliance with Spain against France in 1656, James reluctantly changed sides and commanded the right wing of the Spanish army. In 1660, Charles II agreed to limitations of his power if he was crowned king. Now back in power in England, James was named lord high admiral in charge of the navy and, by extension, the colonies in the New World. He gave the orders to take New Amsterdam from the Dutch. The English marched in, drove the Dutch out, and renamed all the land-marks they passed. In 1664 New Amsterdam became New York for the Duke of York. Farther up the Hudson River, an outpost known as Fort Orange became Albany for James, whose Scottish title was Duke of Albany even though there is no British place of that name. Albany became the capital of New York state in 1797. Albany, Georgia was named for Albany, New York. In fact, there are Albanys in about twenty states. Trivia question for collective-noun buffs: People from Boston are called Bostonians. People from New York are called New Yorkers. What are people from Albany, New York called? Answer: Albanians. Residents of nearby Troy, New York are called Trojans. (For the rest of James II's story *see* William III.)

Jantzen, Carl

In 1910, Danish-born Carl Jantzen and his friends John and Roy Zehntbauer, all in their early twenties, decided to go into business together. They opened the Portland Knitting Company in Oregon. The company used hand-operated machines to make the regular selection of knitted items—sweaters, gloves, scarves, and socks. The business limped along for another three years until a member of the Portland rowing club asked for pair of wool trunks to wear while working out on wintry waters. Carl Jantzen fulfilled his request, sewing the woolen trunks with a machine that normally would make sweater cuffs. The Zehntbauers and Jantzen decided to manu-facture swimsuits of the same material. The suits weighed two pounds when dry and eight pounds when wet. The members of the club liked to swim in them anyway. The partners decided it might be a wise move to market the garments commercially. They became the first to market a stretchable swimsuit. The suits sold very well and people around the country started referring to them as "Jantzens." Thus, in 1918, the business name was changed to *Jantzen Knitting Mills*. Two years later they adopted a new symbol to reflect their new product line. She was the "Diving Girl," a drawing of a woman in a modest red swimsuit with long stockings. It was first used as a catalog illus-tration and then in the company's first national advertisements in *Vogue* and *Life*. Quaint and tame by today's standards, the Diving Girl was a racy emblem in the 1920s. Her appeal became clear when a young man stopped by the shop and asked for a stack of catalogs. He explained that he had pasted the picture of the red diving girl on the windshield of his car and now all his friends wanted to do the same. The idea of giving away car windshield stickers with the icon was born. The emblem was so popular that the company gave out 10 million stickers in the twenties. A number of states considered the stickers a nuisance and tried to block them. They refused to grant a driver's license to anyone whose car sported the sticker. In October 1928, Jantzen Knitting Mills became publicly owned. Carl Jantzen died a year later of a heart attack. His name lives on in one of the most recognizable swimwear brand names.

Jefferies, Walter M.

Walter Matthew Jefferies, "Matt" to his friends, was the long-suffering set designer on the television series "Star Trek." Today "Star Trek" is considered to be one of television's classic shows. It has spawned conventions, spin-off series, films, and some of the most devoted fans in the galaxy. It's hard to believe that in its original run the series never made it higher than number fifty-two in the ratings. It was consistently beaten by competitors "Iron Horse" and "Mr. Terrific." Always teetering on the verge of cancellation, "Star Trek" suffered budget cuts again and again. One of the hardest hit by the cuts was Matt Jefferies. He had to create realistic-looking alien planets and spaceships on a shoestring budget. Nothing could be wasted. The wall of Kirk's cabin in one episode would be redecorated to serve as the wall of Spock's cabin in the next. His plastic, wood, and steel model for the starship *Enterprise* was eleven feet in length and weighed 200 pounds. (The registry number on the original *Enterprise*, NCC-1701, incidentally, was based on that of Jefferies' 1935 Waco airplane.) The model cost $600 in 1964 money. This did not leave much in the budget for constructing a shuttlecraft. The result was one of "Star Trek"'s most memorable features, the transporter beam. Using a special effect to dematerialize and rematerialize future travelers was simply less expensive than another model. Another challenge came in an early script that would show the ship's engineer, Mr. Scott, hard at work on the ship's interior. With set space limited, Jefferies created a tall cylinder that could be rolled out of the way, then rolled back in as needed. The crawlspace came to be known in the script as the "Jefferies tube." The ships of "Star Trek: The Next Generation" and "Voyager" feature their own Jefferies tubes—now as much a part of the Trek lexicon as "Klingon," "warp speed," and "Borg." Jefferies was not the only staff member whose name was included in the series. "Star Trek" is full of inside jokes and references to friends. Early in his career, series creator Gene Roddenberry went by the pen name "Robert Wesley"—Wesley is his middle name. One episode of the original series featured a Commodore Robert Wesley who leads a squadron of starships against the *Enterprise*. "The Next Generation" character Wesley Crusher was also named for Roddenberry. One of the alien races in that series was the Bolians. They were named for director Cliff Bole. "Deep Space Nine" tipped its hat to the television series "Cheers" by including a character that seemed to reside at Quark's bar. The character was named Morn, an anagram of Norm. Another television series that includes frequent references to crew members, and has a loyal enough audience to catch some of them, is "The X-Files". The names of the main characters, Fox Mulder and Dana Sculley, come from series creator Chris Carter's life. He had a boyhood friend named "Fox," and his mother's maiden name is Mulder. The character's birthday is October 13, which is a reference to the production company, Ten Thirteen Productions. That name, in turn, comes from Carter's own birthday. The name Sculley is a reference to one of Carter's favorite radio sportscasters, Vin Sculley. Finally, the highly observant "X-Files" fan will notice 11:21 often appears on clocks. November 21 is Carter's wife's birthday.

Jenkins, Robert

Most wars have been given fairly sensible names. There was the French Revolution, the War of 1812, the Spanish-American War, World War I, and then there was the War of Jenkins' Ear.

The war was sparked by an incident involving Robert Jenkins, the captain of a merchant vessel named the *Rebecca*. The ship was on a regular voyage between Jamaica and England on April 9, 1731 when it was boarded by a Spanish privateer, Captain Fandino. After he had pirated Jenkins' ship he lopped off one of the captain's ears. Jenkins reported the event to the king when he returned to England. At the time, however, the hostilities that had raged for centuries between Spain and England had temporarily subsided. The king did not want to rock the boat so nothing was done. Seven years later, however, tensions mounted again between the nations. The British Parliament desperately wanted an excuse to wage war on Spain. That was when someone remembered Jenkins' missing ear. He was called before the House of Commons to tell the story of Fandino's crimes. He even produced the severed ear itself. The public was duly outraged and England declared war on Spain before the year was out. The War of Jenkins' Ear lasted until 1744, with no great victories on either side.

Jergens, Andrew

Andrew Jergens was a young Dutch immigrant. Upon his arrival in the United States, he found work as a lumberjack. By the time he was twenty, Jergens had managed to save $5,000, dollars which he used to buy a small soap business in Cincinnati, Ohio. He aptly named it *The Jergens Soap Company*. His first product was a coconut-oil soap, specially designed to perform in hard water. By 1894 he'd sold enough of it to bring his brothers, Herman and Al, into the business, now named *Andrew Jergens and Company*. Seven years later, Jergens decided to expand by buying two cosmetics and perfume operations, John H. Woodbury Company and the Robert Eastman Company. One of the Eastman company's chemists had developed a smooth white lotion that had not yet been put on the market. It was first sold under the name "Jergens Benzoin and Almond Lotion Compound." Without any advertising, the compound became the company's biggest seller. With a name change to the simpler *Jergen's Lotion*, it became the best-selling hand lotion in the United States.

Joachim

Little is known about Saint Joachim, except that he lived in Nazareth with his wife, Anne, and that the couple had a daughter, Mary, who would grow up to be the mother of Jesus. A mining town in what was once Bohemia was named Sankt Jochimsthal (the English equivalent would be Saint Jochimstown). The Count of Schick, who owned a huge estate in the town, began minting coins in 1519. The silver coins had a picture of Saint Joachim on the front and were called "Jochimsthalers." This proved to be a bit too much to say on a daily basis—"that will be twelve Jochimsthalers, please"—so people started calling them simply "thalers." In northern German, Dutch, and Danish dialects, the term was pronounced "dalers." The thaler became the main German monetary unit until it was replaced by the mark in 1873. The English called the currency a "daller," which evolved into dollar. By the time they were calling it a dollar, the English had forgotten where the word came from. They were applying it to any foreign coin, especially Spanish pieces of eight. The pieces were commonly seen in America before the Revolution, when currencies from other nations were used along with British pounds. As part of their break with England, the Continental Congress chartered the Bank of North America in Philadelphia as the nation's first "real" bank in 1781. Four years later they "resolved that the money unit of the U.S.A. be one dollar (Spanish)." At that time, private banknote companies printed a variety of paper bills. It would not be until 1792 that the first official American dollars were minted. Coins worth $2.50, $5, and $10 were also minted. The paper money was printed during the Civil War. "Greenbacks" appeared for the first time in 1862. The slang term "buck," meaning "dollar," goes back to the frontier days, when colonists traded deerskins for goods and services.

K

Kashio, Tadao

Tadao Kashio was born in November of 1917 in Nangoku City, Japan. His parents were young farmers whose tiny rice field did not produce enough to feed the growing family. To make ends meet, Tadao's father, Shigeru, would sell the rice they produced and buy cheaper rice to feed the family. To bring in additional income, the family dug up clay from the soil and made ceramic foot warmers and piggy banks. The foot warmers were especially useful, as they sold best during the winter months when the farm was not producing. The family stayed on their ancestors' farm until 1922 when the Great Kanto Earthquake devastated Tokyo. About one hundred thousand people were killed in the disaster. After the quake caused its damage, fires swept through the city, reducing much of it to ash and rubble. The only positive thing to come of it was that it created work for carpenters, who were desperately needed to rebuild. Shigeru Kashio, although conflicted about leaving the land of his ancestors, decided to take advantage of the opportunity. The family, which now numbered four thanks to the birth of a daughter, Sadako, left their home on October 30, 1923. Shigeru faced the house for the last time, bowed his head, and apologized for leaving the land, asking his ancestors for forgiveness. Another son, Toshio, was born the following June. Toshio was a quiet boy. Asked what he wanted to be when he grew up, he said "an inventor" to the amusement of the adults. His brother Tadao found it difficult to adapt to life in Tokyo. He would later recall:

I could only speak the Tosa dialect. I couldn't understand what the teacher and classmates were saying. Some of the kids called me a "hayseed" but it didn't matter because I couldn't understand what they were calling me anyway.

His teacher was not aware of the depth of Tadao's confusion until one day the boy blurted out, "I can't understand what you're saying." The teacher took special care to make the lessons understandable to the boy after that and life improved. As reconstruction work fell off, the Kashios converted part of their home into a store, selling socks and gloves to neighbors. Another brother, Kazuo, was born in September 1928. Kazuo would grow to be a gregarious, popular boy who loved sports. Tadao graduated from the lower level of elementary school in 1929. Another boy, Yukio, was born in November 1930 as Tadao was graduating from the upper level and preparing to enter the professional world. "The toys that were handed down to him were invariably broken," Tadao Kashio wrote. "He did his best to fix them so he could play with them." After his graduation, Tadao got a job at a company that recycled oil cans, then with a company that made medals for military uniforms. His employer was impressed with his performance and introduced him to a manager at the Enomoto Manufacturing Company. At the age of fourteen, Tadao went to work there with a variety of machine tools. One of the Enomotos, Hiroshi, decided to set up his own business, and he asked Tadao Kashio to take part in his new venture. Because the nation was suffering an economic depression, Tadao took his work seriously. This impressed his employer, who suggested Tadao go to trade school and offered to pay him overtime for the time he spent in school. Tadao attended the Waseda's Worker's School. He worked by day in Enomoto's factory and studied by night. Sleep was a luxury. Meanwhile, the Kashio family grew with the addition of a daughter in 1933. In 1936, Hiroshi Enomoto was drafted and died in battle, putting an end to the educational arrangement and eventually the Enomoto Manufacturing Company itself. That year, Tadao went for his military physical. Always a sickly boy, he did not pass. He stayed behind while most of his friends became soldiers. Over the next several years, Tadao worked for a number of companies that made military equipment, parts, and munitions. Since he had never finished his education, Tadao's prospects for advancement were limited. He decided the only way to advance was to start his own business. During the war, however, government regulations made it difficult to start new companies. In 1942, Tadao made an agreement with the Yoshioka company. Since there was a shortage of labor, Tadao would train Yoshioka's employees; in return, Mr. Yoshioka would help Tadao to set up a company. Officially it would be a subsidiary of Yoshioka. After Toshio graduated from the Tokyo Electric School, he got a job as an engineer with the Tokyo Electric Telecommunication Engineering Bureau. At night, he would help his brother. Kazuo also helped, even though he was still a student. In April 1945, an air raid on Tokyo destroyed the operation, leaving only two badly charred lathes. Tadao fixed them and they were up and running again by June. Two weeks later, the war ended. Up to this point Tadao's company had produced nothing but military equipment. He started making pots and pans and was surprised to find he could not keep up with the demand. In April 1946, he'd sold enough of them to start his own, independent company, which he named Kashio Seisakujo. Toshio, the inventor, left his job to join his brother and suggested they try to develop a new product, an electric calculator. Soon after, Kazuo joined the company, then Yukio, who had studied mechanical engineering at Nippon University, joined. It took them seven years to develop Japan's first calculator. In 1956, they were finally ready to demonstrate their invention to potential investors. When they brought the large device to the Haneda airport, the airline staff ordered them to dismantle it. When they arrived at their destination, even though they worked all night, they were not able to put it back together so that it would work. The demonstration was a failure, but the setback was only temporary. They were able to find an investor shortly thereafter and in 1957 they established a company to develop and manufacture the calculators. Since they intended to compete in the international marketplace they changed the spelling of their name to *Casio Computer Company*. The calculators were a huge success. From there the company branched out into digital watches and musical instruments. Today, the company is known as Japan's number-one watchmaker. It is known for its calculators, office computers, pagers, answering machines, and laptop musical keyboards. Tadao Kashio died in 1993 at the age of seventy-five. His three younger brothers still run Casio.

Kidd, William

The legendary pirate Captain Kidd was a real historical figure, and in fact, he was a reluctant pirate. He was born in 1645 in Greenock, Scotland, the son of a Presbyterian minister. He grew up to be a respected ship owner. By the mid-1690s, Kidd and his family were living in an elegant home on Pearl Street in Manhattan. There, he was a respected member of his church and passed the collection plate on Sundays. He was hired as a privateer—a sailor who attacked pirate ships in exchange for a share of the recovered bounty—by the English East India Company in 1695. Kidd set sail on a ship named the *Adventure Galley*. Before heading off in search of pirates, he loaned equipment from his ship to help in the building of Trinity Church on Wall Street, which opened in 1698 under a royal grant. To this day, Kidd's name is engraved on pew number sixteen: "Captain William Kidd, Commander *Adventure Galley.*" After a year at sea, he hadn't nabbed a single pirate. His crew, which had not been paid, was near mutiny. With no other choice, Kidd turned pirate. He allowed the men to plunder one ship. When that proved successful they wanted to rob another. The crew threatened mutiny, and he let them rule. When they finally came across an actual pirate ship the men left Kidd and joined the pirate crew. Kidd was shocked when he was arrested on his arrival in New York. He was extradited to England, found guilty, and sentenced to hang on May 23, 1701. When the floor fell out from under him, the rope broke and he survived. He was carried back up and hanged again. The second time Kidd was dead.

Kimberly, John

Perhaps the most amazing thing about *Kimberly-Clark* is that such a huge corporation could make its fortune selling three products that were originally thought too delicate to discuss. The Kimberly-Clark story began in 1872 when four young men, John A. Kimberly, Havilah Babcock, Charles B. Clark, and Frank C. Shattuck, invested $7,500 each in a Neenah, Wisconsin paper mill. Since the next closest paper mill was 300 miles away, they believed they could capture the market of paper for the new western newspapers. Frank Shattuck and Havilah Babcock were the salesmen of the group, while Kimberly and Clark handled the management duties. By 1880, the company had grown to the point that the partners were able to incorporate. They chose the name Kimberly & Clark Company. They bought land along the Fox River and built an improved mill, around which they also constructed a town including company housing and a hotel. The company grew and prospered, selling newsprint, wrapping paper, wallpaper stock, and ledger paper to American companies. By 1906, three of the original founders had passed away, leaving only John Kimberly. The company was again reorganized and incorporated as the Kimberly-Clark Company. Kimberly gradually withdrew from an active role in the company but he kept the title of president until his death at age ninety on January 21, 1928. Meanwhile, the new company management had become convinced that the company's future lay in two new ways of processing wood. One made bleached paper, which could be used for magazines and catalogs; the other produced a fluffy cellulose product. The second product, known as Cellucotton, became indispensable during World War I. It was more absorbent than cotton and cheaper and more resistant to infection. It was therefore perfect for bandaging wounds. Thin sheets of the material were also used as gas-mask filters. By 1917, Kimberly-Clark had three mills turning out nothing but Cellucotton and it had to build two more to keep up with the demand. When the war ended, however, the company found itself with warehouses full of the stuff. They certainly weren't willing to start another war to get rid of it. One solution came from nurses who had been stationed overseas. When they saw how absorbent the material was they logically chose it for handmade disposable sanitary napkins. This was not due to any great innovation on their part. For centuries women had been using whatever absorbent materials were available to keep themselves clean during menstruation. Linen cloths, rags, and towels were popular solutions. The cloths would be washed and reused. Of course, menstruation was so taboo that this process was carried out with great secrecy. The expression about not "airing your dirty linen in public" refers to the telltale stained cloths. Clearly there was a need for a product that was more absorbent than linen, and that removed the embarrassment of airing the dirty linens. The problem was, how do you advertise a product that no one is supposed to talk about? Afraid that being in the sanitary-napkin business would reflect badly on their other products, the corporation first formed another company, International Cellucotton Corporation, specifically to handle the delicate product. They first chose the name Cellunap, for Cellucotton Napkins, but decided against it because "an article of this nature should carry a trade name which in no way reflects its purpose." They hired an advertising agency, which came up with the name Kotex, for cotton and textile. The firm scripted ads that coyly avoided any reference to the purpose of the product. For example, "To Save Men's Lives Science Discovered Kotex (Cotton Textile)—A Wonderful, Sanitary Absorbent." Even so, most magazines, including top women's magazines like *Ladies' Home Journal,* refused to run the ads. Since the few stores that were willing to stock Kotex hid it in the back room, and most women were too embarrassed to ask for it, there would probably not have been many sales even if the ads had run. After many frustrating attempts to change public perceptions the company hit upon an idea. They created a fictional nurse, Ellen J. Buckland, to answer women's letters about "women's greatest hygiene problem." "Buckland" sent out Kotex samples and booklets providing information on menstruation. At the same time Kotex told retailers to display the product in unmarked packages and to leave a small box where women could deposit the payment without having to face a storekeeper. Once the company had found a nonthreatening way to get the word out about their

product women started to buy it from pharmacies that offered
home delivery and from vending machines especially. By 1945,
the majority of American women were using commercially
made pads instead of the homemade variety. As for the
Cellucotton sheets, the company was not as squeamish in its
plans for them. They decided to release them to the public as
a cold-cream and makeup remover called Kleenex Kerchiefs.
Until then, women had traditionally used a cloth towel to
remove cosmetics, which was usually hung on the back of the
bathroom door. Kleenex never sold well on cosmetics counters
but the few people who did buy it wrote to the company to tell
them how wonderful the sheets were for another, less glamorous purpose, blowing their noses. Instead of carrying the
same cloth handkerchief all day, the customers were happy to
have a paper sheet they could dispose of after use. Kimberly-
Clark responded by printing advertisements that polled customers to find out if they used the kerchiefs for makeup or as
disposable handkerchiefs. The majority of respondents chose
the nose and the company changed its advertising slogan to
"Don't put a cold in your pocket." Kleenex became so ubiqui-
tous that the company's lawyers have continuously had to battle to keep the trade name from becoming a generic substitute
for the word "tissue." In the 1980s Kimberly-Clark expanded its
product line even more, adding Huggies and Pull-Ups diapers
and Depends incontinence products. The company did away
with another longstanding taboo by advertising Depends on
television. In 1995, Kimberly-Clark merged with Scott Paper.
Scott had also come up against public sensibilities when it started selling another unmentionable product—toilet paper—in
1879. Over the years Kimberly-Clark has grown from its initial
4 employees to 55,000 in thirty-eight countries by selling the
things that were once improper to mention.

Knight, Charles Landon

Charles Landon Knight bought the *Akron Beacon Journal* in
1903. Upon his death in 1933, his son John became the editor
and publisher. John Knight did not, initially, want to be associated with the paper. When he first wrote for the *Journal* as a

sportswriter he had used a pseudonym because, as he put it, "I was ashamed of the stuff." He went on to win a Pulitzer Prize, however, for his "Editor's Notebook" column. In 1937, he and his brother, James, bought the *Miami Herald,* and James became editor and publisher. The brothers went on to buy papers in Detroit, Chicago, North Carolina, Georgia, Kentucky, and Philadelphia. Business success, however, did not prevent John Knight from suffering more than his share of personal tragedies. His first wife died eight years after their marriage in 1921. Their oldest son, John, Jr., was killed in action in Germany in 1945. Their youngest son, Frank, died three years later. Knight's grandson, John Knight III, was killed in 1975, stabbed to death while working on the *Philadelphia Daily News.* Ironically, he had written a letter about the Vietnam War five years earlier that had been printed in his grandfather's column in the Knight newspapers. "After more than six years of peaceful protests," he wrote, "kids are still being sent to their deaths in this senseless, unnecessary war." In 1974, the Knight Brothers merged with another newspaper chain, which had been started by a man named Herman Ridder. Ridder's first newspaper was the *Staats-Zeitung,* the leading German-language newspaper in the United States. After his death in 1915, Ridder's three sons, Bernard, Victor, and Joseph, took over the paper. They expanded the company by purchasing the *Journal of Commerce* in New York City and eighteen daily papers in places like Michigan, Indiana, Minnesota, South Dakota, Colorado, Washington State, and California. *Knight Ridder* is today the nation's second-largest newspaper publisher, with products in print and online. The company publishes thirty-one daily newspapers in twenty-eight U.S. markets, with a readership of 9.2 million daily and 13.1 million Sunday.

Knorr, Carl Heinrich

In 1838, Carl Heinrich Knorr built a factory in Heilbronn, Germany. The plant, which he ran with the help of his sons, dried chicory and manufactured various types of flour. The Knorrs eventually came to believe that convenience foods were the wave of the future. They introduced their first packaged soup mix in 1873. They soon expanded into bouillon cubes and other soup concentrates. The products were a hit in Germany and were soon exported to other European nations as well. In 1907, Switzerland set up its own factory to manufacture the foods. Two years later a plant opened in Austria. Two world wars kept the company from expanding to the rest of Europe until 1950, when Belgium opened a plant, followed by France in 1951, Italy in 1952, and Holland and Britain in 1957. By 1957 the little flour factory begun by Carl Heinrich Knorr was bringing in about $3.5 million. Knorr soup mixes were introduced to America in 1958 when the company became part of the Corn Products Company, which later evolved into Bestfoods.

Kreutzer, Rudolphe

Rudolphe Kreutzer was born in 1766 in Versailles to a German family. His father was a musician at the Royal Chapel. Kreutzer studied in Vienna and befriended Haydn. In Vienna, he was appointed conductor at the Imperial Theater. A prolific composer, he was most noted for his violin playing. One person who was inspired by it was Ludwig van Beethoven, who met Kreutzer in 1798. Beethoven dedicated his Piano and Violin Sonata in A Major, op. 47, to Kreutzer. It is now generally known as the *Kreutzer Sonata* and is considered by many to be Beethoven's finest violin sonata. One person who was not a fan of the sonata was Kreutzer. He never played it. Perhaps the British violinist George Bridgetower would have appreciated it more. The sonata had originally been dedicated to him, but Beethoven was fiercely moralistic about women. He heard Bridgetower make an off-color remark about a female friend of his and decided to change the dedication. Had Beethoven's work become known as the *Bridgetower* Sonata, perhaps Tolstoy would have written a novel by that name. Instead he wrote *The Kreutzer Sonata* in 1890. Kreutzer went on to serve as chamber musician to Napoleon and Louis XVIII. In 1998, a world record was set when a Stradivarius owned by Kreutzer fetched £947,500 ($1.6 million) at Christie's Auction House.

Kublai

Kublai, also spelled Khubilai, Kubilai, Koublai, and Kubla, was the Mongol emperor from 1215 to 1294. He founded the Yuan dynasty of China. In 1260 he succeeded his brother as khan of the empire that had been founded by their grandfather Jenghiz Khan. Marco Polo visited the Khan Kublai's capital at what is now Beijing. The historical figure's name found its way into *Purchas His Pilgrimage,* by Samuel Purchas. It was a 1613 survey of peoples and religions of the world. Poet Samuel Taylor Coleridge was an avid reader of such travel literature. In the summer of 1797, he was in ill health, so he took some prescribed opium and fell asleep while reading Purchas's book. He said the last sentence he recalled reading was: "Here the Khan Kubla commanded a palace to be built, and a stately garden thereunto. And thus ten miles of fertile ground were inclosed with a wall." The actual line containing a reference to Kubla Khan read, "In Xanadu did Cublai Can build a stately Palace, encompassing sixteene miles of plaine ground with a wall, wherein are fertile Meddowes, pleasant Springs, delightful Streames, and all sorts of beasts of chase and game, and in the middest thereof a sumptuous house of pleasure." The author fell asleep and dreamed a poem of 300 lines beginning with: "In Xanadu did Kubla Khan/A stately pleasure-dome decree." When he woke up he began scribbling them down. He had written down about 40 lines when there was a knock at the door. It was a "person on business from Porlock." Coleridge talked to him for an hour, and when he returned to his writing he could only remember another 14 lines. The rest "had passed away like the images on the surface of a stream into which a stone has been cast." He printed this explanation as a preface to the original manuscript of "Kubla Khan." Scholars continue to debate whether the poem really was a fragment or whether the poet imagined the story of the poem's composition as well.

L

La Vallière, Louise Françoise de La Baume Le Blanc de

Born in 1644, Louise Françoise de La Baume Le Blanc was a maid of honor to Louis XVI's sister-in-law, Henrietta of England. She became, in 1661, his first "maîtresse en titre," or official mistress. Louis, the Sun King, had married Princess Maria Theresa. It was not a marriage of love, but of politics. She was a member of the Spanish royal family. He had never seen her before their wedding night. Louise Françoise was only one of a string of royal mistresses. She bore Louis four children, two of whom died in infancy. Towards the end of their affair, in 1667, Louis made her a duchess and gave her the estate of Vaujours. The act officially legitimized their children. The duchess was much admired throughout Europe for her glamorous beauty and fashion sense. One of the fashions she introduced was an ornamental jeweled pendant worn on a chain around the neck. It is unclear how early she was identified as de La Vallière, but we do know that this necklace was dubbed the lavallière in her honor. The term was also sometimes used during France's Third Republic to describe a man's silk scarf. In English this became *lavaliere*. The duchess was eventually replaced in the king's affections by Madame de Montespan. In 1674 the duchess retired to a Carmelite convent and became celebrated for her piety. The name of a hanging piece of jewelry was later applied to the small television microphone that hung from a cord around the neck. These days *lavaliere microphones* are usually clipped onto the shirt or jacket collar.

Lacks, Henrietta

She was born in 1920 in Clover, Virginia. She was descended from slaves, the great-granddaughter of a plantation owner and one of his workers. As a young woman she, too, worked on the tobacco plantation. She was attractive, liked to wear nice dresses, and painted her toenails with bright red polish. She caught the eye of a fellow worker, her cousin, David Lacks. They married and later moved to Baltimore, where the booming steel industry promised a better way of life. He found work at the Sparrows Point Shipyard and the couple had five children in quick succession. The youngest was born in 1951. Only a few weeks later Henrietta started to experience sharp pains and excessive vaginal bleeding. She was frightened and told her husband. He convinced her to go to Johns Hopkins Hospital, where Dr. Howard Jones discovered a malignant tumor. This was not any tumor. It was growing at an alarming rate. Without asking or informing the Lackses, he sent a small piece of the tumor to Dr. George Gey. Gey had been trying for years to grow human cells outside the body so they could be tested and safely studied. Most human cells taken from the body are delicate and will die within weeks, but Lacks' cells were different. They thrived and multiplied aggressively outside her body without much help at all. Gey was finally able to achieve his goal using Lacks' cells. He also gave samples of the cells to other scientists so they could do their own research. Descendents of these cells are still alive in vitro. The number of the cells living today, in fact, amounts to 400 times Lacks' original weight. They have been used for hundreds of research projects, such as the development of the polio vaccine, the effect of zero gravity on the body, and the search for a cure for cancer. The cell line was named *HeLa* for *He*nrietta *La*cks. Now the HeLa Line is controlled by the American Type Culture Collection in Rockville, a nonprofit group which sells it to accredited researchers for eighty-five dollars. While her cells may live forever, Lacks herself did not have long to live. Despite radium treatments, the cancer did its work in only ten months. Lacks was buried in an unmarked grave near the plantation her great-grandfather had owned. David Lacks never remarried.

LaCoste, Rene

Born in Paris July 2, 1904, Rene LaCoste was a sickly youth.
When he started playing tennis at the age of fifteen, his father
tried to stop him. He was afraid his son was not healthy enough
to compete. Within a year, LaCoste proved him wrong. He was
nationally ranked in France and well on his way to being an
internationally known tennis champion. In 1925, he built one
of the first ball-lobbing machines so he could practice on his
own. LaCoste was the world's top tennis player in 1926 and
1927. He won seven major singles titles, including Wimbledon
twice. One day he spotted an expensive crocodile bag in a shop
window. His Davis Cup captain said he would buy it for him if
he won. He did not get the bag, but the episode did give him
a lifelong nickname—"the Crocodile." A friend, Robert
George, drew a crocodile for LaCoste and the tennis player
had it embroidered on the blazer he wore on the courts.
LaCoste met and married golf champion Simone Thion de la
Chaume. The couple would go on to have three sons and a
daughter. LaCoste's health forced him to retire from tennis in
1929 when he was only twenty-five. As a second career, he manufactured polo shirts emblazoned with the crocodile logo he
had already made famous on the courts. *La Société Chemise
Lacoste* started operations in 1934. Rene LaCoste ran it "like a
hobby." In 1951 the chairman of David Crystal Inc., Vin
Draddy, imported several thousand of the shirts to the U.S. and
marketed them under the name of a famous English tailor,
Jack Izod. At first, the *Izod Lacoste* shirt did not sell well. At $8
each, they were more expensive than other shirts of their type.
In the late 1970s and early 1980s, however, their higher price
became a selling point. Crocodile shirts, or "alligator shirts" as
they were more often called, became a mark of status and a
uniform of the preppy generation. By the early 1980s U.S.
domestic sales for the shirts climbed to $500 million. They
spawned many imitators in their heyday. In all, the company
estimated in 1996 that it had produced 300 million shirts.
Rene LaCoste passed away on October 12, 1996 at the age of
ninety-two. The polo shirt, incidentally, dates back to 1893
when it was worn at the Hurlingham Club near Buenos Aires.

The first commercially manufactured polo shirts featuring an embroidered logo were made by one of Argentina's top polo stars, Lewis Lacey, who opened his Buenos Aires sports shop in 1920. The shirts featured a logo of a player on a pony. Ralph Lauren introduced his polo shirt in 1972. Polo/Ralph Lauren's shirt has a polo player emblem as well. In 1985, Polo/Ralph Lauren got wind of a Buenos Aires clothier, Alberto Vannucci, who was selling shirts with a polo player on them. Further investigation revealed that the logo was the one designed by Lewis Lacey in 1920. Polo/Ralph Lauren sued for trademark infringement anyway.

Lamourette, Adrien

Adrien Lamourette was bishop of Lyons and a member of the Legislative Assembly during the French Revolution. The Legislative Assembly was divided into factions, the Royalists, Constitutionalists, Girondists, Jacobins, and Orleanists. On July 7, 1792, Lamourette convinced the various groups to lay aside their differences. They were momentarily inspired by the bishop's speech and they hugged one another. The king was summoned to see "how these Christians loved one another." The reconciliation was short-lived, though. After the briefest pause the groups went back to their battles. The expression *"Lamourette's kiss"* has come to refer to a superficial, temporary reconciliation.

Lansing, John

John TenEyck Lansing was born January 30, 1754 in Albany, New York. He became a lawyer after graduating in 1775 and set up a lucrative practice. The following year, he became military secretary to Gen. Philip Schulyer. From there he entered the political arena. He began the first of his six terms in the New York Assembly. in 1780 A year later he married a woman named Cornelia Ray. The couple had ten children, but tragically, five died in infancy. From 1786 to 1790, Lansing was mayor of Albany. In the summer of 1787, Lansing went to Philadelphia as part of the New York delegation to the Constitutional Convention. He believed the purpose of the meeting was to amend the Articles of Confederation, not to write an entirely new constitution. He and fellow delegate Robert Yates withdrew from the convention in protest. Lansing objected to the new Constitution again in 1788. After many years of public service as a Supreme Court judge, chief justice, and regent of the University of the State of New York, Lansing died under mysterious circumstances. He was visiting New York City in 1829. He left his hotel to mail some letters and he was never seen again. It is generally believed he was murdered. Lansing, New York was named for the politician. Later, a group from that city headed west and settled in Michigan. They named their new home Lansing, Michigan. Today it is that state's capital. Michigan, incidentally, most likely takes its name from the Chippewa word for "great water," *micigana*.

Lapostolle, Alexandre Marnier-

Alexandre Marnier-Lapostolle was born into a French distilling family. The Lapostolle distillery was founded in 1827. Under the leadership of its founder, Jean-Baptiste Lapostolle, it acquired a solid reputation and a faithful local clientele. By 1870, Jean-Baptiste's son, Eugene, had taken over the business. It was a difficult time to be a distiller. The German invasion of France in 1870 prevented people from socializing and spending money on anything but necessities. Since production was temporarily halted, Eugene paid a visit to the city of Cognac. There were other distillers in a similar situation there. The prices were low but the famous brandy, slowly aging in oak vats, was every bit as good as before. He bought part of the production and took it back to his hometown, Neauphle le Chateau. The political crisis soon ended and Parisians started, once again, to buy luxury items, including fine cognac. Eugene showed his purchase to his son-in-law, Alexandre, who thought they could have even greater success if they did something unique with the drink. He experimented with several flavors, arriving finally at the unique addition of orange peels and syrup. The mixture was then carefully filtered and aged in oak vats until it was ready for bottling. Once he was convinced it was just right he gathered the family and had them sample his liqueur. They were so impressed they decided to call it *Grand Marnier* for its creator. The liqueur was marketed as a "drink of style, good living and hospitality" and became France's leading liqueur export.

Larousse, Pierre

Pierre Larousse, a blacksmith's son, was born October 23, 1817, in Toucy, France. After studying at Versailles, he returned to Toucy as a schoolmaster. In 1840 he went to Paris, where he began research into the French language. His first work, a basic vocabulary textbook, was published in 1849. Three years later, he founded his own publishing house as a means to bring out more dictionaries, grammar books, and textbooks. The Larousse publishing company thrived, allowing him the financial means to compile the *Grand Dictionnaire universal du XIX siecle*, which was issued in small pieces every two weeks for a period of eleven years. "My first ambition was to teach children," he wrote; "I wanted to continue by trying to teach everyone about everything." The publishing house's logo portrays a young woman blowing softly through a dandelion, sowing knowledge. About a million copies of the Petit Larousse dictionary are sold each year.

Lauderdale, William

Maj. William Lauderdale was described by *Sun-Sentinel* reporter David Cazares as "an obscure soldier in an obscure war." The war was the Seminole War between the Seminole tribe of Florida and the U.S. military. It began in 1817 over attempts by U.S. authorities to recapture runaway slaves who found refuge among the Seminoles. U.S. forces under Gen. Andrew Jackson invaded, seized Spanish territory, and established a reservation for the tribe. In the 1830s a second Seminole war broke out when the tribe was ordered to move west of the Mississippi as part of the Indian Removal Act. Led by Chief Osceola, the Seminoles used guerrilla tactics to defend their homeland. In one battle, which took place Christmas Day 1837, 400 Seminole warriors went up against 1,000 troops under the command of Col. Zachary Taylor. It was the largest battle of the war. Seminole casualties were listed as 11 dead, 14 wounded. Of Taylor's troops, 26 were killed and 112 wounded. Somehow this was recorded as a victory for Taylor, who rode it to the White House. Major Lauderdale entered the conflict the following spring, March 22, 1838, when he led a group of Tennessee volunteers into Florida. Within five days the troops built a thirty-foot-square, two-tiered fort. They held the fort in a minor battle, then went back to Tennessee. Lauderdale never made it back to Tennessee. He died in an army barracks in Baton Rouge, Louisiana. The fort he had built in Florida remained. Years later, in 1893, a man named Frank Stanahan built a trading post at the spot. The city of *Fort Lauderdale* was incorporated in 1911.

Laurie, Annie

Born December 16, 1682, Annie Laurie was the oldest of three daughters of Sir Robert Laurie of Maxwelton, Dumfriesshire, Scotland and his second wife, Jean Riddell. Robert Laurie recorded the blessed event in his personal journal: "At the pleasure of the Almighty God, my daughter, Anna, was born upon this, the 16th day of December, 1682, about 6 o'clock in the morning, and was baptised by Mr. Geofrey Hunter, Minister of Glencairn." As a young woman, she was pursued by a man named William Douglas. Douglas, a Jacobite with a spirited temper, did not meet with the approval of Sir Robert, who was a staunch royalist. Legend has it that the two men fought a duel over bonnie Annie Laurie. Eventually, though, the girl bowed to the will of her father and rejected her suitor. Heartbroken, Douglas wrote her a poem:

> Her braw is like the snow-drift.
> Her throat is like the swan.
> Her face is the fairest
> That e'er the sun shone on.
> And dark blue is her ee
> And for bonnie Annie Laurie
> I'd lay me down and dee.

Laurie went on to marry, in 1709, James Fergusson, of Craigdarroch, and was the mother of Alexander Fergusson, the hero of poet Robert Burns' song "The Whistle." After her husband's death she became known as the Lady Bountiful of Nithsdale. She was also known as the town matchmaker. She died in 1764 at the age of eighty-two. The poem *"Annie Laurie"* was discovered in a library book and set to music by Lady John Douglas Scott. Scott also rewrote the words slightly. The song became a favorite of British troops during the Crimean War. After the war, Scott gave permission for her song to be published for the benefit of the widows and orphans. Thus, 150 years after Annie Laurie's aborted romance with Douglas, her name came to be known throughout the world.

Lawrence, Amos

Amos Adams Lawrence was born in 1814 in Boston. After graduating from Harvard, he became a textile merchant and one of Boston's most wealthy and prominent citizens. A year after his death in 1886, historian John Levering wrote:

> Commercial men in all generations have been the strength and support of all enterprises. They have been the producers, while the classes enumerated above [statesmen, artists, military men], have been the consumers; the dispensers. They have, in most experiences, been inspired by selfish ambition, while the counting rooms of the land have furnished the fuel which vitalizes all activities, as well, the support of all the religious, educational and philanthropic institutions which prosper us. The names of George Peabody, Samuel Appleton, Thomas P. Cope, Stephen Girard, Peter Cooper, Amos Lawrence, John Jacob Astor, et alias, of generations ago, still are graven in the memories of the people, and still deeper in the hearts of their descendants.

In 1844, Lawrence came into the possession of several thousand acres in Wisconsin after the previous owner defaulted on a loan. Two years later, Rev. Reeder Smith purchased the land as a site for a frontier school to afford "gratuitous advantage to Germans and Indians of both sexes." Lawrence offered to make a donation of $10,000 provided that the Rock River Conference of the Methodist Episcopal Church match his endowment, which they did in 1848. Lawrence subsequently gave additional funds to the school. Meanwhile, the Reverend Mr. Smith and several other members of his congregation were laying out plots for a school and a village to surround it. The school was named the *Lawrence Institute,* after its benefactor, and the village was named *Appleton* in honor of Lawrence's wife, Sarah Appleton, whose second cousin, Samuel Appleton, was another prominent Bostonian who donated money to the institute. When classes first began on November 12, 1849, the school's name was changed to *Lawrence College* and later *Lawrence University.* Several years later, in May 1854, the Kansas Territory was opened to settlement. The area was named after the River Kansas, which was in turn named after a Sioux tribe. The tribal name is said to mean "south wind." The actual name of the tribe was most likely Kansa, with the second *s* added by French settlers to make it plural. The *s* on Arkansas, incidentally, was added so it would match Kansas. Arkansas also derives its name from a river. The river was called Akenzea by the Native Americans, which explains the pronunciation. (There is an Arkansas River in Kansas. It is pronounced Ar-KAN-zus not AR-kensaw.) When Kansas was a new territory, the issue of slavery was dividing the nation. According to the concept of "popular sovereignty" settlers could decide whether or not to admit their territory as a free or slave state. Abolitionists decided to stack the decks in their favor by forming organizations that would encourage members of their ranks to move to Kansas. Amos Lawrence served as the treasurer of the most successful of the New England companies, the Emigrant Aid Company. The company, to which Lawrence was a major contributor, sent about 1,240 settlers to the area. They named their settlement *Lawrence* for their benefactor. Lawrence, Kansas, as one of the few cities in the nation founded purely for political reasons, became an important stop on the Underground Railroad. It also attracted a number of proslavery societies that wanted to counteract the effect of the abolitionists. The result was several heated and bloody skirmishes. Although there were a number of abolitionists who advocated the use of military force to ensure that Kansas would become a free state, Lawrence always advocated peaceful protest and financial help to Free Staters. In the end, the Emigrant Aid Company probably had little to do with making Kansas a free state—the credit rests primarily with settlers from Western states—but the movement brought the issue greater exposure, fueled the slavery debate, and may have hastened the onset of the Civil War. Amos Lawrence continued to give generously throughout his life. He established a trust fund for educational purposes, which was the principal factor in the selection of Lawrence as the site for the University of Kansas. He also gave towards the erection of Memorial Hall at his alma mater, Harvard, and he presented a dormitory, Lawrence Hall, to the Episcopal Theological School at Cambridge. An interesting side note—Amos Lawrence believed that there was a giant sea serpent off the coast of Nahant, Massachusetts. He never saw it himself, but in 1849 a number of prominent Nahant citizens reported seeing the creature. Lawrence wrote:

> I have never had any doubt of the existence of the Sea-serpent since the morning he was seen off Nahant by old Marshal Prince, through his famous mast-head spy-glass," Lawrence wrote. "For, within the next two hours, I conversed with Mr. Samuel Cabot, and Mr. Daniel P. Parker, I think, and one or more persons besides, who had spent a part of that morning in witnessing its movements. In addition, Col. Harris, the commander at Fort Independence, told me that the creature had been seen by a number of his soldiers while standing sentry in the early dawn, some time before this show at Nahant; and Col. Harris believed it as firmly as though the creature were drawn up before us in State street, where we then were. I again say, I have never, from that day to this, had a doubt of the Sea-serpent's existence.

L'Ecorcheur, Jacques

According to Robert Hendrickson's *Human Words,* Jacques L'Ecorcheur, or Jack the Scorcher, was the leader of a violent gang that terrorized the French countryside in the wake of the French Revolution. The gang would force its way into a home, tie the residents up, and demand their valuables. If they refused, the gang would put the residents' bare feet in the fire until the residents changed their minds. This is how Jack and his gang came to be known as chauffeurs, or "firemen." Years later the expression was applied to steamship stokers, train engineers, and finally to the stokers who ran steam-powered automobiles. In the days when cars needed stokers, the people who operated them were generally not the owners. This is how the word came to be applied to someone who drives someone else.

Leitz, Ernst

In 1865 Ernst Leitz received a promotion. He was made a partner in an optical institute that had been founded in 1849 in Wetzlar, Germany to develop lenses and microscopes. At the time there were roughly 12 employees in the company. In just four years Leitz took over the management of the entire operation and gave it his name—Leitz Works. He ran the company until 1920 when his son Ernst Leitz II succeeded him. By 1924 the company could boast 1,000 employees, including a man named Oskar Barnack. In the early days of photography, there was nothing portable about a camera. Photographers had to haul large plates, tripods, and darkroom equipment with them. Barnack thought there must be an easier way. He imagined that by reducing the format of negatives and then enlarging the photographs after they had been exposed, he could make a camera that was much less cumbersome. The result was the first 35-mm camera. It was dubbed the *Leica,* for Leitz Camera. It was first released to the public in 1925. Other companies not only copied the cameras, they copied the name. Their own products were dubbed with words ending in "ca" for camera. Konica and Fujica are examples. Konica is a contraction of Konishiroku and camera and Fujica is Fuji (the company was named for Japan's highest mountain) and camera. Minolta, on the other hand, is an acronym for *m*achine, *i*nstrument, *o*ptica*l*, and *Ta*jima. Tajima is a shortened form of Tajima Shoten, a Japanese wholesale silk firm that was run by Minolta's founder, Kazuo Tashima. Nikon is a shortened form of the company's original and official name, Nippon Kogaku, which translates to "Japan optics company." The word "camera," incidentally, was coined by the German astronomer Johannes Kepler. He used a room with light entering through a small hole to make observations on the size of the sun and the moon. He called the "dark chamber" by its Latin name, "camera obscura." A later British physicist, Robert Boyle, used the same technique on a smaller scale. He took a small box with a lens at one end and stretched paper across the back that received an image. This small camera obscura was eventually referred to simply as a camera. In 1802 when Thomas Wedgewood announced to the British Royal Institution that he had discovered a method of "copying paintings upon glass and of making profiles by the agency of light upon nitrate of silver," the first camera as we know it today was born.

Lender, Harry

In 1927, Harry Lender, an immigrant who had arrived only six months earlier from Lodz, Poland, started the first bagel bakery outside New York City. The business began modestly, supplying bagels to Jewish delis and bakeries in the city and in New Haven, Connecticut. One of his biggest customers was a Catskill Mountain hotel. The waiters there were having trouble cutting the bagels. They sliced their fingers so often that the union was prepared to go on strike. Lender responded by selling them presliced bagels. He was the first bagel baker to do so. Lender's sons Murray and Marvin took over the business, developed a bagel-cutting machine, and began shipping presliced frozen bagels around the country in 1963. The presliced bagels not only prevented kitchen accidents but also gave the uninitiated a hint as to how to eat the food. "A lot of people would think of it like a donut and dunk it," Murray Lender told a Gannett reporter in 1995. "We decided to preslice the bagels so customers would know to toast them." Today, *Lender's Bagels* is the leading bagel seller worldwide. Purchased by Kraft General Foods in 1984, the company sells more than 1.5 billion packaged bagels a year.

Lenox, Walter Scott

In the late nineteenth century, Trenton, New Jersey was becoming known as one of the two major pottery centers in the United States, the other being East Liverpool, Ohio. It started, of course, with a single pottery, opened in 1850. It was followed by two more in 1853. By 1870 Trenton boasted fifteen potteries, twenty-three by 1883, and at its zenith in the 1920s, more than fifty. One of the few Trenton potteries from the nineteenth century that has survived to the present was that of Walter Scott Lenox. Lenox began his career as an apprentice at Ott and Brewer. The shop was well known, especially as the employer of Isaac Broome, an outstanding nineteenth-century American ceramic sculptor who produced a line of ceramic ware for the American Centennial in 1876. Broome's works at Ott and Brewer are among the most famous ceramic pieces ever produced in this country. Between 1882 and 1892, Ott and Brewer created some of this nation's most outstanding art porcelain and served as a training ground for many individuals who would become prominent in the field, including Lenox. By 1889, Lenox felt he was ready to open his own shop. With the superintendent of Ott and Brewer, Jonathan Coxon, he founded the Ceramic Art Company. The partnership endured until the spring of 1896 when Coxon sold his interest to Lenox. The company continued as the Ceramic Art Company with the word "Lenox" added beneath the CAC label. In February 1906, the name of the company officially became Lenox, Inc. Lenox's shop was run as an art studio with a staff of designers and artisans. The porcelain they produced was soon ranked in quality with that of Wedgwood. Lenox china's staying power was helped in no small part by Pres. Woodrow Wilson, who, in 1918, commissioned Lenox to produce the first American-made White House serving dishes. The executive mansion continued to order place settings from Lenox. Services would later be commissioned for Presidents Franklin Roosevelt, Harry S. Truman, and Ronald Reagan. Lenox acquired a glass-making company, Lenox Crystal, which has been selected for official use by the vice-president of the United States and by American embassies around the world. Lenox crystal has also been chosen by the White House, the State Department, and Congress for presentation to dignitaries and heads of state throughout the world. The company even presented Bill Clinton's dog, Buddy, with a special glass ornament for the "first dog's first Christmas" in 1997.

Lenya, Lotte

Lotte Lenya was born in 1898 in Austria, the daughter of a washerwoman and a cabdriver. She escaped a tumultuous childhood of abuse and prostitution by teaching herself to dance and sing. By 1926, when she married Kurt Weil, a Jewish cantor's son who had become a noted composer, she was a well-known actress and singer in Berlin. The couple's relationship was stormy, but creatively charged. There were many separations and eventually a divorce followed by a remarriage. They collaborated on many projects, including *Die Dreigroshenoper,* or *Threepenny Opera,* which debuted in Germany in 1929. The production, written by Weil and Bertolt Brecht, was a social commentary with parallels to the rise of Adolf Hitler. The main character was MacHeath, whose killing sprees were recounted in "The Ballad of Mac the Knife." Lenya played Jenny in the show. Shortly thereafter, Weil and Lenya fled to the United States to escape the Nazis. They worked on and off Broadway. After Weil's death in 1950, Lenya continued acting, and was married three more times. She was nominated for an Academy Award for Best Supporting Actress for her role in *The Roman Spring of Mrs. Stone.* In the late 1950s, her name somehow found its way into one of the songs from *Threepenny Opera.* When "Mac the Knife" was first performed in the United States, its lyrics were changed because the original German words were thought to be too violent for American audiences. An instrumental version called "Moritat" was a hit for the Dick Hyman Trio in 1956. Meanwhile, the rewritten version found its way to Louis Armstrong, who also recorded it. In the part of the song that lists women who'd been victims of Mac the Knife, Armstrong added Lotte Lenya's name. Armstrong's version found its way to Bobby Darrin, a pop singer who'd had success with "Splish Splash" and "Dream Lover." The violent song was a departure for him, and he didn't much like it. He recorded it for his album *That's All,* but didn't want it released as a single. His record label, Atco, however, felt differently and over his objections they put it out. It became an instant hit, the biggest seller of 1956, complete with the line "Look out, Miss Lotte Lenya and ol' Lucy Brown."

Lever, William

William Lever, the son of a wholesale grocer, was born in Bolton, England in 1851. When he was only sixteen he started working in the family business and became a partner with his father at the age of twenty-one. As he reached his thirties, Lever became restless and wanted to start a business of his own. He decided to try his hand at soap making and leased a chemical works in Warrington, England. Along with his brother James Darcy Lever, he began experimenting with various soap recipes. At a time when most soap was made of tallow, they used vegetable oil as a base. The result was Sunlight Soap. In 1886, the newly formed Lever Brothers company sold its first sliced bar. It was so successful that they soon outgrew their factory. They decided to build a new plant on the Mersey River in Cheshire. To house the workers Lever built up a town. He vowed "to build houses in which our working people will be able to live and be comfort-able . . . and know more about the science of life, than they can in a back slum." Port Sunlight, as it came to be called, gave Lever employees a higher standard of living than most factory workers of the time and earned William Lever recognition as a social reformer. By 1895 Port Sunlight was producing 40,000 tons of soap a year. Until his death in 1925, Lever continued to give gen-erously to charity. His contributions to society earned him the title Viscount Leverhulme. In America, the name Lever is most-ly associated with the widely advertised Lever 2000 soap. The Unilever corporation, an international manufacturer of food and home products, is made up of three companies: NV Margarine Unie, Margarine Union, and Lever Brothers.

Libby, Arthur and Charles

Arthur Libby was born in 1831. His brother Charles was born in 1838. As young men, they both went to work in Chicago's slaughterhouses. This was not the most pleasant of occupations, and it was not long before the Libbys decided they would rather be in management. They and a friend, Archibald McNeil, scraped together $3,000 to start their own corned-beef produc-tion facility. Arthur Libby had the job of acquiring the best beef from Chicago's stockyards. Charles Libby and Archibald McNeil managed operations at their packaging facility. In 1875, Libby, McNeil & Libby became the first to market meat in cans. By 1879 they were processing 200,000 cattle a year. The name "Libby" was already familiar by 1884, as witnessed by this article on the Zulu wars from the *Chicago Tribune:* "After the battles in the land of the Zulus, and later when the last gun was fired on the banks of the Nile, the battlefields were strewn with empty cans bearing the well-known brand of Libby, McNeil & Libby." Charles Libby died in 1895. Arthur died four years later. Neither did McNeil survive into the next century. Their descendents did not follow them into the business. The company passed into the hands of the largest meat packer in the country, Swift & Company. Somewhere along the line, McNeil's name was dropped. Swift & Company was forced to divest itself of Libby's in 1920 because of a decision that broke up their "meat trust." Libby's was on its own then. It expanded into the canned food business, packing ketchup, vegetables, juices, and fruit along with the meat. They were the first company to pack tomato juice. It was swallowed up by Nestle in 1976. By 1980, 10 percent of the nation's beets and 60 percent of the world's pumpkin ended up in cans with Libby, Libby, Libby on the label, label, label.

Lindt, Rodolphe

In 1879, Bern, Switzerland-based chocolatier Rodolphe Lindt began experimenting with the amount of cocoa butter in his confections. He found that with the right combination he could produce a rich chocolate that melted on the tongue. He also found that the more he mixed the chocolate the smoother it became. Because his first chocolates were produced in the shape of a shell, his process came to be known "conching," from the Spanish word "concha" or shell. Lindt's smooth chocolate and that of his imitators soon overtook the market for hard, strong, dark chocolate. Lindt, along with Henri Nestle and John Tobler, was largely responsible for establishing Switzerland as the land of chocolate. In 1899, Lindt's small but famous factory was sold to Johann Rudolf Sprüngli-Schifferli, who had inherited a thriving fifty-year-old chocolate business from his father, Rudolf Sprüngli-Ammann. The combined company was known as Lindt & Sprüngli. Lindt chocolates are still popular throughout the world.

Loughead, Allan

Allan Loughead was born in 1889 in Niles, California. He grew up to be an auto mechanic. He found himself in Chicago working for an automobile distributor named James Plew. Plew wanted to expand his business to include aircraft. Loughead taught himself to fly in one of Plew's planes and developed a love of aviation himself. He started tinkering and building his own airplanes. Shortly thereafter he was married. Soon after that he crashed a plane. His new bride made him promise to give up the dangerous occupation. He did, briefly. The Lougheads moved back to California. Loughead was reunited with his brother, Malcolm, who had also begun his career as a mechanic. He learned that his brother had caught the flying bug as well. The brothers started to build planes together. They called their company the Alco Hydro-Aeroplane Company. So prospective buyers would not think they were new at the flying game, they called their first aircraft the "Model G." They took their creation out for its first demonstration flight June 15, 1913. No one was impressed enough to order one. The Loughead brothers decided to go back to fixing cars. When World War I began, however, they suspected the demand for aircraft would increase. In 1916 they formed a new company, Loughead Aircraft, with a view to selling seaplanes to the navy. They hired an engineer named John Northrop. Their war efforts, however, were not successful. They managed to sell only two seaplanes to the government. Loughead Aircraft went under in 1921. Malcolm Loughead designed hydraulic brakes for cars. Allan Loughead tried his hand at real estate. Northrop got a job with Douglas Aircraft. Allan never gave up his dream, however, and in 1926 he and Northrop decided to give it another try. The new venture was named Lockheed. The orders were few and far between. After only three years, Lockheed merged with the Detroit Aircraft Company and Loughead left. The combined company teetered on the verge of bankruptcy until it was purchased by an investment group in 1932. It was under their management that Lockheed began to soar. Lockheed Martin Corporation was formed in March 1995 with the merger of Lockheed Corporation and Martin Marietta Corporation. It is the world's number-two aerospace and defense firm behind Boeing. Although his name has become familiar, Loughead's own ventures continued to struggle. His new company, Loughead Brothers Aircraft Corporation, lasted four years and only built one plane. He still did not give up. After legally changing his name to Lockheed in 1934, he started a new company, Alcor, in 1937. It went under as well. Lockheed passed away in 1969.

Louis XVI

Louis was born August 23, 1754 in Versailles, France. He was the third son of the dauphin, Louis, and his consort, Maria Josepha of Saxony. He was thus a member of the House of Bourbon, a noble family that took its title from Bourbon L'Archambault, a town in France that was named for an early lord. The first to hold the title lord of Bourbon was Robert de Clermont, a son of Louis IX, who married Beatrix, the heiress to the Bourbon lands. The Bourbons ascended to the throne in 1589, upon the death of Henri III. Henri's closest relative, Henri de Bourbon, became king and the throne was passed to his successors all the way down to Louis XVI, who became king on May 10, 1774. Louis was not destined to be remembered for his great leadership in a time of crisis. He was dominated by his queen, Marie Antoinette, the daughter of Maria Theresa and the Holy Roman emperor Francis I. Under Louis, French finances fell into confusion and the French Revolution began. The royal couple tried to flee the country in 1791 but in August 1792, Parisians stormed Tuileries palace and took the royal family prisoner. Citizen Capet, as Louis was then called, was found guilty by the National Convention and condemned to death. He was taken to the Place de la Révolution in Paris on January 21, 1793. He met his end in the guillotine. After the blade fell, a revolutionary guard held up the former regent's severed head as the crowd shouted, "Vive la république!" Given his end, it seems unlikely that the king would have many places named in his honor. But thanks to France's support of the American revolutionaries in their battle against Britain, a number of American cities bear his name. "The Western Country," an area that comprised all that is now northeastern Kentucky and part of Virginia, was named *Bourbon County* in his honor. *Louisville* also owes its name to the ruler. Most authorities credit the Rev. Elijah Craig, a Baptist minister, with distilling the first batch of what we now call bourbon whiskey in 1789. As the story goes, he named his concoction after the county where he made it. Charles Cowdery, author of *The Bourbon Country Reader,* however, disputes this claim. Although Elijah Craig was a Kentucky distiller, Cowdery says he was not the originator of bourbon whiskey. "The durable claim that Elijah Craig . . . made the first bourbon whiskey can be traced to Richard Collins, whose *History of Kentucky* was published in 1874," Cowdery writes. "Collins does not attempt to substantiate the claim nor has any evidence ever been produced to support it." Instead, Cowdery traces bourbon's origins to Fort Harrod, the first permanent European settlement west of the Allegheny Mountains. "Since whiskey-making on the frontier was as common as baking bread," Cowdery explains, "it is almost certain that the first batch was cooked as soon as there was enough corn, which means it probably happened within a year of the settlement's establishment in June of 1774." Bourbon County, which was then a much larger region than it is today, did produce a fair amount of whiskey of its own. It and Kentucky's other main product, hemp, were shipped down the Ohio River to New Orleans to market. Eventually, Bourbon County was carved up into smaller counties in two states. The people in New Orleans began to refer to all products that arrived from the region as being from "Old Bourbon County." Eventually, people got used to the new boundaries and they stopped referring to the area as "Old Bourbon," but the appellation stuck on the barrels of whiskey. *Bourbon Street* in New Orleans dates back to pre-Revolutionary War times. In 1722 the French capital in the New World was moved from Biloxi, Mississippi to New Orleans. French engineer Adrien de Pauger laid out the master plan for the city and named one of the main streets after the ruling dynasty in France.

Luger, George

In the 1890s, Austrian George Luger worked at Ludwig Loewe & Company in Karlsruhe, Germany. The company manufactured firearms. Notably, the company made a self-loading pistol designed by one of Luger's co-workers, Hugo Borchardt. While Borchardt's was a fine target arm, it was cumbersome and somewhat fragile, thus unsuitable for use as a military side arm. Using one of the weapons as a model, Luger set to work on a new pistol. The semiautomatic pistols he constructed proved to be quite valuable to the military. The *Luger pistol* is especially associated with Nazi Germany.

Luyon, Solange

In 1680 Solange Luyon arrived in England from France, a Huguenot refugee fleeing from Louis XIV's persecution. She Anglicized her name to Sally Lunn and found a job with a baker in the resort city of Bath. She introduced the baker to French brioche bread and buns. The light, sweet tea biscuits were served at the traditional public breakfasts and afternoon teas and were an immediate hit with the English, who called them *Sally Lunns.* A baker named Dalmer bought her recipe, built some portable ovens mounted on wheelbarrows, and delivered Sally Lunns. He wrote a song about the cakes, which became popular and helped keep the name alive. Nearly a century later, a Gilbert and Sullivan character in *The Sorcerer* sang about "the gay Sally Lunn." She was also the subject of a 1990 historical novel by Pamela Oldfield. The bakery where Lunn worked, which was in a stone coffeehouse on Lilliput Alley close to the Abbey Church, is now a tourist attraction. The recipe was discovered in a "secret cupboard" over the downstairs corner fireplace and is now passed on with the deed of the house. A modern bakery on the second floor continues to make Sally Lunn buns.

Lynch, Charles and John

Charles and John Lynch were the two oldest of the four children of Charles Lynch and his wife, Sarah Clark. Charles, Sr., was an Irish immigrant. As Rev. Edgar Woods recounted in his

1901 *History of Albermarle County in Virginia,* "Taking offence while a mere youth at some ill-treatment, he determined to quit home and country and with this purpose took passage on a vessel bound for America." Once the ship set sail, however, Lynch regretted his hasty decision. He leapt from the deck and attempted to swim to shore but was rescued by the sailors, who kept him on board for the rest of the voyage. Despite his early misgivings, Charles Lynch quickly rose to prominence in his new homeland. Settling in the colonial village of New London, Virginia in 1733, he obtained land patents for more than sixty-five hundred acres over the next seventeen years. Much of the land was passed on to son John upon Charles' death in 1753. At that time, trading was slowed in the area due to the necessity of fording the Fluvanna (now James) River. John solved the problem by establishing a ferry service. Lynch's Ferry became a profitable center of trade. Following the American Revolution, in 1784, he petitioned the General Assembly of Virginia for a town charter on the land surrounding his ferry. It was granted two years later and the town of *Lynchburg* was created. Brother Charles' name would also become familiar in a more infamous way. Prior to the war, Charles worked as a justice of the peace in the South River Meeting House and considered himself a pacifist. When war broke out, however, he became a colonel in the Revolutionary army. He fought in several major battles including the battle of Yorktown. Because of the disrupted political state, Charles Lynch was one of four magistrates—with James Callaway, William Preston, and Robert Adams—called upon to set up an unofficial court to try cases. From this court came the term *Lynch law* and the verb *to lynch*. Whether or not the court's activities matched up to the current sense of the term is disputed. *The Columbia Encyclopedia,* for example, states, "Lynch clearly exceeded his authority." James G. Ryan, in an article for *Irish America,* on the other hand, said that while the word is used to signify unjust punishment, "this was not the case with the court presided over by Lynch." Only in one case, when a criminal was convicted of manslaughter, was a prisoner executed. The most extreme punishment otherwise was "forty save one" lashes on the bare back and the enforced cry "Liberty or Death!" Lynch's court was later reviewed by the Virginia legislature, which found it "justifiable from the imminence of the danger." While most word watchers believe Colonel Lynch's court to be the origin of the word lynch, there have been a few rival theories, most of which have little evidence to support them. One theory is that the term refers to Capt. William Lynch, a justice in the court of Pittsylvania. As Charles Earle Funk points out in his book *Thereby Hangs a Tale,* the origin of the William Lynch story is an article in the May 1859 *Harper's Magazine* which interviewed a man named Richard Venables who had "long been in feeble health and often sat for hours to all appearance unconscious of what was said or done in his presence." Whether his memory was trustworthy or not, Venables never mentioned the first name of "Mr. Lynch" and could have been as easily referring to Charles Lynch as William. The author of the article may have simply made an assumption about who Lynch was. Another of the more dubious stories points to a Mayor Lynch of Galway, Ireland. As the story goes, this Lynch's son was convicted of a crime and sentenced to the gallows. Because the mayor was very popular, the people refused to execute the young man. Mayor Lynch, insisting justice be done, was said to have performed the hanging himself. *Picturesque Expressions: A Thematic Dictionary,* by Gale Research, provides yet another tale, which it describes as "a less credible conjecture." This story attributes the expression to a band of colonists called the "Regulators" who lived in Lynch's Creek, South Carolina. They administered their own style of justice, which came to be known as "Lynch law," after the name of the town.

M

MacCarthy, Cormac MacDermott

Cormac MacDermott MacCarthy, also known simply as Dermot MacCartney, was descended from the noble MacCarthy family of Cork County, Ireland. In 1446, his ancestor Cormac MacCartney built a castle, known as Blarney Castle, on the same ground as the family's two previous castles. The new edifice was impressive. It featured a massive square tower with battlements. It surrounded an eight-acre property and was one of the strongest fortresses in the region, with walls eighteen feet thick in some places. The castle housed a famous stone. The Blarney Stone is situated in the top of a window about one hundred feet off the ground in what are now the ruins of the castle. The stone bears the Latin inscription "Cormac MacCarthy fortis me fieri facit a.d. 1446" ("Cormac MacCarthy caused me to be built strong in 1446"). According to legend, when Cormac was worried about losing his castle in a lawsuit, a fairy came to him in a dream and told him that if he kissed the stone all the right words would pour out of him. Upon waking he did just as the fairy had said and he won his suit. To keep other people from gaining the same powers, he hid the stone in the tower, where it remains to this day. Every year thousands of tourists visit the town and allow themselves to be lowered headfirst from the battlements to kiss the stone in the hopes of gaining the power of flattering and convincing speech. Yet this legend does not appear to date back to Cormac's time. It became current during the rule of Elizabeth I. Cormac's descendent Dermot was then lord of the castle and thus known as Baron Blarney. Elizabeth decreed the lords of Ireland would take their tenure from the

English Crown, rather than from the clan. Dermot was ordered to surrender the family castle to Sir George Carew, the lord president of Munster. He did not refuse the request, but each time sent back letters designed to avoid the question. After one such message the queen is said to have replied, "This is more Blarney; what he says is never what he means!" Thus *blarney* became synonymous with smoothly evasive nonsense. Another word for nonsense—*malarky* or *malarkey*—may also come from a proper name. Mullarkey is an Irish surname and it seems likely that someone of that name was the origin of the expression, which can be traced back to the 1920s. If it was a person who inspired the expression, however, there is no record of him.

McDonnell, James Smith

James Smith McDonnell was born in Denver, Colorado in 1899. He grew up to be an army pilot. After his service, his career could best be described as "nomadic." He worked with five different aircraft manufacturers between 1924 and 1933, when he became the chief engineer in charge of land planes for Martin. After five years he left that business as well and a year later founded his own company in St. Louis. During the war, this firm manufactured aircraft parts. Finally, in 1943, McDonnell got a contract to design the first navy jet. McDonnell's company continued to grow and grow until, by 1967, it was profitable enough to buy a company founded by Donald Wills Douglas. Douglas was born in Brooklyn in 1892. While he was attending the Naval Academy he saw Orville Wright's demonstration of the army's first biplane and he immediately knew what he wanted to do with his life. He left the academy and transferred to MIT, where Jerome Hunsacker had established the first university course in aeronautics. After he graduated, Douglas worked briefly at the Connecticut Aircraft Company. Next he joined Glen Martin, a California aircraft maker, as chief engineer. At the end of World War I, Martin decided to move the company to Ohio and merged with Wright. Douglas went with him, but he missed the California sun, so he moved back. He had only $600 and a dream of starting his own company. In 1920 he found a partner, a barnstormer named David Davis, who invested $40,000 to create the Davis-Douglas Company. Their goal was to create a plane that could cross the country without stopping. It didn't work. Davis crashed the aircraft in Texas and the company folded soon afterwards. Douglas struck out on his own, and soon had secured a contract to build fighters for the navy. Douglas's reputation grew in 1924 when two of his airplanes became the first to circle the world. In 1935, Douglas's company introduced the DC-3. The successful aircraft ensured the business's survival. When McDonnell purchased the company in 1967, McDonnell Douglas, the second-largest military supplier in the country, was formed. McDonnell stayed at the helm of the company until July 1980. He passed away one month after his retirement. Douglas died a year later. In 1996, Boeing bought McDonnell Douglas for $13.3 billion. It was the tenth-largest merger in U.S. history and the largest ever in the aerospace industry.

McKee, Debra

At the beginning of the Great Depression, a man named O. D. McKee was one of the many people out of work. He saw a man selling Virginia Dare cakes from his car. McKee asked if he could do the same, and he was given a territory in Chattanooga, Tennessee. He sold cakes for a nickel from the back of his 1928 Whippet. In 1935 he learned of a bakery called Jack's Cookie Company. With the somewhat reluctant blessing of his wife, Ruth, McKee used his car as collateral to buy the shop. Soon afterward, he put two oatmeal cookies together with a creme filling in the middle. The creme pies, which sold for a nickel, were very popular. O. D., the company's salesman, was often on the road. While he was away, Ruth managed the plant and office. In 1960, McKee decided to market his snack cakes in a family pack. He was not sure exactly what to call the product until a packaging supply salesman, Bob Mosher, suggested McKee name it after his granddaughter, Debra. The *Little Debbie* snack cake was born. Between 1964 and 1979 company sales grew 15 percent, mainly due to the Little Debbie snack family pack. Ruth and

O. D. McKee turned over the presidency of the McKee Baking Company in 1971 to their eldest son, Ellsworth. Ruth McKee died in 1989. O. D. McKee died in 1995 at the age of ninety. Grownup Debbie still works for the family business, which was renamed McKee Foods Corporation in 1991. She serves on the board of directors.

Maginot, André

André Maginot was born February 17, 1877 in Paris. He was elected to the French Chamber of Deputies in 1910 and became undersecretary of war three years later. Despite his high post, he entered the army as a private at the outbreak of World War I. Severely wounded during the defense of Verdun, he was decorated with the Cross of the Legion of Honor and the Médaille Militaire. His service complete, he returned to politics in 1915. He held a number of government posts, eventually becoming Minister of Defense in 1929. Maginot was determined that Germany would never again invade France. He and his generals decided to construct a wall along the eastern border from Switzerland to Belgium. Built at a cost of $2 million per mile, it consisted of semiunderground forts joined by underground passages and was protected by antitank defenses. Maginot died in early 1932, but his project continued and was completed in 1938. Since Maginot never considered Belgium to be a threat to France, the wall was never built along that frontier. The Germans were therefore able to access France by invading Belgium and marching through, which they did in May 1940. *The Maginot line* came to refer not only to the wall itself but to anything that serves only to lull a nation into a false sense of security. The Maginot line's forts still stand. Most are closed to the public for fear of accidents in their steep stairwells and other recesses. Some are kept open by local authorities for guided tours. In January 2000, the Germans invaded again. Two German souvenir hunters were arrested and fined $460 each for breaking into one of the abandoned forts.

Magli, Bruno

In 1936, siblings Bruno, Marino, and Mario Magli followed in the footsteps of their grandfather, a cobbler, and began making women's shoes in a small basement in Bologna, Italy. During the postwar construction years, they were able to step up production, build a manufacturing plant, and increase the line of products to include men's shoes and later belts, handbags, wallets, and jackets. Word of the quality of the Maglis' shoes quickly spread to the fashion conscious of Europe. In 1969, the company built a larger plant and started opening elegant boutiques in various Italian cities. Starlets of no less sophistication than Sophia Loren were regular customers. In the 1980s, the boutiques left the confines of Italy. There are now more than forty Bruno Magli shops located everywhere from China to the United States. In 1992, the firm hired a new shoe designer to refine the look of the shoes. They also hired an advertising and marketing firm to increase their exposure. At the end of that year they retired the sluggish "Lorenzo" shoe after only three seasons. The Lorenzo was a casual lace up with a distinctive heavy-duty rubber sole. It was retired in favor of a similar style that far outsold its predecessor. Although the company generated a few dozen press clippings a month in the fashion pages in this country prior to 1992, the shoes are not for the average buyer. They sell for anywhere from $200 to $1,700 in the U.S. (The $200 Bruno Maglis are slippers.) Magli products are on display at the Museum of Modern Art in New York. "The name Magli is synonymous with quality and that unique Italian flair for design," says a Magli promotion. On June 12, 1994, Bruno Magli would become synonymous with something else in America—the O. J. Simpson murder trial. A distinctive shoe print—that of a size-twelve Bruno Magli Lorenzo-style shoe— was found at the scene of the double homicide of Nicole Brown Simpson and her friend Ronald Goldman. Only 299 size-twelve pairs of the shoes were sold in the United States. Simpson repeatedly denied owning the shoes, which he claimed were ugly. The lawyers in his criminal trial claimed that a photograph of the athlete in the shoes was a forgery. At his civil trial, however, more than thirty-one photographs— taken by two separate photographers—of Simpson apparently wearing a pair were shown. Simpson was found responsible for the wrongful death of the two victims and was hit with a total of $33.5 million in actual and punitive damages. ABC-TV estimates that 80 percent of the people residing in the United States followed the Simpson trials to some extent. They kept track of each piece of evidence, from the slow-speed chase in the white Ford Bronco, to the Isotoner gloves that were the subject of the rhyme "if they don't fit you must acquit," to the Bruno Magli shoes. Even though these products received the negative attention of a murder investigation, sales increased. Ford Bronco sales rose after the televised police chase, as did sales of Bruno Magli shoes after the trials. Some marketing experts estimate that Magli received more than $100 million in free publicity. In 1996, Bruno Magli's business was up 30 percent. The company tried to distance itself from Simpson by attributing its success to an advertising campaign.

Malfatti, Therese

Young Therese Malfatti was a student of Ludwig van Beethoven. The composer, an awkward man who lacked social graces, was smitten with the girl and intended to ask for her hand in marriage. He wanted to let his music speak for him, and he composed a short, light piece for her. He had learned his lesson when it came to writing music for a woman. His previous attempt to woo a potential wife with music was the *Sonata quasi una Fantasia,* which was moody and complex. It failed to win the lady, but a critic, Ludwig Rellstab, said the first movement of the sonata reminded him of the moon setting over Lake Lucerne. This led to its familiar name, *The Moonlight Sonata.* The second time around, Beethoven wanted to write something his student could play. He brought the simple bagatelle to her home and presented it to her father. As he tried to screw up his courage to ask for her hand in marriage, he drank a bit too much of the strong punch that was being served. Too tipsy to play the piano, he just wrote the young woman's name on the top of the manuscript and left it behind. The name "Therese" was barely legible, so years after the composer's death, when a publisher tried to decipher it, he arrived at the title *Für Elise.*

Mambert

In the Dark Ages, long before the Norman invasion of England, a man named Mambert became the owner of a large tract of land in what is now Normandy, France. The area became known as "Mambert's Field." In French this is "Champ de Mambert." Church records from the sixteenth century list the area by the Latin name "Campo Mauberti." Over the years local residents got tired of uttering all those syllables and the area's name evolved into *Camembert.* Camembert is best known throughout the world for the cheese that is manufactured there, also known as Camembert. The food is made of cow's milk, treated with the *Penicillium camemberti* mold. The bicentennial of Camembert cheese was celebrated in France in 1991, even though its origins undoubtedly go back more than two hundred years. The traditional story of its origin, however, begins in 1790, during the French Revolution. Roman Catholic priests were forced to swear allegiance to the new republic. Those who refused were forced into exile. One such priest took refuge on the farm of a woman named Marie Harel. In return for her kindness, he gave her the secret of making Camembert. The problem with the tale is that there are references to Camembert's famous cheese in literature going back to the 1550s, long before Harel was born. Whatever its origins, Camembert is now popular worldwide. Although the people of Normandy say only they make the "real" thing, cheese makers around the world label their concoctions "Camembert." Varieties are produced as far away as China.

Marcus, Herbert

Carrie Marcus and her brother Herbert were born in Louisville, Kentucky. As adults both siblings moved to Hillsboro, Texas, where another brother had a grocery. Herbert got a job selling women's shoes at Sanger Brother's, the oldest and largest store in Dallas. Carrie became an assistant buyer at A. Harris and Company. There, she met a salesman from Cleveland named Al Neiman. They were married in 1905. Around this time Herbert, also newly married, became a father to a boy named Stanley. So he asked for a raise. When his pay was elevated only $1.87 a week, he quit. He and his new brother-in-law opened an advertising agency in Atlanta, Georgia. After only two years they were given an option. They could sell the agency for $25,000 cash or trade it for Coca-Cola stock and a franchise for the drink. They took the cash. Although the Coca-Cola stock would later be worth millions, the businessmen would not regret their decision for long. They took the money and rented a $9,000-a-year, two-story building, which they outfitted with opulent fixtures and carpeting. With Al Neiman's financial know-how, Herbert Marcus's natural salesmanship, and Carrie Marcus Neiman's discriminating taste in fashion, they opened a specialty store, which they advertised with a full-page announcement in the *Dallas News* in 1907. "On September Tenth," it read, "will take place the formal opening of Neiman-Marcus Co. The South's finest and only exclusive ready-to-wear shop, the policy of Neiman-Marcus is to be at all times leaders in their lines and to give buyers in Texas something out of the commonplace." The shop changed the buying habits of well-dressed Texans. Until that time, few stores offered ready-to-wear clothing. The fashion conscious went to Europe for their garments. With a talent for showmanship, the specialty shop soon evolved into, in the words of *Harper's Bazaar,* an "imaginative miniworld that . . . continues its tradition of larger-than-life luxury, first class service and southern hospitality. . . . They were nothing less than pioneers who raised the taste level of the biggest state in the land." Neiman Marcus became the shop of choice for celebrities and the wealthy. A Texas cattleman who visited Neiman Marcus summed up their stock by saying, "In all my time I never saw so many things a body kin get along without." By 1929, sales of things a body kin get along without had reached $3.6 million. Then, after twenty-three years of marriage, the Neimans divorced. Herbert Marcus bought Al Neiman's interest in the company. Neiman founded his own firm, Neiman Associates. Although he became blind in 1946, Herbert continued to be active in the store until his death in 1950. Carrie passed away three years later. Stanley Marcus took over as president of Neiman Marcus after his father's death. Today *Neiman Marcus* has annual revenues of more than $2.5 billion.

Marks, Michael

Marks & Spencer is a British institution. About a quarter of the adult British population visits the department stores each week. Today the stores sell clothing, cosmetics, and food. Many Americans who become aware of the store when traveling incorrectly assume that the "Spencer" in the name has something to do with Princess Diana. In fact, the chain owes its existence to a Russian immigrant and a Yorkshire cashier. Michael Marks was born in Slonim, Russia in 1859. As a young man, with no English-speaking skill, he emigrated to Britain. He landed in Leeds because he heard of a company there called Barran, which was known to employ Jewish refugees. In 1884 Marks met warehouse owner Isaac Dewhurst. Marks agreed to buy goods from Dewhurst and sell them in the numerous villages in the area. Thus Marks was able to raise enough money to open stalls in a few local markets. He tried attracting customers to one of his stalls with a large sign reading Don't Ask the Price, It's a Penny. It was a stunning success. Marks opened several penny stalls after that, each one more successful than the last. In 1894 Marks decided he needed a partner to help him expand the business. His former partner, Isaac Dewhurst was not interested, but he did know someone else who might be. He introduced Marks to a cashier, Tom Spencer. Spencer was born in Yorkshire, England on November 7, 1851. He already knew about Marks and his penny stalls. He was more than willing to part with £300 to become the entrepreneur's partner. Spencer, who had contacts and an ability to haggle for wholesale prices, took over management duties of the office and warehouse. Marks continued to run the market stalls. Within six years, the partners had opened thirty-four penny bazaars. In 1903 *Marks & Spencer* became a limited company. Spencer's original £300 had grown to £15,000. Spencer retired to a farm later that year. He passed away July 25, 1905. Michael Marks passed away the last day of 1907. The company ended up in the hands of Marks' son Simon and Simon's brother-in-law Israel Sieff. In 1928 they registered a trademark that is famous throughout England and Europe—the St. Michael brand. Because it could serve as a tribute to founder Michael

Marks, St. Michael narrowly beat out St. Joan to grace the store's shirts, pajamas, and undergarments. In 1999 there were 470 Marks & Spencer stores employing 71,300 people.

Martin, Christian

Christian Frederick Martin was born January 31, 1796 in Germany. From boyhood, Martin worked in his father's guitar-making shop, learning the trade. As a young man he moved to Vienna, Austria, where he got a job with guitar-maker Johann Stauffer. Next he worked for a man named Karl Kuhle. Kule's daughter Ottile caught Martin's eye. They were married and had a son, Christian F. Martin, Jr., in 1825. The Martins moved back to Germany shortly thereafter. A bitter labor dispute surrounded guitar making in that country in the early 1800s. People like Christian's father, Johann, had started their careers as cabinetmakers. The Violin Makers Guild was opposed to allowing furniture makers to craft musical instruments. The Cabinetmakers Guild argued that its members were clearly able to make quality instruments. Martin, a member of the Cabinetmakers Guild, got tired of dealing with the dispute. He made plans to move his family to America. The Cabinetmakers Guild won the right to legally make guitars in 1832, but a year later, Martin and his family still went to New York. There, Martin opened a music store. Over the next five years, the Martins had two more children and befriended a number of fellow members of the Moravian religion who lived in Nazareth, Pennsylvania. They decided to move there and two more Martins were born. Over the next two decades, Martin's business grew and prospered. Christian Martin died February 16, 1873. Six generations later, *The Martin Guitar Company* is still a family-run business. After Martin's death, his son Christian took the helm. When he died in 1888, his son, Frank Henry Martin, inherited the company. It was, in turn, passed on to his son, Christian Frederick Martin III, in 1948. His son, Frank Herbert Martin, followed his father. The current chairman and CEO is Christian Frederick Martin IV. Martin guitars were used by Gene Autry, Johnny Cash, Willie Nelson, Eric Clapton, and, in the words of C. F. Martin IV, "both Elvises,

Elvis Presley and Elvis Costello." C. F. Martin himself, by the way, does not play guitar. "At least not in public," he says.

Martin, Joe

"Smokey" Joe Martin was the assistant chief of the New York City Fire Department from 1919 to 1930. During World War II, the U.S. government became concerned that the Japanese might target forests, burning up much-needed lumber. They launched a campaign to education the public about forest-fire prevention. They created the Cooperative Forest Fire Prevention Program, which hired the Wartime Advertising Council (now simply the Ad Council) to develop a campaign. They tried a number of different approaches, including patriotic war slogans and posters featuring Walt Disney's Bambi, before arriving at the idea of a fire-prevention bear. Artist Albert Staehle was hired to create the image of the new character. They named him *Smokey Bear* after Martin. In 1950, the character was brought to life. A carelessly discarded cigarette set the Los Tablos in the Lincoln National Forest ablaze. A second blaze, known as the Captain Gap fire, started two days later. Together they destroyed 17,000 acres and the homes of the area's wildlife. On May 9, a fire crew found a scared little black bear cub holding on to the side of a scorched pine tree. Because his buttocks and feet were badly burned, the firefighters affectionately dubbed him "Hotfoot." Game warden Ray Bell had the cub treated at the veterinary hospital in Santa Fe. When he had recovered, he took Hotfoot to his home, where he took naps in a washing machine and was reported to be a "mite domineering" with the other family pets. When U.S. forestry officials heard the story, they adopted him as the real-life Smokey. He was flown to Washington's National Airport in a Piper Cub airplane to begin a life of government service. At the height of Smokey Bear's popularity, surveys showed his image was the second-most recognizable after Santa Claus. He got so much mail from children that he was given his own zip code. At the time, he was the only celebrity besides the U.S. president to have such an honor. He even became the first (and probably the only) bear to appear on the TV game show

"What's My Line?" He stumped the panel. In the 1970s, CB radio enthusiasts noticed the similarity in the hats worn by state highway patrolmen and that worn by the fire prevention character. They started to refer to a state trooper as "Smokey Bear," later truncated to "Smokey." Smokey retired in 1975 and died a year later when he was the physical equivalent of a seventy-year-old human. The *Washington Post* printed an obituary for Mr. Bear. Smokey Bear was buried near his original home, the Capitan Mountains. Visitors regularly visit his grave. Capitan, New Mexico honored its most famous bear by naming the main street Smokey Bear Boulevard. The U.S. Forest Service estimates that forest fires have been reduced by half since the beginning of the Smokey Bear campaign. This fact is especially impressive as the number of people who visit U.S. forests has increased ten times since 1940.

Martinet, Jean

In 1660, King Louis XIV of France appointed a nineteen-year-old war minister named François Michel Le Tellier Louvain to reorganize the army. Until that point there had been little military organization since the fall of the Roman Empire. Louvain's first step was to put the army in the employ of the state. Soldiers in France had previously been hired by the colonels. He put the new Royal Regiment under the command of Col. Jean Martinet. Martinet, in turn, developed a set of drills. To make effective use of inaccurate muskets, concentrated volleys had to be delivered at short range. Martinet had the troops fire together on command and advance in straight battle lines. The order and strict discipline at first amused the British, who made fun of the so-called Martinets. Thus *martinet* became a synonym for "strict disciplinarian." Despite the teasing by the British, eventually all the countries in Europe adopted Martinet's drills. Straight battle lines had seen their day by the time the American Civil War broke out. Soldiers then abandoned the formations and took cover in trenches. In France, Martinet's name was never associated with strict discipline. There he is better known for the small copper pontoons he invented.

Martini, Alessandro

Alessandro Martini was a commercial agent for the vintner and vermouth-maker Distilleria Nazionale di Spirito di Vino in Tuscany, Italy in 1860 when the company's founder died. Along with bookkeeper Teofoilo Sola and winemaker Luigi Rossi, Martini came to the fore to run things. The company was renamed Martini, Sola e Cia in 1863. Their vermouth and liqueurs were exported to the United States for the first time in 1867. In 1879, Sola died. His sons sold his part of the business to Rossi. The company was renamed *Martini and Rossi.* The martini cocktail probably did not take its name from Martini and Rossi vermouth (although it is often used as an ingredient). The cocktail was a favorite by World War I and became even more popular during prohibition because it was easier to make at home than brandy or scotch. Some credit Martini di Armi di Taggia, the head bartender at the Knickerbocker Hotel in New York City, with the invention of the martini. A more farfetched theory is that a German opera composer, J. P. Schwartzendorf, who had the nickname "Martini," was the inspiration for the name. Schwartzendorf drank a blend of gin, Chablis, and cinnamon. It is likely that no one named "Martini" was behind the drink at all. The earliest printed reference to the cocktail, Henry Johnson's *New and Improved Illustrated Bartender's Manual, or How to Mix Drinks of the Present Style,* published in 1888, calls it a "Martinez." According to one common account, the "Martinez" was first mixed by San Francisco bartender Jerry Thomas, who first served it to a traveler bound for the town of Martinez. Another explanation is that the drink actually originated in Martinez. This version of the story credits a bartender named Julio Richelieu with its creation. Should you drink your martini shaken or stirred? It depends on whom you ask. Most martini lovers say you should not follow the example of James Bond. The martini should be stirred, not shaken. Shaking causes too much dilution. A group of scientist begs to differ. According to the *Toronto Star,* scientists at the University of Western Ontario, whose research was published in the *British Medical Journal,* say shaking a martini lets it maintain higher levels of age-delaying chemicals. The researchers concluded that

"007's profound state of health may be due, at least in part, to compliant bartenders."

Martino, Anthony

Anthony A. Martino was born January 7, 1933 in Philadelphia into a family of railroad workers. A high-school dropout, Martino got a job working at an auto-repair shop. When automatic transmissions became popular in the late 1950s, many of the older mechanics did not know how to fix them. Martino sensed an opportunity. With $3,000 his dad had lent him, Martino opened a shop that specialized in automatic transmissions. He called it the Anthony A. Martino Company, or AAMCO for short. Older mechanics referred customers to him and the business grew. He opened five more shops. In 1962, Martino consulted a franchise expert, Robert Morgan. Most people told Martino that auto repair would simply not work as a franchise, but Morgan felt differently. They started offering franchises and in less than five years there were more than 500 AAMCOs in the country. Martino had enough money that he would never have to work again if he didn't want to. So he retired from the company. He found, however, that he preferred to work. In 1972, he started a new company to do automotive body work. He used his initials again in the naming of his venture—MAACO. Along with a partner, Daniel Rhode, Martino sold franchises almost immediately. The first one opened in Tucson, Arizona. It was joined by seven more the next year. The number increased to 200 the year after that. In 1982, the partners started another company, Sparks Tune-Up. Within five years it was a chain of 125 stores. In 1987 they sold the chain to a British company, GKN. A year later, Martino teamed up with the owner of the Goddard School in Pennsylvania and franchised the Goddard Early Learning Centers. In 1997, AAMCO had estimated sales of $450 million. What is more, today, thanks in part to Martino's strategies, consumers are used to going to specialty franchises for service, says AAMCO's vice-president of franchise development Jack Wilki. "Brake, fast-tune, and muffler specialists work in each other's favor," he says. AAMCO has brand recognition of 93 percent and MAACO has become a household brand name thanks to the advertising slogan "Uh-oh, better get MAACO."

Matchabelli, Georges

Georges Matchabelli was the oldest son of a family of Russian nobles. He received his education at the Royal Academy in Berlin, where he studied mining engineering and languages because he expected to take over the management of his family's estates in southern Russia. As an ambassador for his country he traveled throughout Europe and met and married the Italian silent-movie star Maria Carmi. Matchabelli's life was changed forever in 1919. While he was in Europe his family lost its estates during the Bolshevik revolution. He was a prince without a country. Fortunately, Maria was invited to reprise her role in the play *The Miracle on Broadway* in America. The Matchabellis moved to New York, where Maria Carmi was celebrated. Having been treated as royalty in the past, her husband did not want to be known as Mr. Carmi. He opened an antique store called Le Rouge et le Noir on Madison Avenue. With his royal title, his famous wife, and his charming mannerisms, the shop soon became a favorite of wealthy socialites and celebrities. Matchabelli catered to his female clients by mixing individual perfumes to match their personalities. When more women wanted the perfume than the bottles he decided to stop selling antiques all together. Joining him in the perfume business were a number of his old friends—exiled counts and barons. In America they mixed ingredients for perfumes and cosmetics. Matchabelli designed a special bottle for his own signature perfume. It was decorated in gold and was in the shape of a crown taken from his family coat-of-arms. This was the beginning of the *Prince Matchabelli* line of fragrances and bath oils.

Matsuda, Jujiro

The twelfth son of a fisherman in the Hiroshima Prefecture in Japan, Jujiro Matsuda was born August 6, 1875. His father died when he was just a toddler. Matsuda began working at the age of thirteen in a blacksmith shop in Osaka. By the time he was twenty, he was running his own shop, which employed 50 workers.

A recession forced him out of business, but only temporarily. Eleven years later, in a converted cowshed, he and his son Tsuneji invented a pump, which they patented. The result was the Matsuda Pump Partnership. It was taken over by another businessman a few years later. In 1912 he was back with a new enterprise called Matsuda Works. The company produced artillery fuses for the Russian czar. In 1920 Matsuda was one of a group of investors to take over a failing cork company. This was renamed Toyo Kogyo Kaisha (Orient Industry Company). The company quickly expanded into noncork-related production. In 1931 it produced its first motor vehicles. These were three-wheeled trucks for the Chinese market. Toyo Kogyo's executives knew that if they were going to sell automobiles internationally, they would need a name that was easier for foreign tongues to pronounce. They decided to name their vehicles after their president, Matsuda. In Japanese, no syllables are ever stressed and some inner syllables are barely audible. Matsuda, therefore, is generally pronounced "Matsda." To make it even easier to pronounce, the spelling was changed to *Mazda*. The word Mazda already had a meaning. It is the name of a Persian god of light. The full name of the ancient Zoroastrian deity is Ahura Mazda, which means, literally, "Lord Wisdom." Automotive production came to a halt in 1938 as a result of World War II. The machinery was converted to produce munitions and the number of employees swelled from 1,000 to 9,000. Jujiro Matsuda's seventieth birthday, August 6, 1945, would not be a day of celebration. At 8:15 an atomic bomb exploded 1,900 feet above Hiroshima. Those near the center died immediately. Others, farther from the hypocenter, suffered burns, blindness, and slow, painful deaths from radiation. In all, about 140,000 people were killed. Toyo Kogyo was fortunate to be on the city's eastern perimeter. There, partially shielded by a hill, roughly half of the factory survived the blast. Under the leadership of Tsuneji Matsuda, the company quickly got back to business. Jujiro passed away in 1951. The first Mazda passenger car was produced in 1960, but it wasn't until 1984 that the company itself changed its name to *Mazda Motor Corporation*. Today Mazda is Japan's fifth-largest auto maker. It sells some 335,000 vehicles annually in Japan and almost 550,000 more in other countries.

Maxwell, Harriet

In 1859, Col. John Overton began construction on a luxury hotel in Nashville, which then had a population of only 16,986. Some Nashville residents thought he was crazy. They called the project "Overton's Folly." When the city was occupied by Union troops during the Civil War, construction on the hotel stopped. The building was taken over for use as a prison for captured Confederate soldiers. At that time it was called Zollicoffer's Barracks. When the war ended, Overton was able to complete his hotel. He named it the *Maxwell House* in honor of his wife, the former Harriet Maxwell. The hotel became a favorite of celebrities and politicians. In 1873 a traveling salesman named Joel Cheek was promoted to a partnership in his grocery product business. Settling down in Nashville, he began experimenting with coffee. His coffee-roasting hobby took up more and more of his time until he finally decided to quit his day job and devote all his energy to java. When he had a blend he was satisfied with he presented it to the management of the Maxwell House. The brew was popular with the guests, many of whom bought it for use in their homes. Years later Theodore Roosevelt was visiting the old home of Andrew Jackson. The hostess asked him if he would like another cup of Maxwell House coffee. He said, "Delighted! It's good to the last drop." The president's utterance was adopted as the official Maxwell House coffee slogan and is still used today. The famous Maxwell House jingle, featuring the sound of a syncopated percolator, debuted in 1960. The commercial was created by David Ogilvy. It was, in the words of Mark Pendergrast, the author of *Uncommon Grounds: The History of Coffee and How It Transformed Our World,* "a brilliant, evocative commercial, even though it celebrated a dreadful way to brew coffee." The original Maxwell House hotel burned to the ground on Christmas night 1961. A new luxury hotel in Nashville bears its name.

Mercator, Gerardus

Gerardus Mercator was born March 5, 1512 in Rupelmonde, Flanders. His family was German, but they had moved to Flanders shortly before his birth. He studied philosophy and earned his master's degree at the University of Louvain in

1532. His interest soon shifted, however, from religion and philosophy to geography and astronomy. He learned about mathematics under the tutelage of the noted astronomer and mathematician Gemma Frisius. In 1534 Mercator married Barbara Schellekens. They had six children. In the early 1530s, Mercator earned a reputation as a skilled cartographer and globe maker. With Frisius, Mercator made his first globe of the earth in 1535, and a celestial globe a year later. In 1537 he published a map of Palestine. A year later, he made his first world map based on the work of Ptolemy. Charles V, Holy Roman emperor from 1519 to 1558, was his patron. At Charles' court, Mercator met navigators and cartographers from Portugal and Spain who helped him improve the accuracy of his maps. In 1544 he became one of forty-three Louvain residents to be charged with heresy. He was arrested, and jailed for seven months. But the university stood behind him, and after his release, he was permitted to go back to work. Years later, in 1552, he left Louvain and established a cartographic workshop of his own in Duisburg. In a little more than a decade, his reputation was such that he was appointed court "cosmographer" to Duke Wilhelm of Cleve. During this period, he conceived of a system of depicting longitude and latitude on a flat map of a round globe. Using the system, a sailor could use a map to chart straight-line courses. The system came to be known as a Mercator projection. It was the world's most common projection for navigators' maps for nearly four hundred years. Mercator also gave our language the word "atlas," meaning a collection of maps. He published a book of maps in 1569 with a picture on the front of Atlas holding the world on his back. The god's name came to be applied to any such book. Mercator died December 2, 1594 in Duisburg.

Moody, John

John Moody learned the hard way the value of keeping track of business information. Working as an errand boy for Spencer Trask & Company, a Wall Street investment firm in the late 1800s, he delivered bonds to the wealthy J. P. Morgan. One day, Moody forgot to write down the value of his shipment. When

Morgan asked him the value later, Moody said they totaled between $50,000 and $55,000. Morgan reasonably wanted to know which it was, $50,000 or $55,000. Moody didn't remember. "Don't remember?!" Morgan's tirade began. By the time the industrialist had finished with Moody, the young man had resolved never to make that kind of mistake again. The much more careful Moody quickly rose to the head of the statistical department at Spencer Trask. In those days, the Securities and Exchange Commission had not yet come into existence. Information on how companies were doing was a well-guarded secret. Moody wondered how anyone could invest with confidence in such an environment. In his free time, he began compiling a company information guide for potential investors. He convinced a printer to print up a prospectus of the information for free as long as he would get the job of printing the actual manual. Moody mailed the prospectus to 5,000 insurance agencies, brokers, and bankers. To sound like a Wall Street insider, he arranged to have a Wall Street return address. This he did by asking a used bookstore to let him have his mail sent there. In just two weeks, hundreds of orders, containing advance payment, rolled in. *Moody's Manual of Industrial and Miscellaneous Securities* was released in 1900 when Moody was thirty-two. It sold out in only a few months. As he became more prominent, he introduced *Moody's Investors Magazine.* Two years later, the panic of 1907 left Moody in debt and he lost control of his company. He tried again two years later, introducing his *Railroad Manual.* He used the Aaa-through-C symbols that have since become a world standard to rate some fifteen hundred individual securities of over two hundred U.S. railroads. "It raised a storm of opposition, not to mention ridicule from some quarters," Moody would later say. "But it took hold with dealers and investment houses." Later that year he published *Moody's Weekly Review of Financial Conditions. Moody's Investors Service* was launched in 1914. The new enterprise flourished. Purchased by Dun & Bradstreet in 1962, Moody's today publishes credit ratings and other financial information on about 70,000 commercial and 60,000 government entities in seventy countries.

Morgan, Justin

Justin Morgan was an aspiring musician and schoolteacher from Springfield, Vermont. In 1795, he accepted a colt as payment for a loan. Morgan named the two-year-old colt Figure. Figure was small, fourteen hands high and 800 pounds. Morgan's "pony horse" was a cause of mirth among some neighbors. But Morgan trained him to race and pull. It became clear that Figure was exceptionally strong for his size and highly intelligent. The horse proved his worth by winning races against much larger Thoroughbreds. Justin Morgan died of tuberculosis in 1798 when Figure was five. The stallion was then renamed "Justin Morgan" in line with a tradition of naming horses after previous owners. Justin Morgan, the horse, had a number of owners in the course of his twenty-eight-year life. He sired numerous offspring, the beginning of the Morgan breed of horses. More than one hundred thirty thousand horses have been recorded since the American Morgan Horse Registry was formed in 1894. Today, the breed enjoys great popularity in all fifty states and in over twenty foreign countries. Every registered *Morgan horse* traces back to Justin Morgan through his best-known sons, Bulrush, Sherman, and Woodbury.

Mornay, Philippe de

Born November 5, 1549 in Normandy, France, Philippe de Mornay received a Protestant education and attended the University of Heidelberg. He narrowly escaped the massacre of French Protestants on Saint Bartholomew's Day in 1572. He spent the next five years writing on Protestant political issues. He is often credited with writing the *Vindiciae contra tyrannos,* an early tract advocating the people's right to resist an evil king. Mornay became the chief diplomatic agent for the Huguenot leader Henry of Navarre, who would go on to be crowned Henry IV, king of France. Philippe de Mornay remained the king's right-hand man until Henry reconciled with the Roman Catholic Church in 1593. Mornay continued to write and publish. His works influenced the development of Protestant thought in France. He appears in this book, however, for a sauce he whipped up once for his friend the king. The sauce, made with fish broth, Parmesan and Gruyere cheeses, and butter, came to be known as *Mornay sauce.*

Mott, Samuel R.

In 1842, Samuel R. Mott of Brouckville, New York, began selling apple cider and vinegar. He made it by first crushing apples with two large stones pulled by horses. He then shoveled the crushed apples into a crib with slotted sides that was packed in straw. Finally three men would lean on a lever that operated a jackscrew to squeeze out the juice. Later, Mott replaced the horse- and manpower with waterpower and steam. With the help of his son, he enlarged the cider mill. It became the first American mill to use a scientifically controlled oxidation process instead of letting the cider age in open tanks. By the 1880s, he was shipping champagne cider and vinegar to California in 1,000-case lots. In 1900, the S. R. Mott company merged with the W. B. Duffy Cider Company of Rochester, New York creating Duffy-Mott, which was incorporated in 1914. It would be another thirty years before the company would introduce *Mott's Apple Sauce.* Eight years later the company introduced Mott's Apple Juice. Cider had always been thought of as a seasonal product. Thanks to new filtering and pasteurization techniques, apple juice could be sold and consumed year round. The two products helped to make Mott a household name. Today, Mott's makes more than thirteen million cases of apple sauce and apple juice each year.

Moxie, Lieutenant

According to old promotional materials, Lieutenant Moxie was a soldier in the Civil War. Following that service, he went down to the jungles of South America near the Strait of Magellan. There the natives introduced him to a plant that they said had great powers. He brought the plant back to Lowell, Massachusetts and gave some to a physician, Augustin Thompson. The doctor used it as the chief ingredient for a soft drink, which he began selling as a nerve tonic. He named the beverage after the soldier. In all probability, however, this story was concocted for the newspapers. There is no documented history of a Lieutenant Moxie who fought in the Civil War. In any case, Moxie was the nation's first mass-marketed soft drink. In the early twentieth century, Moxie was aggressively market-ed as the drink that promoted vigor. It was billed as a cure for everything from "loss of manhood" to "paralysis, and softening of the brain." The company used celebrity pitchmen and print-ed the name Moxie on every conceivable product: toys, sheet music, candy, china, piano rolls, lap boards for picnics, and fans featuring the most popular movie stars. Soon people all over the country were singing "Just Make It a Moxie for Mine." But as sugar prices rose and Coca-cola and Pepsi gained promi-nence in the beverage market, Moxie sales began to dwindle. It is still made in New England and is lightly distributed on a local basis. Moxie promotional materials from the early twen-tieth century have become prized collectibles. The American language also retains a vestige of the drink's former glory. Moxie has become synonymous with the word "chutzpah" or "spunk" as in the expression, "She's got moxie."

Muffet, Patience

Patience Muffet was the daughter of the Reverend Dr. Thomas Muffet, or Mouffet, who lived from 1553 to 1604. Muffet was an entomologist—a bug scientist, not to be confused with an ety-mologist—a word scholar. Muffet wrote the scholarly book *The Silkwormes and Their Flies*. He had a special fondness for the spi-der because, in his words, "she doth beautify with her tapestry and hangings." He was convinced that spiders had medicinal properties, a belief that dates back to Aristotle's time. He fed ground spiders to his patients, including his daughter, when they were ill. Patience, it is said, was arachnaphobic. (She had a fear of spiders.) Most, but not all, nursery-rhyme watchers credit Thomas Muffet with composing a poem for his daugh-ter, the original Miss Muffet, that said: "Little Miss Muffet sat on a tuffet, eating her curds and whey. Along came a spider that sat down beside her, and frightened Miss Muffet away." Among the authors who doubt the story is Gloria T. Delamar, author of *Mother Goose: From Nursery to Literature*. She points out that the first version of the poem appears in the 1805 *Songs for the Nursery,* whose 1812 edition read, "Little Mary Ester sat upon a tester." An 1842 collection had a verse that read, "Little Miss Mopsey sat in a shopsey." And what is a "tuffet"? According to *The Oxford Dictionary of Nursery Rhymes,* "Miss Muffet probably sat on a grassy hillock, though tuffet has also been described as a 'three-legged-stool.' When she sits on a buffet she is certainly on a stool, and may come from the north country." "Curds and whey" refers to the solid and liquid parts of cottage cheese and similar milk dishes.

Mulholland, William

William Mulholland, an immigrant from Belfast, went to work as a ditch digger in Los Angeles, which was, in 1913, a small town with little hope of growing much because it was practically a desert. Eventually Mulholland worked his way up to the post of chief engineer of the city's municipal water system. The system desperately needed an overhaul. Mulholland got the idea to divert water from the Owens River 238 miles away. He set off in a mule-driven wagon, and when he returned, he convinced Los Angeles residents that it would be possible. They voted for the necessary $24 million bond issues and work began on an aqueduct. It took the crew of 5,000 six years to construct what *Life Magazine* called "one of the most difficult hydraulic feats ever undertaken in the U.S." At the opening ceremony, Mulholland just said, "There it is; take it." *Mulholland Drive* in Los Angeles bears his name. Another of the city's famous streets, *Wilshire Boulevard* (one of the landmarks named in Randy Newman's song "I Love L.A."), was named for H. Gaylord Wilshire, who lived from 1861 to 1927. He was an entrepreneur, inventor, failed politician, and socialist who founded the town of Fullerton and developed the street that bears his name. Not surprisingly, Los Angeles street names are often found in movies and television series. Sometimes they are transformed into the names of characters. The television series "Emergency!" was set at a hospital named "Rampart General" and featured paramedics "John Gage" played by Randolph Mantooth and "Roy DeSoto" played by Kevin Tighe. Rampart, Gage, and DeSoto are all L.A. street names. Another of the city's streets, Balboa Boulevard, was once home to a struggling actor and screenwriter named Sylvester Stallone. Stallone used the name of his street as the surname of his most famous character, Rocky.

Muller, Sandra

When Munich makeup artist Sandra Muller dated David Loubega, she had no idea her name would be familiar to music fans around the world. Born to a Ugandan father and a Sicilian mother in Munich in 1975, Loubega was an aspiring pop musician and a fan of soul and reggae music. He had been writing songs since he was twelve years old. Sometime after his breakup with Sandra, Loubega adopted the stage name Lou Bega and dashed out the lyrics for a little mambo number in about twenty minutes. The number of the mambo, in fact, was five. "Mambo No. 5," one of the tracks on Bega's debut album, mentions the names of nine real-life ex-girlfriends: Angela, Pamela, Sandra, Rita, Monica, Erica, Mary, Tina, and Jessica. "All these ladies meant something to me," he said. Sandra Muller was "like my first real love." Bega's CD, *A Little Bit of Mambo,* went multiplatinum, fueled by the runaway international hit "Mambo No. 5," which reached number one in nineteen countries. In 1999, Muller found herself on the phone with *People* magazine. She said she was "proud and flattered" to be in the song. In case you were wondering what happened to Mambos No. 1, 2, 3, and 4, there weren't any. Bega says the number five refers to the world's five continents (according to European tradition).

Münchhausen, Karl Friedrich Hieronymus, Baron von

Münchhausen was born May 11, 1720, in Bodenwerder, Germany. He served as a soldier with the Russians against the Turks in the service of Frederick the Great. After his retirement in 1760, he became famous for the exaggerated stories he told about his military life and his adventures as a hunter and sportsman. In 1781 a collection of stories called *Vademecum für lustige Leute,* or "Manual for Merry People," was released. The stories were credited to the baron. Four years later, a German author living in England, Rudolph Erich Raspe, published an even more fictionalized collection of adventures under the title: *Baron Munchausen's Narrative of His Marvellous Travels and Campaigns in Russia,* eventually shortened to *The Adventures of Baron Munchausen.* The tales, and the storytelling character, became popular in many languages. In 1850 the term "Munchausenism," meaning exaggerated tales, was applied to the writings of Herodotus, the ancient Greek historian. In the days of old radio, the Munchausen character was played by comedian Jack Peal. Peal, as Munchausen, would tell his inflated stories in a German accent to a sidekick named Charlie. When Charlie would doubt the veracity of the tales, Peal would answer, "Vas you dere, Sharlie?" The expression became a national catchphrase. In 1989, former Monty Python cartoonist Terry Gilliam directed a film version of the adventures. The baron has also made his way into psychological terminology. In 1951, English physician Richard Asher identified a mental illness in which patients fake symptoms of catastrophic illness to get attention. He called the disorder *Munchausen syndrome.* Related is *Munchausen by proxy syndrome.* The first clinical description of this disorder was published in 1977 by the British pediatrician Roy Meadow. Munchausen-by-proxy patients are parents, usually mothers, who systematically invent illnesses for their children. Sometimes they even purposely make their children sick in order to get the attention they crave.

N/O

Nash, Charles

Charles W. Nash was born January 28, 1864 in De Kalb, Illinois. His parents separated when he was a young boy and he was apprenticed to a farmer in Michigan. At the age of twelve he ran away and got a job as farmhand on another man's land. He saved up his tiny wage and bought a flock of sheep. He sold their wool and saved the profits, less a small amount to buy books, which he used to teach himself to read. When he reached the age of eighteen, he sold his flock and bought half a share in a hay-cutting machine. He traveled from farm to farm until 1884 when he met his future wife, Jessie Halleck, and settled down in a home outside Flint, Michigan. He continued to work as a farmhand and sometime carpenter. After another six years he decided to find work in the city. He got a job at a carriage factory. His hard work caught the attention of his boss, who quickly promoted him to supervisor, then general manager, and finally vice-president. As part of this job he attended, in 1897, a trade show in New York. There he drove his first motorized carriage. He fell in love with the automobile and joined with William Durant and David D. Buick to form the Buick Motor Company. He became the company's president and general manager. Then, in 1910, he was hired away by a struggling auto maker named General Motors. As president of GM, Nash turned things around by putting almost all of the company's earnings into paying off old debts. Whatever was left, he channeled back into the company for new equipment and improvements. This did not please the stockholders, who did not see any dividends. Nash felt the dissatisfaction with his performance and he started to look for his next opportunity. He found it in another struggling automotive company. The business had been founded by a Kenosha, Wisconsin bicycle maker named Thomas Jeffrey. Jeffrey had introduced a car he called the Rambler in 1902. It was popular and sold as well as could be expected for a vehicle of its time. When Jeffrey died ten years later, however, his family did not know how to run things. By 1916, they were in desperate financial straits. Nash snapped up the company for $5 million and renamed it the *Nash Motor Company*. In spite of, or perhaps because of, his humble upbringing, Nash had little sympathy for the workers in his factory. He himself worked sixteen-hour days and from 1916 to 1925 he never took a vacation. He did not see why anyone else should work any less. He was a penny pincher. His workers had the lowest pay in the industry and his factories were notoriously dangerous. He had a red light in his office that went on whenever the assembly line stopped. On one occasion, the light went on and he rushed into the plant to find three severed fingers lying next to a machine. He wanted to know why the line had stopped. The foreman explained that the workers were upset by the accident. Nash ordered the foreman to get the crew back to work with a brusque "brush them off and keep going." The workers called this intimidating man "the Chief." But the Chief himself believed he had a good relationship with his workers. He prided himself on knowing each employee by name, although his foreman often prompted him when he toured the plant. He personally handed out the $10 Christmas Eve bonuses, and thought of himself as a beloved, benevolent patriarch. During the labor movement of the 1930s, he predictably opposed the idea of a union. He vowed he would close the plant before he would recognize such an organization. When he was finally forced to recognize a union, he felt personally betrayed. He decided it was time to retire and he sought out someone to take over day-to-day operations. He approached George W. Mason, who had been running the Kelvinator refrigerator company. Mason said he was happy at Kelvinator and didn't want to leave, so Nash bought that company in 1937, forming the Nash-Kelvinator Corporation. He put Mason in charge and moved to Beverly Hills. His personal fortune was estimated at more than $100 million. He died eleven years later at the age of eighty-four. After the ups and downs of the depression and war years, the Nash Motor Company began the 1950s as an important player in the U.S. auto market. In 1950, Nash dusted off the name Rambler, which it introduced as the first "compact car." But the big Detroit auto makers were beginning to dominate the market. Ford and Chevrolet started to introduce new body styles each year, something that had never been done before. Independent auto makers were closing their doors every day. Nash's executives made a proposal. To be competitive, they argued, the biggest of the little guys—Nash, Hudson, Packard, and Studebaker—should merge. By the time consolidations did take place it was too little too late for many of the once-proud automotive names. Nash and Hudson combined to form American Motors in 1954. Studebaker and Packard ceased production in 1956. A year later, the Hudson and Nash nameplates disappeared. American Motors continued to produce the Rambler until 1969. AMC became affiliated with Renault in 1978 and was sold to Chrysler in 1987. Although the Nash Rambler is long gone, it is remembered by collectors and enthusiasts who take part in Nash clubs. Some who are too young to remember the car itself are familiar with the name thanks to the novelty song "Beep Beep" by the Playmates, which was a number-four hit in 1958. The song starts slowly and accelerates as it goes on to tell the story of a Rambler outpacing a Cadillac. The punch line of the song has the driver of the Rambler calling out, "Buddy, how can I get this car out of second gear?" Trivia question for oldies fans: Can you name any of the Playmates' other singles? Answer: Before "Beep Beep" they had a hit with "Jo-Ann." They followed "Beep Beep" with the Top 40 singles "What Is Love?" and "Wait for Me" and another novelty number, "Keep Your Hands in Your Pockets."

Nethercutt, Merle

Merle Nethercutt was born on an Indiana farm January 15, 1887. A lively, gregarious young woman, she embarked on one of the few careers available to women of her day—teaching. She gave up that career, however, when she married Andrew Norman. The couple moved to Ocean Park, California. They had no children of their own, but she often cared for the children of her brother, C.C., a widower. When he remarried, his oldest son, Jack, stayed with the Normans. Not content with the life of a homemaker, Norman worked as a hospital lab technician during the day and studied chemistry at night. Using her training, she set out to create a tonic to improve the complexion. Mixing the ingredients in a large coffeepot on her stove, she finally found a face cream that satisfied her. At first, she gave it away to friends and neighbors. Eventually, however, the demand was so great that she began to sell it. It was not long before her home became insufficient as a place of business. So, in 1931, with only $150 in capital, she opened her own shop and lab in a vacant garage across the street. Although the nation was in the middle of the Great Depression, Norman was convinced that she could make a living selling skin treatments and cosmetics. Her plan was to give away samples. She believed that the majority of the women who received free facials would become paying customers. It was a risky move in such unstable times, but it paid off. *Merle Norman Cosmetics* grew and thrived in spite of the national depression and supply shortages during World War II. Merle Norman continued to run the company personally until the early 1960s. Within a period of a few years Norman lost her husband, her brother C.C., and her mother. The strain caused her own health to deteriorate. She retired and handed the reins over to her nephew Jack Nethercutt. She spent the last decade of her life traveling. She passed away during a trip to Australia on February 1, 1972, at the age of eighty-five. Her name lives on in the more than two thousand independently owned and operated Merle Norman Cosmetic Studios in the United States and Canada.

Nicholas

Nicholas was born into a wealthy family sometime before A.D. 300. He was, right from his birth, full of religious passion. It is said he would refuse his mother's breast on feast days and fast days. When a plague took the lives of his parents, Nicholas dedicated his life to helping others. He tried to do his good works secretly. Once he learned of three young women who were going to sell themselves into prostitution to help their father, who had fallen into poverty. Nicholas, who had inherited his family's wealth, secretly visited their house for three nights and each time he threw a ball of gold through the open window. In some versions of the tale, the balls land in the stockings the daughters had hung by the chimney to dry. Nicholas became a bishop of Myra, Turkey. He was imprisoned by the Roman emperor Gaius Diocletianus, who wanted to put an end to Christianity. He was later freed by the emperor Constantine. By some accounts, Nicholas attended the Council of Nicaea in 325. After becoming a bishop, Nicholas continued to help others, both publicly and in secret. During a time of famine he served "miraculous" bread to the poor, making him the patron saint of bakers. He became the patron saint of children in trouble when he rescued three murdered boys from a butcher's cellar and brought them back to life. The butcher had planned to sell their meat since there was no other food available. Nicholas is also said to have stilled a sea storm, making him the patron saint of sailors. Since his death on December 6, 342, he has often appeared to sailors to guide them through stormy seas. The sailors carried his legends to ports in Asia and Europe. He became the patron saint of Russia when the czar Vladimir converted to Christianity in the tenth century. In 1087 sailors from Bari stole the saint's bones from Myra, which was then under Muslim control. They now rest in the San Nicola basilica in Italy. In the northern European countries, stories of Nicholas merged with tales of Norse gods who rode horses across the skies. His famous habit of leaving gifts at night led to the tradition, in many countries, of secretly leaving gifts for children the night before Saint Nicholas Day, December 6. He is known by a number of variations on his name in different parts of the world. In some places he is called Harry Nicholas, Klaubauf, Pelznichol, Knect Ruprecht, or Krampus. In Holland he is known as Sinter Klaas (Sinter meaning Saint and Klaas being a shortened version of

Nicholas). In England, after the Reformation of the seventeenth century, in which the Catholic Church was replaced by the Church of England as the official state religion, the celebration of Saint Nicholas Day was banned. In the saint's place, the English created a character called Father Christmas, a bearded figure with a crown of holly. This Christmas character came to America with the early settlers. Immigrants from Germany and Holland brought their Saint Nicholas and Sinter Klaas traditions along as well. Their stories merged, creating a character with Father Christmas's white beard who rode through the sky and secretly delivered presents to children. He was called by an Anglicized version of Sinter Klaas—*Santa Claus*. He is still often referred to as *Old Saint Nick*. The name Kris Kringle comes from the German Christkindl, or "Christ child." Our modern ideas about Santa can be traced to Clement Moore's poem "An Account of a Visit from Saint Nicholas," more commonly known as "T'was the Night Before Christmas." Bavarian artist Thomas Nast, the illustrator who popularized the elephant and donkey as symbols for the Republican and Democratic parties, also gave us the image of Santa that we know and love today.

Nordstrom, John

John Nordstrom was sixteen when he left his native Sweden in 1887 bound for New York. He arrived, as legend has it, with $5 in his pocket and a dream to make a better life for himself in America. He traveled across the country working in mines and logging camps. By 1897 he had landed in Seattle. On July 17, the decrepit steamship SS *Portland* arrived from the Yukon carrying 68 men, fresh from the mines of Klondike, Alaska. The miners were carrying boxes and bags loaded with gold. As word spread of their discovery, people flooded the formerly sleepy town. Over the next two years, 100,000 men arrived in the city bound for the Klondike. Nordstrom immediately joined the northward migration. An estimated $10 million in Yukon gold was found the first year. Yet most of the Alaska gold diggers were not successful. Historians estimate maybe 300 struck it rich, and of those only a fraction managed to keep hold of the money. The real beneficiaries were Seattle merchants who supplied the miners. They brought in $25 million—eighty times the sales of 1896. Nordstrom managed to be both a successful miner—he made $13,000 over two years—and a successful Seattle businessman who benefited from the gold boom. While in Alaska, he had met a man named Carl Wallin who owned a shoe store in Seattle. In 1901, Nordstrom invested his money in partnership with Wallin to open a new shoe store, Wallin & Nordstrom. By 1923, the business had grown enough to warrant the opening of a second store. In 1928, John Nordstrom retired and sold his share of the company to his sons, Everett and Elmer. When Carl Wallin retired a year later, he too sold his share to the Nordstroms. A third son, Lloyd, signed on in 1933. The three Nordstrom sons built the company into the largest independent shoe chain in the United States. In the early 1960s the company expanded by buying a number of fashion retailers. In 1968 the second-generation Nordstroms turned the business over to the next Nordstrom generation. Today *Nordstrom, Inc.* employs 47,000 people in seventy Nordstrom stores and twenty-five outlet stores in twenty-three states. Members of the Nordstrom family still own about one-third of Nordstrom stock.

Obsius

Little is known about the ancient Roman Obsius except that back in the days of the naturalist Pliny the Elder, he discovered a volcanic rock while in Ethiopia. The rock is created when magma from a volcano cools so quickly that all the component minerals remain blended and crystals do not have time to form. This gives it a glassy look. It can be black, grey, brown, or green, but when sliced thin it is almost clear. Thus it is known as natural glass. It has been widely used for tools and weapons. Its shiny surface often served as a mirror. The ancient Mexican cultures especially made use of it. Small stones of the material, formed when the magma spray fell as individual droplets, are called "Apache tears," for legend states that the earth cried when Apache warriors were killed in battle. Those who believe in the healing power of stones consider it to have properties that can protect the bearer from emotional draining from others. Pliny the Elder wrote about Obsius's discovery in his natural-history book. He dubbed the stone "obsianus" after its discoverer. Later scholars misread Pliny's handwriting and added a *d* to the name. Thus, it is now known as *obsidian*. *Obsidian Cliff* in Yellowstone is so named because it is composed largely of the rock. In recent times, some surgeons have traded in their steel scalpels for tools made out of the stone. They say it can cut tissue with less trauma and leave a smaller scar. Archaeologists can date artifacts made with the material. Water molecules absorbed by inward diffusion through cut surfaces cause the outer areas of an obsidian article to convert to the mineral perlite. An object may be dated by measuring the thickness of this perlite. The process is called *obsidian hydration-rim dating*.

O'Hare, Edward

Edward ("Butch") O'Hare was born March 13, 1914 in St. Louis, the son of a wealthy attorney and businessman. He was described in the biography *Fateful Rendezvous: The Life of Butch O'Hare*, by Steve Ewing and John B. Lundstrom, as a fat, somewhat lazy little boy. His father, determined to toughen him up, sent him to military school against his will. After O'Hare graduated in the top third of his class, his father used his political connections to get him enrolled in the Naval Academy in the fall of 1933. He graduated 255th out of 323, but he had decided what he wanted to do with his life. He wanted to be a pilot. After his graduation from Annapolis, he was assigned to the USS *Mexico* to begin two requisite years on surface ships before he could specialize in aviation. In 1939, he finally began flight training at the Naval Air Station in Pensacola, Florida. That November his father was slain by a gunman connected with Al Capone. The newspapers speculated on the circumstances of the murder. Some papers printed their suspicions that he was connected with the Mob. Others believed he had given the government information that might be useful in its prosecution of the famous gangster. After completing his aviation training, O'Hare was assigned to the USS *Saratoga*'s Fighting Squadron. In early 1941 he was transferred to the *Enterprise*.

There he met a woman named Rita. He was so taken with her that he proposed marriage that day. They married six weeks later. On February 20, 1942, O'Hare was flying combat air patrol above the carrier *Lexington*. He engaged an incoming flight of eight enemy bombers and single-handedly shot five of them down, forcing the other three to retreat. He became a national hero and a Medal of Honor winner. He was promoted two grades, decorated by President Roosevelt, and sent on a national tour, which he hated, but did anyway. When his public relations duties were concluded, he returned to the Pacific, assigned to training duties at the Naval Air Station on the island of Maui. He returned to combat in 1943, taking part in an assault on Japanese-held Wake Island. He returned to the *Enterprise* in October. While he was stationed there the Japanese attacked with a torpedo operation. O'Hare, now an Air Group commander, decided that radar was essential. He organized teams of Hellcats and slow, radar-equipped torpedo bombers. During the first combat mission, O'Hare's plane disappeared. In 1949, Orchard Place Airport in Chicago was renamed *O'Hare* in his honor. A remnant of the former name remains in the three-letter abbreviation for the airport, ORD, which stands for "orchard." O'Hare International Airport is now the busiest airport in the world. It covers nearly 7,700 acres with fifty commercial, commuter, and cargo airlines and 162 aircraft gates in four terminals. Approximately 180,000 travelers pass through O'Hare each day.

Olds, Ransom E.

Olds was born in Geneva, Ohio. In the late 1800s he began to experiment with horseless carriages. His first successful steam-propelled three-wheeled vehicle was finished in 1885. That done, Olds began work on a gasoline-powered car. Although Henry Ford had driven a gasoline-powered vehicle before Olds, it was Olds who, in 1897, started the first auto company in what would soon be known as the Motor City. To get the working capital to go into production, he traded 95 percent of his company's stock to Samuel L. Smith. In 1899 the factory burned down leaving only one buggy, which they called the Oldsmobile. Out of necessity, they focused on mass-producing the single model. The *Oldsmobile* sold for an affordable $650, becoming America's best-selling car. The song "In My Merry Oldsmobile" became a popular hit, helping Olds to sell 425 of the vehicles in the first year. About 12,000 Oldsmobiles were produced between 1902 and 1904, when Olds sold his interest in the company. By 1905 the Olds Motor Works was producing 6,500 cars a year. Smith, however, wanted to drop the Oldsmobile in favor of a larger automobile. Ransom Olds quit the company and formed his own—the R. E. Olds Company. Smith sued his former partner for infringement and won. Since Olds was prohibited from using his own name, he called his company the Reo Motor Car Company. By 1907, Reo had become the third-largest auto manufacturer. Five years later, Olds retired from day-to-day operations of the company, but he kept veto power. Reo started to lag behind its competitors, and by the time Olds finally let go of the reins in 1934 the company was in no position to survive the Great Depression. The rock band REO Speedwagon took its name from a Reo fire engine. They said they chose the name because Reo had gone up against the big motor companies and REO Speedwagon felt they were going up against the big names in rock.

Osman I

Osman or Othman lived from 1259 to 1326 and led his Muslim followers to become the founder of an empire that covered large areas of Europe, Africa, and Asia. Since the area was centered in what we now call Turkey, *"Ottoman Empire"* and Turkey have sometimes been used interchangeably. The empire lasted until 1918. During the eighteenth century it sparked the imaginations of Europeans, who liked to purchase exotic products imported, or supposedly imported, from the far-off land. Merchants were eager to provide carpets, pillows, and furniture. One of the items that came into vogue at this time was a backless couch that seated two people. The French, who brought it in from the Ottoman Empire, called it an *ottoman*.

The furniture found its way from France to England. There, the term was applied to other furnishings, including a sofa with a back and an *ottoman footstool.*

Oster, John

John Oster began his career in the 1920s making the electric hair clippers that gave the flappers their new bobbed hairstyles. Before Oster came along, most electric clippers were as big as those farmers use to shear sheep. Working out of a basement with fifteen employees, he invented a tiny motor. In 1928 he was able to release the first portable electric hair clipper at a much lower price than his competition. The clippers became such a standard that he was able to buy two of his four largest competitors. A third went out of business. The miniature motor proved useful in other devices. In 1935 he came out with the Oster massager, which was used primarily in hospitals. World War II was a boon to Oster's company. Oster shears were used for the new recruits and Oster motors were placed in mines and artillery. When the war ended, the businessman started looking for other avenues. He purchased the Stevens Electric Company. He and his staff started refining one of that company's most profitable products, its commercial drink mixer. The result was a food blender for use in the home. The *Osterizer* entered the American kitchen in 1946.

Otis, Elisha Graves

Elisha Graves Otis was born in Halifax, Vermont in 1811. He was anxious to leave the family farm and start a business of his own using his mechanical skills. His first job was in Troy, New York, where he briefly worked in construction before returning to his home state to build a gristmill. When that proved unprofitable, he built carriages, but after seven years business slowed so he decided to open a sawmill. This evolved into a water-turbine factory to make machinery. Just when he thought he had found a profitable business for himself, the city of Albany, New York took control of the stream that powered his works and he was once again looking for a new career. He got a job at the

Bedstead Manufacturing Company in Yonkers, New York. He did not intend to stay long, just long enough to earn enough money to head west and join the gold rush. One day, in 1852, he was asked to fix a hoist that the company used for merchandise. In those days, few buildings were taller than four stories. Construction techniques wouldn't allow for much higher structures and even so, no one would want to climb more than four flights of stairs. When freight had to be moved that distance, warehouses built platforms on ropes and pulleys to raise them. Accidents were common with the hoists. If the rope broke, there was nothing to keep the platform from falling and crushing anyone below. Otis decided to design a safer hoist for Bedstead. He took a spring from an old wagon and connected it to the top of the platform where the rope was tied. When the rope was pulled from below, the spring was compressed. If the rope broke, the spring was released, pushing two hooks into a pair of guide rails, preventing it from falling. Otis didn't think much about the safety device. He went back to work until the Bedstead Manufacturing Company went out of business. Otis prepared again for his California excursion. Just as he was about to leave, however, a furniture company that had lost two men in a hoist accident asked him to build two more of his safety hoists. In exchange for his services, the company offered Otis cash, a carriage, and a gun. He decided to build the devices and to go into the elevator business. On September 20, 1853, he opened his own shop to sell "Patented Life and Labor Saving Hoisting Machinery." There were no takers. As it so happened, the nation's first World's Fair, the Crystal Palace Exhibition in New York City, was under way. Otis put together a dramatic exhibition. He climbed into his own hoist, which raised him thirty feet in the air, and then had an assistant cut the rope with a knife. The crowd gasped as the hoist fell a matter of inches and stopped with no harm done. "We may commence by referring to an elevator exhibited by E. G. Otis of Yonkers," wrote the *New York Tribune*, "which attracts attention both by its prominent position and by the apparent daring of the inventor." The spectacle generated some sales—twenty-seven elevators sold in

1856. A year later, Otis's company installed the first passenger elevator in a five-story glass and china store, E. V. Houghwout and Company. The team-powered lift could move 1,000 pounds forty feet per minute. The man credited with making skyscrapers possible died from diphtheria when he was only forty-nine. His sons Charles and Norton inherited a business worth about $5,000 with less than a dozen employees. By 1997, the Otis Elevator Company, now a subsidiary of United Technologies, had about sixty-seven thousand employees and did business in more than two hundred countries, with international revenues of $4.6 billion. It had more than twice the sales of its nearest competitor, Switzerland's Schindler Holding AG. It has put elevators in the White House, Vatican, Eiffel Tower, and space-shuttle launch pad.

P/Q

Pabst, Frederick

Capt. Frederick Pabst came to America from Holland with his parents at the age of twelve. When he was still a teenager, he signed on as cabin boy on a Lake Michigan steamer. He studied navigation and business administration with a view to commanding his own vessel. He moved up the ranks quickly. He was promoted to first mate by the time he was twenty and became the captain of his own ship. But he didn't just want to sail. Pabst also had a financial interest in the fleet. He became co-owner of several vessels. During one of his voyages, Pabst met a young woman named Maria Best. Maria was traveling with her father, Phillip, who owned a brewery in Milwaukee. It had been the first major brewery in that city, built only four years after the creation of the Wisconsin Territory in 1840. Until then the many German immigrants to the region found it difficult to produce a German-style lager of any quality. So they drank British-style porters, stouts, and ales. Traditionally, British brews were cooked up in an open container at room temperature with a top-fermenting yeast that forms a natural air lock. The result of this process is a dark, heavy beer with a yeasty aftertaste. British brewers use a large quantity of hops to mask the yeast flavor. German lager's lighter flavor can be traced back to the Middle Ages when German monks began experimenting with a bottom-fermenting yeast. Living on the bottom of the wort, the yeast did not form a natural air lock, so artificial fermentation locks had to be developed. The monks slowly brewed the mixture in cool caves under the monasteries and kept the fermenting vessels on ice. The name "lager" derives from the long period of storing the liquid. It comes from the German word for "warehouse." The problem for American brewers was that the delicate yeast did not travel well. By the time it arrived on U.S. shores it was generally useless. Another brewer solved the problem by having the yeast mixed with sawdust and dried in bread pans before it was shipped to him. His plan was to rehydrate it when it came. By the time the yeast arrived, however, the brewer's business had gone bust, so he went to Phillip's brother, Jacob Best, who was then running a vinegar factory. The brewer sold the yeast to Best for $5. It had been several years since Best had brewed lager in Metlenheim, Germany but he gave it a shot. He dissolved the dried cakes in water, filtered out the sawdust, and added the result to his experimental batch of beer. It was not the stunning success he hoped it would be, but he kept working on it and eventually arrived at a beer with a satisfying flavor. In 1844, the family changed the focus of their business. They produced the first 300 barrels of beer and renamed the operation the Best & Company Brewery. Beer sold for $4.95 per keg at the brewery, or you could have it delivered by oxcart for $5.00 per keg. By 1850, Best and Company was the fourth-largest brewery in Milwaukee, producing 20,000 barrels a year. But by the time Phillip Best met Frederick Pabst, competition had become fierce in the Milwaukee brewing industry and the Bests were having a hard time keeping their heads above water. Frederick and Maria fell in love and were married in 1862. Everything seemed to fall nicely into place. Frederick Pabst was getting tired of life on the sea and Phillip Best wanted to retire so they formed a partnership in 1864. When Pabst joined the operation, the brewery was selling fewer than 5,000 barrels a year. The next year, sales increased 123 percent and rose another 30 percent the following year. With everything running so smoothly, Best decided the time was ripe to retire completely. Pabst brought Emil Schandein, Maria's sister's husband, on board. They bought a new modern brewery and several other businesses. In 1873 they changed their name to the Phillip Best Brewing Company. By 1871, they were producing 73,585 barrels a year—by 1895, almost a million. And with 20 percent of its holdings in real estate, the brewery was the largest landowner in Milwaukee. The brewery owned saloons, restaurants, rifle ranges, and parks, which they leased to others. The company built the Pabst Theater and an opera house as well. In 1882 the company started tying real blue ribbons around the necks of bottles as a sign of their quality. The silk ribbons were tied by hand. By 1892, 300,000 yards of blue silk ribbon were purchased by the brewery each year, although "Blue Ribbon" would not become the official name of the product for a decade. When Emil Schandein died in 1889, the company's name was changed to *Pabst Brewing Company*. Frederick Pabst died on New Year's Day 1904, but the brewery continued to thrive and was one of the few such businesses to survive prohibition, under the guidance of Frederick Pabst, Jr. In 1946 Pabst was still on the top of the brewing industry. Milwaukee was the city of beer. The big three brands were Pabst, Schlitz, and Miller. They employed generations of families and drew more than a hundred thousand visitors a year. Until the early 1980s, no city in the world produced more beer. Pabst was known as the brew of the city's working-class South Side. Although Frederick Pabst, Jr., sold a controlling interest in the company in 1933, the Pabst family remained involved in the business until 1983 when August Pabst, Frederick's grandson, sold his holdings. As microbrews and imports gained popularity in the 1990s, Pabst, long associated with the blue-collar crowd, found it hard to compete. For several years in a row the company failed to turn a profit. The age of the big family-owned brewery in Milwaukee was coming to an end. Miller was bought by Philip Morris in 1970. Schlitz was purchased by the Detroit-based Stroh Brewing Company in 1981, and in 1996, Pabst's new owner, the California-based S&P Corporation, announced it would close Pabst's Milwaukee brewery. Milwaukee residents responded by boycotting the product. Many pubs stopped serving it. One pub even made an event of getting rid of its Pabst inventory. The Rail's Inn sponsored a "Drink It or Dump It" day. Each Pabst cost $1 and customers had the choice of drinking it or dumping it in a trough outside. Proceeds from the sales, about $700, were given to a fund for retired Pabst workers. One of those workers, Tom O'Brien, told a reporter for the *Washington Post* that Milwaukee had stopped being the beer city years earlier on October 1, 1990. "That was when they said no more beer on the job," he said.

Palmer, Ernest

Ernest ("Chili") Palmer was one of six children born to an Italian housewife and a Spanish waiter in Coney Island, New York. He moved to Miami Beach in 1960. There he started managing nightclubs with money that *GQ* magazine asserts came from the Columbo crime family. Once Palmer chased a man to Las Vegas to collect on a gambling debt. In the early 1970s, he and a partner, Bill Marshall, would sometimes collect on debts for a gambling casino. Palmer says he did not use violence, just a threatening expression called "the look." It usually worked. Palmer was not destined for celebrity of any kind until he crossed paths with a writer named Elmore Leonard. Leonard is the type of author who carries a notebook to scribble down slang and memorable phrases to use in his novels. Palmer did research for several of Leonard's books and the writer was inspired by many of his mannerisms and especially his name. Leonard once said when he settles on a character's name, "that tells me who the person is." As Palmer recounted to the *Los Angeles Times*, Leonard called him up and said, "Chili, I love your name, and I like your background. I'd like to do a book with Chili Palmer." Palmer replied, "Dutch, be my guest." The fictional Chili Palmer was the protagonist of the novels *Get Shorty* and *Be Cool*. How much of the character's past resembles that of its original? Palmer remains vague on the point. "About 25 percent" is all he'll say, but Leonard has claimed that Palmer's old hoodlum friends love the books for their authenticity. In 1995, *Get Shorty* was made into a movie starring John Travolta as Chili Palmer. When Leonard told the filmmakers that there was a real Chili Palmer, they gave him a bit part in the movie. You can see him at the beginning of the film in a scene where the character Ray Bones, played by Dennis Farina, makes jokes at Chili's expense. To his side are two men. The real Chili Palmer is the one on the right who says, "That was a good one." "We are all incredibly lucky I didn't know there was a Chili

Palmer," John Travolta told the *Los Angeles Times,* "because I
would have insisted on going down to Miami and living with
him, and I would have ruined my performance."

Pamphilus

Little is known about the life of twelfth-century author
Pamphilus, except that he was the writer of an erotic love
poem called *"Pamphilus, seu de Amore."* The publication, only a
few pages long, was a big hit in the Middle Ages. In French, the
name of the poem was soon shortened in common parlance to
"Pamphilet." Translated into English it became "Pamflet" and
later *"Pamphlet."* Eventually any small booklet came to be
known by this name.

Parker, George

George Parker was born November 1, 1863 in Shullsburg,
Wisconsin. The family moved, by covered wagon, to Iowa,
where Parker was raised on a farm. He attended Upper Iowa
University, where he prepared for a career as a railroad man.
After spotting an advertisement for the Valentine School of
Telegraphy in Janesville, Wisconsin, he saved up enough for a
train ticket and $55 tuition. He was a quick study and in less
than a year he was teaching classes. The pay was low, however,
and Parker earned extra cash as a distributor for the Cincinnati
Fountain Pen Company. He sold the products mostly to his students. He was embarrassed to discover they were of poor quality and broke frequently. So he set to work to design a better
pen. After a number of experiments, he arrived at an ink feed-
er and holder that seemed sufficiently reliable. He patented the
design in 1889. He hired a company to make pens meeting his
design and had his name printed on them. One day a traveling
salesman came to the boardinghouse where Parker lived.
Parker convinced him to add the pens to his product line. On
another occasion, an insurance salesman approached Parker
about a policy. Parker said he couldn't afford it, but he used the
opportunity to talk about his pens. The salesman, W. F. Palmer,
was impressed and agreed to go into business with Parker.
Parker sold half the interest in his patent to Palmer for $1,000
and the *Parker Pen Company* was formed.

Paul, John

It's a seafood shocker! Mrs. Paul was really a mister. Although the frozen-seafood company was not named for a Mrs. Paul, the "Paul" at least comes from a real person. He was John R. Paul, who in 1946 was working as a short-order cook in Philadelphia. There he met a twenty-nine-year-old entrepreneur named Edward J. Piszek. Piszek was born in Chicago, the son of Polish immigrants. He spent five years with the Campbell's Soup Company while earning a degree in business administration at the University of Pennsylvania through night classes. He had met and married Olga McFadden in 1937. The couple would go on to have four children. Piszek had perfected a method for freezing fishcakes, but he had only managed to scrounge up $400, which wasn't enough to launch his business. He talked Paul into investing an additional $350. To be sure he wouldn't back out, Piszek named the company after him. They decided, however, that the name "Mrs. Paul's" brought to mind the kitchen and good food more than "John Paul" did. Mrs. Paul's first product was frozen crab cakes, but the menu grew quickly. Mr. and Mrs. Piszek came up with sixty-five different varieties before a bad investment forced them to sell the company to Campbell's Soup for $55 million in 1982. Piszek became one of Philadelphia's best-known businessmen. He was famous for supporting Polish-American causes. He convinced author James A. Michener to write a novel about Poland. He waged a campaign to wipe out Polish jokes. A friend of Pope John Paul II, he once sent 250 trailers of fishcakes to Polish workers who were confronting their communist government. Mrs. Paul's was sold by Campbell's to Van de Kamp's. Van de Kamp's closed Philadelphia's last Mrs. Paul's plant. Today, Mrs. Paul's and Van de Kamp's together have a leading 28.1 percent share of the frozen seafood market. Trivia question for advertising fans: When Campbell's Soup owned Mrs. Paul's, they ran a series of ads featuring a former narcotics agent, John L. Kelly, as Mr. Paul. Kelly once held a very odd job. What was it? Answer: He was a bodyguard to Elvis Presley's bodyguards.

Pearle, Stanley

Stanley Pearle was one of a set of twins, along with brother Merle, born in 1918 in Pittsburgh, Pennsylvania. He graduated from high school during the Great Depression, but was fortunate enough to find work as a sales trainee for a jeweler. He traveled throughout the state to various jewelry stores, many of which had optical departments. He made friends with a number of the optometrists and was inspired to enter the field himself. He worked his way through the Northern Illinois College of Optometry by working nights as a hotel clerk. He graduated in 1940 and took the Pennsylvania State Board of Optometry exam. At that time, it took two months to process the results. Pearle didn't want to continue waiting, so he and a fellow graduate went to Texas, which announced the results the day after the test. Pearle passed and immediately went into business. Two months later, when he learned he had also passed the Pennsylvania exam, he returned to the state and married his high-school sweetheart. They would go on to have four children together. During World War II, Pearle entered the navy. After his tour of duty, he moved back to Texas and joined Lee Optical as a junior partner in 1948. He stayed with the operation until 1955. Three years later, shortly after his fortieth birthday, Pearle decided to take a chance and open his own practice and shop. His idea was to offer optical services and products in one location. The first Pearle Vision Center opened in Savannah, Georgia in 1961. It grew throughout the next two decades, eventually becoming the only optical chain to advertise on national television. It became the world's largest network of eyewear and eye-care outlets. It became a subsidiary of Cole National Corporation in 1996. There are now around seven hundred Pearle Vision Centers in the United States.

Perdue, Arthur

Arthur Perdue worked in Salisbury, Maryland as a Railway Express agent after World War I. He loved the area, so when his employer told him he would be transferred elsewhere, he quit. He built a chicken coop, in which he raised 50 Leghorn chickens. He sold the eggs to markets in cities as far away as New York. His flock continued to grow during the depression. By 1940 there were 2,000 chickens in all. Then an avian disease, leukosis, decimated his stock. Not wanting to face such a crisis again, Perdue bought New Hampshire Red chickens. The hardy breed was generally sold for broilers, not used for harvesting eggs. During the Second World War Perdue managed to land accounts with Armour and Swift. In 1953, Perdue was incorporated. The firm was raising 2.6 million chickens a year, which brought in $8 million. That year he turned the day-to-day operations over to his son, Frank, who was then thirty-three. Today Perdue is one of the largest companies in the U.S. poultry market, selling 42 million pounds of chicken products and 3.5 million pounds of turkey products each week.

Perignon, Dom Pierre

Dom Perignon was a blind man who became a Benedictine monk at the age of fifteen. He became the cellar master of the abbey in Hautvillers, a quiet town near Epernay, France. Residents of that region will tell you that the monk was impatient waiting for the wine to be ready and he tried to speed up the slow winemaking process by adding yeast. As the story goes, he tried stopping the bottles with rags, and many exploded before he tried using corks. They remained tight in the bottlenecks and retained the effervescent gasses. When he first tasted the result of his experiment, Dom Perignon exclaimed: "Come quickly, I am tasting stars!" It is not clear whether Dom Perignon was real or a creation of the Champagne's largest producer, Moet & Chandon. A British wine specialist claims the process was developed in England. Regardless, Dom Perignon's name graces Moet & Chandon's most famous product, and a statue of the monk stands in front of the Moet & Chandon Champagne house in Epernay.

Pernod, Henri-Louis

In the late eighteenth century, Henri-Louis Pernod purchased the recipe for a type of absinthe from a physician called Pierre

Ordinaire. The blend used aniseed, fennel, hyssop, lemon balm, and wormwood. (The wormwood or *Artemisia absinthium* gives absinthe its name.) The mixture was left to sit, water was added, and it was distilled. Then more dried herbs were added and diluted with alcohol resulting in about 75 percent alcohol by volume. Absinthe was a popular drink among artists and bohemians of the 1800s. It was the subject of paintings by Manet, Degas, and Picasso. Toulouse Lautrec drank it from a hollowed-out walking stick. English poet Ernest Dowson wrote *Absinthia Taetra,* which as been called "confessions of an English absinthe drinker." The drink was said to have contributed to Vincent Van Gogh's madness. When produced with wormwood, absinthe contains the chemical thujone, which has an effect similar to THC, the active ingredient in marijuana. Along with its high alcoholic wallop, the drink was reputed to have a hallucinogenic effect. It was also popularly thought to be an aphrodisiac. As with most reputed aphrodisiacs, however, there was no evidence that this was true. In the 1850s the French government became concerned about the effects of chronic use of the drink. It was believed to produce a syndrome called absinthium. Absinthe was banned in France a year after the United States banned cocaine from over-the-counter medicines. Modern *Pernod* is produced without the wormwood. Instead, the current recipe substitutes more aniseed. While we're on the subject of alcohol, the term "proof" used to describe alcoholic strength originally referred to "gunpowder proof." Early distillers proved their alcohol's strength by mixing the drink with gunpowder and applying a flame. If the powder did not burn, it meant the whiskey was too weak. If it burned too brightly the spirit was too strong. If it burned with a blue flame it was said to be "proved." If it was "100 percent perfect" or 100 proof it was about 50 percent alcohol by volume.

Petri, Julius

Julius Richard Petri, a German scientist, lived from 1852 to 1921. Petri worked as an assistant to Robert Koch during "The Golden Age of Microbiology," the late 1800s. Koch was the first scientist to introduce a rationalized system of bacteria culturing. He was also one of the first to demonstrate that steam was a useful sterilizer for surgical instruments and dressings. German surgeons, aware of Koch's work, started to practice aseptic surgery. Another doctor who found Koch's discoveries compelling was Joseph Lister, who would lead an American crusade against unsanitary medical practices. *Listerine* was named in his honor. Petri tried to devise a way to make it easier to keep pure samples in the laboratory. The result was a circular, shallow glass dish with a larger dish fitting over it to serve as a lid. Conceived in 1887, the idea was so straightforward that it quickly caught on. *Petri dishes* have been used ever since.

Pfizer, Charles

Charles Pfizer worked as an apothecary's apprentice in Germany before emigrating to New York in the mid-1840s with his cousin Charles Erhard, a confectioner. In America, the cousins went into business together. They opened a chemical firm, Charles Pfizer & Company, in Brooklyn in 1849. Combining Erhard's skills as a confectioner with Pfizer's background in chemistry, they produced mostly food flavorings, iodine preparations, and citric acid, which they sold to soft-drink makers. Charles Pfizer died October 19, 1906 and was buried in Green-Wood Cemetery in Brooklyn, New York before the name Pfizer became associated with pharmaceuticals. In the 1920s, Pfizer's chemists discovered a new source of citric acid in black bread molds. They stepped up their mold fermenting production just as the federal government was looking for companies to make penicillin on a large scale. Their fermenting vats, as it turned out, were ideal. By the time Allied troops hit the beaches in Normandy, Pfizer provided 95 percent of the penicillin used to treat them and half of the penicillin used in the world. There was so much penicillin competition, however, that profit margins fell to almost nothing by the end of 1948. Shortly thereafter, John McKeen became president of the company. He decided to take Pfizer farther into the pharmaceutical business and he pushed his researchers to "come up with something." They did, oxytetracycline, a new antibiotic sold to hospitals under the name Terramycin. McKeen also started a Pfizer tradition of aggressive marketing of drugs. The company became the largest advertiser in the *Journal of the American Medical Association* from 1952 to 1956. According to company legend, McKeen asked an assistant in 1961 what else he could do to keep the company growing. The assistant shrugged and said, "Buy another company." McKeen is said to have replied, "Fine, which one?" Pfizer bought fourteen companies in the next four years. McKeen stepped down as president in 1965, but the push to develop new drugs and aggressively market them has remained. Pfizer is now known as the producer of Norvasc, a hypertension drug, Zoloft, an antidepressant often prescribed to help people quit smoking, Zithromax, used to fight infection, and Viagra, a well-known treatment for erectile dysfunction and punch line for standup comics' routines. In 1999, Pfizer had about $6.4 billion in annual revenue and more medicines are on the drawing board. *Forbes* magazine reported that Pfizer is close to developing drugs to combat heart disease, schizophrenia, and even cancers of the colon, breast, and pancreas. "Its stable of 50-plus drugs, now in various stages of human trials, is probably the strongest in the industry. At least half a dozen look like blockbusters that might win approval in the next five years." The magazine speculated that those drugs alone could result in sales of $10 billion a year.

Philips, Gerard

Gerard Philips of Eindhoven, the Netherlands, was a twenty-one-year-old engineering student when Thomas Alva Edison demonstrated his electric light bulb. Philips was excited by the cutting-edge technology. He began tinkering with filaments of his own and in 1891, with the help of his father, Philips was able to open his own lighting factory in an abandoned tannery. Within a year the company received an order for bulbs for a candle plant. By 1895 the factory was producing 500 light bulbs a day. Philips, exhausted by the workload, convinced his younger brother Anton to join the business. Anton took charge of international sales to great success. His biggest coup was securing a contract to supply bulbs for Czar Nicholas's Winter Palace in St. Petersburg. The czar demanded the bulbs be changed annually, whether they needed it or not. With a standing order for 50,000 bulbs a year, the small family business grew to the point that Anton felt he could no longer keep up with it. In 1912, he sold most of the family's shares because he believed he could not make objective business decisions if his personal wealth was tied up with the company. The name Philips & Company was changed to *Philips Gloeilampenfabrieken,* or Philips Incandescent Lamp Works, a name it retained until 1991. Now known as *Royal Philips Electronics,* the firm is the world's number-one manufacturer of light bulbs and third in the manufacture of consumer electronics. It is for the latter that the company is best known in America. Philips is credited with developing the cassette tape, videocassette recorder, and compact disc. The name is familiar to 86 percent of U.S. consumers, who, in the words of CEO Robert Minkhorst, "know it's not oil or magnesia powder or screwdrivers."

Pitney, Arthur

Arthur Pitney was born in Quincy, Illinois in 1871. He was stricken with polio as an infant and was left with a shortened left leg. In 1890, he moved to Chicago, where he found work as a clerk in a wallpaper store. His imagination was sparked when the 1893 Columbian World's Fair was held in his city. He wanted to be an inventor and he turned his attention to the tedious bulk mailing he had to do at work. Instead of licking all those stamps, Pitney believed a machine that printed envelopes with postage would make life easier for a lot of sticky-tongued clerks. It would also help their bosses, who had to deal with the serious problem of stamp theft. In 1902 he patented his first double-locking, hand-cranked "postage stamp device." With a partner, he launched the Pitney Postal Machine Company to produce them. When he got the chance to demonstrate his machine to the U.S. postmaster general, he was so sure it would be approved that he rented a large office and started promoting the idea of a postage meter to businesses. But Pitney had underestimated the power of bureaucracy. It would be another eighteen years and several changes in postmasters general before his device would find official acceptance. During that almost two-decade-long wait, Pitney never gave up on his dream. He went back to the wallpaper store, but spent all his money and energy promoting the idea of the postal meter. He collected testimonials from businesspeople and changed the name of his company—which could sell nothing without approval of its product by the U.S. Postal Service—to the American Postage Meter Company. His postal obsession led to the dissolution of his marriage in 1910. That year he tried again to get approval and was rejected again. Two years later he improved his design and presented it to the post office again but still no approval. A discouraged Pitney moved from Chicago and took an advertising job in Joliet, Illinois. While he was there, the postal service agreed to try a full-scale test. He placed machines in Chicago offices for three months. The experiment seemed to be a success. The machine received favorable reviews in the press. Yet the postal service was still unimpressed: "We see no need for such a machine as an adjunct to the Postal Service." Pitney, dejected, started selling insurance. In 1918, word of the device found its way to Walter Harold Bowes. Born in 1882, Bowes ran a business that manufactured check-endorsing machines. In 1909, he had purchased another company, the Universal Stamping Machine Company, which made a machine to cancel postage stamps. Bowes had been toying with the idea of a machine that could affix postage and then cancel it automatically. Bowes contacted Pitney and the two men met in October 1919. They agreed to form the Pitney Bowes Postage Meter Company, based in Bowes' home state of Connecticut. Unlike Pitney, Bowes was a natural salesman. The two men agreed to have Pitney work on improving the postal meter, while Bowes went off to Washington to sell the idea. Finally, on September 1, 1920, the U.S. Postal Service gave its approval. Within two years, the Post Office was selling $4 million in postage through Pitney Bowes equipment. It would seem that everything had finally fallen into place for Arthur Pitney. Unfortunately, Pitney and Bowes did not get along. In 1924, Pitney resigned in anger from the company that bore his name. He sold his entire stock for $200,000. He suffered a stroke three years later and died in 1933. Bowes never had Pitney's passion for running the company. He gave up control of the day-to-day operations in 1938. He was named chairman, a mostly honorary title. He retired in 1940 to focus on his hobbies, horses and yachts. Walter Bowes died on June 24, 1957. Pitney Bowes is now the world's largest producer of postage meters, with annual sales of more than $4 billion. Pitney's frustrations might have been enough to make anyone, to use a modern expression, "go postal." While we're on the subject of postal workers, it seems an opportune time to talk about the origin of the word "disgruntled," which has recently gained great currency in the wake of a few highly publicized cases of workplace violence, often at post offices. "Is 'disgruntled' a registered trademark of the U.S. Postal Service?" asks the "Disgruntled Postal Workers Zone" Web page, a tongue-in-cheek look at "difficult working conditions and bad days." According to *Webster's Dictionary*, the word "disgruntled" comes from "gruntle," meaning "sulky." A person who is "disgruntled" is, therefore, someone who has "become sulky." This is why you never hear of happy, gruntled employees. A gruntled employee is a sulky one. A disgruntled employee is also sulky but has only recently come to be that way.

Pond, Theron T.

Theron T. Pond was a chemist in Utica, New York. He did the normal work of a chemist, selling and dispensing drugs from his shop. In the early 1840s, however, he became interested in how the Oneida Native Americans, a tribe based in central New York, treated burns and wounds. Their medicine man made a "tea" from a shrub known as witch hazel. (Witch hazel was so named because its branches were used as divining rods to find water underground.) By steeping the shrub in an ordinary teakettle, he obtained a clear liquid, which he used for all variety of maladies. Pond was convinced that there was some value in the extract. He spent several months with the tribesman learning which species of shrub to use and which to avoid. Pond then took the plants back to the lab in the rear of his shop. The elixir created by the medicine man was effective, but had to be used

immediately. Pond wanted to find a way to preserve it. He discovered that distilling the extract, combining it with pure grain
alcohol, and aging it in oak barrels did the trick. Pond named
the product "Golden Treasure." In the beginning he mostly sold
it to his friends. Local physicians praised the product, so in 1849,
Pond formed the T. T. Pond Company to market it. Three years
later, however, Pond fell ill and had to sell his interest to partners. He died shortly thereafter. Pond's company continued and
added cosmetics including cold cream and vanishing cream. By
the 1920s the J. Walter Thompson ad agency helped make
Pond's the leading manufacturer of skin creams in the U.S. by
running a series of ads featuring socially prominent women
endorsing the products. On July 1, 1955, the company merged
with a business formed by Robert A. Chesebrough and
Chesebrough-Pond's, Inc. was the result.

Ponzi, Charles

Italian immigrant Charles Ponzi was a symbol of financial success. His Securities Exchange Company was bustling with
investors. From 1919 to 1920, Ponzi attracted thousands of
Bostonians to his firm, many of whom had never invested
before. They invested $15 million with the entrepreneur. They
came to him because he said he could make them a fortune by
buying International Postal Union coupons from certain countries at a discount and redeeming them in the United States for
their full value. He promised to return a fifty-cent profit on
investments in forty-five days. As investors lined up, Ponzi grew
rich and famous. He bought a hundred suits, drove in a blue
stretch limousine, and smoked expensive cigars from a diamond
holder. As the spotlight shone on the millionaire, some people
became suspicious of his financial scheme. In the summer of
1920 the Feds announced that all the postal coupons cashed in
the nation could not account for the profits Ponzi was claiming.
In August, after Ponzi's bank account became overdrawn, the
public discovered that he had been twice imprisoned, once for
forgery, a second time for smuggling illegal aliens. Ponzi could
not repay the investors who stormed his offices. He declared
bankruptcy and was arrested on August 13. In the ensuing trial

it was revealed that there had, in fact, never been any postal coupons. Instead, Ponzi had used later investors' money to pay the earlier investors. Such strategies have since been dubbed *Ponzi schemes.* Ponzi served five years in federal prison for his conniving. He never gave up his fraudulent ways and was eventually deported to Italy, where he died broke.

Price, Emily

Emily Price was born to a wealthy Baltimore family in 1872. She attended Miss Graham's Finishing School for Young Ladies in New York. In June 1892 she married a banker named Edwin M. Post. They were divorced in 1906. She became a writer, producing newspaper articles and serials for such magazines as *Harper's, Scribner's,* and the *Century.* Her novels include *Flight of the Moth, Purple and Fine Linen, Woven in the Tapestry, The Title Market,* and *The Eagle's Feather.* One thing she never planned to write was a book of etiquette. She hated such books. The etiquette books of her day were elitist treatises based on exclusivity and what she saw as outmoded European values. A friend of hers, Frank Crowninshield, then editor of *Vanity Fair,* teased her by giving her a copy of an etiquette book as a gift. She was inspired to write a new etiquette book that would lay to rest all of the snobbishness of the past. Instead of relying on rules that showed a person to be well bred, Post's book would say proper behavior evolved naturally out of common sense and consideration of others. *Etiquette in Society, in Business, in Politics, and at Home* was released in 1922. By 1945 it had sold 666,000 copies and "Post, Emily" had become an entry in the dictionary. Emily Post, the novelist, was forgotten, but Emily Post, the authority on etiquette, is remembered today.

Quadracci, Harry V.

Harry V. Quadracci was born in 1936 in an apartment above his family's grocery store in Racine, Wisconsin. He started working in the store almost as soon as he was able to walk. Behind the store was a small print shop, which Quadracci's father (also named Harry Quadracci) had started when he was only sixteen to help supplement the grocery income. In 1934, the older Quadracci sold the print shop to a man named W. A. Krueger. Harry V. Quadracci went to work for Krueger part time when he was fifteen. After he graduated from high school, he attended Regis College in Denver, Colorado, where he earned a degree in philosophy. When the offers from large philosophy corporations failed to roll in, Quadracci returned to school. He earned his Juris Doctor from Columbia University's School of Law in 1960. He went back to Wisconsin and started a private law practice. He found that he enjoyed the business part of his job more than the legal aspects. He left the practice of law and returned to Krueger's print shop, working his way up to the position of vice-president and general manager of the Wisconsin printing division. There he worked alongside his father, Harry R. Quadracci. Tensions between labor and management convinced him to leave the company in 1969. He mortgaged his house and launched his own printing venture in a 20,000-square-foot abandoned warehouse in Pewaukee, Wisconsin. He called his company *Quad/Graphics*. In 1972, he was joined by his father, who retired from Krueger, having served as director of manufacturing, executive vice-president, and a board member. The Quadraccis' new company grew to be the largest private printer in the U.S. and the third-largest printer, public or private, in the Western Hemisphere.

Quinn, Anthony

Here's a trivia question for you: Who wrote "The Mighty Quinn," the song that became a chart hit for Manfred Mann's Earth Band? The answer is Bob Dylan. Dylan had heard and enjoyed recordings of other versions of his songs that the band had done so he decided to give them the song, which is subtitled "Quinn the Eskimo." Although Dylan has not said so himself, authors Bob Shannon and John Javna in their book *Behind the Hits* logically speculate that the "Quinn" of the song was Anthony Quinn, who played an Eskimo in the movie *The Savage Innocents*. The Eskimo was only one of many ethnic roles Quinn has taken on in his lifetime. Born Antonio Quiñones April 21, 1915 in Chihuahua, Mexico, and raised in Los

Angeles, he got his first film role by convincing director Cecil B. DeMille that he was a pureblood Cheyenne. During the filming of the 1937 production, Quinn pretended he did not understand a word of English. He went on to play Chinese and Italian characters and, most famously, Zorba the Greek. In all he has appeared in more than 147 pictures. His private life, on the other hand, could best be described as a soap opera. He first married actress Katherine DeMille, daughter of the famous director, in 1936. They had five children and divorced in 1963. He met second wife Iolanda, a Venice-born wardrobe assistant, in 1961 on the set of the movie *Barabbas*. Even though Quinn was still married to his first wife, the couple had two children. She was pregnant with a third when she and Quinn finally wed in 1966. During the twenty-nine years of their marriage, Quinn fathered four illegitimate children. Iolanda forgave all his affairs until the seventy-nineyear-old fathered his twelfth child with his thirty-two-year-old secretary, Kathy Benvin. A heated legal battle took place. Iolanda initially refused to grant the actor a divorce. Quinn responded by claiming his divorce from DeMille was invalid and therefore his marriage to Iolanda had never been legal. The discussions went downhill from there. August 18, 1997, Quinn, then eighty-two, appeared before New York's state supreme court, drew an unflattering sketch of his estranged wife, presented it, and said, "There's an angry mouth with spikes coming out." The couple's son Danny also appeared in court and accused the actor of beating his wife. He and another son, Francesco, broke all ties with their father. In the end Quinn agreed to settle for half of his $15 million estate. On December 7, 1997 the octogenarian married his thirty-five-year-old girlfriend. As *People* magazine put it: "Among couples there are May-December romances—and then there are those that don't fit on the same calendar." You'll not see nothing like the Mighty Quinn.

R

Redding, Jheri

In 1930, Jheri Redding, a former Illinois farm boy, became one of the first men in America to be licensed as a cosmetologist. He had ambitions that reached far beyond simple hairstyling. That same year he founded Jheri Redding Products to produce his own line of beauty treatments. He is credited with introducing the first cream rinse and setting lotion to American consumers. The setting lotion helped maintain a hairstyle that came to be known as *Jheri curls*. Redding was a master marketer. While other shampoo makers were simply promising to get hair clean, Redding appealed to consumers' desire for scientifically enhanced products. He was the first to advertise a "pH-balanced shampoo" and to put vitamins and minerals in the mix. He went on to found two other companies with names based on his own—*Redken* in 1960 and *Jhirmack* in 1968. By the 1980s, however, the Redding family no longer owned those businesses. The family still owns his 1979 venture, Nexxus Products. The name Nexxus comes from a Greek word meaning to be joined. The name was chosen because the products "unite nature and earth with science." Jheri Redding continued to be active in the company into his eighties. At age seventy-eight he was featured in *Fortune* magazine for using a new technique to hawk his "botanically fortified" shampoos and "polymeric tridimensional" conditioners—advertising products only available in salons direct to the consumer on television. Jheri Redding passed away in 1998 at the age of ninety-one.

Remington, Eliphalet

Eliphalet Remington was born in Suffield, Connecticut in 1793, the son of a blacksmith. Young Remington was trained at his father's forge in Ilion Gulph, New York, a small shop powered by a waterwheel. Remington was not satisfied with the firearms that were available on the market. He was sure he could make a better one himself. He and his father worked on a new rifle, which was completed in the fall of 1816. Remington decided to show off his handiwork by entering a shooting match. He finished in second place. Impressed by the weapon's accuracy, many of the other contestants ordered rifles from Remington. When his father died in 1828, Remington took over the firm and moved it closer to the new Erie Canal. He supplied the U.S. Army with the rifles it used in the Mexican War. Remington rifles were also standard issue for Union troops in the Civil War. The firm later supplied the armies of several European countries with breech-loading rifles. The business became known as E. Remington and Sons. One of the "sons" was Philo Remington. Philo was largely responsible for expanding the family business to include products other than guns.

Remington, Philo

Philo Remington was born in 1816 in Litchfield, New York. He directed the family firearms business during the Civil War. Once the war had ended, however, Philo suspected rifle sales would fall dramatically. Under his guidance, E. Remington and Sons began selling agricultural equipment and sewing machines. In 1872, a Milwaukee journalist and printer, Christopher Latham Sholes, brought Remington the first workable typewriter. Remington was convinced this was a promising product. Sholes and several associates had patented their device in 1868. The version they presented had the keys in alphabetical order. It soon became clear that was not the best layout. There was another problem. The type was suspended by wires in a small, circular nest inside the machine. Anyone who started to get the hang of the machine and type quickly would jam up the machine. Sholes tried to solve the problem by keeping the most frequently used keys apart and by slowing down the typist. He went to his son-in-law, James Densmore, a school superintendent, and asked him which letters appeared most often in the English language. He placed those as far apart as possible in the type basket. The result was the familiar keyboard arrangement, known as "qwerty" for the first line on the first row of letters. The early typewriters sold poorly. They were expensive—$125 each—and many people considered typewritten documents impersonal. By 1878, Remington typewriters included a new feature—upper- and lowercase letters. The company began to target office workers and secretaries and by the early 1880s they were selling 1,200 typewriters a year. Unfortunately, the economy took a turn for the worse and Remington sold off its typewriter plant in 1886. One thing that has stayed with us is the qwerty keyboard. Even though modern computer keyboards and electric typewriters make the less-efficient keyboard unnecessary, generations of typists have learned on qwerty keyboards and changing would require everyone to learn a new system. Even though a number of people, notably a man named August Dvorak, have proposed simpler arrangements, qwerty seems likely to persist. Lefties will be pleased to know that the qwerty keyboard is one of the few modern inventions to favor the left hand. With Sholes' keyboard, the left hand is responsible for 57 percent of the work.

Revson, Charles

Charles Haskell Revson was the middle son of a cigar maker and a saleswoman. Born October 11, 1906 in Somerville, Massachusetts, outside Boston, Revson grew up in Manchester, New Hampshire. His parents were both Russian-born Jews. The Revsons were the only Jewish family in their six-unit tenement house and one of only a few Jewish families in their neighborhood. Growing up, Charles was forced to share a bed with his younger brother, Martin. After he graduated from high school, Charles moved to New York, where he worked as a piece-goods buyer for a dress company. In 1930, he fell in love with a woman named Ida Tompkins. They married and moved to Chicago. There Revson tried to make a living selling sales-motivation plans. At the beginning of the Great Depression, there was not a big market for them. The business failed, as did the marriage. Revson liked to say the marriage fell apart because Tompkins' parents said he would never amount to anything. Broke and with no place to go, Revson returned to his parents' home, but he didn't stay long. With his older brother, Joseph, and a nail-polish supplier named Charles Lachman he formed a new company in New Jersey. The team decided to give their new venture a moniker made up of both their last names. Their first idea was Revlac, but they decided it didn't sound good. In the end, Lachman's only contribution to the name was the letter *l*. They called their company *Revlon*. (One of Revlon's later products, the perfume *Charlie*, comes from the first name of both company founders.) Charles Revson was twenty-five years old when Revlon was created. He personally tested the first Revlon nail polish by painting his own nails. Then he went cross-country by train to sell it. In only six years the company became a multimillion-dollar organization and Revson became one of the most famous—or notorious—characters in New York. Described by some as "the Elvis Presley of the cosmetics industry," Revson continued to actively run the company for another forty-three years. He earned a reputation for his dictatorial, even abusive management style, which supposedly included wiretapping executives. Revson's younger brother, Martin, joined his two other brothers at Revlon. Both brothers ended up leaving after bitter feuds with Charles. Joseph left in 1955 because he didn't think Revlon should go public. Martin left in 1959 and sued the company. Martin and Charles Revson did not speak to each other for thirteen years. Charles Revson was also known for lavish spending. He loved to sail on a yacht that burned up $20,000 worth of fuel each time the tank was filled, and he reportedly spent $5,000 a day on little luxuries. He passed away in 1975 with only his nurse at his side. He left behind three ex-wives, including one whose name he couldn't remember. His estate was valued at only $100 million—a drop in the bucket compared to the money he had earned as head of Revlon.

Roberts, Flori

Flori Roberts was born in New York. She majored in drama at

Carnegie-Mellon Institute in Pittsburgh and pursued a life on the stage. She appeared in several Broadway productions in small roles. Her biggest moment came while she was Carol Channing's understudy in the musical *Lend an Ear*. Channing developed laryngitis, and Roberts took the leading role, something she says gave her great confidence. Finding acting work is never easy, so Roberts started a sideline business, a fashion consulting firm. She married an ophthalmologist named Craig Roberts and the couple had two children. In the 1960s, Roberts was working on a fashion show and she heard some of the African-American models complaining that they always had to mix and match the makeups designed for white women. Roberts, being Caucasian, had never thought about this before. As she would later tell a *Tampa Tribune* reporter, "I thought, 'Could this be possible that an industry like this is not making colors for black women?'" When she looked around, Roberts realized that almost all makeup on the market at that time had pink undertones. She went home and told her husband that she had an idea for a new business. Roberts designed "the Mahogany collection" and used the family's savings to fund the Flori Roberts cosmetics line. They went from store to store in black neighborhoods, talked to beauty-shop owners, and went on black radio stations to spread the word. At first, many people were skeptical of this white couple trying to peddle brown-toned makeup. The Robertses remember being thrown out of a number of stores. A few vendors were willing to take a chance on the products, though. Every store that did saw the cosmetics snapped up by women who were relieved to finally have makeup designed with them in mind. Today *Flori Roberts* is one of the biggest names in the ethnic cosmetic market, a market that is growing by leaps and bounds. In the early 1980s, Roberts underwent surgery to remove skin cancer from the bridge of her nose. She was frustrated to find that there were no cosmetics on the market designed to hide scars. She set to work again, designing a new product line called Dermablend in 1985, but it is the Flori Roberts line that will always be her biggest claim to fame. In 1993, the Robertses sold their multimillion-dollar company to IVAX Corp. That company subsequently negotiated a merger with Johnson Products, maker of Ultra Wave, Ultra Sheen, and Fashion Fair cosmetics. In recent years, the big players in the cosmetics game have all tried to get a piece of the ethnic makeup market. As recently as 1989, there were only a few small companies making cosmetics for black women, but the number increased exponentially in the 1990s. The industry awoke to women of color. "And the color was green," Vince Staten wrote in *Do Pharmacists Sell Farms?* "The African-American woman has gone from being the invisible woman to the woman of the hour." In the early 1990s, Covergirl, Estee Lauder, and Revlon all rolled out new products aimed at this segment of the market, and no wonder. In 1997, sales of such products topped $730 million. "I'm happy now because I go in the store and I see almost every line has a choice, and black women deserve that choice," Roberts says. "Even though you have competition, it's wonderful because there's a choice." Flori Roberts has not slowed down to enjoy her retirement. She is active in many civic organizations and was the first woman inducted into the Sales and Marketing Executive International Academy of Achievement. In 1998 she started again with a new cosmetics line, this one designed for older women. Smart Cover is available only on the Home Shopping Network. It is designed to cover varicose veins and age spots.

Roosevelt, Alice Lee

Alice Lee Roosevelt was born February 12, 1884 and named for her mother, the beloved wife of Theodore Roosevelt, who was then a New York politician. Two days later, Alice, Sr., died of kidney failure. On the same day, Roosevelt's mother died of typhoid fever. Roosevelt was heartbroken. He traveled to the Dakota Territory and left his new daughter in the care of an aunt. He never again spoke of his first wife, even to little Alice. Two years later, he was married again to a woman named Edith Carow. According to biographer Carol Felsenthal Putnam, Carow "took care to let the child know that her mother had been stupid and boring." As a political daughter, Alice moved on a regular basis. The family followed Theodore Roosevelt from Long Island to Washington, D.C., back to New York City, to Albany, and in 1901 again to Washington and the White House. To avoid being lost in the shuffle, Alice developed a keen sense of humor and unconventional, headstrong ways. She became a favorite of celebrity watchers of her day. Her favorite color, a shade of blue-grey, became known as *Alice blue.* It also inspired the Joseph McCarthy song "In My Sweet Little Alice Blue Gown."

Russell, John

Born in 1795, John Russell had two passions, religion and fox hunting, earning him the nickname "The Sporting Parson." When he was studying divinity at Oxford University, he imagined a terrier that could root out foxes from their holes. One day, the story goes, he spotted a milkman walking a small dog named Trump. Russell thought she would be the perfect fox hunter and he bought the dog from her owner then and there. In the mid- to late 1800s, he bred a strain of dogs that were noted for their fox-hunting ability. He was a founding member of England's Kennel Club in 1873. In his day, Russell was known as "The Father of the Wire-Haired Fox Terrier." Because of the reputation of both the terriers and their flamboyant breeder, they came to be known as *Jack Russell terriers,* as did many other dogs. According to the Jack Russell Terrier Association of America, "After Russell's death, the name *Jack Russell* was misused to describe all mix and manner of working and hunt terriers, many of which bore little, if any, similarity to Russell's own terriers. . . . Unfortunately, it was this kind of terrier; bull-headed, long-backed, short-legged, prick-eared, frequently achondroplastic and of questionable temperament; that was imported to America incorrectly bearing the name *Jack Russell* and who can be found all over the media today." One of the most famous Jack Russells today is Eddie on the television series "Frasier." The canine actor who plays Eddie is actually named Moose. Should Moose be insulted by the association's characterization of his breed? Most breeds of dog are named for their physical traits or the purpose for which they were bred. Cocker spaniels, for example, were originally bred to hunt woodcocks. They were thus originally known as cocking spaniels. The dachshund is similarly named. The German name translates to "badger hound." Basset hounds were originally bred to hunt rabbits. Their name comes from the French "bas" meaning low, a reference to the short legs that keep bassets close to the ground. Rottweilers get their name from a place, the town of Rottweil. The dogs were first bred in Rome and taken to Rottweil along with Roman soldiers, who left them behind. When it comes to dog breeds and place names, however, it's best not to trust what you hear. French poodles do not come from France. They were first bred in Germany and "poodle" came from "pudel," the German word for puddle. The dogs, apparently, are good swimmers. Great Danes are not Danish. They, too, come from Germany. The French were the first to think they came from Denmark. Pekinese, however, really did come from China. The dogs were so precious to the Chinese royal family that when British troops overtook the Imperial Palace in 1860, their owners killed most of the pets rather than let them be taken by the enemy. The emperor's aunt, however, was so distraught that she killed herself instead. Her five dogs were found hiding in her quarters and were taken back to England, where one was presented to Queen Victoria.

S

Saud, Abdul Aziz ibn Abdul Rahman al-

Abdul Aziz ibn Abdul Rahman al-Saud, better known in the West as Ibn Saud, was born in 1880 in Riyadh, the capital of Nejd, of which his father was sultan. His family was the traditional leader of the ultraorthodox Wahhabi movement in Islam. In 1891, a rival group seized Riyadh and the family was driven into exile in Kuwait. There Ibn Saud studied military strategy, religion, and Arab politics. His father resigned the throne in his son's favor. In 1902 Ibn Saud put his training to the test. He and a small group made up mostly of relatives recaptured Riyadh. Using a mixture of military strategy, diplomacy, coopting conquered opponents into important positions in his government, and multiple marriages, he was able to bring all of central Arabia under his rule by 1921. (Ibn Saud had hundreds of wives and fathered at least sixty-four children.) In 1924 he invaded the Hejaz and was proclaimed king in 1926. Nejd and the Hejaz were united soon afterwards. The united lands needed a new name, and the king gave them his own—*Saudi Arabia*.

Schlitz, Joseph

In 1856 Joseph Schlitz was working as a bookkeeper for August Krug's seven-year-old brewery. When Krug passed away, Schlitz married his former boss's widow and took over the business. The timing was fortuitous. During the Civil War, alcohol was taxed to help the war effort. Each gallon of whiskey and barrel of beer was taxed the same amount—one dollar. It didn't take tavern owners or patrons long to realize that with thirty-one gallons of beer in a barrel, beer was going to be a much better value than the former favorite drink. Schlitz was able to increase production and later invited Krug's young nephews August, Henry, Alfred, and Edward Uihlein to join him. They renamed the operation the Joseph Schlitz Brewing Company. Schlitz died in a shipwreck a year later and the Uihleins took over, but they kept the name. Tragedy in Chicago was a boon to the brewery. Following the great Chicago Fire of 1871, Schlitz sent down several shipments of beer to the city that had lost all its own breweries. The move helped gain consumers farther afield. The following year the company's sales doubled. In 1893 Schlitz decided to boast on this success with the slogan "The Beer That Made Milwaukee Famous." The slogan was so well known that Glenn Sutton wrote a song called "What Made Milwaukee Famous (Has Made a Loser Outta Me)." Jerry Lee Lewis recorded it in 1968. By 1900 Schlitz was Milwaukee's largest brewery, with an annual production of over 1 million barrels. The business thrived until prohibition took effect. The company sold a special nonalcoholic brew and waited. Prohibition was repealed and the brewing began again. It wasn't long before Schlitz was setting sales records. In 1952 it became the first brewery to produce 6 million barrels of beer in a year. To celebrate, 2,000 employees and more than 1,000 guests drank beer and ate hamburgers to the tune of "Roll Out the Barrel." In the early 1970s Schlitz was the country's best-selling brand of beer. Since they were already selling to a large portion of the beer-drinking public, they decided to look for other ways to save money. They decided to lower costs by replacing the expensive barley malt with corn syrup and to adopt a process they called "automated balance fermentation," which allowed a batch of beer to be brewed in roughly half the time. The idea was that a lower-cost beer with a quicker turnaround would equal higher profits. The problem with the plan was that Schlitz drinkers weren't buying it. They didn't like the new and "improved" taste. They could even see the change—there was no head on the beer and yeast flakes were often found floating in the brew. In 1976 the company was even forced to recall and destroy 10 million cans. Sales of Schlitz plummeted, dropping from 24 million barrels a year to just 15 million barrels by 1980. By the time the company mercifully reverted back to its old recipe, it had lost most of its customers. In 1981 "the beer that made Milwaukee famous" closed its Milwaukee brewery. The ornate building they left behind was converted into elegant apartments. In 1982, shareholders voted overwhelmingly to sell the company to the Detroit-based Stroh Brewery Company. Old Milwaukee was ironically one of the famous Schlitz brands to be brewed in Detroit. By 1985, Schlitz had just 1 percent of the U.S. beer market. In the late 1990s, *Stroh Brewery*, in trouble itself, sold the Schlitz brand to *Pabst*. This would have put Schlitz back in Milwaukee were it not for the fact that Pabst itself was sold to a California-based company and moved out of the famous brewing city.

Schwab, Charles

Charles Schwab, Chuck to his friends, was always interested in money and how to make it. He was born in 1937 in Sacramento, California, the son of the Yolo County district attorney. He was dyslexic. While he was challenged by reading, he was always comfortable with numbers and mathematics. He spent most of his childhood looking for ways to collect money. "Other kids wanted to be doctors or lawyers or farmers or teachers," he would later say. "I knew from the start I would be an entrepreneur; my instincts for it were almost hard-wired." His first job was picking walnuts and selling them for $5 a bag. Next he sold eggs door to door. As a teenager he worked as a golf caddy. In college he worked as a bank teller and an insurance salesman. After graduating from Stanford with a degree in economics, he went straight into an MBA program, all the while working at a small investment-advisory service. In 1961 he earned his MBA and was promoted to vice-president of the company. A year later, he was one of three partners to launch *Investment Indicator,* an investment advisory newsletter. At its height, the newsletter had 3,000 subscribers. As the enterprise grew, it drew the attention of Texas authorities, who ordered it to stop soliciting investments by mail. The lengthy court battle left Charles Schwab $100,000 in debt. It also took a toll on his marriage, which eventually fell apart. Schwab borrowed money from family members and founded the First Commander brokerage firm. In 1974, the SEC mandated a thirteen-month trial period for the deregulation of certain brokerage transactions. Schwab used the opportunity to create a new kind of brokerage, a discount brokerage. A year later, the SEC officially approved "negotiated" commissions, marking the birth of the discount brokerage industry. Charles Schwab sold the company to BankAmerica in 1983 for $55 million. He ended up buying it back for $325 million and selling stock, which was valued at more than $400 million. He named it Charles Schwab & Company.

Seagram, Joseph Emm

Joseph Emm Seagram was born in Ontario on April 15, 1841. A racing enthusiast, he was known for his physical resemblance to King Edward VII. In the mid-1800s Seagram made his home in Waterloo, Ontario, which was a center for German immigration to Canada after the Napoleonic Wars in Europe. The Germans brought with them their skills in brewing and distilling. In 1857, Granite Mills and Waterloo Distillery was constructed by two men, William Hespeler and George Randall. Joseph E. Seagram became a partner in 1869 and bought the business outright in 1883, renaming it the Joseph Seagram Flour Mill and Distillery Company. That same year he created Seagram's '83, which became one of Canada's most popular whiskeys. Seagram's VO, first blended in 1907, is now the best-selling Canadian whiskey worldwide. His business success helped him to become one of the area's most prominent citizens. He served as a town councilor from 1879 to 1886, and was the Conservative member of Parliament for Waterloo from 1896 to 1908. He was also known for his extracurricular and philanthropic activities. In 1888 he opened the Seagram Stables, which won eight consecutive Queen's Plates from 1891 to 1898. He later became the president of the Ontario Jockey Club and the founder of the Canadian Racing Association. In 1893, Seagram donated the land for the site of the Berlin-Waterloo Hospital. He died in 1919 and the distillery was purchased by Samuel Bronfman's

Distillers Corporation in 1928. The head office was moved to Montreal. The name Seagram was so strongly associated with the product that it remained. The original Seagram plant in Waterloo closed in 1992 and was torn down the following year. A fire that same year destroyed the original flourmill and still house. Today, the Seagram Company Ltd. owns 80 percent of Universal Studios as well as the spirits business. Some of the entertainment companies that they own all or part of are USA Networks, MCA Records, and Polygram. On the drinks side, Seagram sells distilled spirits, wines, coolers, beers, and mixers throughout more than 190 countries and territories. Their brands include Grolsch Beer, Sterling Vineyards, Captain Morgan, and Glenlivet Distillers.

Sealth, Noah

Born around 1786 on Blake Island in Puget Sound, Sealth grew to be the chief of the Suquamish and Duwamish tribes. Chief Sealth was known for his speaking skills and his ability to main-tain peace with the European settlers who came to fish in the salmon-filled water of the Duwanmps settlement. His tribe traded with the whites and Sealth even encouraged Dr. David Manyard to open a store. Because the settlers had difficulty pro-nouncing Sealth in the native language, they called the leader Chief Seattle. In 1855, Sealth led the American Indian council that ceded the settlement to the United States. In spite of fric-tions between Native Americans and the United States govern-ment, Sealth remained friendly with the settlers. They decided to change the name of Duwanmps to Seattle in the chief's honor. Sealth was strongly opposed to the appellation. It violated tribal custom that forbade naming a place after a person; the Native Americans believed a spirit would be disturbed if its name was spoken after death. The townspeople refused to change it. Sealth's tribe was eventually exiled to the Port Madison Indian Reservation. The chief converted to Catholicism and was buried in a Catholic cemetery on Bainbridge Island. A canopy of dugout canoes marks his grave, which has a tombstone bearing the inscription I.H.S., Latin for "in this spirit." Members of the Suquamish interpreted the letters as "I have suffered."

Shea, William Alfred

William Alfred Shea was born June 21, 1907 in Manhattan. From his youth he had a keen interest in sports, fueled in no small part by his high-school Spanish teacher, whose nephew, Herb Pennock, was a star pitcher for the New York Yankees. He went to New York University on a basketball scholarship before transferring to Georgetown University, from which he received a law degree in 1931. He was admitted to the New York bar a year later. After many years in private practice, he became reacquainted with an old high-school friend, Milton S. Gould. Gould had also become a lawyer. Together they formed a twenty-two-lawyer firm, Shea, Gallop, Climenko and Gould, in 1964. After a number of personnel and name changes, the organization settled on the short and simple Shea & Gould. "It's no great secret that this firm is run by Mr. Shea and myself," Gould said. "For the first time, the name of the firm is accurate." In fact, Gould and Shea drove to work together for twenty-five years. They arrived together each morning at exactly 8:15. Employees called them autocratic and strongly dedicated to their practice, but agreeable. The firm became known for "getting around the law without breaking the law," Jack Newfield and Paul DuBrul wrote in their 1983 book, *The Permanent Government*. William Shea's political skills and Milton Gould's preeminence as a litigator attracted the powerful and prominent from Albany and New York City, including congressmen and the staffs of several presidents. Shea came to be known, in the words of a 1974 *New York* magazine profile, as "the city's most experienced power broker." When the Brooklyn Dodgers and New York Giants left for California in 1957, Mayor Robert F. Wagner called upon Shea to help fill the void. He was asked to lead a four-member committee of prominent citizens who would try to bring a National League team to the city. The committee tried first to bring three existing teams to New York— Pittsburgh, Cincinnati, and Philadelphia. When that didn't work, Shea announced his plan to start a third baseball league, which he planned to call the Continental League. The league would be made up of eight new teams. "It was," wrote David Margolick in the *New York Times,* "in some ways, an elaborate bluff; few actually expected the new teams ever to take the field. But the major league owners, unwilling to risk their treasured exemption from federal antitrust laws, gave in anyway." In August 1960, William Shea and former Dodgers manager Branch Rickey met with the major-league owners in Chicago. The leagues agreed to include the teams that would have made up the Continental League, including the team that would become the New York Mets. The team began playing in the Polo Grounds in 1962. Two years later they moved to a new stadium in Queens. Mayor Wagner dubbed the new field *Shea Stadium*. As for Shea & Gould, the original partners handed over the reins in 1985. Shea suffered a stroke and passed away in 1991. At the time of his death, there were nearly three hundred lawyers employed by the firm. The firm's partners were unable to fall in behind any new leader. Senior partner Thomas Constance tried to steer Shea & Gould after the founders stepped down, but he was never able to engender sufficient loyalty to rule effectively. The firm disbanded in 1994. Milton S. Gould passed away in March 1999 at the age of eighty-nine.

Shelumiel

Shelumiel, the son of Zurishaddai and the leader of the tribe of Simeon, appears four times in the Book of Numbers. Little was recorded about him except that at the Lord's command he made an appropriate offering for the dedication of the altar. It is believed, however, that somehow this biblical character had the dubious honor of lending his name to the Yiddish term *schlemiel,* meaning a person who makes a foolish bargain, or a fool in general. The common use of the word dates back to poet Adelbert Von Chamisso's 1814 fable *Peter Schlemihls Wunderbare Geschicte* (Peter Schlemiel's Wonderful Story). Chamisso probably took the name of his character from the Bible. In the story Peter Schlemiel makes a deal with the devil. He sells his shadow for a purse that is never empty. His wealth buys him no happiness, because when people see he has no shadow, they are frightened of him and he is shunned from society. The story was translated into many languages, retaining the original name of the character with variations in spelling here and there. Thus *schlemiel* became a household word.

Shem

Noah had three sons, Shem, Ham, and Japheth. According to biblical tradition, God destroyed all the world in a great flood. Only Noah, his family, and one pair of each beast on earth survived in the ark Noah had built. When the waters receded, they started anew and repopulated the world. Thus all human beings descend from one of Noah's children. Shem was the common ancestor of various ancient peoples. In 1781, a German historian, August Ludwig von Schloyer, identified a language group consisting of Hebrew, Aramaean, Arabic, Ethiopic, and ancient Assyrian. The name he chose for the group, *Semitic,* derived from Shem's name. The word later came to be applied to the people who had spoken the common tongue from which all the above languages are believed to have evolved. In the past century, the word has come to be applied primarily to Jewish people.

Shillibeer, George

George Shillibeer, born in 1797, introduced the first buses to London. These were not the red double-decker buses that are so closely associated with that city. Known as omnibuses, they were pulled by horses and carried twenty-two passengers. Shillibeer later adapted his coaches to carry mourners to burials and funerals. A combined hearse and mourning coach came to be known as a *shillibeer.* It is also thought that the word *shill,* meaning a swindler's helper, derived from his name. The story here is that Shillibeer hired people to lure tourists onto his coaches. There are other candidates for the title of the original shill, however. Some attribute the word's source to humorist Benjamin Penhallow Shilaber, who was widely criticized for borrowing the name of the legendary Dame Partington from a speech by politician and author Sydney Smith. Although Shilaber admitted the name came from the woman who had tried to sweep the flooding Atlantic Ocean out of her cottage, the character of Mrs. Partington, who appeared in a number of Shilaber's books, was entirely his creation. Even so, accusations of plagiarism were damaging to Shilaber's reputation. Some say that his name became associated with dishonesty and somehow evolved into shill.

Simmons, Zalmon

Zalmon Simmons was born September 10, 1828. On his twenty-first birthday, he moved from Illinois to Southport (now Kenosha), Wisconsin determined to make his fortune. He began his career as a store clerk earning $200 a year. The thrifty Simmons was able to put money aside. When his employer took ill, he bought the store for $14,000 and paid off the mortgage in five years. Shortly thereafter he met and married Emma E. Robeson. The couple had six children. Simmons learned of a struggling telegraph company. The owner of the firm owed Simmons a fair amount of money. Telegraph technology was new then and all manner of aspiring entrepreneurs rushed to enter the emerging field. Most of these startups failed. It was said that Simmons never gave up trying to collect a bad debt. In this case, Simmons agreed to write off the debt and take over some of the company. He sold his store to his brother, and with $500 bought half-interest in the new venture. Nine years later, the Northwestern Telegraph Company had 2,300 miles of wire and a value of $1.5 million. The firm seemed to naturally transition into the railroad business. Simmons built the first cogwheel railway up Pikes Peak. He eventually became president of the Rock Island Railroad. During the Civil War, Simmons avoided the draft by hiring someone else to go in his place, a common practice in his day. In 1870, Simmons bought a little factory that made wooden insulators for his telegraph lines as well as for cheese boxes. Through that enterprise, in 1875, Simmons met an inventor who had come up with something called the woven-wire mattress. It was a frame with strands of wire woven through it. Simmons bought the invention and, with a $5,000 investment, converted part of his factory to bed production. It was not long before the company was turning out 1,500 mattresses a day. In 1892, a fire spread through the factory and burned it to the ground. Simmons rebuilt and by 1910, the year of his death, the company had annual sales of $5 million. Zalmon Simmons II took over the business. By the time the Simmons Beautyrest mattress hit the market in 1925, the company had dropped all its sidelines and was focusing entirely on mattresses. Annual sales increased to $43 million by 1936. Simmons is now the number-three U.S. mattress maker, behind Sealy and Serta.

Sinatra, Nancy

Nancy Sinatra was born June 8, 1940 in Jersey City, New Jersey, the first child of Nancy and Frank Sinatra. When she was only five years old, family friends Jimmy Van Heusen and comedian Phil Silvers wrote a song about the little girl, which they named "Nancy with the Laughing Face." Her father later recorded it and made it famous. Nancy had musical aspirations of her own. She made her television debut with her father and Elvis Presley in 1959, and a year later married teen idol Tommy Sands. Her family connections helped her get her start. With her father's new label, Reprise, she waxed a novelty record, "Cuff Links and a Tie Clip," in the style of Annette Funicello. Her second single, "Like I Do," went to number one in Japan, Italy, and other countries but flopped at home. During this time she appeared on "Hullabaloo" and "American Bandstand" and in supporting roles in movies like *Get Yourself a College Girl, The Ghost in the Invisible Bikini,* and the Elvis movie *The Oscar and Speedway.* Ironically, during the filming of a picture called *Marriage on the Rocks,* her own marriage ended. She decided to revamp her image and recorded a new song that was full of attitude. "These Boots Are Made for Walking" went to number one on the American record charts in just four weeks. She had several follow-up hits, including a number-one debut with her father, "Something Stupid," but she seemed destined always to be in the elder Sinatra's shadow. In a 1999 interview with *Washington Times* reporter Corey Levitan she snapped at the suggestion her new album was a "comeback." After five questions, the name "Frank Sinatra" came up, and she stopped the interview cold by pushing the stop button on the reporter's tape recorder.

Slosberg, Pete

A 1998 Internet survey found that more people believed in Mr. Whipple than Pete of Pete's Wicked Ale fame. Only 26 percent of the respondents thought Pete was a real person while 40 percent believed the fictional Charmin toilet-paper spokesman was real. Another 1 percent of the people who took the time to reply to the poll said they believed Tony the Tiger was real. The poll results, it should be mentioned, were released as part of a campaign to promote a book. (Conducted by "a qualified third party," the survey was filled out by only 500 people.) The book, *Beer, for Pete's Sake,* was written by the very real Pete Slosberg of Pete's Brewing Company. Slosberg studied rocket science but ended up as an expert in beer and marketing. He attended Columbia University's engineering school. After he graduated he entered the University of Colorado's doctoral program in astrophysics. He left Denver, he says, because the beautiful setting distracted him from his studies. He went back to Columbia and graduated from the business school in 1974. He worked for three years for Xerox in Rochester, New York and was able to get a transfer to Los Angeles by calling people from the Columbia engineering alumni directory. There, he got a job with Rolm, a company that offered employees a paid sabbatical every seven years. During his three months of paid vacation, Slosberg and a friend decided to go into business together. Slosberg had recently taken up a hobby, homebrewing. He had never been much of a drinker, but his wife introduced him to wine and after some time, he decided to try making some of his own. He went out and bought all the equipment, but found he was too impatient. Wine needed to ferment. It would take a good five to ten years before he could sample what he had made. A friend told him he could use the same equipment to make beer and he would only have to wait a few weeks. Slosberg had never much liked beer, but he decided to give it a try, anyway. He sampled a number of less common beers and developed a taste for some of them, notably Samuel Smith's Nut Brown Ale. He set out to imitate the British brew. He tried four times and was met with failure and then success. His concoction never tasted anything like Samuel Smith's, but on the fourth try, Slosberg hit on something he liked even better. So during his vacation he met with his friend, Mark Bronder, at the Jew and Gentile Deli in Mountain View, California to map out a plan to turn the hobby into a business. Bronder, interestingly, was not a beer fan either. Since Slosberg was the one who had become a beer fan, they decided to name the company after him. They arrived at the word "wicked" when they heard a radio announcer use it repeatedly. Pete's Wicked Ale was launched, featuring Slosberg's bull terrier,

Millie, on the label. The partners were fortunate to be located in California's Bay Area, a region dense with young, college-educated, affluent consumers who were willing to pay $6 or $7 for a six-pack for quality and because it fit their image. They also entered the business at the right time. It was 1986, America's first brewpub opened in the 1980s, and the production of domestic specialty beers, also known as "microbrews," steadily increased 40 to 50 percent a year. Six months after Pete's Wicked hit the shelves, Anheuser-Busch launched an ad campaign around a spokesdog, a bull terrier named Spuds McKenzie. The huge brewer's lawyers contacted Slosberg. He decided it wasn't worth fighting with the King of Beers, so Millie was dropped. The Millie-less beer's sales soared from $444,000 in 1989 to $33 million in 1994. Pete Slosberg personally promotes his product with speaking engagements. He studied up on beer and collected facts and trivia from the archives of many major and minor brewers. Now he crosses the country giving "beer education" or, as he puts it, an educational "standup routine." The underlying purpose of the talks is, of course, to plug his own products. People come for the fun facts and the entertainment value and, hopefully, go away and buy a six-pack of Pete's Wicked Ale. In 1998, he even spent several hours on a San Francisco billboard waving. He said he wanted to prove to the doubters that he exists.

Smith, Henry Walton

In 1792 it seemed as if everything was just beginning for fifty-four-year-old Henry Walton Smith, a London Custom House official. He had just started a new business—a newspaper shop in London's Mayfair section. He increased newspaper sales by setting up something he called a "newswalk," basically a paper delivery round. That year his wife gave birth to a son, William Henry Smith. Unfortunately, Henry Walton did not live long enough to enjoy either the business he created nor the son who would go on to run it. He died two weeks after his son's birth. William's mother took charge of the business and ran it until her own death in 1816, when William and his brother Henry took over. Even though William was the younger brother, he soon became the dominant partner. In 1828 Henry left the news business entirely in the hands of William. At this time a new, and controversial, form of transportation—the railroad—was being debated in England. Samuel Smiles, a writer of the era, described the reaction when a bill to build a railway between Liverpool and Manchester, England, was introduced in Parliament in 1825:

> Pamphlets were written and newspapers were hired to revile the railway. It was declared that its formation would prevent cows grazing and hens laying. The poisoned air from the locomotives would kill birds as they flew over them, and render the preservation of pheasants and foxes no longer possible. Householders adjoining the projected line were told that their houses would be burnt up by the fire thrown from the engine-chimneys, while the air around would be polluted by clouds of smoke. There would no longer be any use for horses; and if railways extended, the species would become extinguished, and oats and hay unsalable commodities. Traveling by road would be rendered highly dangerous, and country inns would be ruined. Boilers would burst and blow passengers to atoms. But there was always this consolation to wind up with—that the weight of the locomotive would completely prevent its moving, and that railways, even if made, could never be worked by steam-power!

William Henry Smith, being of an earlier generation, did not consider the new system. He built a countrywide newspaper distribution network based on the mail-coach system and was still able to boast, "First with the News." His son William Henry Smith II, however, instantly recognized the potential in rail delivery. In 1846, at the peak of "railway mania," the younger Smith turned twenty-one. He joined his father and the firm of W. H. Smith and Son was created. William Henry II made the company what it is today. He recognized that railways offered a faster and more reliable way of distributing newspapers. This allowed him to sell papers on a truly national scale. To make delivery even more efficient, and to serve the needs of travelers, he set up the first W. H. Smith bookstall in a railway station. It opened at London's Euston Station in 1848 and stocked candles and rugs along with the reading material. Today the company has more than eleven hundred stores internationally.

Smith, Maria Ann

Maria Ann Smith lived in Ryde, Australia. One day she left a pile of old apples on the ground and after some time had passed she returned to find a sapling was growing. She cultivated the green fruit that grew from the tree. Today the apple is popular worldwide and known as *Granny Smith,* after its discoverer. The variety was sold for the first time in the United States in 1960. It gained popularity, in part because of a fruit-fly infestation that prevented the importation of Australian apples that year. (Apples come from the Southern Hemisphere during the summer, when few U.S.-grown apples are available.) The average American eats approximately 19.6 pounds of fresh apples a year, compared to about 46 pounds consumed annually by the average European. There are more than 7,000 varieties of domestic apples grown in the world, and about 2,500 in North America. Author Elizabeth Hellfman listed 8,000 past and present varieties in her aptly named book, *Apples, Apples, Apples.* Even so, the American marketplace is dominated by just a few varieties. "Red Delicious is the red apple; Golden Delicious is the yellow apple; the Granny Smith is the green apple," writes Vince Staten in *Can You Trust a Tomato in January?* "No clerk is required to explain all the different varieties." In the United States, Red Delicious, Golden Delicious, and Granny Smith account for two-thirds of the apples grown. Granny Smith might not even be one of the varieties found at your local grocery were it not for a study that shows 20 percent of shoppers want a tart apple.

Sousa, John Philip

John Philip Sousa was born in Washington, D.C. in 1864, the son of Portuguese refugees. When he was thirteen, he became an apprentice musician with the United States Marine Corps Band. He learned to play the trombone, violin, and several other band instruments and studied musical composition. He became bandmaster at only nineteen. His band toured the world. He began to write music and showed his interest in musical theater by composing several operettas. The most successful of these was *El Capitan,* which contained a march by the same name. He wrote "Semper Fidelis," which became the official march of the Marine Corps Band, as well as such famous marches as "The Stars and Stripes Forever," "Washington Post March," "High School Cadets," and "Liberty Bell," which is known to Monty Python fans as the comedy team's theme song. He was dubbed the "March King." Additionally, he invented an instrument, a large tuba that encircles the player, known as the *sousaphone*.

Spencer, Marge

Marge Spencer was not an entrepreneur. She did not supply the idea for a new business, nor did she fund a venture. She was an Easton, Pennsylvania, secretary. Her boss, Max Adler, decided, in 1947, to start his own mail-order enterprise. He funded his gift catalog with less than $500. For some reason, "Adler Gifts" just didn't sound quite right to him. So he borrowed his secretary's name. *Spencer Gifts* grew quickly. Within a year it moved its headquarters to Atlantic City. By 1958 sales volume reached $3 million. It was not until 1963 that the first Spencer Gifts retail store opened in the Cherry Hill Mall in New Jersey. Spencer Gifts was acquired by MCA in 1968 and today it has more than six hundred retail stores, all bearing the name of Max Adler's secretary.

Sperry, Thomas A.

In 1996, Clancy Stock began an article for *Reminisce* magazine by observing that hers might be the last generation to have used the words "I'm saving up for . . ." "These are the days of instant gratification," she wrote. "See it now, buy it now." The article was an ode to the bygone days of saving trading stamps. Saving up thousands of stamps seemed daunting, but rewards like electric mixers were "at the end of the rainbow." In the mid-twentieth century, trading stamps were everywhere. Grocery stores, gas stations, and even beauty parlors gave away stamps and booklets of competing brands. The first trading stamps were issued in 1890 by the Schuster and Company department store in Milwaukee. The Blue Trading Stamp System, as it was called, came to the attention of a silverware salesman from Jackson, Michigan. Thomas A. Sperry had frequent business in Milwaukee and he watched carefully what the department store was doing. He came to believe that an independent stamp company could make a killing by supplying stamps to several merchants in one community. He shared his concept with another Michigan businessman, Shelly B. Hutchinson. Hutchinson agreed to help finance such a venture and Sperry and Hutchinson Company was formed in 1896. They sold large pads of stamps to retailers for a small fee. Each stamp had a value of one mill, or one-tenth of a cent. For every ten cents a customer spent, he would receive one stamp, which he could paste into a booklet. When he saved up enough he could redeem the booklets for merchandise at a Sperry and Hutchinson "premium parlor." The system was designed to keep customers coming back to the same store so they could save up enough *S&H Green Trading Stamps. USA Today* described the system as "a prehistoric ancestor of frequent-flier miles." By 1904 the company was boasting capital of $1 million and it spawned a host of imitators. That year Hutchinson sold his interest to Thomas Sperry's brother William. In 1915, however, he regretted the decision and sued for $6 million, claiming he had actually been forced out of the company. The lawsuit was dismissed, but Hutchinson appealed all the way to the Supreme Court. The higher court also ruled against him. In 1923, Sperry's heirs sold the company to Edwin J. Beinecke of New York. The business survived the ups and downs of the Great Depression and World War II to thrive in the 1950s and 1960s. By 1964, S&H was printing and distributing more stamps than the U.S. Postal Service. It was printing 32 million copies of its catalog and 140 million savers books. It redeemed more than a billion stamps a week and was the largest wholesale purchaser of General Electric small appliances, Bissell carpet sweepers, and Coleman lanterns. The stamps, along with Campbell's Soup, were among the few consumer brands painted by artist Andy Warhol. Community groups saved the books for charitable causes. The city of Erie, Pennsylvania once collected 4,500 books to buy the city zoo a pair of gorillas, which they named Samantha and Henry or

"S&H." Green Stamps began to fall out of use in the 1970s. The increasingly impatient consumer was not the main factor in its demise, however. Advertisers are always looking for new ways to catch the attention of potential shoppers. By the 1970s, so many stores were giving away stamps that there was little novelty in the practice. Stores began to advertise that they offered lower prices instead of stamps, and premiums as a way to differentiate themselves. Then the gasoline crisis struck the nation. Gas stations, which accounted for about a quarter of S&H's business, didn't need to offer incentives to get people to the pumps when already there were long lines. Consumers were also discovering manufacturer's coupons and discount stores at this time. All of these economic trends cut into the company's profit margins. An insurance company bought S&H in early 1980. It soon went bankrupt. As part of a financial settlement, Sperry and Hutchinson ended up the property of Leucandia National Corporation. It continued to dwindle during the 1980s from a high of 85,00 participating stores, 700 redemption centers, and 9,000 employees servicing them to 32 employees handling the business of about 400 small stores, primarily in the Southeast. Green stamps, interestingly, survived mostly among truck stops and truckers. In 1999, a group of investors, including Sperry's grandson and great-grandson, bought the company and announced a new approach for a new millennium. Instead of stamps, online shoppers accumulate points on a credit card. The operation is run through www.greenpoints.com.

Spiegel, Joseph

On May 18, 1848, Germany's first democratically elected parliament took power. The Paulskirche Assembly concluded months of demonstrations, pitched street battles, and political wrangling known as the March Revolution. Although it was not as bloody as the French Revolution or some of the other European uprisings around that time, hundreds of people had died for the cause. The parliament was short-lived. After a little more than a year, the constitution it had drawn up had been nullified and the revolutionary movement forcibly quashed in violent clashes all over the country. Many Germans who had hoped for the revolution's success were unwilling to return to a life under the restored authoritarian regimes. They chose emigration—mostly to the United States. Numbers of German immigrants almost tripled, reaching a peak of 252,000 in 1854. The Spiegels were such a family. Moses Spiegel had been the town rabbi of Abendheim, Germany. He had four children, Sara, Marcus, Theresa, and Joseph. The Spiegels, less Marcus, who stayed behind to fight the Prussians, settled in Manhattan, where Moses served as both a rabbi and a tailor. Marcus rejoined the family later. Sara eventually married and moved to Chicago. Marcus followed her to the city. There, he married. Always seeking adventure, he moved to Ohio and joined the Union forces during the Civil War. He was commissioned a lieutenant, and charged with putting together his own military unit. He called on his younger brother, who was still a teenager. Joseph Spiegel joined up. In 1864 the brothers were serving together on a transport boat in Texas. The Confederates attacked. There were 270 survivors. Joseph was among them; Marcus was not. Joseph was taken prisoner. He was released a year later. By then, sister Theresa had also married and settled in Chicago. Her husband was a successful furniture wholesaler. They helped Spiegel open his own store, J. Spiegel and Company, in 1865. Joseph Spiegel married his brother-in-law's niece in 1870. They had a son a year later and named him after Spiegel's father. Moses Spiegel was given the nickname "Modie" by an aunt, and it stuck. That same year, the Chicago Fire wiped out Spiegel's store. He opened a new store shortly before the depression of 1873 struck. During this difficult economic period, Spiegel joined forces with a partner and formed Spiegel and Cahn, Retail Furniture Dealers. Cahn retired in 1879 and the company was renamed J. Spiegel and Company. Two more sons were added to the family during these years. When Modie was a grown man, he joined his father's business. As Chicago residents started moving away from the downtown shopping district, Modie convinced his father to offer credit and add new products. At the turn of the twentieth century, Spiegel started to sell through a mail-order catalog. The catalog business eventually eclipsed the retail side. *Spiegel, Inc.* now ships more than a billion dollars worth of clothing, home furnishings, and electronics each year.

Standish, Myles

Myles Standish was born in England around 1586. He came to the New World on the *Mayflower* in 1620 with his wife, Rose. Also on board the *Mayflower* was John Alden, who was roughly ten years younger than Standish. Both men settled in Plymouth, where they signed the Mayflower compact and became prominent citizens. Sadly, Rose Standish died shortly after her arrival in Massachusetts. According to legend, shortly thereafter the most famous episode in Standish's life took place—his courtship of Priscilla Mullins. As recorded in Henry Wadsworth Longfellow's poem "The Courtship of Miles Standish," Standish sent his friend John Alden to woo the young woman for him. As described in a 1902 text, Alden "sought to fathom the breast of the maiden on the delicate question. In her lonely condition she evidently had the acuteness to prefer a young gentleman, rather than become an 'old man's slave,' and naively replied: 'Prithee, John, why do you not speak for yourself?' It is needless to add that 'he tumbled.'" "The Courtship of Miles Standish" continues to be required reading in many high schools. One of the most revered poets of the nineteenth century, Longfellow used a bit of poetic license with Standish's story. While Standish and Alden both lived in Plymouth and Alden did marry Priscilla Mullins, the love triangle was entirely the product of Longfellow's imagination. Standish married a woman named Barbara sometime before 1627. He moved to Duxbury in 1631 and remained there until his death in 1656.

Stanhope, Philip Dormer

Philip Dormer Stanhope was born September 22, 1694 in London to an aristocratic family that bore the title "Chesterfield." He succeeded to the earldom in 1726 and became the fourth earl of Chesterfield and an ambassador to Holland in 1728. There he fathered an illegitimate son, also named Philip Stanhope, in 1732. That year he returned to England and took up a parliamentary career. He served as lord lieutenant of Ireland and as secretary of state before retiring because of increasing deafness. The earl is most famous for two books of letters published posthumously called *Letters to His Son* and *Letters to His Godson*. The letters, full of the older man's advice and wisdom, reflected the morality of the age. His son, however, did not appear to benefit from the advice. He was described by contemporaries as "loutish." Stanhope's godson did not appear to have been touched by the sentiment either. He was once described by Fanny Burney as having "as little good breeding as any man I ever met." Stanhope's last words were "Give Dayrolles a chair," referring to the diplomat Solomon Dayrolles, a lifelong friend who was with him at his deathbed in 1773. Stanhope was famous for his gracious lifestyle and impeccable taste. The *chesterfield coat*, a single-breasted overcoat with concealed buttons, and the overstuffed *chesterfield sofa* were introduced in the nineteenth century. Because of the earl's fame, they are generally believed to have been named for him, although it is likely that they commemorate a later earl of Chesterfield. Which earl is unclear. *The Oxford English Dictionary* cites the terms only as deriving from "an Earl of Chesterfield." The earl did, however, definitely bestow his title on at least one inanimate object- a brand of cigarettes. Because the earl had made "Chesterfield" synonymous with the finer things in life, the Drummond Tobacco Company decided to give the name to its product. In 1898 Drummond was sued by a New York company that claimed they had already used the Chesterfield name on a cigar, and therefore had the rights to it. The New York Supreme Court ruled in favor of Drummond, saying that "Chesterfield" was a geographical name and the name of an actual person. Drummond was eventually absorbed by the American Tobacco Company, which was broken up in 1911. One of the other companies that had become part of American, Liggett & Myers emerged with twelve manufacturing branches and 625 brand names, including Chesterfield, which they reintroduced in 1912.

Stayner, Steven

Steven Stayner was seven years old in 1972. On December 4 of that year, he was on his way home from school in Merced, California, when a man approached him and said he wanted to talk to his mother about making a contribution to a church. The man led him to a car. Inside the car was Kenneth Eugene Parnell, who kidnapped the boy and told him his parents had abandoned him. Parnell kept Stayner's identity a secret for seven years by changing his name and moving often. During that period he psychologically and sexually abused the boy. In 1980, Parnell kidnapped another boy, five-year-old Timmy White. Stayner, then fourteen, escaped with the child and hitchhiked forty miles to the nearest police station. Stayner finally returned to his parents' home, where he was hailed as a hero. It was not an easy adjustment for the family, especially older brother Cary, who was used to having his own room and now had to share with a brother he didn't know. Steven later found work as a pizza delivery driver. He married and had two children. His story formed the basis of the 1989 NBC mini-series *I Know My First Name Is Steven*. The real Steven Stayner had a cameo in the production as a police officer. It must have seemed, at the time, that there was finally a happy ending for the Stayner family. Unfortunately, this was not the case. Stayner was killed in a motorcycle accident one day before the 1989 Emmy Awards show, in which *I Know My First Name Is Steven* was nominated for four awards. An even stranger turn of events happened ten years later. In 1999, Cary Stayner confessed to killing three people near Yosemite National Park. Police continue to investigate whether he had killed before. Although relatives deny that his killing spree had anything to do with Steven's kidnapping and subsequent fame, the elder Stayner said in a jailhouse interview that maybe they would make a movie of him now.

Stroh, Bernhard

Bernhard Stroh was born in Kirn, Germany to a family that had been brewing beer for two generations. In 1848, political turmoil in his native land convinced him to head for a German settlement in Brazil. He was not happy with life in South America and decided to seek his fortune in America. He got on a steamer bound for Chicago. It made a stop in Detroit and Stroh was so happy with the city that he decided to stay. Upon his arrival in 1850, he had $150 left from his journey. So he did what his family training had equipped him to do. He cooked up some beer in a small copper kettle and started delivering it in a wheelbarrow. At the time, dark Scottish and English brews were the only beers to be found. His light, fire-brewed lager was a welcome change to Detroit palates. He sold enough to open a more permanent business, which he called the Lion Brewery. He adopted the lion crest from Kyrburg Castle in Kirn as its emblem. As the business grew, Stroh was joined by his two sons, Bernhard, Jr., and Julius. They took over the operations when their father died in 1882. They kept the lion symbol but renamed the business the B. Stroh Brewing Company. Under their leadership, it became the largest brewery in Michigan and one of the nation's ten largest. By 1919, sales topped 300,000 barrels a year. The next year Stroh's sold 0 barrels because the Volstead Act, passed that year, closed the country's 1,568 breweries and made prohibition the law of the land. The Stroh family did what it could to stay in business. They sold nonalcoholic beer, soft drinks, ice cream, and malt syrup for homebrewers. The alternative products were sufficiently lucrative to allow the family to build a nineteen-story corporate headquarters in downtown Detroit. In 1933, prohibition was repealed, and by the next year 756 breweries were in operation, including Stroh's. The next forty years were a period of great prosperity for the brewery. They bought several breweries and by the 1980s they were the third largest brewer in the country, behind Anheuser-Busch and Miller. By the middle of that decade, however, consumers were turning to imported and designer beers. By 1985, Stroh's closed its Detroit brewery, and four years later, it was looking for a partner or buyer. In 1999 it found one. Stroh's announced it was selling off its brands to former rivals Miller and *Pabst Brewing* for $400 million. Pabst bought Old Milwaukee, Old Style, and

Schlitz and a brewery in Pennsylvania, and Miller, which is owned by the Philip Morris tobacco company, took the Henry Weinhard's and Mickeys brands from Stroh's and Hamm's and Olde English from Pabst.

Stuart, Mary

Mary Stuart, or Mary Queen of Scots, was the only child of James V of Scotland and Mary of Guise. She was born in December 1542 and became queen of Scotland only six days later when her father died. Mary of Guise betrothed her daughter to the French dauphin and sent her to France when she was only six. In 1558, Mary and Francis II were married under an agreement that would unite the crowns of Scotland and France if they had a son. At the same time Mary signed a secret contract that bequeathed Scotland to France should she die without issue. That same year Mary's cousin Elizabeth became queen of England. England was deeply divided at the time over the question of religion. Elizabeth was the child of Henry VIII and Jane Seymour, a marriage viewed by Catholics as unlawful. Many Catholics saw Mary as the logical person to take the throne from the Protestant Elizabeth. Through her grandmother Margaret Tudor, she had the strongest claim to the throne of England after the children of Henry VIII. Only a year after Mary and Francis were jointly crowned monarchs of France and Scotland in 1559, Francis died. Mary returned to Scotland in 1561 at the age of eighteen. On her return trip from Calais to Leith, one story goes, Mary became seasick and to calm her stomach she mixed orange and crushed sugar. The word *"marmalade"* was thus born, deriving from the words "Marie est malade" or "Mary is sick." Not everyone believes that story, however. Other etymologists are convinced marmalade came from the Portuguese *marmelo,* for "quince." In any case, when Mary found herself back on dry land she thought she would do best to stay out of the battle between the Protestants and Catholics. She accepted the establishment of the Presbyterian Church and, under pressure, consented to certain laws against Catholics, despite the fact that she was Catholic herself. She refused, however, to approve a law for compulsory attendance at Protestant services. In 1565 she married her Catholic cousin Henry Stuart, Lord Darnley, whose descent from Margaret Tudor also gave him a claim to the English throne. Some Protestant nobles opposed the marriage and tried to raise a revolt, but they were defeated and fled to England. This was not the end of Mary's troubles, however. She soon grew tired of Darnley's arrogance and she made a move to ensure that he would play no role in ruling the kingdom. Meanwhile, she was spending a great deal of time with her Italian secretary, David Rizzio. Darnley was so enraged that he murdered Rizzio before Mary's eyes. When Mary gave birth to son James, Darnley refused to attend the baptism. Mary soon found a new lover, the earl of Bothwell, with whom she plotted to kill Darnley. Although Bothwell was acquitted of the crime, most citizens believed he was guilty. When Bothwell and Mary wed, the Scots could take no more. Bothwell escaped but Mary was imprisoned and the baby, James VI, became king. She fled to England and asked her cousin for asylum. Elizabeth feared Mary might try to seize her throne and had her imprisoned for nineteen years. Mary was finally convicted of plotting to assassinate Elizabeth. She refused to admit she was guilty, but was beheaded February 8, 1587 at Fortheringhay Castle. After Elizabeth's death, Mary's son became King James I of England. Some of Mary's more peaceful days were captured in a poem that refers to the queen and her royal maids of honor, Mary Beaton, Mary Seaton, Mary Fleming, and Mary Livingston. The rhyme goes: *"Mistress Mary, quite contrary, how does your garden grow? With silver bells, and cockleshells, and pretty maids all in a row."*

Sumter, Thomas

Thomas Sumter was born in Virginia on August 14, 1734. A tenacious soldier, he earned the nickname the "Carolina Gamecock" during the Revolutionary War. In 1780, things looked bleak for the rebels of the Carolinas. On May 12, Charleston had been taken by the British in the worst American defeat of the war. To discourage Carolina residents from joining the Continental Army, the British had a habit of burning the farms and homes of American soldiers. Many rebels gave up the fight in fear that their families would suffer the consequences. On August 16, 1780, General Cornwallis led a charge against a poorly armed, inexperienced militia. The Americans dropped their guns and ran. Many members of the Continental Congress had already given up on the Carolinas as lost to the British. Thomas Sumter, a colonel in the South Carolina Continentals, fled to the woods of western South Carolina after he discovered his plantation had been burned. There he met a ragtag group of American soldiers. Their leader, Joseph McJunkin, had hidden gunpowder and ammunition in hollow logs and bushes. When McJunkin asked Sumter how he felt about fighting, he is said to have replied: "Our interests are the same. With me it is liberty or death." The group named Sumter its new general. The small army had an uphill battle convincing men to fight the British, but little by little they attracted more fighters to their cause. Word of the group's existence found its way to the British, who sent Benjamin Tarleton after them. Tarleton was known to Carolina residents as "The Butcher" or "Bloody Tarleton." He was said to be the most feared and hated English soldier in the South. Fresh from a victory in Camden, Tarleton and his men set out to destroy Sumter's partisans. Tarleton caught Sumter unprepared. When he arrived at their camp, most of the men were sleeping or sitting around the fire preparing an evening meal. Virtually the entire army of 400 soldiers was killed or captured. Sumter escaped riding bareback on a horse. Tarleton was hailed as a hero in England for his victory. Sumter, however, had not given up. He began gathering a new fighting force. Meanwhile, Tarleton's forces set out to crush any last resistance by harassing and burning the homes of anyone who would not declare loyalty to King George. Tarleton's men were exhausted from the spree when they received orders once again to find Sumter. On November 20, 1780, Tarleton caught up with Sumter and his new band of soldiers. He ordered his 200-member cavalry to charge. Sumter's army now numbered more than 1,000. Instead of taking on the British head-on, Sumter ordered his men to spread out and hide in the trees. The battled ended in a bloody draw. Sumter was badly wounded, and his militia dispersed. Tarleton reported to Cornwallis, "Sumter is defeated. His corps dispersed. But my Lord I have lost men—50 killed and wounded." Sumter was remembered as a hero of the Revolutionary War. His wounds did not kill him. He went on to serve in the House of Representatives for two terms and in the Senate from 1801 to 1810. When he passed away on June 1, 1832 he was the last surviving general officer of the Revolution. He was buried in a city that bears his name, *Sumter, South Carolina.* Joel Poinsett, for whom the poinsettia is named, is also buried there. Following the War of 1812, Pres. James Madison ordered the "immediate extension and gradual completion of the works of defense, both fixed and floating, on our maritime frontier." It would be another twelve years before plans were drawn up for a fort at the mouth of Charleston Harbor. It was named *Fort Sumter* in honor of the Carolina Gamecock. The U.S. government didn't consider Charleston Harbor to be of special military significance, so construction on Fort Sumter progressed slowly. It was still incomplete in 1861. When the South threatened to leave the Union, however, it became one of only two forts in the South to remain under federal jurisdiction. Sumter took on strategic importance as a symbol of national union. The Confederates demanded Union troops evacuate the fort. President Lincoln refused to pull out. The Confederates captured the fort in the first action of the Civil War, earning Fort Sumter a place in American history.

T

Tamanend

Tamanend, of the Lenni-Lenape Nation of Native Americans, resided in the Delaware valley when Philadelphia or "Coaquannok" was established. In 1683, the leader ceded land to the Society of Friends, including William Penn, which led to the founding of the city. Until 1868, the colonists recognized Tamanend's contributions by celebrating Tamanend Day on May 1. After the American Revolution, a number of patriotic societies came into being. One such organization was the *Tammany Society* or *Tammany Hall* of New York City, named in honor of Tamanend. The group was formed around 1786 and incorporated in 1789. The members copied Native American social structures and called their officials "chiefs." Because Tammany Hall and the Democratic Party had the same leaders, Tammany became identified with the Democrats. Tammany Hall stood for reform until the 1860s when Boss Tweed made the name synonymous with corruption. The Atlanta Braves baseball team also takes its name, indirectly, from Tamanend. In 1912, James Gaffney bought a Boston team. A New Yorker, Gaffney was a veteran of Tammany Hall. He decided to give his team an Indian name and Brave sounded good with Boston. The team subsequently moved to Milwaukee and finally to Atlanta. While we're on the subject of team names, here are a few interesting sports-name origins: When Madison Square Garden boss Tex Ricard announced his plan to start a hockey team, the newspapers labeled the organization "Tex's Rangers." The "Rangers" portion stuck, and the New York Rangers were born. The Green Bay Packers got their name in 1919 when Curly Lambeau funded his team with $500 donated by his employer, the Indian Packing Company. The only condition was that the company name be put on the uniforms. The Detroit Pistons basketball franchise seems like an obvious reference to its Motor City location. In fact, the team was founded in Fort Wayne, Indiana in 1957. Sixteen years before it moved to Detroit, it was organized by Fred Zollner, owner of a machine-works plant, hence the name.

Tandy, Charles

Charles David Tandy was born May 15, 1918 in Brownsville, Texas. Shortly after his birth, his father, David Tandy, moved the family to Fort Worth, where he established a leather company. As a boy, Charles earned pocket change by selling scrap leather from his father's factory to classmates. When he was eighteen, he and a friend managed to get a contract to fix the shoes of the dancers in a touring stage show that had come to Fort Worth. Each of the fifty-five dancers wore gold boots that were frequently in need of repair, at five dollars each fix. After graduating from Texas Christian University, Tandy entered Harvard Business School but World War II prevented him from finishing his MBA. Stationed in Hawaii, he noticed that leather crafts were popular in base hospitals and recreation centers. He wrote home to his father and suggested the family business sell leather craft kits. In 1947, Tandy returned to Fort Worth and took a job with the family business. The sale of leather craft kits to veterans hospitals had helped the Hinckley-Tandy Leather Company, as it was then called, to expand in the late 1940s. Norton Hinckley, however, did not like the idea of selling purse- and moccasin-making kits. He believed the real money in the future would be in shoe sales. David Tandy and Norton Hinckley split the partnership. Hinckley kept the shoe business; the Tandys kept the crafts business. In 1950, the company was renamed the Tandy Leather Company. Charles Tandy became the driving force behind the company. He decided to move further into the crafts business by buying American Handicrafts of East Orange, New Jersey in 1952. Using direct mail and advertisements in magazines like *Popular Science*, Tandy was able to sell its craft supplies to 150 stores in the

1950s. In 1960, Charles Tandy became president of the Tandy Corporation. He opened Tandy Marts in Fort Worth in 1961. He bought a saddle-making firm, a tannery, and Cost Plus, which evolved into Pier 1 Imports and was sold off. In 1961, Tandy also bought a nearly bankrupt Boston electronics chain called Radio Shack. At the time Radio Shack had only 9 outlets. Tandy increased the chain's sales through mail order and then put stores in the cities that had generated the most orders through the mail. By the late 1960s, there were nearly 250 Radio Shack stores. In 1971 there were 1,100. In the mid-1980s there were 3,000. The company also went into the computer business, rolling out the TRS-80 computer. Today there are nearly 7,000 Radio Shack stores and the Tandy Corporation has annual sales of around six billion dollars. Charles Tandy considered himself to be such a lucky man that he used the name Mr. Lucky as his CB handle in the 1970s. Tandy was a gregarious, talkative man, well liked by his peers and employees. It was said he never fired anyone. Instead, he would move the less capable from the front lines to less demanding positions. Charles Tandy died in 1978 at the age of sixty.

Tappan, W. J.

Bill Tappan began his career in the Ohio valley of the 1880s as a door-to-door iron-stove salesman. Often he would barter with the poor farmers he visited, trading stoves for food from the farm. In 1891, he changed the name of his company from the Ohio Valley Foundry Company to the Eclipse Company, after a solar eclipse fell over the eastern half of the United States. His Eclipse stove became a big seller; it even sold beyond the borders of Ohio. The company made its greatest strides during World War I, when it developed and supplied cooking equipment to the armed forces. In the 1940s the company changed its name to the Tappan Stove Company. Today the name Tappan is most closely associated with the microwave oven. Tappan did not invent the oven; that honor goes to Dr. Percy Spencer, a self-taught engineer with the Raytheon Corporation. While he was experimenting with a new tube called the magnetron he discovered that a chocolate bar in his pocket had melted. He decided to try a second experiment.

He placed popcorn kernels near the tubes and sure enough he ended up with the world's first microwave popcorn. After experiments with various other foodstuffs, he began construction on a full-fledged oven. The first commercial microwaves, released in 1947, were far from portable. They stood five and a half feet tall, weighed more than 750 pounds, and required plumbing installations for water-cooling of the tubes. Not only that, the behemoths cost about five thousand dollars each. Needless to say, they were practical for very few consumers. Tappan, in 1955, released the first relatively small microwave priced for household use. Of course, the "small" microwave was large by today's standards and it was seen as a novel luxury in its time. By 1975, sales of microwave ovens exceeded that of gas ranges for the first time. In 1976, the microwave oven became a more commonly owned kitchen appliance than the dishwasher, reaching nearly 60 percent of (about fifty-two million) U.S. households.

Termen, Lev Sergeivitch

Termen, whose name was later Anglicized to Leon Theremin, was born in St. Petersburg on August 15, 1896. In 1919, the physicist and inventor was working for the Russian government trying to fix local oscillations in a radio. He created a device whose odd electronic hum changed with the proximity of an approaching body. By waving his hands around the machine, he could play recognizable melodies. In 1928, Theremin received a U.S. patent for his new instrument, which he dubbed the "thereminvox." The device is generally recognized as the first electronic music instrument and the ancestor of the keyboard synthesizer. It is also unusual in that it is played without being touched—the musician simply waves his hands in its electronic field. The *theremin,* as it came to be called, was commercially licensed by RCA in the same year. Its sound is an acquired taste. The *London Times* likened it to "a cow in dyspeptic distress." Although it is not often used today, you can hear the theremin's distinctive warble in the Beach Boys' "Good Vibrations." It was also used to create the buzz of the Green Hornet for the radio drama.

Tetrazzini, Luisa

Luisa Tetrazzini was born in 1871 and made her opera debut in Florence at the age of nineteen. The coloratura soprano was known as much for her zest for life as for her brilliant high tones. As she traveled around the world her reputation grew. She was already a hit in Latin America and most of Europe when she made a triumphant American debut in San Francisco in 1905. Her voice made her famous and her multiple marriages, affairs with other opera stars, and appetite for fine, rich foods made her a great subject for gossip. The San Francisco papers printed the details of her lawsuits, amorous connections, and favorite dishes. The public noted, for example, that one of the diva's favorite dishes was chicken combined with pasta and cream sauce and topped with cheese. This came to be known as *chicken tetrazzini*.

Tobler, Jean

Jean Tobler was born Johann Jakob Tobler in Appenzell, Switzerland. After learning his craft in Paris, he opened his own confectionery in Bern. The shop sold mostly handmade candies with coatings made of chocolate supplied by other manufacturers. He was going through so much chocolate that it became clear it would be cheaper to make it himself. In 1899, he and his sons founded the "Fabrique de Chocolat de Berne, Tobler & Cie." Eventually son Theodor took over the business and in 1908, along with his cousin, production manager Emil Baumann, set out to develop a special chocolate. As the story goes, Theodor was visiting a Parisian cabaret where he saw the Folies Bergères. The dancers ended their routine with a human pyramid. Theodor had an epiphany—his factory should produce a triangular chocolate. The triangle would represent Switzerland's most famous landmark, the Matterhorn. The confection would place honey-almond nougat in the base with triangular chocolate peaks. For a name they combined the Italian word for such nougat, "terrone," with the name of the manufacturer. The result was *Toblerone*.

Toof, Grace

Grace Toof grew up in Memphis, Tennessee, the daughter of a prominent businessman. In 1894 she bought a 323-acre parcel of land, which she increased by another 157 acres in 1901. She never built on the land, but used it for entertaining and outings. Eventually the property was divided among relatives. One parcel found its way to Toof's great-niece, the former Ruth Toof, and her husband, Dr. Thomas Moore. The Moores built a cattle farm and a Southern estate designed to acoustically enhance their daughter Ruth Marie's harp playing. They named the twenty-three-room estate at 3764 South Bellvue Boulevard *Graceland* in honor of Aunt Grace. In 1957 Elvis Presley went looking for a new home. He had bought a house on the city's posh Audubon Drive less than a year before. It soon became apparent that the Presleys were a disruption to the neighborhood. It wasn't anything they did so much as the constant stream of Elvis fans who surrounded the house trying to catch glimpses of their hero. Neighbor Peggy Jemison would later tell *USA Today* that young Elvis played touch football with the kids in the area until his fame made it impossible. "The Greyhound bus tours began to come by," as well as individual fans, she said. "The police had to install a 'No Parking' sign on the street." Graceland, on the other hand, was secluded enough to offer the Presleys and their neighbors some privacy. Elvis bought it for a little more than a hundred thousand dollars. He liked the name, so he kept it. Today Graceland is the most famous American home after the White House. More than seven hundred thousand visitors flock there annually. They pay their respects at Elvis's grave and shop at the Graceland Plaza, an 18-acre museum and shopping complex across the street. John Strausbaugh, author of *E: Reflections on the Birth of the Elvis Faith*, calls Graceland "the American Lourdes." Of course, if the crowds are too much for you, you could always go to Holly Springs, Mississippi, where Elvis superfan Paul MacLeod has created his own Elvis Presley shrine, Graceland Too. According to MacLeod, his wife asked him to choose between her and Elvis Presley. The King won. He is aided in his never-ending search for Elvis blurbs in the media, however, by his son and fellow tour guide, Elvis Aaron Presley MacLeod.

Travis, Andy

Andy Travis was a Colorado policeman. His cousin, Hugh
Wilson of Florida, grew up, moved to Hollywood, and became
a writer for such programs as the "The Bob Newhart Show and
"The Tony Randall Show." In 1977, Wilson finally came up with
an idea for a program that would not have the word "show" in
the title. He wanted to write and produce a character-driven
sitcom that took place in a radio station. He based his fictional station, WKRP in Cincinnati, on real-life radio station WQXI
in Atlanta. One of the first characters he scripted was a DJ
named Johnny Fever, who was based on one of WQXI's an-
nouncers, Skinny Bobby Harper, a morning man who could
never get used to rising at 4 A.M. In Wilson's pilot, the station
manager, Arthur Carlson, hires a new program director who
changes WKRP's elevator-music format to rock 'n' roll. Wilson
decided to base his viewpoint character on his own cousin. He
gave the character many of his cousin's personal habits—his
fondness for cowboy hats, for example—and his cousin's
name, *Andy Travis*. The fictional Andy Travis ran WKRP for
ninety televised episodes. In its original run, "WKRP" was never
a sustained hit, but it became very popular after the fact in syndication. In 1990, *Entertainment Weekly* voted the show as the
sixth most popular syndicated television program of all time.

Trophimus of Arles

Trophimus of Arles died in 280. A bishop, he was sent from
Rome to Gaul about 240-20. He is often confused with the biblical Trophimus mentioned by Saint Paul. The confusion is
exacerbated by the fact that they share the same feast day,
December 29. Saint Gregory of Tours testified that this
Trophimus was one of several bishops associated with Saint
Sernin of Toulouse. Writing to the bishops of Gaul in 417,
Pope Zozimus mentioned him as being sent by the papacy to
preach and found the church of Arles. His church contains a
third-century crypt, which was discovered in 1835. It was for
this Trophimus that the city of *St. Tropez* on the Mediterranean
was named. The other Trophimus was a gentile from Ephesus.
He accompanied Paul to Jerusalem. The presence of a gentile
in the Temple provoked violent protests against Paul that

almost resulted in his death. This Trophimus is the patron saint of children, invoked against gout.

Trumbull, Jonathan

Jonathan Trumbull was born in 1710, the younger of two sons of a Lebanon, Connecticut farmer and merchant. When he was old enough, Trumbull went to Harvard in preparation for a career as a minister. An unexpected tragedy in 1732 changed his plans. His brother, Joseph, was lost at sea en route to Barbados. Trumbull abandoned his ministerial plans and took Joseph's place working at the family shop. Soon his father's health was failing, and Trumbull took over all of the shop duties. As a well-respected, successful member of the community Jonathan Trumbull was elected to the General Assembly. In 1735, he married a woman named Faith Robinson, eight years his junior. The couple had six children, Joseph, Jonathan, Jr., Faith, Mary, David, and John. Trumbull went on to hold a number of military and political positions. During the French and Indian War, he was a colonel of the Twelfth Connecticut Regiment. From 1766 until 1769, he was deputy governor of Connecticut. From there he went on to serve as governor. He served until his retirement in 1784, becoming the only colonial governor to serve both before and after the Revolutionary War. During the war, he became one of George Washington's most trusted advisors. He managed to get supplies to Washington's starving troops in Valley Forge and Morristown, earning Connecticut the nickname "The Provisions State." Because of Trumbull's tireless assistance, Washington referred to him as *"Brother Jonathan."* The British soon adopted the term as a derisive nickname for Americans in general. Like the song "Yankee Doodle," which the British first sang to taunt and ridicule the Americans, the expression was soon adopted by the Americans themselves and given a positive spin. Jonathan Trumbull died in 1785. Two of his sons became highly prominent—one by following in his father's footsteps, the other by rebelling. Jonathan Trumbull, Jr., like his father before him, became governor of Connecticut. The town of Trumbull, Connecticut was most likely named in his honor. The youngest son, John Trumbull, became an artist over his father's strong protests. With the encouragement of Thomas Jefferson, Trumbull painted scenes from the nation's short history. The most famous were a series of scenes commissioned by the U.S. Congress for the Capitol Rotunda in Washington, D.C., including the often-seen rendering of the signing of the Declaration of Independence.

Tso Tsung-t'ang, Pinyin

Tso was born into a well-connected family. He gained his doctoral degree around 1840 and devoted himself to geographic and agricultural studies. In 1853 he was sent to join Tsen Kuofan's army against the Taiping Rebellion. Tso helped organize the defenses and moved quickly up the ranks. By 1860 he was governor general of Checkiang and Fukien, making him one of the most powerful men in China. Six years later he was made governor general of Shenshi and Kansu, the northwest provinces, where a Muslim rebellion was under way. Not only did he quell the uprising, he also improved the area's economic and agricultural systems by building his own arsenal and woolen mill and ordering his troops to grow grain and cotton in their spare time. Tso continued to have military successes despite increasing ill health. He suffered from bouts of malaria and dysentery and became blind in one eye. He tried to retire in 1882, but was recalled two years later to help plan defense of the Fujian coast during the war with France for control of what is now Vietnam. He died soon after the peace settlement on September 5, 1885. Julie Jindal, a writer with a background in Chinese history, publishes essays on the Web at She says General Tso stories are told to Chinese children in much the same way the story of George Washington and the cherry tree is told to American children, as a kind of morality tale. As to the sugar-encrusted chicken dish that is a staple of American Chinese food restaurants, it was probably not a favorite dish of the general's. In fact, it is doubtful that he ever tasted it. The dish was invented in the mid-1970s, by a man named Chef Peng who ran a Chinese restaurant on East Forty-fourth Street in New York City. Most Chinese restaurants in those days served Cantonese food. Around 1974, Hunan and Szechuan food were introduced to the city. General Tso's chicken was representative of the new style. Next time you order *General Tso's chicken,* how should you pronounce the name? The *Encyclopedia Britannica* lists the pronunciation of Tso as "zuo." The *Columbia Encyclopedia* lists it as "dzo." But don't worry, Jindal writes, you're probably going to pronounce it wrong. Even if you get all the consonant and vowel sounds right, it can still come out comically wrong if you use the wrong tone. "You could accidentally claim you want the chicken to play some music. However, the hapless person taking your order has already heard the name butchered often and imaginatively." If you're feeling overwhelmed, order by number.

Tudor, Mary

When Henry VIII's daughter, Mary Tudor, took the English throne in 1553, her main goal was to restore the Roman Catholic Church to England. (*See also* Stuart, Mary.) Henry VIII had created the Protestant Anglican Church in order to divorce Mary's mother. Both the Tudor family and the nation were divided over the Protestant/Catholic issue. Mary's advisors warned her that as long as her Protestant cousin, Lady Jane Grey, was alive, she would be a threat to Mary's throne. Mary gave her cousin a choice—she could convert to Catholicism or be executed for treason. Lady Jane did not convert. She and her husband were beheaded in 1554. When Mary announced that she would marry her cousin, the future Philip II of Spain, her subjects feared that a Catholic foreigner would become king. Her council advised her against the union, but she married anyway on July 25, 1554. The wedding threatened the Protestants and riots broke out. Mary battled the riots with public executions. Some three hundred people were burned at the stake during Mary's reign, including the archbishop of Canterbury, Thomas Cranmer. This earned her the nickname *Bloody Mary.* The cocktail containing vodka, tomato juice, and a dash of chili and Worcestershire sauce was so dubbed because of its color.

Tull, Jethro

Jethro Tull was born at Basildon, Berkshire, England. Although he was a sickly youth, he managed to earn a law degree in 1699 after studying at St. John's College, Oxford. The fast-paced life of a lawyer began to take a toll on his health, however, and he decided to return to the country and take up farming. Up to this point in history, the strip system was still generally practiced in most parts of Britain. Fields were divided up into half-acre strips separated from each other by pathways. The strips would be cultivated in rotation—two in use, one fallow. Tull envisioned a simpler way. In 1701, he invented a seed-planting drill that sowed three parallel rows of seeds at once. Then he experimented with implements for plowing, paying particular attention to the different requirements for different types of soil. Local farmers found the inventions interesting, but they'd been planting seeds for years and didn't see any reason to change what they were doing. Tull spent the next three decades trying to convince farmers that his system was a vast improvement. Towards this end, he published a book, *The New Horse Houghing Husbandry,* in 1733. The book was a big seller and helped to spread word of his innovations farther than he had ever been able to before. Centuries later, Blackpool musicians Ian Anderson, Mick Abrams, Glenn Cornick, and Clive Bunker formed a rock band. They decided to name it *Jethro Tull* for no other reason than they liked the sound of it. Outside of agricultural circles, this is the most common use of the man's name.

Tyson, John

In 1929, a Kansas produce hauler named John Tyson ran out of gas in Springdale, Arkansas. He decided to stay and use his truck to haul fruit for Ozark Mountain orchards. During the depression he started selling chickens to support his family. In 1935 he heard chickens were fetching a better price in Chicago. He bought 500 of them, loaded them into his truck, and drove north. He sold the birds for a profit of $235. He sent $220 of it home to pay on his debts and buy another load of birds. As his venture grew, Tyson found that the Arkansas farmers didn't always have as many chickens as he could sell, so he bought a hatchery in 1937. Later, when a local feed mill told Tyson he would have to wait for feed, he decided to mill his own. By 1940, he had become a commercial feed dealer for Ralston Purina. His business expanded even further in the next few years with the purchase of a number of small farms. In 1947, *Tyson Feed and Hatchery* was incorporated. In 1963, the company went public and changed its name to *Tyson Foods*. In 1966, Tyson's son, Don, became president of the company. John Tyson and his wife, Helen, were killed a year later when the car he was driving was struck by a train. Today, another John Tyson, the founder's grandson, is chairman of the board. The company sells about 7.2 billion pounds of chicken a year or 45 million birds a week. In 1999 it employed 65,000 people and had sales of $7.4 billion.

U/V

Uncle Ben

According to the rice company that bears his name, there was an Uncle Ben. He was an African-American rice farmer known in and around Houston for consistently producing the highest-quality rice. Other farmers in the area were said to have boasted their crop was "good as Uncle Ben's." Little more is known about the real Uncle Ben, except that his name was familiar to a man named Gordon L. Harwell who, during World War II, was the first president of a company called Converted Rice, Inc. Harwell's company had invented a new process for milling rice that resulted in a more nutritious grain. By steaming the rice while still in its hull, the nutrients in the outer bran layers penetrated the grains. The resulting rice cooked faster and was fluffier and more nutritious. At the time, the company supplied its rice exclusively to the armed forces. Now that the war was over, Harwell wanted to sell directly to American consumers. As he discussed the company's marketing strategy with a business partner he remembered Uncle Ben. The farmer had passed away years earlier. Since the name Uncle Ben was synonymous with quality rice in the minds of many Houstonians, they decided to change the name of their product to *Uncle Ben's Converted Brand Rice*. But this is probably nothing more than a marketing fable. Another version is that the name Uncle Ben was given to the rice after Harwell sold his company to chocolate mogul Forrest Mars in 1942. Mars went from farm to farm determined to learn everything about the rice industry. After visiting farms in a number of Southern states, he decided to buy his grain from a farmer named Ben, and this is where the name came from. Or maybe there was no Uncle Ben at all. According to Paul Dickson, author of *What's in a Name?* published by Merriam Webster, the company simply made Uncle Ben up. In any case, everyone agrees the man whose likeness appears on the box is not the real Uncle Ben. He was a Chicago maitre d' by the name of Frank Jones, or Frank Brown, depending on whom you ask. He became the Uncle Ben model by chance. In 1943, he was serving lunch to a couple of businessmen, Mars and Leo Burnett, an adman who would go on to create Charlie the Tuna, Tony the Tiger, Morris the Cat, the Marlboro Man, and the Pillsbury Doughboy. At the time, rice accounted for less than 10 percent of the nation's starch consumption. Mars obviously wanted to change this. Burnett pointed to the waiter and said, "If you want everybody eating your rice, you better have somebody really friendly like him serving it." Mars asked the waiter, then and there, to pose for a portrait for fifty dollars and the rights to the image. The image of Uncle Ben we know today made its debut a year later. Today Uncle Ben's produces 200,000 tons of rice a year.

Van Dyck, Anthony

Born March 22, 1599 in Den Berendans, Antwerp, Anthony Van Dyck the seventh of twelve children of a wealthy silk merchant. Van Dyck's brother became a priest, and three sisters became Beguines. Van Dyck demonstrated his skill for painting at an early age, creating a self-portrait when he was only thirteen. He became one of Peter Paul Rubens' most notable pupils. A prodigious artist, he was hired by James I shortly after his twenty-first birthday. After a few years, Van Dyck set off for Italy on a horse supplied by Rubens. In 1632 in England, he became one of Charles I's court painters and received the active patronage of the earl of Arundel. Honor upon honor followed. He was knighted, appointed principal painter in ordinary, and installed at Blackfriars. A celebrity of his day, Van Dyck painted and hung out with the aristocrats, who copied his style of dress and distinctive pointed beard. The beard came to be known as a *Van Dyck*. The artist married a lady-in-waiting to the queen. Their daughter, Justina, was born December 1, 1641. Van Dyck died eight days later.

Van Wye, Harmen Jansen

Harmen Jansen Van Wye came to America from Bommel in Holland sometime around 1682. Although genealogists have yet to uncover documentary evidence to support it, family legend has it that he was in the Dutch navy and was wounded in the Battle of Solebay, fought June 7, 1672. After his arrival in what is now the Albany, New York area, he came to be known by the name Knickerbacker—a name that does not exist in his native land. Katherine Knickerbacker Viele, in her 1916 book *Sketches of Allied Families Knickerbacker-Viele*, suggests that the appellation was a reference to wounds he received in battle. In 1673 the same fleet in which Harmen Jansen supposedly fought was engaged in another battle at a place called Kijk. Viele speculated that her ancestor was wounded in the cheek, which is called "back" in Dutch. He was thus called Harmen Jansen Van Wye-Kijk-Back or "Harmen Jansen Van Wye whose cheek was marked at Kijk." "In the effort to read the name, the Wye, which might easily be mistaken for Nye (it has been read in both ways by different clerks), was so interpreted and the name became Niekicbacker-Niekerbacker, from which the transition was easy to the final form of Knickerbacker," she wrote. As Harmen Jansen Knickerbacker, the immigrant raised seven children, to whom he left a sizeable parcel of land. His oldest son, Johannes Harmensen Knickerbacker, added land along the river Schaghticoke. This even greater estate passed to his grandson Harmen, who was born in 1779. This wealthy heir was known for his lavish parties and was dubbed "the prince of Schaghticoke." He was, nevertheless, not known outside of greater Albany—that is, until the satirical writer Washington Irving wrote a comical guidebook, *A History of New York from the Beginning of the World to the End of the Dutch Dynasty.* He wrote the guide under the alias of Diedrich Knickerbocker, a thinly veiled reference to the wealthy Knickerbacker family. The work became known in popular parlance as *Knickerbocker's History.* The most well known edition of the book was illustrated with pictures of Dutchmen in traditional costume with breeches fastened just below the knee. In the 1850s the fashion was widely copied and the distinctive garment became known as knickerbockers, often shortened to knickers.

Vancouver, George

George Vancouver, born in 1757, was one of nine children of a prominent family. He began his career as an explorer at the age of fourteen when he joined the crew of Capt. James Cook. Assigned in 1791 to survey the West Coast, he sailed more than thirty thousand miles in four years and charted more than four thousand miles of coastline from California to Alaska. His highly accurate charts were used into the twentieth century. "To describe the beauties of this region will, on some future occasion, be a very grateful task to the pen of a skilled panegyrist," the explorer wrote. "The serenity of the climate, the innumerable pleasing landscapes, and the abundant fertility that unassisted nature puts forth, requires only to be enriched by the industry of man with villages, mansions, cottages, and other buildings to render it the most lovely country that can be imagined; whilst the labour of the inhabitants would be amply rewarded, in the bounties which nature seems ready to bestow on cultivation." Vancouver gave a number of locations their present names—Mount Baker, Mount Rainier, Port Orchard, and Puget Sound—but the city of Vancouver in Canada, and another Vancouver in Washington State, were named *for* him, not *by* him. It was a member of Vancouver's crew, Lt. William Broughtan, who made a trek up the Columbia River naming Mount Hood, Mount Saint Helens, and a city in honor of his captain. During his travels, incidentally, Captain Vancouver carried with him a book, a handwritten guide to the flags and signals used by ships to communicate. The rare manuscript was briefly lost in 1999 when an official of Vancouver's Maritime Museum borrowed it to show a visiting cruise-ship captain and found it had been stolen from his car. A city parks employee found the priceless book in a park trashcan a week later. George Vancouver is celebrated in Ocean Shores, Washington in a unique way. When Vancouver was sailing along the Northwest coast, he never stopped at the site of what is now Ocean Shores. Each year the people of the city gather to celebrate "Undiscovery Day." They have a huge party and finish the evening by wading out into the ocean and shouting, "Hey, George!" The annual celebration was established in 1973.

Vernor, James

Ask a person from Michigan where he lives and he is likely to raise his right hand and point to a place on his palm. People outside the state are often amused to hear a straight-faced Michigander say she lives in "the thumb." Ask a Detroiter about his favorite ginger ale and he is likely to say "Vernors." Vernors ginger ale was first served in Detroit in the 1860s, making it the nation's first soda pop. In 1858, James Vernor was fifteen. He got his first job at Higby and Sterns' Drug Store as an errand boy. He worked his way up to the position of junior clerk. At the age of nineteen, he enlisted in the Fourth Michigan Cavalry and fought in the Civil War. As the story goes, before Vernor left for the war, he put an experimental ginger extract in an oak barrel to age. When he came back he opened his own drugstore on Detroit's main drag, Woodward Avenue, and, if the tale is to be believed, he opened the vat he had waiting for him and discovered the perfect aged blend of his new ginger soft drink. In any case, golden ginger ale had been imported from Ireland for some time and Vernor started to sell his own version at the soda fountain in his Detroit pharmacy. His beverage was made of nineteen ingredients, including ginger, vanilla, and spices, then "barrel aged," as the bottles boast. Meanwhile, as a member of the State Board of Pharmacy, a post he held for eight years, Vernor was instrumental in getting Michigan's first pharmacy law passed. The state's first pharmacy license went to Vernor. His son, James Vernor II, was born in 1877. He joined his father's business in 1896. That same year, Vernor decided to abandon the pharmacy and concentrate full-time on ginger-ale production. He bought a plant down the street from the old drugstore near the Detroit River. Besides his father, the younger James Vernor was the only employee of the company for many years. The father-and-son team worked sixteen-hour days, doing everything from brewing and bottling the soda to bookkeeping and delivery. Before the days of prohibition, most pharmacists sold golden ginger ale. As speakeasies became the rage, "dry" ginger ale, the colorless, milder version we know today, started to eclipse the golden variety. It was designed to be a mixer. The "wets" started drinking clear ginger ale and the "drys" avoided ginger ale in general because of its association with alcohol. Vernor's was one of the few golden ginger ales left after prohibition. Vernor retired, according to his family "a few hours before he died." This was in 1927 when he was eighty-four. Vernor's Ginger Ale continued to grow. In 1941, the plant moved to another spot on Woodward that could accommodate "the most modern bottling facility in the world." With a giant electric Vernor's sign decorated with a bearded gnome, it became a Detroit landmark. Shortly before the second James Vernor's death in 1952, his nephew Vernor Davis became president of the company. James Vernor III was named vice-president. (James Vernor III's son, incidentally, was also named James Vernor.) Around this time they dropped the apostrophe and Vernor's became Vernors. Between 1961 and 1963 sales increased from $6 million to more than $9 million. In 1966, Vernors was sold to a group of investors. It would continue to change hands over the next few decades. In 1971 it was purchased by American Consumer Products. Eight years later, United Brands bought it. In 1985, it closed the landmark bottling plant in downtown Detroit. The property was sold a year later and the plant torn down to make way for apartments. United sold Vernors two years later. It was acquired by A&W, which was itself swallowed up by Dr. Pepper/Cadbury in 1993. Three years later, Dr. Pepper merged with 7UP. Yet, in the words of Keith D. Wunderlich writing for *Soda Pop Dreams,* "even with all the changes, all the owners, and the closing of the bottling plant, Vernors remains Detroit's drink." As a Canadian vendor put it, "It's a niche brand. As you get farther up the highway, it gets smaller." It has the kind of taste that people tend to love or hate. Its nippy, spicy flavor and aroma tickle the nose. It has been described by at least one critic as "liquid pain." Fans of the beverage, however, go to great lengths to find it. There are Internet forums where people from every state discuss where to buy it, mail-order vendors to supply those who don't have a shop within driving distance, and collectors who seek out Vernors ads from the past.

W

Wake, William

Many place names are taken from some aspect of their geography. Wake Island, an atoll in the north-central Pacific, certainly sounds as if it could have gotten its name that way. In fact, it takes its name from a British sailor, William Wake, who visited it in 1796. The island was probably discovered many years earlier, in 1568, by the Spanish explorer Álvaro de Mendaña de Neira. Located about two-thirds of the way from Hawaii to the Northern Mariana Islands, with an area roughly eleven times the size of the Mall in Washington, D.C., the island was not the site of frequent visits. After Wake's voyage, it was basically forgotten for almost five decades. In 1841, an expedition by the U.S. Navy under the command of Lt. Charles Wilkes rediscovered the land and mapped it. The United States was not particularly interested in Pacific islands until the late 1800s. In 1898, the nation annexed Hawaii and took the Philippines from Spain. A year later it claimed tiny Wake Island. It was placed under the jurisdiction of the navy in 1934. A commercial seaplane base and hotel were constructed the next year so airplanes could stop and refuel on their way across the Pacific. During World War II, Wake Island was captured by the Japanese, who attacked it on the same day they attacked Pearl Harbor. It was recovered after the war. It is now an unincorporated territory of the United States administered by the Department of the Interior. There is no indigenous population. In 1980, the population of the island numbered 302 people. As of 1999, most military personnel had left the island. A small civilian population stayed behind to operate airstrips as well as research stations for the National Oceanographic and Atmospheric Administration and the National Weather Service.

Waldo, Peter

In 1176, a wealthy merchant named Peter Waldo (pronounced "Valdo") gave away all his property and went about the French city of Lyons preaching the values of apostolic poverty. He attracted a number of followers, who called themselves the Poor Men of Lyons. Other people called them the Vaudois, in English, Waldenses. The Waldenses were not permitted to preach because they were not Catholic priests. So they traveled to Rome in 1179, where Pope Alexander III refused to grant them permission. He did, however, bless their lifestyle. They returned to France and, ignoring the pope's orders, began to preach. What they preached got them in big trouble with the religious establishment. Centuries before Martin Luther's Protestant Revolution, they taught that any Christian could read and interpret the Bible. The Waldenses rejected the papacy, the mass, purgatory, and the selling of indulgences. Pope Lucius II declared them heretics in 1184. More than eighty of Waldo's followers were burned at the stake in 1211. The Waldenses survived, despite continued persecution, for hundreds of years. A group of them settled in the United States in an area that came to be known as *Valdese, North Carolina.* Centuries of opposition to the papacy made the name Vaudois synonymous with heresy in France. According to etymologist Ernest Weekley, when French missionaries traveled to the West Indies they viewed the rituals there as primitive and heretical. They called the witchcraft Vaudois as well, which eventually evolved into *voodoo.* Not all etymologists agree, however. *The Oxford English Dictionary* records the origin of voodoo as the African *vodun,* a form of the Ashanti *obosum,* "a guardian spirit or fetish."

Walgreen, Charles

Charles Rudolph Walgreen was born October 9, 1873 in Illinois. He came to his life's work quite literally by accident.

He was employed by the Henderson Shoe Factory and he cut off part of his finger in one of the stitching machines. Over the course of the many doctor's visits that followed, Walgreen developed a friendship with the physician, who helped him find safer work at a drugstore. He was not satisfied with his small-town life or his $4-per-week job as a drugstore clerk so he borrowed $20 from his sister and headed to Chicago to seek his fortune. He worked for a number of pharmacies before landing a job at William Valentine's drugstore. There, Walgreen worked seventy-nine hours a week for $35 a month. Walgreen's plan for revenge against his dictatorial boss backfired. He put in longer hours and worked harder than before. The idea was that he would make himself indispensable and then quit, leaving Valentine high and dry. Instead, Valentine gave him a raise and took him under his wing, inspiring the younger man to become a registered pharmacist. During the United States war with Spain in 1898, Walgreen enlisted and served in Cuba. There, he contracted yellow fever and was unconscious for so long that he was actually listed among the dead. He surprised the physicians by recovering. He returned to Illinois with a military pension and was able to buy a drugstore of his own in 1901. Feeling stable for the first time, Walgreen married his sweetheart, Myrtle Norton, a year later. They had three children together, one of whom died in infancy. By 1907, the drugstore had become so successful that Walgreen was able to buy Valentine's store. Myrtle Walgreen once said:

> He always said that he wanted to make better products and sell them cheaper than anyone else. He always based his prices on a percentage of profits. I used to say that it would be a world's wonder if the first words our children learned were not "percent."

In 1909, he built a counter to sell his own brand of "double rich ice cream," and soup and sandwiches prepared by Myrtle Walgreen. It was the first drugstore soda fountain. From that point on, the chain kept growing and growing. By 1925 there were 65 Walgreens. Four years later there were 397. Charles R. Walgreen said the secret to his success was that "I know enough to hire men who are smarter than I am." Walgreen passed away in 1939. His son, also named Charles Walgreen, took over operations, but he did not have long to enjoy it. He, too, died in 1939. The business lived on, however, and in 1974 it became the first drugstore chain to top $1 billion in sales. The company now has about 3,000 Walgreens stores in forty-one states and Puerto Rico.

Warner, Ty

Ty Warner, named after baseball great Ty Cobb, was the older of two children born to Harold Warner, a jewelry and toy salesman, and his wife, a pianist named Georgia. He grew up in the Chicago suburbs and was educated at Michigan's Kalamazoo College. After graduation, Warner joined his father at the Dakin toy company in San Francisco. There he worked as a salesman. To get in to see the buyers, Warner dressed in a fur coat and top hat and drove up to their stores in a Rolls-Royce Silver Shadow. "I figured if I was eccentric looking, people would think, 'What is he selling?'" Warner once told writer Joni Blackman. With a confidence that acquaintances say sometimes crossed the line into arrogance, Warner was a master of marketing. In no time at all he was earning more than $100,000 a year. But in 1980, Warner left Dakin. According to some reports he was fired for designing a competing line of toys. Warner, on the other hand, says he left to pursue other career options. In either case, Warner's new product idea would soon pay off. He believed that there was a need for a line of toys that were affordable—about $5 each—but not, in his words, "real garbage." In 1993, after his father died of a heart attack, Warner inherited $50,000. This he used to create a line of understuffed toys filled with pellets. *Beanie Babies* made their debut at a Chicago trade show that fall, each with a heart-shaped tag on the ear reading *Ty, Inc.* By limiting to thirty-six the number of beanies any single store could have, Warner's company created a demand. Beanies were an instant smash with collectors, who enjoyed hunting down the missing pets to complete their sets. Some of the rarest beanies have fetched up to $13,000 at resale. In November 1998, to celebrate shipping sales of $1 billion, Ty Warner gave each of his employees two special-edition Beanie Babies called the Billionaire Bear and autographed the tags on each one. Those bears are now valued at $3,500 each. Today Warner's fortune is estimated at $2 to $4 billion. As for toys of his own, Warner collects luxury cars and he recently bought the famous Four Seasons Hotel in Manhattan.

Warner, William Richard

William Richard Warner was born in 1836 in Maryland. As a young man, he worked at a drugstore doing odd jobs. His employer could not afford to part with cash, so Warner traded his services for merchandise that he then sold door to door. Thus he was able to pay for an education at the Philadelphia College of Pharmacy. After graduating in 1856, the nineteen-year-old opened his own drugstore. He put most of his attention into mixing new medicines that could be taken in one dose instead of repeated doses. He also worked on pleasant-tasting coatings for otherwise foul-tasting pills. By 1886 he decided to give up the store entirely and focus on drug manufacturing. He created William R. Warner and Company, which released a volume entitled the *Therapeutic Reference Book* two years later. William Warner passed away in 1901 and the company was willed to the oldest of his three sons, also named William. Seven years later, the company merged with the St. Louis-based Pfeiffer Chemical Company. In 1955 it merged again, this time with a company founded by Jordan Wheat Lambert. Lambert had his first major success with a product developed by Dr. Joseph Lawrence based on the work of Dr. Joseph Lister. Listerine, originally marketed to hospitals and physicians, was a stunning success. Lambert promoted it to dentists in 1895 and in 1914 to the general public. The product ensured the Lambert Pharmaceutical Company's future. The Warner-Lambert Pharmaceutical Company, formed in 1955 as the result of the merger of the two men's companies, went on to buy Parke, Davis and Company in 1970. As of 2000, more than twenty Warner-Lambert products were generating more than $100 million in annual sales. In February of that year, Pfizer Inc. bought Warner-Lambert for about $91.4 billion, creating the largest drug maker in the U.S. and the second biggest in the world. The combined company, they announced, would be named Pfizer Inc.

Wesson, David

In 1898, thirty-eight-year-old David Wesson was an employee of the Southern Cotton Oil Company. The company had been founded in 1887. With cottonseed crushing mills in North Carolina, South Carolina, Georgia, Louisiana, Texas, Arkansas, and Tennessee, it was the largest producer of cottonseed oil in the country. Wesson's contribution was the introduction of a new method for deodorizing the oil. Previously, cottonseed oil was unpopular because the only way to deodorize it was by heating it with a steam coil and blowing steam through it at atmospheric pressure. Wesson's vacuum and high-temperature process revolutionized the cooking-oil industry and brought cottonseed oil, under the name *Wesson oil*, into American homes. The product was put on the market by the Southern Cotton Oil Company in 1900. A reorganization of the company in 1925 resulted in the creation of Wesson Oil and Snowdrift Company. In 1960 Hunt Foods merged with Wesson Oil and Snowdrift, creating the Hunt Wesson Company. Hunt Wesson sales were about $2.3 billion in 1998.

West, Thomas

Thomas West, born in 1577, succeeded to the peerage in 1602. He became Baron de la Warr. In 1609 he was appointed first governor of Virginia, replacing the deputy governor Sir Thomas Gates. He was granted the appointment for life. He sailed there in April 1610, with three ships equipped at his own expense and an expedition of 150 people, including Sir Samuel Argall. When he got to Jamestown he found the settlers hungry, bereft of supplies, and ready to give up this whole "New World" idea and return to England. He rebuilt Jamestown, constructed forts, and brought order to the colony. He encouraged the settlers to stay, and sent Argall back for more supplies. On his voyage, Argall sailed into a bay, which he named *Delaware Bay* for the governor. Lord de la Warr returned to England himself shortly thereafter, and left the colony under the leadership of Thomas Gates and Sir Thomas Dale. Back in England in 1611, de la Warr pleaded for more funds and supplies for the colonists. He wrote an account of his experiences titled *Relation . . . of the Colonies Planted in Virginia*. He remained in England as nominal governor until 1618, when complaints against his deputy inspired him to return to Virginia. He never made it there. He died on the voyage and was buried at sea. The state of *Delaware* and the *Delaware Indian tribe* both take their names from Delaware Bay.

Whipple, George

Believe it or not, there really was a Mr. Whipple. George Whipple was head of the public-relations department of the ad agency Benton & Bowles in 1964. One of its biggest clients was Procter & Gamble. Procter & Gamble had purchased the regional toilet-paper supplier in Madison, Wisconsin in 1957. They experimented with the manufacturing process and discovered that if they dried the pulp with hot air instead of pressing the water out of it, as most companies did at the time, the result was softer and fluffier paper. Better yet, it required less wood pulp. The result was a product that cost less to manufacture that could be sold at a higher price as a "premium" paper. All that was left was to find the right way to advertise it. They came up with an ad featuring a cartoon dog that went to court to legally change its name from "Gentle" to "Gentler." Test audiences hated it. So the ad writers went back to the drawing board. They were sitting around a table with a few rolls of the product on hand for inspiration. One of the copywriters, John Chervokas, was playing with one and started to squeeze it. Someone said, "Please don't squeeze the Charmin," and that was it. The writers were off and running. They came up with a script featuring a store manager who scolds his customers for squeezing the Charmin, but who can't resist squeezing it himself when no one is watching. They named the grocer "Edward Bartholomew." Procter & Gamble's executives were not thrilled with the concept, but they reluctantly agreed to pay for three test commercials. A casting call went out for potential Mr. Bartholomews. The actor they chose was Dick Wilson. The veteran of vaudeville, TV, and movies would later recall:

> My agent asked me, "What do you think of toilet paper?" And I told him I think everybody should use it. "No, no, no," he said, "I'm asking you how would you like to do a commercial for toilet

paper. There's an audition tomorrow." I said, "How do you audition for toilet paper?" And my agent said, "Please go and take the screen test."

With their actor cast, all that was left was to shoot the test ad. Usually, when a fictional name is used in a commercial, an ad agency finds someone with that name and licenses the right to use it for a small fee. They do this to avoid lawsuits from other people of that name who claim the character is meant to depict them. The problem was, Benton & Bowles' lawyers could not find anyone named Edward Bartholomew. They decided to change the character's name. Just to be safe, they went through the list of employees of their own firm. They liked the sound of George Whipple. He sold them the right to use his name for one dollar. When they tested the first Mr. Whipple ad they found it scored higher than any other commercial in viewer recall. The ads were a hit with real viewers as well. Charmin became the top-selling toilet tissue and the ads continued to run for twenty-one years. Wilson earned about three hundred thousand dollars a year and a "lifetime free supply" of Charmin for his work. He became so closely identified with the character that he was unable to find other acting work, but he remained in good spirits about it. "It was like a paid vacation," he said. Procter & Gamble retired Mr. Whipple in 1985. None of their new campaigns caught viewers' attention the way Mr. Whipple had, and Mr. Whipple never seemed to fade from the public's imagination. A&W Rootbeer hired him to do a parody ad in the late 1980s. In the commercial Mr. Whipple couldn't pick up a can of root beer without squeezing it and making a mess. In 1995, Dick Wilson's lifetime supply of Charmin inexplicably expired. The story made *USA Today*. The publicity forced Procter & Gamble to give him back his Charmin the next day. "He *is* Mr. Whipple," they said. "He will always be Mr. Whipple and certainly we want to make sure nothing but Charmin goes in his bathroom." Twelve years after Mr. Whipple left the airwaves, readers of humor columnist Dave Barry voted it the most hated commercial of all time. As Barry put it, "Mr. Whipple and various idiot housewives lived in a psycho pervert community where everybody was obsessed with squeezing toilet paper. . . . Americans still, after all these years, feel more hostility toward that ad campaign than they ever did toward international communism." It was clearly a love/hate relationship, though. Procter & Gamble brought Mr. Whipple back in 1999 to great fanfare. Dick Wilson hopes that when his contract expires this time Procter & Gamble will hire his son, Stuart, as the next Mr. Whipple. "He looks like me if he puts on the glasses," he said.

Whitman, Stephen

When Stephen F. Whitman went into business in 1842, most candies were imported from France and Switzerland. The finest were individually wrapped chocolates with cream, caramel, nougat, or fondant in the center. Whitman opened a small candy and fruit shop near Philadelphia's shipyard and began buying exotic candies from sailors. He added to his inventory with chocolates he produced in a little kitchen. His company ran ads in a local newspaper by 1860. Whitman's boxed chocolates gained national distribution in 1907. Whitman then became the first candy company to advertise nationally. In 1912, Whitman introduced a box of assorted chocolates called a *Whitman's Sampler*. That year, a man named J. E. Brandenberger perfected a cellophane material he had patented in 1908. Whitman used the new technology to wrap the sampler. It was the first candy box to be so wrapped. For the cover design, the company's president, Walter B. Sharp, was inspired by a cross-stitch sampler of his grandmother's. An illustration was created to resemble a cross-stitch design. Despite appearances to the contrary, today there is only one company that makes midpriced gift-boxed chocolates. In 1993, former competitor Russell Stover Candies, Inc., bought out Whitman Chocolates, for $35 million.

Wian, Bob

In 1936, Bob Wian owned a small restaurant called Bob's Pantry in Glendale, California. One of the neighbors was a six-year-old named Richard Woodruff. The chubby boy used to do odd jobs for Wian. He'd rake the yard and clean the ice-cream containers and the restaurateur would feed him. According to Woodruff's brother Glenn, Richard always asked for a hamburger with two pieces of meat on it. Thus, Wian got the idea to sell the first double-decker hamburger. He named it, and renamed his restaurant, for the child. Wian created a stylized image for his new symbol, a chubby youngster with wavy brown hair, checkered overalls, and a huge grin. By 1955 *Bob's Big Boy* had sold 5 million Big Boy burgers. Wian had become mayor of Glendale and his franchise had spread east to Kansas, Oklahoma, Michigan, West Virginia, Pennsylvania, and Massachusetts under several different names, including Elias, JB's, Frisch's, and Shoney's. Richard Woodruff lived to be fifty-four years old. When he died he weighed 300 pounds. Marriott bought the Big Boy chain in 1967. The Big Boy advertising icon was so popular that when Marriott considered dropping him in the mid-1980s, customers voted by a landslide to save him.

William III

The son of William II, Prince of Orange, and of Mary, the daughter of Charles I of England, William was born in The Hague in November 1650, eight days after his father's death. He stood fourth in the English succession. In November 1677 he married Mary, the daughter of James, Duke of York, who would later be known as James II of England, and his first wife, a Protestant named Anne Hyde. After James, Mary was the next in line for the throne. James went on to marry a Catholic named Marry of Modena and to try to restore Catholicism as the official religion of England. When the couple had a son, the Anglicans and Puritans were afraid of what would happen now that there was a Catholic heir (this son now replaced James' daughter as next in line for the throne). Some people believed that James had smuggled a male orphan into the palace just to have a Catholic successor. So they invited William to "invade." William saw this as an opportunity to unite the Protestant powers of Holland and England against his arch rivals, the French. William landed at Torbay in Devon on November 5, 1688. He advanced to London, where James' discontented subjects joined him. James fled to France.

Parliament interpreted this as abdication of the throne, which they bestowed jointly on William and Mary on April 1, 1689. One of the first things they did was to enact the Toleration Act, which granted freedom of worship to everyone—everyone, that is, except Catholics and Unitarians. Not surprisingly, this was not good news to the Catholics. They gave William, who was short in stature, the derisive nickname *Wee Willie Winkie.* They wrote a number of rhymes and songs referring to the king, one of which evolved into the nursery rhyme we know today. The verse was a favorite in Germany, where it was known in German as "Der Kleine Villee Vinkee."

Wise, Earl V.

In 1921, a grocer named Earl V. Wise discovered he had stocked far too many potatoes. Instead of letting them rot, he peeled and sliced them and used his mother's recipe for potato chips. He put the chips in brown paper bags and sold them. They sold so well that he decided to order more potatoes and make more chips. In the early 1930s he decided to wrap the product in cellophane and sell it more widely. *Wise Potato Chips* were a hit. By 1964 Wise Foods had become the largest potato-chip manufacturer in the Eastern United States. That year it was purchased by Borden, Inc.

Woolf, Virginia

Virginia, the daughter of Sir Leslie Stephen, was born in 1882. She was educated at home using her father's huge library. In 1912, now a young novelist, she married Leonard Woolf, a critic and writer on economics. The pair established the Hogarth Press five years later. They became the center of a circle of artists, critics, and writers known as the Bloomsbury group. As a novelist Woolf focused more on characters' thoughts and feelings than on plot or characterization. Despite suffering mental breakdowns in 1895 and 1915, Woolf was able to produce a number of highly praised works. They include *Mrs. Dalloway, To the Lighthouse, The Waves, The Common Reader, The Second Common Reader, The Death of the Moth and Other Essays,* and *A Room of One's Own.* Literary success was not enough to save Woolf from the ravages of depression. She took her own life in 1941. After her death, her husband continued to edit her work and published a number of titles posthumously. Along with her own work, her name has become familiar as part of the title of a 1962 play by Edward Albee, *Who's Afraid of Virginia Woolf?* The playwright discovered the title written on a big graffiti-covered mirror in a Greenwich Village bar. Albee thought it was a typical college joke and appropriate for a play set on a college campus. "Who's afraid of Virginia Woolf," Albee once said, "means who's afraid of the big bad wolf . . . who's afraid of living without false illusions."

Woollcott, Alexander

Alexander Woollcott was born January 19, 1887 in Phalanx, New Jersey. He graduated from Hamilton College, in Clinton, New York, in 1909 and joined the staff of the *New York Times* as cub reporter. He eventually worked his way up the ranks, becoming the drama critic in 1914. During World War I, he spent a year in the army, reporting for the *Stars and Stripes,* then returned to his old job. He went on to write for the *New York Herald, New York World,* and *The New Yorker.* He was given his own radio show in 1929. He billed himself as "The Town Crier," which meant a "critic, lecturer, wit, radio orator, and intimate friend to the great and nearly great." As a literary and theater critic he wielded great influence over the public's taste. His reviews were so sharp tongued that some theater managers tried to have him barred from first-night performances. He himself inspired George Kaufman's play, *The Man Who Came to Dinner.* Woollcott was such a terrible houseguest, constantly complaining, that Kaufman got to joking with a friend about how awful it would be if he broke his leg and had to stay for an extended period. That became the theme of the play. A character named Sheridan Whiteside breaks an ankle while staying with a Midwestern family and turns their lives upside down. In 1941, Woollcott himself took the role that he had inspired. Woollcott was the self-appointed leader of the Algonquin Round Table, an informal luncheon club at New York City's Algonquin Hotel in the 1920s and 1930s. His favorite drink, a combination of creme de cacao, brandy, and sweet cream, was a "lethal mixture," according to actress Helen Hayes. "It tasted like cream. I drank one down and took another and drank it down, and I was blind." The cocktail is called an *Alexander* after its inventor. Woollcott died in 1943. He was engaged in an argument on his radio show as to whether all Germans were effectively Nazis and he suffered a fatal heart attack.

Worth, William Jenkins

William Jenkins Worth was born in Hudson, New York in 1794. After receiving a common school education, he worked at a Hudson shop before moving to Albany, where he got a job in another store. When he turned nineteen he applied for a commission in the army. He became a first lieutenant and served as an aide to Gen. Winfield Scott in the War of 1812. He distinguished himself in a number of battles. At the outbreak of the Mexican War, Worth was second in command to Gen. Zachary Taylor and was awarded numerous medals and honors for his service. When the war finished he was placed in command of the Department of Texas. He died there of cholera in 1849. His remains were buried in Worth Square in New York City under an obelisk built in his honor. At the time of Worth's death, Maj. Ripley Arnold was turning a stopping point on cattle drives into a military outpost against Comanche Indian raids. Although no fort was ever built there, it was named Fort Worth in William Worth's honor. After the Civil War, Fort Worth became a major shipping depot for cattlemen. When the Texas & Pacific Railway put a stop there, one of the speakers on hand to welcome the railroad executives predicted that Fort Worth would one day have a population of 5,000. It seemed overly optimistic at the time, but today Fort Worth has a population of 490,500.

X/Y/Z

Yale, Linus

Linus Yale, Jr., was born in Salisbury, New York in 1821. He spent the first decade of his career barely getting by as a portrait artist. Meanwhile, his father, Linus Yale, Sr., was starting to design and manufacture locks around 1840. He opened up the Yale Lock Shop in Newport, New York in 1847. He encouraged his son to take up the trade. Yale, Jr., did. He designed the "Yale Infallible Bank Lock." Its combination could be changed by separating and reassembling parts of the key. Many improvements were to follow. There was the "Yale Magic Bank Lock" and the "Yale Double Treasury Bank Lock," one of the most secure bank locks operated by keys. When the Crystal Palace Exhibition in London was broken into, Yale traveled to England to find out how it had been done. He came back to his factory, tried the technique on his own much-touted Double Treasury lock, and found it to be fallible. Bank robbers were also demonstrating the fallibility of key locks. They broke into many a vault by filling the keyholes with explosives and blasting the doors off. So Yale set to work on a new kind of lock, one without keyholes. The result was the Monitor Bank Lock, the first combination bank lock. Around 1860, he started to work on a small key lock based on the pin-tumbler mechanism used by the ancient Egyptians. The completed lock was patented in 1861. The design called for a serrated key that would be inserted into a cylinder that housed spring-loaded pins. The serrations on the key raise the pins. If the key raises all the pins to the proper height, the cylinder can be turned and the lock can be opened. Yale's design allowed a large number of individual key shapes, each of which will open only one lock, and a master key that will open all of the locks of its series. In 1868 Yale entered into a partnership with J. H. and H. R. Towne to found the Yale Lock Manufacturing Company. Unfortunately, Linus Yale would not live to see the fruits of his labors. He suffered a massive heart attack on Christmas Day 1868, before the partners had brought their first Yale cylindrical locks to market. Today, Yale's lock remains the most commonly used design in door locks and padlocks.

Yuengling, David

David G. Yuengling came to the United States from Wurtemburg, Germany in 1828 when he was twenty-one. He settled in Pottsville, Pennsylvania and, in 1829, opened the Eagle Brewery. Things seemed to be going well until 1831 when a fire reduced his brewery to ash. He found a new location on a mountainside where tunnels provided natural cold temperatures. In 1873, David's son Frederick joined his father as a partner and the name of the company was changed to D. G. Yuengling and Son. At that point, the brewery was producing 23,000 barrels a year. David Yuengling died that year. After adding bottling to the plant in 1895, Frederick also passed away, in 1899 at the age of fifty-one. His son, Frank, took over management duties. The passage of prohibition made Yuengling's product illegal. For the next few years the Yuenglings made do by building a dairy and selling nonalcoholic beer. The company celebrated its 100th anniversary in 1929 without producing a single drop of actual beer. When prohibition ended in 1933, the brewery introduced "Winner Beer" and shipped a truckload to Pres. Franklin D. Roosevelt. The company began using the slogan "America's Oldest Brewery" in 1957. Frank Yuengling died in 1963 at the age of eighty-six and his sons, Richard L. Yuengling and F. Dohrman Yuengling, took control. In the United States' bicentennial year, the Yuengling brewery was placed on the National Register of Historic Places. When the company applied for federal registration of the "oldest brewery" phrase as a trademark in 1993, the Molson company, which has brewed in Canada since 1786, opposed what they called a "misdescription," arguing that "America" refers to Canada as well as the United States. The U.S. Patent and Trademark Office, however, felt differently. They ruled, in 1998, that D. G. Yuengling and Sons, Inc. could continue to use the slogan because most beer buyers associate the word "America" with the U.S. Molson can properly claim to be "North America's oldest brewery."

Ziebart, Kurt

Kurt Ziebart, a mechanic, emigrated to the United States from Germany with his wife, Edith, in 1950. The couple settled in Detroit, hub of the nation's automobile industry. Ziebart found work at a car dealership, but his English was so limited that he had trouble understanding the customers. After less than a year he took a job at a collision shop—the customers needed only point to the dents. In 1954 he moved on again. This time, he found work at a Packard dealership. He didn't have enough money to buy a new automobile, but his employer was willing to sell him a beat-up Packard that had been in a collision. It needed to be almost entirely rebuilt. Ziebart spent his days at the dealership, working on cars, and his evenings working on his own car. Having put so many hours into it, he wanted to be sure the vehicle wouldn't rust. He spent six years experimenting on a rustproofing system. One of his biggest challenges was getting a sealant into the hard-to-reach areas inside doors and panels. After experimenting for six years, he solved the problem by drilling small holes and inserting the sealant with a sprayer. He showed his system to his employer, who started to offer it as an option on the Packards in the lot. In 1960, with the help of a partner, Rudy Herman, Ziebart decided to leave the dealership and set up a business of his own. His first major contract came a year later, for rustproofing 150 General Motors cars. GM used the sealant as a selling point in an advertising campaign and before long Ziebart's small shop had more business than it could handle. The first franchise opened in 1962. Shortly thereafter, the partners parted ways and an investment group bought the company and renamed it *Ziebart Process Corporation.* Now known as *Ziebart International,* the organization has some six hundred franchised stores in more than fifty-five countries. It is the world's largest installer of automotive accessories, including window tint, sunroofs, alarms, hitches, running boards, and truck-bed liners. Mr. and Mrs. Ziebart moved to northern Michigan, where they bought a Mercedes Benz dealership.

Ziegfeld, Florenz

Born March 21, 1869 in Chicago, Florenz Ziegfeld began his career managing the strong man at the World's Columbian Exposition of 1893 in that city. He married a French beauty, Anna Held, in 1897 and promoted her with press releases about her milk baths. His first variety show was staged in New York in 1907. The Follies of 1907 featured fifty women he called "Anna Held Girls." The press dubbed them "Ziegfeld Girls." The chorus, personally selected by the showman, was made up of slender girls. At the time, thinness was considered a mark of ill health. A rounded figure was then thought to be a mark of robust well-being and, therefore, desirable. Until 1917, patent medicines that promised a remedy for "underweight" outsold those promising weight loss. The slim Follies girls, along with artist Charles Dana Gibson's "Gibson Girls," began to change Americans' ideas of the ideal female form. Ziegfeld and Held divorced in 1913. Ziegfeld later married actress Billie Burke, best known as Glenda the Good Witch in *The Wizard of Oz*. The Ziegfeld Follies thrived into the 1930s and, after Ziegfeld's death, continued off and on directed by Burke. A 1936 film, *The Great Ziegfeld*, tells the couple's story. It won the 1936 Academy Award for Best Picture.

Zinn, Johann Gottfried

Johann Gottfried Zinn was a physician and professor of medicine at Göttingen, Germany in the 1750s. In 1750, he published what is said to be the first book on the anatomy of the eye. He was the first to give a detailed description of the iris and to document the fact that a man's eyeball is bigger than a woman's. An amateur botanist, Zinn was also the first European to record a description of a Mexican flower. The Spanish conquistadors had dubbed the purple, desert blooms

"Mal de Ojos," or "Sickness of the Eye." The species is an annual flower that grows quickly and just as quickly dies when the first frost rolls in. Thus, Swedish botanist Carolus Linnaeus named the bloom for a scientist whose life was also brief. Zinn died in 1759 at the age of thirty-two. It wasn't until the late nineteenth century that the *zinnia* became popular. Selective breeding in Germany, Holland, and Italy resulted in a bigger, brighter flower. There are now fifteen different species of zinnia. It is the state flower of Indiana, and the National Garden Bureau named 2000 "the year of the zinnia."

Index